Socialism

Socialism

Dharmendra Kumar

RANDOM

RANDOM PUBLICATIONS

NEW DELHI (INDIA)

Socialism

ISBN 978-93-5111-628-8

Published in 2015 in India by

RANDOM PUBLICATIONS

4376-A/4B, Gali Murari Lal, Ansari Road
New Delhi-110 002
Phone : +9111-43580356, 011-23289044, 011-43142548
e-mail: sales@randompublications.com,
info@randompublications.com, randomexports@gmail.com
Reprinted 2019

Type Setting by : Friends Media, Delhi-110089
Digitally Printed at : Replika Press Pvt. Ltd.

Preface

Socialism is an economic system characterised by public ownership and centralized planning of all major industries (manufacturing, services, and energy), banks and insurance companies, agribusiness, transportation, the media, and medical facilities. Under capitalism, these giant enterprises dominate the economy but are privately owned and operated for the purpose of generating wealth for their owners by extracting it from working people who are paid only a small fraction of what their labour produces. Socialism turns this around so that the class that produces the wealth can collectively decide how it will be used for the benefit of all.

Socialism is a political term applied to an economic system in which property is held in common and not individually, and relationships are governed by a political hierarchy. Common ownership doesn't mean decisions are made collectively, however. Instead, individuals in positions of authority make decisions in the name of the collective group. Regardless of the picture painted of socialism by its proponents, it ultimately removes group decision making in favour of the choices of one all-important individual.

Socialism is rule by the working people. They will decide how socialism is to work. This was how Marx and Engels defined socialism, as a scientific term in sociology or social history, to differentiate it from the multitudinous social schemes or daydreams that men have produced since social classes first developed and so split humanity into the haves and have nots. The task of socialists therefore is to help and guide the transfer of power from capitalists to working people. As working people, socialists have and will continue to have the duty both to initiate working people's power, by revolution, and to continue to increase it - "permanent revolution".

The political and economic theory of socialism was created with the vision of a utopian society in mind. Contrary to other economic systems, there is no real consensus on how the ideal socialist society should function. Dozens of forms of socialism exist, all with differing ideas about economic planning, community size and many other factors. Despite the variations in socialist thought, every version advocates the benefits of cooperation among the people, steering clear of the "evils" of competition associated with capitalism.

The book will be found immensely informative and useful for all and for students and scholars.

I would like to thank my team for standing beside me throughout my career and writing this book. My special thanks go to "Random Publications" who have published the book.

– Dharmendra Kumar

Contents

1

Introduction to Socialism

SOCIALISM

Socialism is a social and economic system characterised by social ownership of the means of production and co-operative management of the economy. as well as a political theory and movement that aims at the establishment of such a system."Social ownership" may refer to cooperative enterprises. common ownership. state ownership. citizen ownership of equity. or any combination of these. There are many varieties of socialism and there is no single definition encapsulating all of them. They differ in the type of social ownership they advocate. the degree to which they rely on markets or planning. how management is to be organised within productive institutions. and the role of the state in constructing socialism.

A socialist economic system is based on the organisational precept of production for use. meaning the production of goods and services to directly satisfy economic demand and human needs where objects are valued based on their use-value or utility. as opposed to being structured upon the accumulation of capital and production for profit. In the traditional conception of a socialist economy. coordination. accounting and valuation would be performed in kind (using physical quantities). by a common physical magnitude. or by a direct measure of labour-time in place of financial calculation. On distribution of output there have been two proposals. one which is based on the principle of *to each according to his contribution* and another on the principle of *from each according to his ability. to each according to his need*. The advisability. feasibility and exact methods of resource allocation and valuation are the subject of the socialist calculation debate.

The socialist political movement includes a diverse array of political philosophies. Core dichotomies within the socialist movement include the distinction between reformism and revolutionary socialism and between state socialism and libertarian socialism. State socialism calls for the nationalisation of the means of production as a strategy for implementing socialism. while libertarian socialists generally place their hopes in decentralized means of direct democracy such as libertarian municipalism. citizens' assemblies. trade unions. and workers' councils coming from a general anti-authoritarian stance. Democratic socialismhighlights the central role of democratic processes and political systems and is usually contrasted with non-democratic political movements that advocate socialism. Some socialists have adopted the causes of other social movements. such as environmentalism. feminism and liberalism.

Modern socialism originated from an 18th-century intellectual and working class political movement that criticised the effects of industrialisation and private property on society. The revival of republicanism in the American Revolution of 1776 and the egalitarian values introduced by the French Revolution of 1789 gave rise to socialism as a distinct political movement. In the early 19th century. "socialism" referred to any concern for the social problems of capitalism irrespective of the solutions to those problems.

However. by the late 19th century. "socialism" had come to signify opposition to capitalism and advocacy for an alternative post-capitalist system based on some form of social ownership. During this time. German philosopher Karl Marx and his collaborator Friedrich Engels published works criticizing the utopian aspects of contemporary socialist trends and applied a materialist understanding of socialism as a phase of development which will come about through social revolution instigated by escalating and conflicting class relationships within capitalism. Alongside this there appeared other tendencies such as anarchism. revolutionary syndicalism. social-democracy. Marxism–Leninism anddemocratic socialism as well as the confluence of socialism with anti-imperialist and anti-racist struggles around the world. The socialist movement came to be the most influential worldwide movement and political-economic worldview of the 20th century. Today. socialist parties and ideas remain a political force with varying degrees of power and influence in all continents leading national governments in many countries.

ETYMOLOGY

For Andrew Vincent "The word 'socialism' finds its root in the Latin *sociare*. which means to combine or to share. The related. more technical term in Roman and then medieval law was *societas*. This latter word could mean companionship and fellowship as well as the more legalistic idea of a consensual contract between freemen." The term "socialism" was created by Henri de Saint-Simon. one of the founders of what would later be labelled "utopian socialism". The term "socialism" was created to contrast against the liberal doctrine of "individualism". which stressed that people act or should act as if they are in isolation from one another. The original socialists condemned liberal individualism as failing to address social concerns of poverty. social oppression. and gross inequality of wealth. They viewed liberal individualism as degenerating society into supporting selfish egoism that harmed community life through promoting a society based on competition. They presented socialism as an alternative to liberal individualism. that advocated a society based on cooperation. The term socialism is attributed to Pierre Leroux. and to Marie Roch Louis Reybaud in France; and in Britain to Robert Owen in 1827. father of the cooperative movement.

The modern definition and usage of the term "socialism" settled by the 1860s. becoming the predominant term among the earlier associated words "co-operative". "mutualist" and "associationist". The term "communism" also fell out of use during this period. despite earlier distinctions between socialism and communism from the 1840s. An early distinction between "socialism" and "communism" was that the former aimed to only socialize production while the latter aimed to socialize both production and consumption.However. by 1888 the term "socialism" was used by Marxists in place of "communism". which was now considered an old-fashion term synonymous with socialism. It was only until 1917 after the Bolshevik revolution that "socialism" came to refer to a distinct stage between capitalism and communism. introduced by Vladimir Lenin as a means to defend the Bolshevik seizure of power against traditional Marxist criticisms that Russia was not sufficiently developed for socialist revolution.

HISTORY

Early socialism

Socialist models and ideas espousing common or public ownership have existed since antiquity. Mazdak. a Persian communal proto-socialist. instituted communal possessions and advocated the public good. And it has been claimed. though controversially. that there were elements of socialist thought in the politics of classical Greek philosophers Plato and Aristotle. In the post-revolutionary period right after the French Revolution activists and theorists like François-Noël Babeuf. Étienne-Gabriel Morelly.

Filippo Buonarroti. and Auguste Blanqui influenced the early French labour and socialist movements. In Britain Thomas Paine proposed a detailed plan to tax property owners to pay for the needs of the poor in *Agrarian Justice* while Charles Hall wrote *The Effects of Civilization on the People in European States* denouncing capitalism´s effects on the poor of his time which influenced the utopian schemes of Thomas Spence. The first "self-conscious socialist movements developed in the 1820s and 1830s. The Owenites. Saint-Simonians and Fourierists provided a series of coherent analyses and interpretations of society. They also. especially in the case of the Owenites. overlapped with a number of other working-class movements like the Chartists." A later important socialist thinker in France was Pierre Joseph Proudhon who proposed his philosophy of mutualism in which "everyone had an equal claim. either alone or as part of a small cooperative. to possess and use land and other resources as needed to make a living". There were also currents inspired by dissident Christianity of christian socialism "often in Britain and then usually coming out of left liberal politics and a romantic anti-industrialism" which produced theorists such as Edward Bellamy. Frederick Denison Maurice and Charles Kingsley.

The first advocates of socialism favoured social levelling in order to create a meritocratic or technocratic society based upon individual talent. Count Henri de Saint-Simon is regarded as the first individual to coin the term *socialism*. Saint-Simon was fascinated by the enormous potential of science and technology and advocated a socialist society that would eliminate the disorderly aspects of capitalism and would be based upon equal opportunities. He advocated the creation of a society in which each person was ranked according to his or her capacities and rewarded according to his or her work. The key focus of Saint-Simon's socialism was on administrative efficiency and industrialism. and a belief that science was the key to progress.

This was accompanied by a desire to implement a rationally organised economy based on planning and geared towards large-scale scientific and material progress. and thus embodied a desire for a more directed or planned economy. Other early socialist thinkers. such as Thomas Hodgkin and Charles Hall. based their ideas on David Ricardo's economic theories. They reasoned that the equilibrium value of commodities approximated to prices charged by the producer when those commodities were in elastic supply. and that these producer prices corresponded to the embodied labour – the cost of the labour (essentially the wages paid) that was required to produce the commodities. The Ricardian socialists viewed profit. interest and rent as deductions from this exchange-value.

West European social critics. including Robert Owen. Charles Fourier. Pierre-Joseph Proudhon. Louis Blanc. Charles Hall and Saint-Simon. were the first modern socialists who criticised the excessive poverty and inequality of the Industrial Revolution. They advocated reform. with some such as Robert Owen advocating the transformation of society to small communities without private property. Robert Owen's contribution to modern socialism was his understanding that actions and characteristics of individuals were largely determined by the social environment they were raised in and exposed to. On the other hand Charles Fourier advocated phalansteres which were communities that respected individual desires (including sexual preferences). affinities and creativity and saw that work has to be made enjoyable for people. The ideas of Owen and Fourier were tried in practice in numerous intentional communities around Europe and the American continent in the mid-19th century.

Linguistically. the contemporary connotation of the words *socialism* and *communism* accorded with the adherents' and opponents' cultural attitude towards religion. In Christian Europe. of the two. communism was believed the atheist way of life. In Protestant England. the word *communism* was too culturally and aurally close to the Roman Catholic *communion rite*. hence English atheists denoted themselves socialists. Friedrich Engels argued that in 1848. at the time when the *Communist Manifesto* was published. "socialism was respectable on the continent. while communism was not." The Owenites in England and the Fourierists in France were considered "respectable" socialists. while working-class movements that "proclaimed the necessity of total social change" denoted themselves communists.

This latter branch of socialism produced the communist work of Étienne Cabet in France and Wilhelm Weitling in Germany. The British moral philosopher John Stuart Mill also came to advocate a form of economic socialism within a liberal context. In later editions of his *Principles of Political Economy* (1848). Mill would argue that "as far as economic theory was concerned. there is nothing in principle in economic theory that precludes an economic order based on socialist policies." While democrats looked to the Revolutions of 1848 as a democratic revolution. which in the long run ensured liberty. equality. and fraternity. marxists denounced 1848 as a betrayal of working-class ideals by a bourgeoisie indifferent to the legitimate demands of the proletariat.

The Paris Commune was a government that briefly ruled Paris from 18 March (more formally. from 28 March) to 28 May 1871. The Commune was the result of an uprising in Paris after France was defeated in the Franco-Prussian War.

The Commune elections held on 26 March elected a Commune council of 92 members. one member for each twenty thousand residents. Despite internal differences. the Council began to organise the public services essential for a city of two million residents.

It also reached a consensus on certain policies that tended towards a progressive. secular. and highly-democratic social democracy. Because the Commune was only able to meet on fewer than sixty days in all. only a few decrees were actually implemented. These included the separation of church and state. the remission of rents owed for the entire period of the siege (during which. payment had been suspended). the abolition of night work in the hundreds of Paris bakeries. the granting of pensions to the unmarried companions and children of National Guards killed on active service; the free return. by the city pawnshops. of all workmen's tools and household items valued up to 20 francs. pledged during the siege.

The Commune was concerned that skilled workers had been forced to pawn their tools during the war; the postponement of commercial debt obligations. and the abolition of interest on the debts; and the right of employees to take over and run an enterprise if it were deserted by its owner; the Commune. Non-etheless. recognised the previous owner's right to compensation.

Socialism expands and the First and Second Internationals

The International Workingmen's Association (IWA). also known as the First International. was founded in London in 1864. The International Workingmen's Association united diverse revolutionary currents including French followers of Proudhon. Blanquists. Philadelphes. English trade unionists. socialists and social democrats. The IWA held a preliminary conference in 1865. and had its first congress at Geneva in 1866. Due to the wide variety of philosophies present in the First International. there was conflict from the start. The first objections to Marx's came from the Mutualists who opposed communism and statism. However. shortly after Mikhail Bakunin and his followers (called *Collectivists* while in the International) joined in 1868. the First International became polarised into two camps. with Marx and Bakunin as their respective figureheads. The clearest differences between the groups emerged over their proposed strategies for achieving their visions of socialism. The First International became the first major international forum for the promulgation of socialist ideas.

The followers of Bakunin were called collectivist anarchists and sought to collectivize ownership of the means of production while retaining payment proportional to the amount and kind of labour of each individual. but the anarcho-communists sought to extend the concept of collective ownership to the products of labour as well. While both groups argued against capitalism. the anarchist communists departed from Proudhon and Bakunin. who maintained that individuals have a right to the product of their individual labour and to be remunerated for their particular contribution to production. But. Errico Malatesta put it: "...instead of running the risk of making a confusion in trying to distinguish what you and I each do. let us all work and put everything in common. In this way each will give to society all that his strength permits until enough is produced for every one; and each will take all that he needs. limiting his needs only in those things of which there is not yet plenty for every one."

Anarchist communism as a coherent. modern economic-political philosophy was first formulated in the Italian section of the First International by Carlo Cafiero. Emilio Covelli.Errico Malatesta. Andrea Costa and other ex-Mazzinian Republicans. Out of respect for Mikhail Bakunin. they did not make their differences with collectivist anarchism explicit until after Bakunin's death. Syndicalism emerged in France from the inspiration in part by the ideas of Pierre Joseph Proudhon and later by Fernand Pelloutier and Georges Sorel. Syndicalism developed at the end of the 19th century "out of the French trade-union movement—syndicat being the French word for trade union. It was a significant force in Italy and Spain in the early 20th century until it was crushed by the fascist regimes in those countries. In the United States. syndicalism appeared in the guise of theIndustrial Workers of the World. or "Wobblies." founded in 1905." Syndicalism is a type of economic system proposed as a replacement for capitalism. which proposes that industries be organised into confederations or syndicates. It is a form of communism and economic corporatism that advocates interest aggregation of multiple non-competitive categorised units composed of specialists and representatives of workers in each respective field to negotiate and manage an economy. Syndicalism also refers to the political movement and tactics used to bring about this type of system. An influential anarchist movement based on syndicalist ideas is anarcho-syndicalism. TheInternational Workers Association is an international anarcho-syndicalist federation of various labour unions from different countries.

The Fabian Society' is a British socialist organisation which was established with the purpose of advancing the principles of socialism viagradualist and reformist means. The society laid many of the foundations of the Labour Party and subsequently affected the policies of states emerging from the decolonisation of the British Empire. most notably India and Singapore. Originally. the Fabian society was committed to the establishment of a socialist economy. alongside a commitment to British imperialism as a progressive and modernizing force.

Today. the society functions primarily as a think tank and is one of 15 socialist societies affiliated with the Labour Party. Similar societies exist in Australia (the Australian Fabian Society). Canada (the Douglas-Coldwell Foundation and the now disbanded League for Social Reconstruction) and in New Zealand. Guild socialism is a political movement advocating workers' control of industry through the medium of trade-related guilds "in an implied contractual relationship with the public". It originated in the United Kingdom and was at its most influential in the first quarter of the 20th century. Inspired by the medieval guild theorists such as Samuel G. Hobson and G.D.H. Cole advocated the public ownership of industries and their organization into guilds. each of which would be under the democratic control of its trade union. On the other hand the guild socialists were less inclined to invest power in the state than were the Fabians. At some point "like the American Knights of Labour. guild socialism wanted to abolish the wage system"

As the ideas of Marx and Engels took on flesh. particularly in central Europe. socialists sought to unite in an international organisation. In 1889. on the centennial of the French Revolution of 1789. the Second International was founded. with 384 delegates from 20 countries representing about 300 labour and socialist organisations. It was termed the "Socialist International" and Engels was elected honorary president at the third congress in 1893. In 1889. on the centennial of the French Revolution of 1789. the Second International was founded. with 384 delegates from 20 countries representing about 300 labour and socialist organizations. Anarchists were ejected and not allowed in mainly because of the pressure from marxists. It has been argued that at some point the Second International turned "into a battleground over the issue oflibertarian versus authoritarian socialism. Not only did they effectively present themselves as champions of minority rights; they also provoked the German Marxists into demonstrating a dictatorial intolerance which was a factor in preventing the British labour movement from following the Marxist direction indicated by such leaders as H. M. Hyndman".

Eduard Bernstein was a leading social democrat in Germany who proposed the concept of evolutionary socialism. Reformism was quickly targeted by revolutionary socialists. with Rosa Luxemburg condemning Bernstein's *Evolutionary Socialism* in her 1900 essay *Reform or Revolution?*. Revolutionary socialism encompasses multiple social and political movements that may define "revolution" differently from one another. The Social Democratic Party (SPD) in Germany became the largest and most powerful socialist party in Europe. despite working illegally until the anti-socialist laws were dropped in 1890. In the 1893 elections it gained 1.787.000 votes. a quarter of the total votes cast. according to Engels. In 1895. the year of his death. Engels emphasised the Communist Manifesto's emphasis on winning. as a first step. the "battle of democracy".

The early 20th century and the revolutions of 1917–1936

In 1904. Australians elected the first Australian Labour Party prime minister: Chris Watson. who became the first democratically elected social democrat. In 1909 the first Kibbutz was established in Palestine by Russian Jewish Immigrants. The Kibbutz Movement will then expand through the 20th century following a doctrine of zionist socialism. The British Labour Party first won seats in the House of Commons in 1902.

The International Socialist Commission (ISC. also known as Berne International) was formed in February 1919 at a meeting in Berneby parties that wanted to resurrect the Second International. By 1917. the patriotism of World War I changed into political radicalism in most of Europe. the United States. and Australia. Other socialist parties from around the world who were beginning to gain importance in their national politics in the early 20th century included the Italian Socialist Party. the French Section of the Workers' International. theSpanish Socialist Workers' Party. the Swedish Social Democratic Party. the Russian Social Democratic Labour Party. the Socialist Party of America in the United States. the Argentinian Socialist Party and the Chilean Partido Obrero Socialista.

In February 1917. revolution exploded in Russia. Workers. soldiers and peasants established soviets (councils). the monarchy fell. and aprovisional government convoked pending the election of a constituent assembly. In April of that year. Vladimir Lenin. leader of the *Majority*(or in Russian: "Bolshevik") faction of socialists in Russia and known for his profound and controversial expansions of Marxism. was allowed to cross Germany to return to his country from exile in Switzerland. Lenin had published essays on his analysis of imperialism. the monopoly and globalization phase of capitalism as predicted by Marx. as well as analyses on the social conditions of his contemporary time. He observed that as capitalism had further developed in Europe and America. the workers remained unable to gain class consciousness so long as they were too busy working and concerning with how to make ends meet. He therefore proposed that the social revolution would require the leadership of a vanguard party of class-conscious revolutionaries from the educated and politically active part of the population. Upon arriving in Petrograd. he declared that the revolution in Russia was not over but had only begun. and that the next step was for the workers' soviets to take full state authority. He issued a thesis outlining the Bolshevik's party programme. including rejection of any legitimacy in the provisional government and advocacy for state power to be given to the peasant and working class through the soviets.

The Bolsheviks became the most influential force in the soviets. and on 7 November. the capitol of the provisional government was stormed by Bolshevik Red Guards in what afterwards known as the "Great October Socialist Revolution". The rule of the provisional government was ended and the Russian Socialist Federative Soviet Republic - the world's first constitutionally socialist state - was established. On 25 January 1918. at the Petrograd Soviet. Lenin declared "Long live the world socialist revolution!" He proposed an immediate armistice on all fronts. and transferred the land of the landed proprietors. the crown and the monasteries to the peasant committees without compensation.

On 26 January 1918. the day after assuming executive power. Lenin wrote *Draft Regulations on Workers' Control*. which granted workers control of businesses with more than five workers and office employees. and access to all books. documents and stocks. and whose decisions were to be "binding upon the owners of the enterprises". Governing through the elected soviets. and in alliance with the peasant-based Left Socialist-Revolutionaries. the Bolshevik government began nationalising banks. industry. and disavowed the national debts of the deposed Romanov royal régime.

It sued for peace. withdrawing from World War I. and convoked a Constituent Assembly in which the peasant Socialist-Revolutionary Party (SR) won a majority. The Constituent Assembly elected Socialist-Revolutionary leader Victor Chernov President of a Russian republic. but rejected the Bolshevik proposal that it endorse the Soviet decrees on land. peace and workers' control. and acknowledge the power of the Soviets of Workers'. Soldiers' and Peasants' Deputies. The next day. the Bolsheviks declared that the assembly was elected on outdated party lists. and the All-Russian Central Executive Committee of the Soviets dissolved it. In March 1919 world communist parties formed Comintern (also known as the Third International) at a meeting in Moscow. Parties which did not want to be a part of the resurrected Second International (ISC) or Comintern formed the International Working Union of Socialist Parties (IWUSP. also known as Vienna International/Vienna Union/Two-and-a-Half International) on 27 February 1921 at a conference in Vienna. The ISC and the IWUSP joined to form the Labour and Socialist International (LSI) in May 1923 at a meeting in Hamburg Left wing groups which did not agree to the centralisation and abandonment of the soviets by the Bolshevik Party led Left-wing uprisings against the Bolsheviks which were a series of rebellions and uprisings against the Bolsheviks led or supported by left wing groups including Socialist Revolutionaries. Left Socialist Revolutionaries. Mensheviks. and anarchists. Within this left wing discontent the most large scale events were the worker's Kronstadt rebellion and the anarchist led Revolutionary Insurrectionary Army of Ukraine uprising which controlled an area known as the Free Territory.

The Bolshevik Russian Revolution of January 1918 engendered Communist parties worldwide. and their concomitant revolutions of 1917–23. Few Communists doubted that the Russian success of socialism depended upon successful. working-class socialist revolutions in developed capitalist countries. In 1919. Lenin and Trotsky organised the world's Communist parties into a new international association of workers – the Communist International. (Comintern). also called the Third International.

The Russian Revolution also influenced uprisings in other countries around this time. The German Revolution of 1918–1919 resulted in the replacement of Germany's imperial government with a republic. The revolutionary period lasted from November 1918 until the formal establishment of the Weimar Republic in August 1919 and included an episode known as the Bavarian Soviet Republic and the Spartacist uprising. In Italy the events known as the *Biennio Rosso* was characterised by mass strikes. worker manifestations as well as self-management experiments through land and factories occupations. In Turin and Milan. workers councils were formed and many factory occupations took place under the leadership of anarcho-syndicalists organised around the Unione Sindacale Italiana.

By 1920. the Red Army. under its commander Trotsky. had largely defeated the royalist White Armies. In 1921. War Communism was ended and. under the New Economic Policy (NEP). private ownership was allowed for small and medium peasant enterprises. While industry remained largely state-controlled. Lenin acknowledged that the NEP was a necessary capitalist measure for a country unripe for socialism. Profiteering returned in the form of "NEP men" and rich peasants (Kulaks) gained power in the countryside.Nevertheless the role of Trotsky in this episode has been questioned by other socialists incluiding ex-trostkists. In the United States Dwight Macdonald broke with Trotsky and left the trotskyist Socialist Workers Party. by raising the question of the Kronstadt rebellion. which Trotsky as leader of the Soviet Red Army and the other Bolsheviks had brutally repressed. He then moved towards democratic socialism and anarchism. A similar critique on Trotsky's role on the events around the Kronstadt rebellion was raised by the American anarchist Emma Goldman. In her essay "Trotsky Protests Too Much" she says "I admit. the dictatorship under Stalin's rule has become monstrous. That does not. however. lessen the guilt of Leon Trotsky as one of the actors in the revolutionary drama of which Kronstadt was one of the bloodiest scenes."

In 1922. the fourth congress of the Communist International took up the policy of the United Front. urging Communists to work with rank and file Social Democrats while remaining critical of their leaders. whom they criticised for betraying the working class by supporting the war efforts of their respective capitalist classes. For their part. the social democrats pointed to the dislocation caused by revolution. and later. the growing authoritarianism of the Communist Parties. When the Communist Party of Great Britain applied to affiliate to the Labour Party in 1920 it was turned down. In 1923. on seeing the Soviet State's growing coercive power. a dying Lenin said Russia had reverted to "a bourgeois tsarist machine... barely varnished with socialism." After Lenin's death in January 1924. the Communist Party of the Soviet Union – then increasingly under the control of Joseph Stalin – rejected the theory that socialism could not be built solely in the Soviet Union. in favour of the concept of *Socialism in One Country*. Despite the marginalised Left Opposition's demand for the restoration of Soviet democracy. Stalin developed a bureaucratic. authoritarian government. that was condemned by democratic socialists. anarchists andTrotskyists for undermining the initial socialist ideals of the Bolshevik Russian Revolution.

In 1924 the Mongolian People's Republic was established and was ruled by the Mongolian People's Party. The Russian Revolution and the appearance of the Soviet State motivated a worldwide current of national Communist parties which ended having varying levels of political and social influence. Among these there appeared the Communist Party of France. the Communist Party USA. the Italian Communist Party. the Chinese Communist Party. the Mexican Communist Party. the Brazilian Communist Party. the Chilean Communist Party and theCommunist Party of Indonesia.

In Spain in 1936. the national anarcho-syndicalist trade union Confederación Nacional del Trabajo initially refused to join a popular front electoral alliance. and abstention by CNT supporters led to a right wing election victory. But in 1936. the CNT changed its policy and anarchist votes helped bring the popular front back to power. Months later. the former ruling class responded with an attempted coup causing the Spanish Civil War (1936–1939). In response to the army rebellion. an anarchist-inspired movement of peasants and workers. supported by armed militias. took control of Barcelona and of large areas of rural Spain where they collectivised the land. The events known as the Spanish Revolution was a workers' social revolution that began during the outbreak of the Spanish Civil War in 1936 and resulted in the widespread implementation of anarchist and more broadly libertarian socialist organisational principles throughout various portions of the country for two to three years. primarily Catalonia. Aragon. Andalusia. and parts ofthe Levante. Much of Spain's economy was put under worker control; in anarchist strongholds like Catalonia. the figure was as high as 75per cent. but lower in areas with heavyCommunist Party of Spain influence. as the Soviet-allied party actively resisted attempts at collectivization enactment. Factories were run through worker committees. agrarianareas became collectivised and run as libertarian communes. Anarchist historian Sam Dolgoff estimated that about eight million people participated directly or at least indirectly in the Spanish Revolution

The mid-20th century: World War II and post war radicalization

The rise of Nazism and the start of World War II led to the dissolution of the LSI in 1940. The Socialist International was formed in Frankfurt in July 1951 as a successor to the LSI. Trotsky's Fourth International was established in France in 1938 when Trotskyists argued that the Comintern or Third International had become irretrievably "lost to Stalinism" and thus incapable of leading the international working class to political power.

Post-World War II social democratic governments introduced social reform and wealth redistribution via state welfare and taxation. Social Democratic parties dominated post-war politics in countries such as France. Italy. Czechoslovakia. Belgium and Norway. At one point. France claimed to be the world's most state-controlled capitalist country.

The nationalised public utilities included Charbonnages de France (CDF). Electricité de France (EDF). Gaz de France (GDF). Air France. Banque de France. and Régie Nationale des Usines Renault. In 1945. the British Labour Party. led by Clement Attlee. was elected to office based upon a radical socialist programme. The UK Labour Government nationalised major public utilities such as mines. gas. coal. electricity. rail. iron. steel. and the Bank of England. British Petroleum. privatised in 1987. was officially nationalised in 1951. and there was further government intervention during the 1974–79 Labour Government Anthony Crosland said that in 1956. 25 per cent of British industry was nationalised. and that public employees. including those in nationalised industries. constituted a similar percentage of the country's total employed population.

Labour re-nationalised steel (1967. British Steel) after the Conservatives denationalised it. and nationalised car production (1976. British Leyland). The National Health Service provided taxpayer-funded health care to everyone. free at the point of service. Working-class housing was provided in council housing estates. and university education became available via a school grant system. The Nordic model refers to the economic and social models of the Nordic countries (Denmark. Iceland. Norway. Sweden and Finland). During most of the post-war era. Sweden was governed by the Swedish Social Democratic Party largely in cooperation with trade unionsand industry. In Sweden. the Social Democratic Party held power from 1936 to 1976. 1982 to 1991. and 1994 to 2006. From 1945 to 1962. the Norwegian Labour Party held an absolute majority in the parliament led by Einar Gerhardsen who was Prime Minister with 17 years in office. This particular adaptation of the mixed market economy is characterised by more generous welfare states (relative to other developed countries). which are aimed specifically at enhancing individual autonomy. ensuring the universal provision of basic human rights and stabilising the economy. It is distinguished from other welfare states with similar goals by its emphasis on maximising labour force participation. promoting gender equality. egalitarian and extensive benefit levels. large magnitude of redistribution. and liberal use of expansionary fiscal policy.

After World War II the USSR became a recognised superpower. which played a decisive role in the Allied victory in World War II. The Soviet era saw some of the most significant technological achievements of the 20th century. including the world's first spacecraft. and the first astronaut. The economy of the Soviet Union was the modern world's first centrally planned economy. It was based on a system of state ownership of industry managed through Gosplan (the State Planning Commission). Gosbank (the State Bank) and the Gossnab (State Commission for Materials and Equipment Supply). Economic planning was conducted through a series of Five-Year Plans.

The emphasis was put on a very fast development of heavy industry and the nation became one of the world's top manufacturers of a large number of basic and heavy industrial products. but it lagged behind in the output of light industrial production and consumer durables. The Eastern Bloc was the former communist states of Central and Eastern Europe. generally theSoviet Union and the countries of the Warsaw Pact which included the People's Republic of Poland. the German Democratic Republic. the People's Republic of Hungary. the People's Republic of Bulgaria. the Czechoslovak Socialist Republic. the Socialist Republic of Romania. the People's Socialist Republic of Albania and the Socialist Federal Republic of Yugoslavia. The Hungarian Revolution of 1956 was a spontaneous nationwide revolt against the government of the People's Republic of Hungary and its Soviet-imposed policies. lasting from 23 October until 10 November 1956. Both Soviet leader Nikita Khrushchev´s denunciation of the excesses of Stalin´s regime during theTwentieth Party Congress of the Communist Party of the Soviet Union on 1956 and the events in Hungary produced ideological fractures and disagreements within the communist and socialist parties of Western Europe.

In the postwar years. socialism became increasingly influential throughout the so-called Third World. Countries in Africa. Asia. and Latin America frequently nationalised industries held by foreign owners. The Chinese Revolution was the second part of Chinese Civil War which ended in the establishmente of the People's Republic of China. The term "Third World" was coined by French demographer Alfred Sauvy in 1952. on the model of the Third Estate. which. according to the Abbé Sieyès. represented everything. but was nothing: "...because at the end this ignored. exploited. scorned Third World like the Third Estate. wants to become something too" (Sauvy). The emergence of this new political entity. in the frame of the Cold War. was complex and painful. Several tentatives were made to organise newly independent states in order to oppose a common front towards both the US's and the USSR's influence on them. with the consequences of the Sino-Soviet split already at works.

Thus. the Non-Aligned Movement constituted itself. around the main figures of Jawaharlal Nehru. the leader of India. Sukarno. the Indonesian president. Josip Broz Tito the Communist leader of Yugoslavia. and Gamal Abdel Nasser. head of Egypt who successfully opposed the French and British imperial powers during the 1956 Suez crisis. After the 1954 Geneva Conference which put an end to the French war against Ho Chi Minh in Vietnam. the 1955 Bandung Conference gathered Nasser. Nehru. Tito. Sukarno. the leader of Indonesia. and Zhou Enlai. Premier of the People's Republic of China. As many African countries gained independence during the 1960s. some of these newly formed governments rejected the ideas of capitalism in favour of a more afrocentric economic model. Julius Nyerere of Tanzania.

Léopold Senghor of Senegal. Kwame Nkrumah of Ghana and Sékou Touré of Guinea. were the main architects of African Socialism. The Cuban Revolution (1953-1959) was an armed revolt conducted by Fidel Castro's 26th of July Movement and its allies against the government of Cuban President Fulgencio Batista. The revolution began in July 1953. and finally ousted Batista on 1 January 1959. replacing his government with Castro's revolutionary state. Castro's government later reformed along communist lines. becoming the Communist Party of Cuba in October 1965.

The New Left was a term used mainly in the United Kingdom and United States in reference to activists. educators. agitators and others in the 1960s and 1970s who sought to implement a broad range of reforms on issues such as gay rights. abortion. gender roles and drugs in contrast to earlier leftist or Marxist movements that had taken a morevanguardist approach to social justice and focused mostly on labour unionisation and questions of social class. They rejected involvement with the labour movementand Marxism's historical theory of class struggle. In the U.S.. the "New Left" was associated with the Hippie movement. anti-war college campus protest movements as well as the black liberation movements such as the Black Panther Party. While initially formed in opposition to the "Old Left" Democratic party. groups composing the New Left gradually became central players in the Democratic coalition. In 1968 in

Carrara. Italy the International of Anarchist Federations was founded during an international anarchist conference held there in 1968 by the three existing European federations of France. the Italian and the Iberian Anarchist Federation as well as the Bulgarian federation in French exile.

The protests of 1968 comprised a worldwide escalation of social conflicts. predominantly characterised by popular rebellions against military. capitalist. and bureaucratic elites. who retorted with an escalation of political repression. In capitalist countries. these protests marked a turning point for the Civil Rights movement in the United States. which produced revolutionary movements like the Black Panther Party.

In that country the prominent civil rights leader Martin Luther King Jr. organised the "Poor People's Campaign" to address issues of economic justice while personally showing sympathy with democratic socialism. In reaction to the Tet Offensive. protests also sparked a broad movement in opposition to the Vietnam War all over the United States and even into London. Paris. Berlin and Rome. Mass socialist or communist movements grew not only in the United States but also in most European countries. The most spectacular manifestation of this were the May 1968 protests in France. in which students linked up with wildcat strikes of up to ten million workers. and for a few days the movement seemed capable of overthrowing the government. In many other capitalist countries. struggles against dictatorships. state repression. and colonization were also marked by protests in 1968. such as the beginning of the Troubles in Northern Ireland. the Tlatelolco massacre in Mexico City. and the escalation of guerrilla warfare against the military dictatorship in Brazil. In communist party led countries there were also protests against bureaucratic and military elites.

It was amidst the Great Proletarian Cultural Revolution in China (1966–1976). and in Eastern Europe there were also widespread protests that escalated particularly in thePrague Spring in Czechoslovakia. Like the Italian and French Communist parties. the Communist Party of Finland denounced the occupation. The Portuguese communist secretary-general Álvaro Cunhal was one of few political leaders from western Europe to have supported the invasion for being counter-revolutionary. along with the Luxembourg party and conservative factions of the Greek party. In the Chinese Cultural Revolution. a social-political youth movement movilized against "bourgeois" elements which were seen to be infiltrating the government and society at large. aiming to restore capitalism. This movement motivated maoism inspired movements around the world in the context of the Sino-Soviet split.

In Indonesia. a right wing military regime led by Suharto killed between 500.000 and one million people mainly to crush the growing influence of the Communist Party of Indonesia and other leftist sectors with support from the United States government. which provided kill lists to the Indonesian military containing thousands of names of suspected high-ranking Communists. In Latin America in the 1960s a socialist tendency within the catholic church appeared which was called Liberation theology which enden motivating even the Colombian priest Camilo Torres to enter the ELN guerrilla. In Chile. Salvador Allende. a physician and candidate for theSocialist Party of Chile. was elected president through democratic elections in 1970. In 1973. his government was ousted by the American-backed military dictatorship ofAugusto Pinochet. which lasted until the late 1980s. In Italy Autonomia Operaia was a leftist movement particularly active from 1976 to 1978. It took an important role in theautonomist movement in the 1970s. aside earlier organisations such as *Potere Operaio*. created after May 1968. and *Lotta Continua*. Out of this experience came out the contemporary socialist radical movement known as autonomism.

Late 20th century

The Nicaraguan Revolution encompassed the rising opposition to the Somoza dictatorship in the 1960s and 1970s. the campaign led by the Sandinista National Liberation Front(FSLN) to violently oust the dictatorship in 1978-79. the subsequent efforts of the FSLN to govern Nicaragua from 1979 until 1990 and the socialist measures which included widescale agrarian reform and educational programmes.

The People's Revolutionary Government was proclaimed on 13 March 1979 in Grenada which was overthrown by armed forces of the United States in 1983. The Salvadoran Civil War (1979–1992) was a conflict between the military-led government of El Salvador and the Farabundo Martí National Liberation Front (FMLN). a coalition or 'umbrella organization' of five socialist guerrilla groups. A coup on October 15. 1979 led to the killings of anti-coup protesters by the government as well as anti-disorder protesters by the guerillas. and is widely seen as the tipping point towards the civil war.

In 1982 the newly elected French socialist government of François Mitterrand carried out nationalizations in a few key industries incluiding banks and insurance companies.Eurocommunism was a trend in the 1970s and 1980s within various Western European communist parties to develop a theory and practice of social transformation that was more relevant for a Western European country and less aligned to the influence or control of the Communist Party of the Soviet Union. Some Communist parties with strong popular support. notably the Italian Communist Party (PCI) and the Communist Party of Spain (PCE) adopted Eurocommunism most enthusiastically.

The Communist Party of Finland was dominated by Eurocommunists while the French Communist Party (PCF) and many smaller parties strongly opposed to Eurocommunism and stayed aligned to the positions of the Communist Party of the Soviet Union until the end of the USSR. Outside of Western Europe. it is sometimes referred to as "Neocommunism." In the late 1970s and in the 1980s the Socialist International had extensive contacts and discussion with the two leading powers of the Cold War period. the United States and the Soviet Union. on issues concerning East-West relations and arms control. Since then. the SI has admitted as member parties not only the Nicaraguan FSLN but also the left-wingPuerto Rican Independence Party. as well as former Communist parties such as the Democratic Party of the Left of Italy and the Front for the Liberation of Mozambique(FRELIMO). The Socialist International aided social democratic parties in re-establishing themselves when dictatorship gave way to democracy in Portugal (1974) and Spain (1975). Until its 1976 Geneva Congress. the SI had few members outside Europe and no formal involvement with Latin America.

After Mao's death in 1976 and the arrest of the faction known as the Gang of Four. who were blamed for the excesses of the Cultural Revolution. Deng Xiaoping took power and led the People´s Republic of China to significant economic reforms. The Communist Party of China subsequently loosened governmental control over citizens' personal lives and the communes were disbanded in favour of private land leases. This turn of events marked China's transition from a planned economy to a mixed economy named as "socialism with Chinese characteristics" which maintained state ownership rights over land. state or cooperative ownership of much of the heavy industrial and manufacturing sectors and state influence in the banking and financial sectors. China adopted its current constitution on 4 December 1982.President Jiang Zemin and Premier Zhu Rongji led the nation in the 1990s.

Under their administration. China's economic performance pulled an estimated 150 million peasants out of poverty and sustained an average annual gross domestic product growth rate of 11.2per cent. At the Sixth National Congress of the Communist Party of Vietnam in December 1986. reformist politicians replaced the "old guard" government with new leadership. The reformers were led by 71-year-old Nguyen Van Linh. who became the party's new general secretary. Linh and the reformers implemented a series of free-market reforms – known as *Đ-i M-i* ("Renovation") – which carefully managed the transition from a planned economy to a "socialist-oriented market economy". Mikhail Gorbachev wished to move the USSR in the direction of Nordic-style social democracy. calling it "a socialist beacon for all mankind." Prior to its dissolution in 1991. the USSR had the second largest economy in the world after the United States. With the collapse of the Soviet Union. the economic integration of the Soviet republics was dissolved. and overall industrial activity declined substantially. A lasting legacy remains in the physical infrastructure created during decades of combined industrial production practices.

Many social democratic parties. particularly after the Cold war. adopted Neo-liberal market policies including privatisation. deregulation andfinancialisation. They abandoned their pursuit of moderate socialism in favour of market liberalism. By the 1980s. with the rise of conservative Neo-liberal politicians such asRonald Reagan in the United States. Margaret Thatcher in Britain. Brian Mulroney in Canada and Augusto Pinochet in Chile. the Western welfare state was attacked from within.Monetarists and Neo-liberals attacked social welfare systems as impediments to private entrepreneurship. In the UK. Labour Party leader Neil Kinnock made a public attack against the entryist group Militant at the 1985 Labour Party conference.

The Labour Party ruled that Militant was ineligible for affiliation with the Labour Party. and the party gradually expelled Militant supporters. The Kinnock leadership had refused to support the 1984–1985 miner's strike over pit closures. a decision that the party's left wing and theNational Union of Mineworkers blamed for the strike's eventual defeat. In 1989. at Stockholm. the 18th Congress of the Socialist International adopted a new *Declaration of Principles*. saying:

Democratic socialism is an international movement for freedom. social justice. and solidarity. Its goal is to achieve a peaceful world where these basic values can be enhanced and where each individual can live a meaningful life with the full development of his or her personality and talents. and with the guarantee of human and civil rights in a democratic framework of society.

In the 1990s. the British Labour Party. under Tony Blair. enacted policies based upon the free market economy to deliver public services via the Private finance initiative. Influential in these policies was the idea of a "third Way" which called for a re-evalutation of welfare state policies. In 1995. the Labour Party re-defined its stance on socialism by re-wording Clause IV of its constitution. effectively rejecting socialism by removing all references to public. direct worker or municipal ownership of the means of production. The Labour Party stated: "The Labour Party is a democratic socialist party. It believes that. by the strength of our common endeavour we achieve more than we achieve alone. so as to create. for each of us. the means to realise our true potential. and. for all of us. a community in which power. wealth. and opportunity are in the hands of the many. not the few."

CONTEMPORARY SOCIALIST POLITICS

AFRICAN

African socialism has been and continues to be a major ideology around the continent. Julius Nyerere was inspired by Fabian socialist ideals. He was a firm believer in rural Africans and their traditions and ujamaa. a system of collectivisation that according to Nyerere was present before European imperialism. Essentially he believed Africans were already socialists. Other African socialists include Jomo Kenyatta. Kenneth Kaunda.Nelson Mandela and Kwame Nkrumah. Fela Kuti was inspired by socialism and called for a democratic African republic. In South Africa the African National Congress (ANC) abandoned its partial socialist allegiances after taking power. and followed a standard Neo-liberal route. From 2005 through to 2007. the country was wracked by many thousands of protests from poor communities. One of these gave rise to a mass movement of shack dwellers. Abahlali baseMjondolo that. despite major police suppression. continues to work for popular people's planning and against the creation of a market economy in land and housing.

ASIAN

The People's Republic of China. North Korea. Laos and Vietnam are Asian countries remaining from the wave of Marxism-Leninist implemented socialism in the 20th century. States with socialist economies have largely moved away from centralised economic planning in the 21st century. placing a greater emphasis on markets. Forms include the Chinese socialist market economy and the Vietnamese socialist-oriented market economy.

They utilise state-owned corporate management models as opposed to modelling socialist enterprise on traditional management styles employed by government agencies. In China living standards continued to improve rapidly despite the late-2000s recession. but centralized political control remained tight. Brian Reynolds Myers in his book *The Cleanest Race*. and later supported by other academics. dismisses the idea that *Juche* is North Korea's leading ideology. regarding its public exaltation as designed to deceive foreigners and that it exists to be praised and not actually readpointing out that North Korea's latest constitution. of 2009. omits all mention of communism.

Though the authority of the state remained unchallenged under the government of Vietnam encourages private ownership of farms and factories. economic deregulation and foreign investment. while maintaining control over strategic industries. The Vietnamese economy subsequently achieved strong growth in agricultural and industrial production. construction. exports and foreign investment. However. these reforms have also caused a rise in income inequality and gender disparities. Elsewhere in Asia. some elected socialist parties and communist parties remain prominent. particularly in India and Nepal. The Communist Party of Nepal in particular calls for multi-party democracy. social equality. and economic prosperity.

In Singapore. a majority of the GDP is still generated from the state sector comprising government-linked companies. In Japan. there has been a resurgent interest in the Japanese Communist Party among workers and youth.

In Malaysia. the Socialist Party of Malaysia got its first Member of Parliament. Dr. Jeyakumar Devaraj. after the 2008 general election. In 2010. there were 270 kibbutzim in Israel. Their factories and farms account for 9per cent of Israel's industrial output. worth US$8 billion. and 40per cent of its agricultural output. worth over $1.7 billion. Some Kibbutzim had also developed substantial high-tech and military industries. For example. in 2010. Kibbutz Sasa. containing some 200 members. generated $850 million in annual revenue from its military-plastics industry.

EUROPEAN

The United Nations *World Happiness Report 2013* shows that the happiest nations are concentrated in Northern Europe where the Nordic model of social democracy persists. with Denmark topping the list. The Nordics ranked highest on the metrics of real GDP per capita. healthy life expectancy. having someone to count on. perceived freedom to make life choices. generosity and freedom from corruption.The objectives of the Party of European Socialists. the European Parliament's socialist and social-democratic bloc. are now "to pursue international aims in respect of the principles on which the European Union is based. namely principles of freedom. equality. solidarity. democracy. respect of Human Rights and Fundamental Freedoms. and respect for the Rule of Law." As a result. today. the rallying cry of the French Revolution – "Egalité. Liberté. Fraternité" – which overthrew absolutism and ushered industrialisation into French society. are promoted as essential socialist values.

To the left of the PES at the European level is the Party of the European Left. (PEL; also commonly abbreviated "European Left") which is a political party at the European level and an association of democratic socialist. socialist and communist political parties in the European Union and other European countries. It was formed in January 2004 for the purposes of running in the 2004 European Parliament elections. PEL was founded on 8–9 May 2004 in Rome. Elected MEPs from member parties of the European Left sit in the European United Left–Nordic Green Left (GUE/NGL) group in the European parliament.

The socialist Left Party in Germany grew in popularity due to dissatisfaction with the increasingly Neo-liberal policies of the SPD. becoming the fourth biggest party in parliament in the general election on 27 September 2009. Communist candidate Dimitris Christofiaswon a crucial presidential Run-off in Cyprus. defeating his conservative rival with a majority of 53per cent. In Greece. in the general election on 17 June 2012. Coalition of the Radical Left (Syriza) won 26.89per cent of the votes and became the second largest party in parliament. It came in first in the 2014 European Parliament election.

In Ireland. in the2009 European election. Joe Higgins of the Socialist Party took one of three seats in the capital Dublin European constituency. In Denmark. the Socialist People's Party (SF or Socialist Party for short) more than doubled its parliamentary representation to 23 seats from 11. making it the fourth largest party. In 2011. the socialist parties of Social Democrats. Socialist People's Party and the Danish Social Liberal Party formed government. after a slight victory over the liberal parties. They were led by Helle Thorning-Schmidt. and had the Red-Green Alliance as a supporting party. In Norway. the Red-Green Coalition consists of the Labour Party (Ap). the Socialist Left Party (SV). and theCentre Party (Sp). and governed the country as a majority government from the 2005 general election until 2013.

In the UK. the National Union of Rail. Maritime and Transport Workers put forward a slate of candidates in the 2009 European Parliament elections under the banner of No to EU – Yes to Democracy. a broad left-wing alter-globalisation coalition involving socialist groups such as the Socialist Party. aiming to offer an alternative to the "anti-foreigner" and pro-business policies of the UK Independence Party. In the following May 2010 UK general election. the Trade Unionist and Socialist Coalition. launched in January 2010 and backed by Bob Crow. the leader of the National Union of Rail. Maritime and Transport Workers union (RMT). other union leaders and the Socialist Party among other socialist groups. stood against Labour in 40 constituencies. The Trade Unionist and Socialist Coalition plans to contest the 2011 elections. having gained the endorsement of the RMT June 2010 conference.

In France. the Revolutionary Communist League (LCR) candidate in the 2007 presidential election. Olivier Besancenot. received 1.498.581 votes. 4.08per cent. double that of the Communist candidate. The LCR abolished itself in 2009 to initiate a broad anti-capitalist party. the New Anticapitalist Party. whose stated aim is to "build a new socialist. democratic perspective for the twenty-first century". On 25 May 2014 in Spain the left wing party Podemos entered candidates for the 2014 European parliamentary elections. some of which were unemployed. In a surprise result. it polled 7.98per cent of the vote and thus was awarded five seats out of 54. while the older United Left was the third largest overall force obtaining 10.03 per cent and 5 seats. 4 more than the previous elections. All around Europe and in some places of Latin America there exists a social centre and Squatting movement mainly inspired by autonomist and anarchist ideas.

NORTH AMERICAN

According to a 2013 article in *The Guardian*. "Contrary to popular belief. Americans don't have an innate allergy to socialism. Milwaukee has had several socialist mayors (Frank Zeidler. Emil Seidel and Daniel Hoan). and there is currently an independent socialist in the US Senate.Bernie Sanders of Vermont." Sanders has described himself as a democratic socialist and has praised Scandinavian-style social democracy.

Anti-capitalism. anarchism and the anti-globalisation movement rose to prominence through events such as protests against the World Trade Organization Ministerial Conference of 1999 in Seattle. Socialist-inspired groups played an important role in these movements. which nevertheless embraced much broader layers of the population and were championed by figures such as

Noam Chomsky. In Canada. theCo-operative Commonwealth Federation (CCF). the precursor to the social democratic New Democratic Party (NDP). had significant success in provincial politics. In 1944. the Saskatchewan CCF formed the first socialist government in North America. At the federal level. the NDP is currently the Official Opposition. after winning 103 out of 308 seats (up from 37) in the 2011 Canadian federal election.

SOUTH AMERICAN AND CARIBBEAN

For the *Encyclopaedia Britannica* "the attempt by Salvador Allende to unite Marxists and other reformers in a socialist reconstruction of Chile is most representative of the direction that Latin American socialists have taken since the late 20th century.... Several socialist (or socialist-leaning) leaders have followed Allende's example in winning election to office in Latin American countries." Venezuelan President Hugo Chávez. Nicaraguan President Daniel Ortega. Bolivian President Evo Morales. and Ecuadorian president Rafael Correa refer to their political programmes as socialist. Chávez has adopted the term *socialism of the 21st century*. After winning re-election in December 2006. Chávez said. "Now more than ever.

I am obliged to move Venezuela's path towards socialism." Hugo Chávez was also reelected in October 2012 for his third six-year term as President. but he died in March 2013 from cancer. After Chávez's death on 5 March 2013. vice-president from Chavez's party Nicolás Maduro assumed the powers and responsibilities of the President. A special election was held on 14 April of the same year to elect a new President. which Maduro won by a tight margin as the candidate of theUnited Socialist Party of Venezuela; he was formally inaugurated on 19 April. "Pink tide" is a term being used in contemporary 21st-century political analysis in the media and elsewhere to describe the perception that Leftist ideology in general. and Left-wing politics in particular. are increasingly influential in Latin America.

Foro de São Paulo is a conference of leftist political parties and other organizations from Latin America and the Caribbean. It was launched by the Workers' Party (Portuguese: *Partido dos Trabalhadores - PT*) of Brazil in 1990 in the city of São Paulo. The Forum of São Paulo was constituted in 1990 when the Brazilian Workers' Party approached other parties and social movements of Latin America and the Caribbean with the objective of debating the new international scenario after the fall of the Berlin Wall and the consequences of the implementation of what were taken as Neo-liberal policies adopted at the time by contemporary right-leaning governments in the region. the stated main objective of the conference being to argue for alternatives to Neo-liberalism. Among its member include current socialist and social-democratic parties currently in government in the region such as Bolivia´s Movement for socialism. Brazil´sWorkers Party. the Communist Party of Cuba. the Ecuadorian PAIS

Alliance. the Venezuelan United Socialist Party of Venezuela. theSocialist Party of Chile. the Uruguayan Broad Front. the Nicaraguan Sandinista National Liberation Front and the salvadorean Farabundo Martí National Liberation Front.

INTERNATIONAL

The Progressive Alliance is a political international founded on 22 May 2013 by political parties. the majority of whom are current or former members of the Socialist International. The organisation states the aim of becoming the global network of "the progressive". democratic. social-democratic. socialist and labour movement".

PHILOSOPHY

Early socialist thought took influences from a diverse range of philosophies such as civic republicanism. Enlightenment rationalism. romanticism. forms of materialism. Christianity (both Catholic and Protestant). natural law and natural rights theory. utilitarianism and liberal political economy.

The philosophical basis for a lot of early socialism was heavily influenced by the emergence of positivism during the European Enlightenment. Positivism held that both the natural and social worlds could be understood through scientific knowledge and be analyzed using scientific methods. This core outlook influenced early social scientists and different types of socialists ranging from anarchists like Peter Kropotkin to technocrats like Saint Simon.

The fundamental objective of socialism is to attain an advanced level of material production and therefore greater productivity. efficiency and rationality as compared to capitalism and all previous systems. under the view that an expansion of human productive capability is the basis for the extension of freedom and equality in society.Many forms of socialist theory hold that human behaviour is largely shaped by the social environment. In particular. socialism holds that social mores. values. cultural traits and economic practices are social creations and not the result of an immutable natural law. The object of their critique is thus not human avarice or human consciousness. but the material conditions and man-made social systems (*i.e.*: the economic structure of society) that gives rise to observed social problems and inefficiencies.

In the 20th century socialist economists were heavily influenced by Neo-classical economics and its precepts in analytic philosophy. Notable socialists often combined Neo-classical economics with Marxian analysis and historical materialism. Bertrand Russell. often considered to be the father of analytic philosophy. identified as a socialist. Bertrand Russell opposed the class struggle aspects of Marxism. viewing socialism solely as an adjustment of economic relations to accommodate modern machine production to benefit all of humanity through the progressive reduction of necessary work time.

FREEDOM AND CREATIVITY

Socialists tend to argue that "capitalism necessarily leads to unfair and exploitative concentrations of wealth and power in the hands of the relative few who emerge victorious from free-market competition—people who then use their wealth and power to reinforce their dominance in society. Because such people are rich. they may choose where and how to live. and their choices in turn limit the options of the poor."

From the socialist perspective. freedom is conceived of as a concrete situation as opposed to a purely abstract or moral concept. and is closely related to human creativity and the importance socialists ascribe to creative freedom. Socialists view creativity as an essential aspect of human nature. and define freedom as a state of being where individuals are able to express their creativity unhindered by constraints of both material scarcity and coercive social institutions. Marxists stress the importance of freeing the individual from coercive. exploitative and alienating social relationships they are compelled to partake in merely to survive. as well as the importance of economic development as providing the material basis for the existence of a state of society where there are enough resources to allow for each individual to pursue his or her genuine creative interests. In Marxist terminology. this is the goal of transcending alienation through material abundance.

The socialist concept of individuality is thus intertwined with the concept of individual creative expression. Karl Marx believed that expansion of the productive forces and technology was the basis for the expansion of human freedom. and that socialism. being a system that is consistent with modern developments in technology. would enable the flourishing of "free individualities" through the progressive reduction of necessary labour time. The reduction of necessary labour time to a minimum would grant individuals the opportunity to pursue the development of their true individuality and creativity.

PERSPECTIVES ON EQUALITY

In general. models of socialism often include some form of co-operative management of economic affairs based on equal power relationships. and socialists generally oppose hierarchies of a non-technical nature.

Karl Marx eschewed theorizing on moral concepts. Instead of advocating principles of justice or equality. Marx's case for socialism was grounded in economic and materialist logic and his analysis of the development of the productive forces. Although Karl Marx is sometimes mistaken as an egalitarian. Marx opposed idealism and the concept of "equality". Marx did. however. have a theory of the evolution of moral principles in relation to specific economic systems. In Marxist theory. upper-stage communism is based on a principle whereby access to goods and services is based on need. stressing equal access to the articles of consumption. The "equality" in a communist society is not about equality of outcome. but about equal access to the articles of consumption so that individuals are free from dependency on other individuals or groups. and are thus able to overcome alienation.

The American socialist economist John Roemer has put forth a new perspective of equality and its relationship to socialism. Roemer attempts to reformulate Marxist analysis to accommodate normative principles of distributive justice. shifting the argument for socialism away from purely technical and materialist reasons to one of distributive justice. Roemer argues that. according to the principle of distributive justice. the traditional definition of socialism based on the principle that individual compensation be proportional to the value of the labour one expands in production is inadequate. Roemer concludes that egalitarians must therefore go beyond socialism as it is classically defined.

CRITIQUE OF CAPITALISM

Socialists do not base their critique of capitalism on the denunciation of greed. vilification of human nature or capitalists. or on human avarice but on the structural causes of social and economic problems that emerge from the normal functioning of the capitalist system.

Socialists generally argue that capitalism concentrates power and wealth within a small segment of society that controls the means of production and derives its wealth through economic exploitation. This creates unequal social relations which fail to provide opportunities for every individual to maximise their potential. and after a certain stage of development. fails to utilise available technology and resources to their maximum potential due to restrictive property relations.

ECONOMICS

Socialist economics starts from the premise that "individuals do not live or work in isolation but live in cooperation with one another. Furthermore. everything that people produce is in some sense a social product. and everyone who contributes to the production of a good is entitled to a share in it. Society as a whole. therefore. should own or at least control property for the benefit of all its members."

The original conception of socialism was an economic system whereby production was organised in a way to directly produce goods and services for their utility (or use-value in classical and Marxian economics): the *direct allocation* of resources in terms of physical units as opposed to financial calculation and the economic laws of capitalism. often entailing the end of capitalistic economic categories such as rent. interest. profit and money. In a fully developed socialist economy. production and balancing factor inputs with outputs becomes a technical process to be undertaken by engineers. Market socialism refers to an array of different economic theories and systems that utilise the market mechanism to organise production and to allocate factor inputs among socially owned enterprises. with the economic surplus (profits) accruing to society in a social dividend as opposed to private capital owners. Variations of market socialism include Libertarian proposals such as mutualism. based on classical economics. and Neo-classical economic models such as the Lange Model.

The ownership of the means of production can be based on direct ownership by the users of the productive property through worker cooperative; or commonly owned by all of society with management and control delegated to those who operate/use the means of production; or public ownership by a state apparatus. *Public ownership* may refer to the creation of state-owned enterprises. nationalisation. municipalisation or autonomous collective institutions. The fundamental feature of a socialist economy is that publicly owned. worker-run institutions produce goods and services in at least the *commanding heights* of the economy.

Management and control over the activities of enterprises are based on self-management and self-governance. with equal power-relations in the workplace to maximise occupational autonomy. A socialist form of organisation would eliminate controlling hierarchies so that only a hierarchy based on technical knowledge in the workplace remains. Every member would have decision-making power in the firm and would be able to participate in establishing its overall policy objectives. The policies/goals would be carried out by the technical specialists that form the coordinating hierarchy of the firm. who would establish plans or directives for the work community to accomplish these goals.

The role and use of money in a hypothetical socialist economy is a contested issue. Socialists including Karl Marx. Robert Owen. Pierre-Joseph Proudhon and John Stuart Milladvocated various forms of labour vouchers or labour-credits. which like money would be used to acquire articles of consumption. but unlike money. they are unable to becomecapital and would not be used to allocate resources within the production process. Bolshevik revolutionary Leon Trotsky argued that money could not be arbitrarily abolished following a socialist revolution. Money had to exhaust its "historic mission". meaning it would have to be used until its function became redundant. eventually being transformed into bookkeeping receipts for statisticians. and only in the more distant future would money not be required for even that role.

The economic anarchy of capitalist society as it exists today is. in my opinion. the real source of the evil... I am convinced there is only one way to eliminate these grave evils. namely through the establishment of a socialist economy. accompanied by an educational system which would be oriented toward social goals. In such an economy. the means of production are owned by society itself and are utilized in a planned fashion. A planned economy. which adjusts production to the needs of the community. would distribute the work to be done among all those able to work and would guarantee a livelihood to every man. woman. and child. The education of the individual. in addition to promoting his own innate abilities. would attempt to develop in him a sense of responsibility for his fellow men in place of the glorification of power and success in our present society.

— Albert Einstein. *Why Socialism?*. 1949

PLANNED ECONOMY

A planned economy is a type of economy consisting of a mixture of public ownership of the means of production and the coordination of production and distribution througheconomic planning. There are two major types of planning: decentralised-planning and centralised-planning. Enrico Barone provided a comprehensive theoretical framework for a planned socialist economy. In his model. assuming perfect computation techniques. simultaneous equations relating inputs and outputs to ratios of equivalence would provide appropriate valuations in order to balance supply and demand.

The most prominent example of a planned economy was the economic system of the Soviet Union. and as such. the centralised-planned economic model is usually associated with the Communist states of the 20th century. where it was combined with a single-party political system. In a centrally planned economy. decisions regarding the quantity of goods and services to be produced are planned in advance by a planning agency. The economic systems of the Soviet Union and the Eastern Bloc are further classified as *command economies*. which are defined as systems where economic coordination is undertaken by commands. directives and production targets.

Studies by economists of various political persuasions on the actual functioning of the Soviet economy indicate that it was not actually a planned economy. Instead of conscious planning. the Soviet economy was based on a process whereby the plan was modified by localized agents and the original plans went largely unfulfilled. Planning agencies. ministries and enterprises all adapted and bargained with each other during the formulation of the plan as opposed to following a plan passed down from a higher authority. leading some economists to suggest that planning did not actually take place within the Soviet economy and that a better description would be an "administered" or "managed" economy.

Although central planning was largely supported by Marxist Leninists. some factions within the Soviet Union before the rise of Stalinism held positions contrary to central planning. Leon Trotsky rejected central planning in favour of decentralised planning. He argued that central planners. regardless of their intellectual capacity. would be unable to coordinate effectively all economic activity within an economy because they operated without the input and tacit knowledge embodied by the participation of the millions of people who in the economy. As a result. central planners would be unable to respond to local economic conditions.

SELF-MANAGED ECONOMY

A self-managed. decentralised economy is based on autonomous self-regulating economic units and a decentralised mechanism of resource allocation and decision-making. This model has found support in notable classical and Neo-classical economists including Alfred Marshall. John Stuart Mill and Jaroslav Vanek. There are numerous variations of self-management. including labour-managed firms and worker-managed firms. The goals of self-management are to eliminate exploitation and reduce alienation. Guild socialism is a political movement advocating workers' control of industry through the medium of trade-related guilds "in an implied contractual relationship with the public". It originated in the United Kingdom and was at its most influential in the first quarter of the 20th century. It was strongly associated with G. D. H. Cole and influenced by the ideas of William Morris.

One such system is the cooperative economy. a largely free market economy in which workers manage the firms and democratically determine remuneration levels and labour divisions. Productive resources would be legally owned by the cooperative and rented to the workers. who would enjoy usufruct rights. Another form of decentralised planning is the use of cybernetics. or the use of computers to manage the allocation of economic inputs. The socialist-run government of Salvador Allende in Chile experimented with Project Cybersyn. a real-time information bridge between the government. state enterprises and consumers. Another. more recent. variant is participatory economics. wherein the economy is planned by decentralised councils of workers and consumers. Workers would be remunerated solely according to effort and sacrifice. so that those engaged in dangerous. uncomfortable. and strenuous work would receive the highest incomes and could thereby work less. A contemporary model for a self-managed. non-market socialism is Pat Devine's model of negotiated coordination. Negotiated coordination is based upon social ownership by those affected by the use of the assets involved. with decisions made by those at the most localised level of production.

Michel Bauwens identifies the emergence of the open software movement and peer-to-peer production as a new. alternative mode of production to the capitalist economy and centrally planned economy that is based on collaborative self-management. common ownership of resources. and the production of use-values through the free cooperation of producers who have access to distributed capital. Anarchist communism is a theory of anarchism which advocates the abolition of the state. private property. and capitalism in favour of common ownership of the means of production. Anarcho-syndicalism as practiced in Catalonia and other places in the Spanish Revolution during the Spanish Civil War. Sam Dolgoff estimated that about eight million people participated directly or at least indirectly in the Spanish Revolution..

The economy of the former Socialist Federal Republic of Yugoslavia established a system based on market-based allocation. social ownership of the means of production and self-management within firms. This system substituted Yugoslavia's Soviet-type central planning with a decentralised. self-managed system after reforms in 1953.

The Marxian economist Richard D. Wolff argues that "reorganizing production so that workers become collectively self-directed at their work-sites" not only moves society beyond both capitalism and state socialism of the last century. but would also mark another milestone in human history. similar to earlier transitions out of slavery and feudalism. As an example. Wolff claims that Mondragon is "a stunningly successful alternative to the capitalist organisation of production."

STATE-DIRECTED ECONOMY

State socialism can be used to classify any variety of socialist philosophies that advocates the ownership of the means of production by the state apparatus. either as a transitional stage between capitalism and socialism. or as an end-goal in itself. Typically it refers to a form of technocratic management. whereby technical specialists administer or manage economic enterprises on behalf of society (and the public interest) instead of workers' councils or workplace democracy.

A state-directed economy may refer to a type of mixed economy consisting of public ownership over large industries. as promoted by various Social democratic political parties during the 20th century. This ideology influenced the policies of the British Labour Party during Clement Attlee's administration. In the biography of the 1945 UK Labour Party Prime Minister Clement Attlee. Francis Beckett states: "the government... wanted what would become known as a mixed economy".

Nationalisation in the UK was achieved through compulsory purchase of the industry (*i.e.* with compensation). British Aerospace was a combination of major aircraft companiesBritish Aircraft Corporation. Hawker Siddeley and others. British Shipbuilders was a combination of the major shipbuilding companies including Cammell Laird. Govan Shipbuilders.

Swan Hunter. and Yarrow Shipbuilders; the nationalisation of the coal mines in 1947 created a coal board charged with running the coal industry commercially so as to be able to meet the interest payable on the bonds which the former mine owners' shares had been converted into.

MARKET SOCIALISM

Market socialism consists of publicly owned or cooperatively owned enterprises operating in a market economy. It is a system that utilises the market and monetary prices for the allocation and accounting of the means of production. thereby retaining the process of capital accumulation. The profit generated would be used to directly remunerate employees or finance public institutions. In state-oriented forms of market socialism. in which state enterprises attempt to maximise profit. the profits can be used to fund government programmes and services through a social dividend. eliminating or greatly diminishing the need for various forms of taxation that exist in capitalist systems. The Neo-classical economist Léon Walras believed that a socialist economy based on state ownership of land and natural resources would provide a means of public finance to make income taxes unnecessary. Yugoslavia implemented a market socialist economy based on cooperatives and worker self-management.

Mutualism is an economic theory and anarchist school of thought that advocates a society where each person might possess ameans of production. either individually or collectively. with trade representing equivalent amounts of labour in the free market.Integral to the scheme was the establishment of a mutual-credit bank that would lend to producers at a minimal interest rate. just high enough to cover administration. Mutualism is based on a labour theory of value that holds that when labour or its product is sold. in exchange. it ought to receive goods or services embodying "the amount of labour necessary to produce an article of exactly similar and equal utility".

The current economic system in China is formally referred to as a Socialist market economy with Chinese characteristics. It combines a large state sector that comprises the 'commanding heights' of the economy. which are guaranteed their public ownership status by law. with a private sector mainly engaged in commodity production and light industry responsible from anywhere between 33per cent (People's Daily Online 2005) to over 70per cent of GDP generated in 2005. Although there has been a rapid expansion of private-sector activity since the 1980s. privatisation of state assets was virtually halted and were partially reversed in 2005. The current Chinese economy consists of 150 corporatised state-owned enterprises that report directly to China's central government. By 2008. these state-owned corporations had become increasingly dynamic and generated large increases in revenue for the state. resulting in a state-sector led recovery during the 2009 financial crises while accounting for most of China's economic growth. However. the Chinese economic model is widely cited as a contemporary form of state capitalism. the major difference between Western capitalism and the Chinese model being the degree of state-ownership of shares in publicly listed corporations. The Socialist Republic of Vietnam has adopted a similar model after the Doi Moi economic renovation.

but slightly differs from the Chinese model in that the Vietnamese government retains firm control over the state sector and strategic industries. but allows for private-sector activity in commodity production.

SOCIAL AND POLITICAL THEORY

In this context. *socialism* has been used to refer to a political movement. a political philosophy and a hypothetical form of society these movements aim to achieve. As a result. in a political context socialism has come to refer to the strategy (for achieving a socialist society) or policies promoted by socialist organisations and socialist political parties; all of which have no connection to socialism as a socioeconomic system.

MARXISM

At a certain stage of development. the material productive forces of society come into conflict with the existing relations of production or – this merely expresses the same thing in legal terms – with the property relations within the framework of which they have operated hitherto. Then begins an era of social revolution. The changes in the economic foundation lead sooner or later to the transformation of the whole immense superstructure. – Karl Marx. *Critique of the Gotha Programme*

Karl Marx and Friedrich Engels argued that socialism would emerge from historical necessity as capitalism rendered itself obsolete and unsustainable from increasing internal contradictions emerging from the development of the productive forces and technology. It was these advances in the productive forces combined with the old social relations of production of capitalism that would generate contradictions. leading to working-class consciousness.

Marx and Engels held the view that the consciousness of those who earn a wage or salary (the working class in the broadest Marxist sense) would be moulded by their conditions of wage slavery. leading to a tendency to seek their freedom or emancipation by overthrowing ownership of the means of production by capitalists. and consequently. overthrowing the state that upheld this economic order. For Marx and Engels. conditions determine consciousness and ending the role of the capitalist class leads eventually to a classless society in which the state would wither away.

The Marxist conception of socialism is that of a specific historical phase that will displace capitalism and precede communism. The major characteristics of socialism (particularly as conceived by Marx and Engels after the Paris Commune of 1871) are that the proletariat will control the means of production through a workers' state erected by the workers in their interests. Economic activity would still be organised through the use of incentive systems and social classes would still exist. but to a lesser and diminishing extent than under capitalism. For orthodox Marxists. socialism is the lower stage of communism based on the principle of "from each according to his ability. to each according to his contribution" while upper stage communism is based on the principle of "from each according to his ability. to each according to his need"; the upper stage becoming possible only after the socialist stage further develops economic efficiency and the automation of production has led to a superabundance of goods and services.

Marx argued that the material productive forces (in industry and commerce) brought into existence by capitalism predicated a cooperative society since production had become a mass social. collective activity of the working class to create commodities but with private ownership (the relations of production or property relations). This conflict between collective effort in large factories and private ownership would bring about a conscious desire in the working class to establish collective ownership commensurate with the collective efforts their daily experience. Che Guevara and Mao Zedong sought socialism based on the rural peasantry rather than the urban working class. Che Guevara attempted to inspire the peasants of Bolivia by his own example into a change of consciousness. Guevara said in 1965:

Socialism cannot exist without a change in consciousness resulting in a new fraternal attitude Towards humanity. both at an individual level. within the societies where socialism is being built or has been built. and on a world scale. with regard to all peoples suffering from imperialist oppression.

EVOLUTIONARY AND INSTITUTIONAL ECONOMICS

Thorstein Veblen. a leading American institutionalist and evolutionary economist. argued that a subset of the working-class. the technical specialists and engineers. would become the driving force behind socioeconomic change within capitalism. There is an antagonism between industry and business. where industry refers to the process of producing goods and services and business is defined as the process of "making money". Thorstein Veblen saw socialism as an immediate stage in an ongoing evolutionary process in economics that would result from the natural decay of the system of business enterprise. In contrast to Marx. he did not believe socialism would be the result of political struggle or political revolution by the working class as a whole and did not believe it to be the ultimate goal of humanity. But like Marx. Veblen saw technology as the underlying force driving social change. Joseph Schumpeter viewed intellectuals and the intelligentsia as the group within society that would gradually move society Towards socialism. Socialism would be partially a result of socio-economic evolution. the growth of workers' self-management. industrial democracy and social planning. and partially from political pressure on the part of intellectuals in Western society.

ROLE OF THE STATE

Socialists have taken different perspectives on the state and the role it should play in revolutionary struggles. in constructing socialism. and within an established socialist economy. In the 19th century the philosophy of state socialism was first explicitly expounded by the German political philosopher Ferdinand Lassalle. In contrast to Karl Marx's perspective of the state. Lassalle rejected the concept of the state as a class-based power structure whose main function was to preserve existing class structures. Thus Lassalle also rejected the Marxist view that the state was destined to "wither away". Lassalle considered the state to be an entity independent of class allegiances and an instrument of justice that would therefore be essential for achieving socialism.

Preceding the Bolshevik-led revolution in Russia. many socialists including reformists. orthodox Marxist currents such as council communism and the Mensheviks. Anarchists and Libertarian socialists criticised the idea of using the state to conduct central planning and own the means of production as a way to establish socialism. Following the victory of Leninism in Russia. the idea of "state socialism" spread rapidly throughout the socialist movement. and eventually "state socialism" came to be identified with the Soviet economic model.

Joseph Schumpeter rejected the association of socialism (and social ownership) with state ownership over the means of production. because the state as it exists in its current form is a product of capitalist society and cannot be transplanted to a different institutional framework. Schumpeter argued that there would be different institutions within socialism than those that exist within modern capitalism. just as feudalism had its own distinct and unique institutional forms. The state. along with concepts like property and taxation were concepts exclusive to commercial society (capitalism) and attempting to place them within the context of a future socialist society would amount to a distortion of these concepts by using them out of context

UTOPIAN VERSUS SCIENTIFIC

Utopian socialism is a term used to define the first currents of modern socialist thought as exemplified by the work of Henri de Saint-Simon. Charles Fourier. and Robert Owen. which inspired Karl Marx and other early socialists. However. visions of imaginary ideal societies. which competed with revolutionary social-democratic movements. were viewed as not being grounded in the material conditions of society and as reactionary.

Although it is technically possible for any set of ideas or any person living at any time in history to be a utopian socialist. the term is most often applied to those socialists who lived in the first quarter of the 19th century who were ascribed the label "utopian" by later socialists as a negative term. in order to imply naivete and dismiss their ideas as fanciful or unrealistic. Religious sects whose members live communally. such as the Hutterites. for example. are not usually called "utopian socialists". although their way of living is a prime example. They have been categorized as religious socialists by some. Likewise. modern intentional communities based on socialist ideas could also be categorized as "utopian socialist".

For Marxists. the development of capitalism in western Europe provided a material basis for the possibility of bringing about socialism because. according to the *Communist Manifesto*. "What the bourgeoisie produces above all is its own grave diggers". namely the working class. which must become conscious of the historical objectives set it by society.

REFORM VERSUS REVOLUTION

Revolutionary socialists believe that a social revolution is necessary to effect structural changes to the socio-economic structure of society. Among revolutionary socialists there are differences in strategy. theory and the definition of "revolution". Orthodox Maxists and Left Communists take an Impossibilist stance. believing revolution should be spontaneous as a result of contradictions in society resulting from technological changes in the productive forces.

Lenin theorized that under capitalism the workers cannot achieve class consciousness beyond organising into unions and making demands of the capitalists. Therefore. Leninists advocate that it is historically necessity for a vanguardof class conscious revolutionaries to take a central role in coordinating the social revolution to overthrow the capitalist state and. eventually. the institution of the state altogether. "Revolution" is not necessarily defined by revolutionary socialists as violent insurrection. but as a complete dismantling and rapid transformation of all areas of class society led by the majority of the masses: the working class.

Reformism is generally associated with social democracy and gradualist democratic socialism. Reformism is the belief that socialists should stand in parliamentary elections within capitalist society. and if elected. utilize the machinery of government to pass political and social reforms for the purposes of ameliorating the instabilities and inequities of capitalism.

POLITICS

The major socialist political movements. Independent socialist theorists. utopian socialist authors. and academic supporters of socialism may not be represented in these movements. Some political groups have called themselves socialist while holding views that some consider antithetical to socialism. The term *socialist* has also been used by some politicians on the political right as an epithet against certain individuals who do not consider themselves to be socialists. and against policies that are not considered socialist by their proponents. There are many variations of socialism and as such there is no single definition encapsulating all of socialism. However there have been common elements identified by scholars. Angelo S. Rappoport in his *Dictionary of Socialism* (1924) analysed forty definitions of socialism to conclude that common elements of socialism include: general criticisms of the social effects of private ownership and control of capital – as being the cause of poverty. low wages. unemployment. economic and social inequality. and a lack of economic security; a general view that the solution to these problems is a form of collective control over the means of production. distribution and exchange (the degree and means of control vary amongst socialist movements); agreement that the outcome of this collective control should be a society based upon social justice. including social equality. economic protection of people. and should provide a more satisfying life for most people.

Bhikhu Parekh in *The Concepts of Socialism* (1975) identifies four core principles of socialism and particularly socialist society: sociality. social responsibility. cooperation. and planning. Michael Freeden in his study *Ideologies and Political Theory* (1996) states that all socialists share five themes: the first is that socialism posits that society is more than a mere collection of individuals; second. that it considers human welfare a desirable objective; third. that it considers humans by nature to be active and productive; fourth. it holds the belief of human equality; and fifth. that history is progressive and will create positive change on the condition that humans work to achieve such change.

ANARCHISM

Anarchism is a political philosophy that advocates stateless societies often defined as self-governed voluntary institutions. but that several authors have defined as more specific institutions based on non-hierarchical free associations. Anarchism holds the state to be undesirable. unnecessary. or harmful. While anti-statism is central. some argue that anarchism entails opposing authority or hierarchical organisation in the conduct of human relations. including. but not limited to. the state system. Mutualists advocate market socialism. collectivist anarchists workers cooperatives and salaries based on the amount of time contributed to production. anarcho-communists advocate a direct transition from capitalism to libertarian communism and a gift economy and anarcho-syndicalists worker's direct action and the general strike.

DEMOCRATIC SOCIALISM

Modern democratic socialism is a broad political movement that seeks to promote the ideals of socialism within the context of a democratic system. Some Democratic socialists support social democracy as a temporary measure to reform the current system. while others reject reformism in favour of more revolutionary methods. Modern social democracy emphasises a programme of gradual legislative modification of capitalism in order to make it more equitable and humane. while the theoretical end goal of building a socialist society is either completely forgotten or redefined in a pro-capitalist way. The two movements are widely similar both in terminology and in ideology. although there are a few key differences.

The major difference between social democracy and democratic socialism is the object of their politics: contemporary social democrats support awelfare state and unemployment insurance as a means to "humanize" capitalism. whereas democratic socialists seek to replace capitalism with a socialist economic system. arguing that any attempt to "humanize" capitalism through regulations and welfare policies would distort the market and create economic contradictions.

Democratic socialism generally refers to any political movement that seeks to establish an economy based on economic democracy by and for the working class. Democratic socialists oppose authoritarian "socialists" as Marxists-Leninists. Stalinists and Maoists. Democratic socialism is difficult to define. and groups of scholars have radically different definitions for the term. Some definitions simply refer to all forms of socialism that follow an electoral. reformist or evolutionary path to socialism. rather than a revolutionary one.

You can't talk about ending the slums without first saying profit must be taken out of slums. You're really tampering and getting on dangerous ground because you are messing with folk then. You are messing with captains of industry. Now this means that we are treading in difficult water. because it really means that we are saying that something is wrong with capitalism. There must be a better distribution of wealth. and maybe America must move Towards a democratic socialism.

— Martin Luther King. Jr.. 1966.

RELIGIOUS SOCIALISM

Christian socialism is a broad concept involving an intertwining of the Christian religion with the politics and economic theories of socialism.

Islamic socialism is a term coined by various Muslim leaders to describe a more spiritual form of socialism. Muslim socialists believe that the teachings of the Qur'an andMuhammad are compatible with principles of equality and public ownership drawing inspiration from the early Medina welfare state established by the Prophet Muhammad. Muslim Socialists are more conservative than their western contemporaries and find their roots in Anti-imperialism. anti-colonialism and Arab nationalism. Islamic Socialist leaders believe in Democracy and deriving legitimacy from public mandate as opposed to religious texts.

LENINISM AND PRECEDENTS

Blanquism refers to a conception of revolution generally attributed to Louis Auguste Blanqui which holds that socialist revolution should be carried out by a relatively small group of highly organised and secretive conspirators. Having seized power. the revolutionaries would then use the power of the state to introduce socialism. It is considered a particular sort of 'putschism' – that is. the view that political revolution should take the form of a *putsch* or *coup d'état*. Rosa Luxemburg and Eduard Bernstein have criticised Lenin that his conception of revolution was elitist and essentially 'Blanquist'. Marxism–Leninism is a political ideology combining Marxism (the scientific socialistconcepts theorised by Karl Marx and Friedrich Engels) and Leninism (Vladimir Lenin's theoretical expansions of Marxism which include anti-imperialism. democratic centralism. and party-building principles). Marxism–Leninism was the official ideology of the Communist Party of the Soviet Union and of the Communist International (1919–43) and later it became the main guiding ideology for trotskists. maoists. and stalinists.

SOCIAL DEMOCRACY

Social democracy is a political ideology which "is derived from a socialist tradition of political thought. Many social democrats refer to themselves as socialists or democratic socialists. and some use these terms interchangeably. Others have opined that there are clear differences between the three terms. and preferred to describe their own political beliefs by using the term 'social democracy' only." There are two main directions. either to establish democratic socialism. or to build a welfare state within the framework of the capitalist system. The first variant has officially its goal by establishing democratic socialism through reformist and gradualist methods.

In the second variant Social democracy becomes a policy regime involving a welfare state. collective bargaining schemes. support for publicly financed public services. and a Capitalist-based economy like a mixed economy. It is often used in this manner to refer to the social models and economic policies prominent in Western and Northern Europe during the later half of the 20th century. It has been described by Jerry Mander as "hybrid" economics. an active collaboration of capitalist and socialist visions. and. while such systems aren't perfect. they tend to provide high standards of living. Numerous studies and surveys indicate that people tend to live happier lives in social democratic societies rather than Neo-liberal ones.

Social democrats supporting the first variant. advocate for a peaceful. evolutionary transition of the economy to socialism through progressive social reform of capitalism. It asserts that the only acceptable constitutional form of government is representative democracy under the rule of law. It promotes extending democratic decision-making beyond political democracy to include economic democracy to guarantee employees and other economic stakeholders sufficient rights of co-determination. It supports a mixed economy that opposes the excesses of capitalism such as inequality. poverty. and oppression of various groups. while rejecting both a totally free market or a fully planned economy. Common social democratic policies include advocacy of universal social rights to attain universally accessible public services such as education. health care. workers' compensation. and other services. including child care and care for the elderly. Social democracy is connected with the trade union labour movement and supports collective bargaining rights for workers. Most social democratic parties are affiliated with theSocialist International.

SYNDICALISM

Syndicalism is a social movement that operates through industrial trade unions and rejects state socialism and the use of establishment politics to establish or promote socialism. They reject using state power to construct a socialist society. favouring strategies such as the General strike. Syndicalists advocate a socialist economy based on federated unions or syndicates of workers who own and manage the means of production. Some Marxist currents advocate Syndicalism. such as DeLeonism. Anarcho-syndicalism is atheory of anarchism which views syndicalism as a method for workers in capitalist society to gain control of an economy and. with that control. influence broader society. The Spanish anarcho-syndicalist trade union CNT led the events known as Spanish revolution during the Spanish Civil War. The International Workers' Association is an international federation of anarcho-syndicalist labour unions and initiatives.

SOCIALISM AND PROGRESSIVE SOCIAL MOVEMENTS

Socialist feminism is a branch of feminism that focuses upon both the public and private spheres of a woman's life and argues that liberationcan only be achieved by working to end both the economic and cultural sources of women's oppression. Marxist feminism's foundation is laid by Friedrich Engels in his analysis of gender oppression in *The Origin of the Family. Private Property. and the State* (1884). August Bebel's *Woman under Socialism* (1879). the "single work dealing with sexuality most widely read by rank-and-file members of the Social Democratic Party of Germany (SPD)".. In the late nineteenth and early twentieth centuries. both Clara Zetkin and Eleanor Marx were against the demonization of men and supported a proletariat revolution that would overcome as many male–female inequalities as possible.

As their movement already had the most radical demands in women's equality. most Marxist leaders. including Clara Zetkin and Alexandra Kollontai. counterposed Marxism against liberal feminism. rather than trying to combine them. Anarcha-feminism began with late 19th and early 20th century authors and theorists such as anarchist feminists Emma Goldman and Voltairine de Cleyre In the Spanish Civil War. an anarcha-feminist group. Mujeres Libres ("Free Women") linked to the Federación Anarquista Ibérica. organized to defend both anarchist and feminist ideas. In 1972. the Chicago Women's

Liberation Union published "Socialist Feminism: A Strategy for the Women's Movement." which is believed to be the first to use the term "socialist feminism." in publication.

Many socialists were early advocates for LGBT rights. For early socialist Charles Fourier. true freedom could only occur without suppressing passions; the suppression of passions is not only destructive to the individual. but to society as a whole. Writing before the advent of the term 'homosexuality'. Fourier recognised that both men and women have a wide range of sexual needs and preferences which may change throughout their lives. including same-sex sexuality and *androgénité*. He argued that all sexual expressions should be enjoyed as long as people are not abused. and that "affirming one's difference" can actually enhance social integration.

In Oscar Wilde's *The Soul of Man Under Socialism*. he passionately advocates for an egalitarian society where wealth is shared by all. while warning of the dangers of social systems that crush individuality. Wilde's libertarian socialist politics were shared by other figures who actively campaigned for homosexual emancipation in the late 19th century such as Edward Carpenter. *The Intermediate Sex: A Study of Some Transitional Types of Men and Women* was a book from 1908 and an early work arguing for gay liberation written by Edward Carpenter who was also an influential personality in the foundation of the Fabian Society and the Labour Party. After the Russian Revolution under the leadership of Vladimir Lenin and Leon Trotsky. the Soviet Union abolished previous laws against homosexuality.

Harry Hay was an early leader in the American LGBT rights movement as well as a member of the Communist Party USA. He is known for his roles in helping to found several gay organizations. including the Mattachine Society. the first sustained gay rights group in the United States which in its early days had a strong marxist influence. The *Encyclopaedia of Homosexuality* reports that "As Marxists the founders of the group believed that the injustice and oppression which they suffered stemmed from relationships deeply embedded in the structure of American society".Also emerging from a number of events. such as the May 1968 insurrection in France. the anti-Vietnam war movement in the US and theStonewall riots of 1969. militant Gay Liberation organisations began to spring up around the world. Many saw their roots in left radicalism more than in the established homophile groups of the time. The Gay Liberation Front took an anti-capitalist stance and attacked thenuclear family and traditional gender roles.

Eco-socialism. green socialism or socialist ecology is an political position merging aspects of Marxism. socialism. and/or libertarian socialismwith that of green politics. ecology and alter-globalization. Eco-socialists generally believe that the expansion of the capitalist system is the cause of social exclusion. poverty. war and environmental degradation through globalization and imperialism. under the supervision of repressive states and transnational structures. Contrary to the depiction of Karl Marx by some environmentalists. social ecologistsand fellow socialists as a productivist who favoured the domination of nature. eco-socialists have revisited Marx's writings and believe that he "was a main originator of the ecological world-view".

Eco-socialist authors. like John Bellamy Foster and Paul Burkett.point to Marx's discussion of a "metabolic rift" between man and nature. his statement that "private ownership of the globe by single individuals will appear quite absurd as private ownership of one man by another" and his observation that a society must "hand it [the planet] down to succeeding generations in an improved condition".

The English socialist William Morris is largely credited with developing key principles of what was later called eco-socialism. During the 1880s and 1890s. Morris promoted his eco-socialist ideas within the Social Democratic Federation and Socialist League. Green anarchism. or ecoanarchism. is a school of thought within anarchism which puts a particular emphasis on environmental issues. An important early influence was the thought of the American anarchist Henry David Thoreau and his book *Walden* as well as Leo Tolstoy and Élisée Reclus.

In the late 19th century there emerged anarcho-naturism as the fusion of anarchism and naturist philosophies within individualist anarchist circles in France. Spain. Cuba and Portugal.Social ecology is closely related to the work and ideas of Murray Bookchin and influenced by anarchist Peter Kropotkin. Bookchin´s first book.*Our Synthetic Environment.* was published under the pseudonym Lewis Herber in 1962. a few months before Rachel Carson's *Silent Spring*. His groundbreaking essay "Ecology and Revolutionary Thought" introduced ecology as a concept in radical politics.

In the 1970s. Barry Commoner. suggesting a left-wing response to the *Limits to Growth* model that predicted catastrophic resource depletion and spurred environmentalism. postulated that capitalist technologies were chiefly responsible for environmental degradation. as opposed to population pressures. The 1990s saw the socialist feminists Mary Mellor and Ariel Salleh address environmental issues within an eco-socialist paradigm. With the rising profile of the anti-globalization movement in the Global South. an "environmentalism of the poor". combining ecological awareness and social justice. has also become prominent. David Pepper also released his important work. *Ecosocialism: From Deep Ecology to Social Justice*. in 1994. which critiques the current approach of many within Green politics. particularly deep ecologists.

Currently. many Green Parties around the world. such as the Dutch Green Left Party (GroenLinks). contain strong eco-socialist elements. Radical Red-green alliances have been formed in many countries by eco-socialists. radical Greens and other radical left groups. InDenmark. the Red-Green Alliance was formed as a coalition of numerous radical parties. Within the European Parliament. a number of far-left parties from Northern Europe have organized themselves into the Nordic Green Left Alliance.

CRITICISM

Socialism has been critiqued from numerous different perspectives. Because there are many models of socialism. most critiques are only focused on a specific type of socialism.

Economic liberals and right libertarians view private ownership of the means of production and the market exchange as natural entities or moral rights which are central to their conceptions of freedom and liberty. and view the economic dynamics of capitalism as immutable and absolute. Therefore. they perceive public ownership of the means of production. cooperatives and economic planning as infringements upon liberty.

According to the Austrian school economist Ludwig von Mises. an economic system that does not utilize money. financial calculation and market pricing will be unable to effectively value capital goods and coordinate production. and therefore these types of socialism are impossible because they lack the necessary information to perform economic calculation in the first place. Another central argument leveled against socialist systems based on economic planning is based on the use of dispersed knowledge. State socialism is unfeasible in this view because information cannot be aggregated by a central body and effectively used to formulate a plan for an entire economy. because doing so would result in distorted or absent price signals.

Many economic criticisms of socialism focus on the experiences of Soviet-type planned economies. It is argued that a lack of budget constraints in enterprises operating in a planned economy reduces incentives for enterprises to act on information efficiently. thereby reducing overall welfare for society.

Other economists criticize models of socialism based on Neo-classical economics for their reliance on the faulty and unrealistic assumptions of economic equilibrium and pareto efficiency.

2

History of Socialism

The history of socialism has its origins in the French Revolution of 1789 and the changes brought about by the Industrial Revolution. although it has precedents in earlier movements and ideas. The *Communist Manifesto* was written by Karl Marx andFriedrich Engels in 1848 just before the Revolutions of 1848 swept Europe. expressing what they termed 'scientific socialism'. In the last third of the 19th century in Europe social democratic parties arose in Europe drawing mainly from Marxism. The Australian Labour Party was the world's first elected socialist party when the party won the 1899 Queensland state election. In the first half of the twentieth century. the Soviet Union and the Communist parties of the Third International around the world mainly came to represent socialism in terms of the Soviet model of economic development. the creation of centrally planned economies directed by a state that owns all the means of production. although other trends condemned what they saw as the lack of democracy. In the UK Herbert Morrison said "Socialism is what the Labour government does". whereas Aneurin Bevan argued that socialism requires that the "main streams of economic activity are brought under public direction". with an economic plan and workers' democracy. Some argued that capitalism had been abolished. Socialist governments established the 'mixed economy' with partial nationalisations and social welfare.

By 1968. the prolonged Vietnam War (1959–1975). gave rise to the New Left. socialists who tended to be critical of the Soviet Union and social democracy. Anarcho-syndicalists and some elements of the New Left and others favored decentralized collective ownership in the form of cooperatives or workers' councils. At the turn of the 21st century. in Latin America. Venezuelan PresidentHugo Chávez championed what he termed 'Socialism of the 21st Century'. which included a policy of nationalisation of national assets such as oil. anti-imperialism. and termed himself a Trotskyist supporting 'permanent revolution'.

ORIGINS OF SOCIALISM

Some of the verses of the Bible which inspired the communal arrangements of the Anabaptist Hutterites are Acts 2. verses 44 and 45: "All the believers were together and had everything in common. Selling their possessions and goods. they gave to anyone as he had need."

Acts 4. verse 32: "All the believers were one in heart and mind. No one claimed that any of his possessions were his own. but they shared everything they had." and Acts 4. verses 34 and 35: "There were no needy persons among them. For from time to time those who owned lands or houses sold them. brought the money from their sales and put it at the apostles' feet. and it was distributed to anyone as he had need."

In Britain Thomas Paine proposed a detailed plan to tax property owners to pay for the needs of the poor in *Agrarian Justice* while Charles Hall wrote *The Effects of Civilization on the People in European States* denouncing capitalism effects on the poor of his time

By 1842 socialism "had become the topic of a major academic analysis by a German scholar. Lorenz von Stein. in his Socialism and Social Movement. According to an 1888 volume of *A New English Dictionary on Historical Principles*. the word *socialism* was coined on 13 February 1832 in *Le Globe*. a liberal French newspaper of Pierre Leroux. The term "socialism" was further described in 1834 by Leroux and Marie Roch Louis Reybaud in France. In England Robert Owen was also using the term independently around the same time. Owen is considered the father of the cooperative movement.

The first modern socialists were early 19th century Western European social critics. In this period socialism emerged from a diverse array of doctrines and social experiments associated primarily with British and French thinkers—especially Robert Owen. Charles Fourier. Pierre-Joseph Proudhon. Louis Blanc. and Saint-Simon. "Associationism" was a term used by early-19th-century followers of the utopian theories of such thinkers as Robert Owen. Claude Henri de Saint-Simon and Charles Fourier to describe their beliefs.T

hese social critics criticized the excesses of poverty and inequality of the Industrial Revolution. and advocated reforms such as the egalitarian distribution of wealth and the transformation of society into small communities in which private property was to be abolished. Outlining principles for the reorganization of society along collectivist lines. Saint-Simon and Owen sought to build socialism on the foundations of planned. utopian communities. According to Sheldon Richman. "[i]n the 19th and early 20th centuries. 'socialism' did not exclusively mean collective or government ownership of the means or production but was an umbrella term for anyone who believed labour was cheated out of its natural product under historical capitalism."

According to some accounts. the use of the words "socialism" or "communism" was related to the perceived attitude Towards religion in a given culture. In Europe. "communism" was considered to be the more atheistic of the two. In England. however. that sounded too close to communion with

Catholic overtones; hence atheists preferred to call themselves socialists. By 1847. according to Frederick Engels. "Socialism" was "respectable" on the continent of Europe. while "Communism" was the opposite; the Owenites in England and the Fourierists in France were considered Socialists. while working class movements which "proclaimed the necessity of total social change" termed themselves "Communists". This latter was "powerful enough" to produce the communism of Étienne Cabet in France and Wilhelm Weitling in Germany. In the post-revolutionary period right after the French Revolution activists and theorists like François-Noël Babeuf. Filippo Buonarroti. and Auguste Blanqui influenced the early French labour and socialist movements.

Josiah Warren is widely regarded as the first American anarchist. and the four-page weekly paper he edited during 1833. *The Peaceful Revolutionist*. was the first anarchist periodical published.. Anarchist Peter Sabatini reports that in the United States "of early to mid-19th century. there appeared an array of communal and "utopian" counterculture groups (including the so-called free love movement). William Godwin's anarchism exerted an ideological influence on some of this. but more so the socialism of Robert Owen and Charles Fourier. After success of his British venture.

Owen himself established a cooperative community within the United States at New Harmony. Indiana during 1825. One member of this commune was Josiah Warren (1798–1874). considered to be the first individualist anarchist". For American anarchist historian Eunice Minette Schuster "It is apparent... that Proudhonian Anarchism was to be found in the United States at least as early as 1848 and that it was not conscious of its affinity to the Individualist Anarchism of Josiah Warren and Stephen Pearl Andrews... William B. Greene presented this Proudhonian Mutualism in its purest and most systematic form.". There were also currents inspired by dissident Christianity of christian socialism "often in Britain and then usually coming out of left liberal politics and a romantic anti-industrialism" which produced theorists such as Edward Bellamy. Frederick Denison Maurice and Charles Kingsley.

HENRI DE SAINT-SIMON

Henri de Saint-Simon. and Karly Roesling. who is called the founder of French socialism. argued that a brotherhood of man must accompany the scientific organization of industry and society. He proposed that production and distribution be carried out by the state. and that allowing everyone to have equal opportunity to develop their talents would lead to social harmony. and the traditional state could be virtually eliminated. or transformed. "Rule over men would be replaced by the administration of things."

CHARLES FOURIER

François Marie Charles Fourier (7 April 1772 – 10 October 1837) was a

French utopian socialist and philosopher. Fourier is credited by modern scholars with having originated the word féminisme in 1837; as early as 1808. he had argued. in the Theory of the Four Movements. that the extension of the liberty of women was the general principle of all social progress. though he disdained any attachment to a discourse of 'equal rights'. Fourier inspired the founding of the communist community called La Reunion near present-day Dallas. Texas as well as several other communities within the United States of America. such as the North American Phalanx in New Jersey and Community Place and five others in New York State. Fourierism manifested itself "in the middle of the 19th century (where) literally hundreds of communes (phalansteries) were founded on fourierist principles in France. N. America. Mexico. S. America. Algeria. Yugoslavia. etc."

ROBERT OWEN

Robert Owen advocated the transformation of society into small. local collectives without such elaborate systems of social organization. Owen was a mill manager from 1800 to 1825. He transformed life in the village of New Lanark with ideas and opportunities which were at least a hundred years ahead of their time. Child labour and corporal punishment were abolished. and villagers were provided with decent homes. schools and evening classes. free health care. and affordable food.

The UK government's Factory Act of 1833 attempted to reduce the hours adults and children worked in the textile industry. A fifteen hour working day was to start at 5.30 a.m. and cease at 8.30 p.m. Children of nine to thirteen years could be worked no more than 9 hours. and those of a younger age were prohibited. There were. however. only four factory inspectors. and this law was broken by the factory owners. In the same year Owen stated:

" Eight hours' daily labour is enough for any [adult] human being. and under proper arrangements sufficient to afford an ample supply of food. raiment and shelter. or the necessaries and comforts of life. and for the remainder of his time. every person is entitled to education. recreation and sleep. "

Leaving England for the United States. Robert Owen and his sons began an experiment with a socialist community in New Harmony. Indiana in 1825. Advertisements announced the experiment for the cooperative colony. bringing various people to attempt an 8-hour work day of which Owen was a proponent. The town banned money and other commodities for trade. using "labour tickets" denominated in the number of hours worked.

Owen's son. Robert Dale Owen. would say of the failed socialism experiment that the people at New Harmony were "a heterogeneous collection of radicals. enthusiastic devotees to principle. honest latitudinarians. and lazy theorists. with a sprinkling of unprincipled sharpers thrown in." The larger community lasted only until 1827 at which time smaller communities were formed. which led to further subdivision. until individualism replaced socialism in 1828. New Harmony was dissolved in 1829 due to constant quarrels as parcels of land and property were sold and returned to private use.

Individualist anarchist Josiah Warren. who was one of the original participants in the New Harmony Society. asserted that the community was doomed to failure due to a lack of individual sovereignty and private property. He wrote of the community: "It seemed that the difference of opinion. tastes and purposes increased just in proportion to the demand for conformity. Two years were worn out in this way; at the end of which. I believe that not more than three persons had the least hope of success. Most of the experimenters left in despair of all reforms. and conservatism felt itself confirmed. We had tried every conceivable form of organization and government. We had a world in miniature. —we had enacted the French revolution over again with despairing hearts instead of corpses as a result....It appeared that it was nature's own inherent law of diversity that had conquered us...our 'united interests' were directly at war with the individualities of persons and circumstances and the instinct of self-preservation... and it was evident that just in proportion to the contact of persons or interests. so are concessions and compromises indispensable." (*Periodical Letter II* 1856).

In a *Paper Dedicated to the Governments of Great Britain. Austria. Russia. France. Prussia and the United States of America* written in 1841. Owen wrote: "The lowest stage of humanity is experienced when the individual must labour for a small pittance of wages from others."

PIERRE-JOSEPH PROUDHON

Pierre-Joseph Proudhon pronounced that "Property is theft" and that socialism was "every aspiration towards the amelioration of society". Proudhon termed himself an anarchist and proposed that free association of individuals should replace the coercive state. Proudhon. Benjamin Tucker. and others developed these ideas in a mutualist direction. while Mikhail Bakunin. Piotr Kropotkin. and others adapted Proudhon's ideas in a more conventionally socialist direction.

In a letter to Marx in 1846. Proudhon wrote:

" I myself put the problem in this way: to bring about the return to society. by an economic combination. of the wealth which was withdrawn from society by another economic combination. In other words. through Political Economy to turn the theory of Property against Property in such a way as to engender what you German socialists call community and what I will limit myself for the moment to calling liberty or equality. "

MIKHAIL BAKUNIN

Mikhail Bakunin. the father of modern anarchism. was a libertarian socialist.

a theory by which the workers would directly manage the means of production through their own productive associations. There would be "equal means of subsistence. support. education. and opportunity for every child. boy or girl. until maturity. and equal resources and facilities in adulthood to create his own well-being by his own labour."

While many socialists emphasized the gradual transformation of society. most notably through the foundation of small. utopian communities. a growing number of socialists became disillusioned with the viability of this approach and instead emphasized direct political action. Early socialists were united. however. in their desire for a society based on cooperation rather than competition.

MARXISM AND THE SOCIALIST MOVEMENT

The French Revolution of 1789. Karl Marx and Frederick Engels wrote. "abolished feudal property in favour of bourgeois property". The French Revolution was preceded and influenced by the works of Jean-Jacques Rousseau. whose *Social Contract* famously began. "Man is born free. and he is everywhere in chains." Rousseau is credited with influencing socialist thought. but it was François-Noël Babeuf. and his *Conspiracy of Equals*. who is credited with providing a model for left-wing and communist movements of the 19th century.

Marx and Engels drew from these socialist or communist ideas born in the French revolution. as well as from the German philosophy of GWF Hegel. and English political economy. particularly that of Adam Smith and David Ricardo. Marx and Engels developed a body of ideas which they called scientific socialism. more commonly called Marxism. Marxism comprised a theory of history (historical materialism) as well as a political. economic and philosophical theory.

In the *Manifesto of the Communist Party*. written in 1848 just days before the outbreak of the revolutions of 1848. Marx and Engels wrote. "The distinguishing feature of Communism is not the abolition of property generally. but the abolition of bourgeois property." Unlike those Marx described as utopian socialists. Marx determined that. "The history of all hitherto existing society is the history of class struggles".

While utopian socialists believed it was possible to work within or reform capitalist society. Marx confronted the question of the economic and political power of the capitalist class. expressed in their ownership of the means of producing wealth (factories. banks. commerce – in a word. 'Capital'). Marx and Engels formulated theories regarding the practical way of achieving and running a socialist system. which they saw as only being achieved by those who produce the wealth in society. the toilers. workers or "proletariat". gaining common ownership of their workplaces. the means of producing wealth. Marx believed that capitalism could only be overthrown by means of a revolution carried out by the working class: "The proletarian movement is the self-conscious. independent movement of the immense majority. in the interest of the immense majority." Marx believed that the proletariat was the only class with both the cohesion. the means and the determination to carry the revolution forward. Unlike the utopian socialists. who often idealised agrarian life and deplored the growth of modern industry. Marx saw the growth of capitalism and an urban proletariat as a necessary stage towards socialism.

For Marxists. socialism or. as Marx termed it. the first phase of communist society. can be viewed as a transitional stage characterized by common or state ownership of themeans of production under democratic workers' control and management. which Engels argued was beginning to be realised in the Paris Commune of 1871. before it was overthrown. Socialism to them is simply the transitional phase between capitalism and "higher phase of communist society". Because this society has characteristics of both its capitalist ancestor and is beginning to show the properties of communism. it will hold the means of production collectively but distributes commodities according to individual contribution.

When the socialist state (the dictatorship of the proletariat) naturally withers away. what will remain is a society in which human beings no longer suffer from alienation and "all the springs of co-operative wealth flow more abundantly." Here "society inscribe[s] on its banners: From each according to his ability. to each according to his needs!" For Marx. a communist society entails the absence of differing social classes and thus the end of class warfare. According to Marx and Engels. once a socialist society had been ushered in. the state would begin to "wither away". and humanity would be in control of its own destiny for the first time.

INTERNATIONAL WORKINGMEN'S ASSOCIATION (FIRST INTERNATIONAL)

In Europe. harsh reaction followed the revolutions of 1848. during which ten countries had experienced brief or long-term social upheaval as groups carried out nationalist uprisings. After most of these attempts at systematic change ended in failure. conservative elements took advantage of the divided groups of socialists. anarchists. liberals. and nationalists. to prevent further revolt. The International Workingmen's Association (IWA). also known as the First International. was founded in London in 1864. Victor Le Lubez. a French radical republican living in London. invited Karl Marx to come to London as a representative of German workers.

The IWA held a preliminary conference in 1865. and had its first congress at Geneva in 1866. Marx was appointed a member of the committee. and according to Saul Padover. Marx and Johann Georg Eccarius. a tailor living in London. became "the two mainstays of the International from its inception to its end". The First International became the first major international forum for the promulgation of socialist ideas. In 1864 the International Workingmen's Association (sometimes called the "First International") united diverse revolutionary currents including French followers of Proudhon. Blanquists. Philadelphes. English trade unionists. socialists and social democrats.

In 1868. following their unsuccessful participation in the League of Peace and Freedom (LPF). Russian revolutionary Mikhail Bakunin and his collectivist anarchist associates joined the First International (which had decided not to get involved with the LPF). They allied themselves with the federalist socialist sections of the International. who advocated the revolutionary overthrow of the state and the collectivization of property.

The Social Democratic Workers' Party of Germany was founded in 1869 under the influence of Marx and Engels. In 1875. it merged with theGeneral German Workers' Association of Ferdinand Lassalle to become what is known today as the German Social Democratic Party (SPD). Socialism became increasingly associated with newly formed trade unions. In Germany. the SPD founded unions. In Austria. France and other European countries. socialist parties and anarchists played a prominent role in forming and building up trade unions. especially from the 1870s onwards. This stood in contrast to the British experience. where moderate New Model Unions dominated the union movement from the mid-nineteenth century. and where trade unionism was stronger than the political labour movement until the formation and growth of the Labour Party in the early twentieth century.

At first. the collectivists worked with the Marxists to push the First International in a more revolutionary socialist direction. Subsequently. the International became polarised into two camps. with Marx and Bakunin as their respective figureheads. Bakunin characterised Marx's ideas as centralist and predicted that. if a Marxist party came to power. its leaders would simply take the place of the ruling class they had fought against. In 1872. the conflict climaxed with a final split between the two groups at the Hague Congress. where Bakunin and James Guillaume were expelled from the International and its headquarters were transferred to New York. In response. the federalist sections formed their own International at the St. Imier Congress. adopting a revolutionary anarchist programme.

PARIS COMMUNE

In 1871. in the wake of the Franco-Prussian War. an uprising in Paris established the Paris Commune. The Paris Communewas a government that briefly ruled Paris from 18 March (more formally. from 28 March) to 28 May 1871. The Commune was the result of an uprising in Paris after France was defeated in the Franco-Prussian War. Anarchists participated actively in the establishment of the Paris Commune. The 92 members of the *Communal*

Council included a high proportion of skilled workers and several professionals. Many of them were political activists. ranging from reformist republicans. various types of socialists. to the Jacobins who tended to look back nostalgically to the Revolution of 1789. The "reforms initiated by the Commune. suchas the re-opening of workplaces as co-operatives. anarchists can see their ideas of associated labour beginning to be realised...Moreover. the Commune's ideas on federation obviously reflected the influence of Proudhon on French radical ideas. Indeed. the Commune's vision of a communal France based on a federation of delegates bound by imperative mandates issued by their electors and subject to recall at any moment echoes Bakunin's and Proudhon's ideas (Proudhon. like Bakunin. had argued in favour of the "implementation of the binding mandate" in 1848...and for federation of communes).

George Woodcock manifests that "a notable contribution to the activities of the Commune and particularly to the organization of public services was made by members of various anarchist factions. including the mutualists Courbet. Longuet. and Vermorel. the libertarian collectivists Varlin. Malon. and Lefrangais. and the bakuninists Elie and Elisée Reclus and Louise Michel." The veteran leader of the Blanquist group of revolutionary socialists. Louis Auguste Blanqui. was hoped by his followers to be a potential leader of the revolution. but he had been arrested on March 17 and was held in prison throughout the life of the Commune.

The Commune unsuccessfully tried to exchange him. first against Georges Darboy. Archbishop of Paris. then against all 74 hostages it detained. but Thiers flatly refused. Some women organized a feminist movement. following on from earlier attempts in 1789 and 1848. Thus. Nathalie Lemel. a socialist bookbinder. and Élisabeth Dmitrieff. a young Russian exile and member of the Russian section of the First International (IWA). created the *Union des femmes pour la défense de Paris et les soins aux blessés* ("Women's Union for the Defence of Paris and Care of the Wounded") on April 11. 1871. The Women's Union also participated in several municipal commissions and organised cooperative workshops.

According to Marx and Engels. for a few weeks the Paris Commune provided a glimpse of a socialist society. before it was brutally suppressed by the French government.

- From the outset the Commune was compelled to recognise that the working class. once come to power. could not manage with the old state machine; that in order not to lose again its only just conquered supremacy. this working class must. on the one hand. do away with all the old repressive machinery previously used against it itself. and. on the other. safeguard itself against its own deputies and officials. by declaring them all. without exception. subject to recall at any moment. "

- Engels' 1891 postscript to *The Civil War In France* by Karl Marx Following the 1871 Paris Commune. the socialist movement. as the whole of the workers' movement. was decapitated and deeply affected for years.

THE SECOND INTERNATIONAL

As the ideas of Marx and Engels took on flesh. particularly in central Europe. socialists sought to unite in an international organisation. In 1889. on the centennial of the French Revolution of 1789. the Second International was founded. with 384 delegates from 20 countries representing about 300 labour and socialist organizations. Anarchists were ejected and not allowed in mainly because of the pressure from marxists.

Just before his death in 1895. Engels argued that there was now a "single generally recognised. crystal clear theory of Marx" and a "single great international army of socialists". Despite its illegality due to the Anti-Socialist Laws of 1878. the Social Democratic Party of Germany's use of the limited universal male suffrage were "potent" new methods of struggle which demonstrated their growing strength and forced the dropping of the Anti-Socialist legislation in 1890. Engels argued. In 1893. the German SPD obtained 1.787.000 votes. a quarter of votes cast. However before the leadership of the SPD published Engels' 1895 Introduction to Marx's *Class Struggles in France 1848–1850*. they removed certain phrases they felt were too revolutionary.

Marx believed that it was possible to have a peaceful socialist transformation in England. although the British ruling class would then revolt against such a victory. America and Holland might also have a peaceful transformation. but not in France. where Marx believed there had been "perfected... an enormous bureaucratic and military organisation. with its ingenious state machinery" which must be forcibly overthrown. However. eight years after Marx's death. Engels argued that it was possible to achieve a peaceful socialist revolution in France. too.

GERMANY

The SPD was by far the most powerful of the social democratic parties. Its votes reached 4.5 million. it had 90 daily newspapers. together with trade unions and co-ops. sports clubs. a youth organization. a women's organization and hundreds of full-time officials. Under the pressure of this growing party. Bismarck introduced limited welfare provision and working hours were reduced. Germany experienced sustained economic growth for more than forty years. Commentators suggest that this expansion. together with the concessions won. gave rise to illusions amongst the leadership of the SPD that capitalism would evolve into socialism gradually. Beginning in 1896. in a series of articles published under the title "Problems of socialism". Eduard Bernstein argued that an evolutionary transition to socialism was both possible and more desirable than revolutionary change. Bernstein and his supporters came to be identified as "revisionists" because they sought to revise the classic tenets of Marxism. Although the orthodox Marxists in the party. led by Karl Kautsky. retained the Marxist theory of revolution as the official doctrine of the party. and it was repeatedly endorsed by SPD conferences. in practice the SPD leadership became increasingly reformist.

RUSSIA

Bernstein coined the aphorism: "The movement is everything. the final goal nothing". But the path of reform appeared blocked to the Russian Marxists while Russia remained the bulwark of reaction. In the preface to the 1882 Russian edition to the Communist Manifesto. Marx and Engels had saluted the Russian Marxists who. they said. "formed the vanguard of revolutionary action in Europe". But the working class. although many were organised in vast modern western-owned enterprises. comprised no more than a small percentage of the population and "more than half the land is owned in common by the peasants". Marx and Engels posed the question: How was Russia to progress to socialism? Could Russia "pass directly" to socialism or "must it first pass through the same process" of capitalist development as the West? They replied: "If the Russian Revolution becomes the signal for a proletarian revolution in the West. so that both complement each other. the present Russian common ownership of land may serve as the starting point for a communist development."

In 1903. the Russian Social Democratic Labour Party began to split on ideological and organizational questions into Bolshevik ('Majority') and Menshevik ('Minority') factions. with Russian revolutionary Vladimir Lenin leading the more radical Bolsheviks. Both wings accepted that Russia was an economically backward country unripe for socialism. The Mensheviks awaited the capitalist revolution in Russia.

But Lenin argued that a revolution of the workers and peasants would achieve this task. After the Russian revolution of 1905. Leon Trotsky argued that unlike the French revolution of 1789 and the European Revolutions of 1848 against absolutism. the capitalist class would never organise a revolution in Russia to overthrow absolutism. and that this task fell to the working class who.

liberating the peasantry from their feudal yoke. would then immediately pass on to the socialist tasks and seek a "permanent revolution" to achieve international socialism. Assyrian nationalist Freydun Atturaya tried to create regional self-government for theAssyrian people with the socialism ideology. He even wrote the Urmia Manifesto of the United Free Assyria. However. his attempt was put to an end by Russia.

UNITED STATES

In 1877. the Socialist Labour Party of America was founded. This party. which advocated Marxism and still exists today. was a confederation of small Marxist parties and came under the leadership of Daniel De Leon. In 1901. a merger between opponents of De Leon and the younger Social Democratic Party joined with Eugene V. Debs to form theSocialist Party of America. In 1905. the Industrial Workers of the World formed from several independent labour unions. The IWW opposed the political means of Debs and De Leon. as well as the craft unionism of Samuel Gompers. In 1910. the Sewer Socialists. the main group of American socialists. elected Victor Berger as a socialist Congressman and Emil Seidel as a socialist mayor of Milwaukee. Wisconsin. most of the other elected city officials being socialist as well. This Socialist Party of America grew to 150.000 in 1912 and polled 897.000 votes in the presidential campaign of that year. 6 percent of the total vote. Socialist mayor Daniel Hoan. was elected in 1916 and stayed in office until 1940. The final Socialist mayor. Frank P. Zeidler. was elected in 1948 and served three terms. ending in 1960. Milwaukee remained the hub of Socialism during these years. The Socialist Party declined after the First World War. By the 1880s anarcho-communism was already present in the United States as can be seen in the publication of the journal *Freedom: A Revolutionary Anarchist-Communist Monthly* by Lucy Parsons and Lizzy Holmes. Around that time these American anarcho-communist sectors entered in debate with the individualist anarchist group around Benjamin Tucker.

FRANCE

French socialism was beheaded by the suppression of the Paris commune (1871). its leaders killed or exiled. But in 1879. at the Marseille Congress. workers' associations created the Federation of the Socialist Workers of France. Three years later. Jules Guesde and Paul Lafargue. the son-in-law of Karl Marx. left the federation and founded theFrench Workers' Party.

The Federation of the Socialist Workers of France was termed "possibilist" because it advocated gradual reforms. whereas the French Workers' Party promoted Marxism. In 1905 these two trends merged to form the French Section Française de l'Internationale Ouvrière (SFIO). led by Jean Jaurès and later Léon Blum. In 1906 it won 56 seats in Parliament. The SFIO adhered to Marxist ideas but became. in practice. a reformist party. By 1914 it had more than 100 members in the Chamber of Deputies.

[M]WORLD WAR I

When World War I began in 1914. many European socialist leaders supported their respective governments' war aims. The social democratic parties in the UK. France. Belgium and Germany supported their respective state's wartime military and economic planning. discarding their commitment to internationalism and solidarity. Lenin. in his April Theses. denounced the war as an imperialist conflict. and urged workers worldwide to use it as an occasion for proletarian revolution. The Second International dissolved during the war. while Lenin. Trotsky. Karl Liebknecht and Rosa Luxemburg. together with a small number of other Marxists opposed to the war. came together in theZimmerwald Conference in September 1915.

ANARCHISM

Anarchism as a social movement has regularly endured fluctuations in popularity. Its classical period. which scholars demarcate as from 1860 to 1939. is associated with the working-class movements of the 19th century and the Spanish Civil War-era struggles against fascism.

In 1864 the International Workingmen's Association (sometimes called the "First International") united diverse revolutionary currents including French followers of Proudhon. Blanquists. Philadelphes. English trade unionists. socialists and social democrats. Proudhon's followers. the mutualists. opposed Marx's state socialism. advocating political abstentionism and small property holdings.

The anti-authoritarian sections of the First International were the precursors of the anarcho-syndicalists. seeking to "replace the privilege and authority of the State" with the "free and spontaneous organization of labour."

In 1907. the International Anarchist Congress of Amsterdam gathered delegates from 14 different countries. among which important figures of the anarchist movement. including Errico Malatesta. Pierre Monatte. Luigi Fabbri. Benoît Broutchoux. Emma Goldman. Rudolf Rocker. and Christiaan Cornelissen. Various themes were treated during the Congress. in particular concerning the organisation of the anarchist movement. popular education issues. the general strike or antimilitarism.

A central debate concerned the relation between anarchism and syndicalism (or trade unionism). The Spanish Workers Federation in 1881 was the first major anarcho-syndicalist movement; anarchist trade union federations were of special importance in Spain. The most successful was the Confederación Nacional del Trabajo (National Confederation of Labour: CNT). founded in 1910. Before the 1940s. the CNT was the major force in Spanish working class politics. attracting 1.58 million members at one point and playing a major role in the Spanish Civil War. The CNT was affiliated with the International Workers Association. a federation of anarcho-syndicalist trade unions founded in 1922. with delegates representing two million workers from 15 countries in Europe and Latin America.

Some anarchists. such as Johann Most. advocated publicizing violent acts of retaliation against counter-revolutionaries because "we preach not only action in and for itself. but also action as propaganda." Numerous heads of state were assassinated between 1881 and 1914 by members of the anarchist movement. For example. U.S. President McKinley's assassin Leon Czolgosz claimed to have been influenced by anarchist and feminist Emma Goldman.

Anarchists participated alongside the Bolsheviks in both February and October revolutions. and were initially enthusiastic about the Bolshevik coup. However. the Bolsheviks soon turned against the anarchists and other left-wing opposition. a conflict that culminated in the 1921 Kronstadt rebellion which the new government repressed. Anarchists in central Russia were either imprisoned. driven underground or joined the victorious Bolsheviks; the anarchists from Petrograd and Moscow fled to the Ukraine. There. in the Free Territory. they fought in the civil war against the Whites (a Western-backed grouping of monarchists and other opponents of the October Revolution) and then the Bolsheviks as part of the Revolutionary Insurrectionary Army of Ukraine led by Nestor Makhno. who established an anarchist society in the region for a number of months.

In the 1920s and 1930s. the rise of fascism in Europe transformed anarchism's conflict with the state.

In Spain. the CNT initially refused to join a popular front electoral alliance. and abstention by CNT supporters led to a right wing election victory. But in 1936. the CNT changed its policy and anarchist votes helped bring the popular front back to power. Months later. the former ruling class responded with an attempted coup causing the Spanish Civil War (1936–1939).

In response to the army rebellion. an anarchist-inspired movement of peasants and workers. supported by armed militias. took control of Barcelona and of large areas of rural Spain where they collectivised the land. But even before the fascist victory in 1939. the anarchists were losing ground in a bitter struggle with the Stalinists. who controlled the distribution of military aid to the Republican cause from the Soviet Union. Stalinist-led troops suppressed the collectives and persecuted both dissident Marxistsand anarchists.

A surge of popular interest in anarchism occurred during the 1960s and 1970s. In 1968 in Carrara. Italy the International of Anarchist Federations was founded during an international Anarchist conference in Carrara in 1968 by the three existing European federations of France. the Italian and the Iberian Anarchist Federation as well as theBulgarian federation in French exile. In the United Kingdom this was associated with the punk rock movement. as exemplified by bands such as Crass and the Sex Pistols. The housing and employment crisis in most of Western Europe led to the formation of communes and squatter movements like that of Barcelona. Spain.

In Denmark.squatters occupied a disused military base and declared the Freetown Christiania. an autonomous haven in central Copenhagen. Since the revival of anarchism in the mid 20th century. a number of new movements and schools of thought emerged. Around the turn of the 21st century. anarchism grew in popularity and influence as part of the anti-war. anti-capitalist. and anti-globalisation movements. Anarchists became known for their involvement in protests against the meetings of the World Trade Organization (WTO). Group of Eight. and the World Economic Forum. Some anarchist factions at these protests engaged in rioting. property destruction. and violent confrontations with police. and the confrontations were selectively portrayed in mainstream media coverage as violent riots.

These actions were precipitated by ad hoc. leaderless. anonymous cadres known as *black blocs*; other organisational tactics pioneered in this time include security culture. affinity groups and the use of decentralised technologies such as the internet. A landmark struggle of this period was the confrontations at WTO conference in Seattle in 1999.

International anarchist federations in existence include the International of Anarchist Federations. the International Workers' Association. and International Libertarian Solidarity.

SOCIAL DEMOCRACY TO 1917

The Social Democratic Party (SPD) in Germany became the largest and most powerful socialist party in Europe. despite working illegally until the anti-socialist laws were dropped in 1890. In the 1893 elections it gained 1.787.000 votes. a quarter of the total votes cast. according to Engels. In 1895. the year of his death. Engels emphasised the Communist Manifesto's emphasis on winning. as a first step. the "battle of democracy". Since the 1866 introduction of universal male franchise the SPD had proved that old methods of. "surprise attacks. of revolutions carried through by small conscious minorities at the head of masses lacking consciousness is past". Marxists. Engels emphasised. must "win over the great mass of the people" before initiating a revolution.

Marx believed that it was possible to have a peaceful socialist revolution in England. America and the Netherlands. but not in France. where he believed there had been "perfected... an enormous bureaucratic and military organisation. with its ingenious state machinery" which must be forcibly overthrown. However. eight years after Marx's death. Engels regarded it possible to achieve a peaceful socialist revolution in France. too.

In 1896. Eduard Bernstein argued that once full democracy had been achieved. a transition to socialism by gradual means was both possible and more desirable than revolutionary change. Bernstein and his supporters came to be identified as "revisionists". because they sought to revise the classic tenets of Marxism. Although the orthodox Marxists in the party. led by Karl Kautsky. retained the Marxist theory of revolution as the official doctrine of the party. and it was repeatedly endorsed by SPD conferences. in practice the SPD leadership became more and more reformist.

In Europe most Social Democratic parties participated in parliamentary politics and the day-to-day struggles of the trade unions. In the UK. however. many trade unionists who were members of the Social Democratic Federation. which included at various times future trade union leaders such as Will Thorne. John Burns and Tom Mann. felt that the Federation neglected the industrial struggle. Along with Engels. who refused to support the SDF. many felt that dogmatic approach of the SDF. particularly of its leader. Henry Hyndman. meant that it remained an isolated sect. The mass parties of the working class under social democratic leadership became more reformist and lost sight of their revolutionary objective. Thus the French Section of the Workers' International (SFIO). founded in 1905. under Jean Jaurès and later Léon Blum adhered to Marxist ideas. but became in practice a reformist party.

In some countries. particularly Britain and the British dominions. labour parties were formed. These were parties largely formed by and controlled by the trade unions. rather than formed by groups of socialist activists who then appealed to the workers for support. In Britain. the Labour Party. (at first the Labour Representation Committee) was established by representatives of trade unions together with affiliated socialist parties. principally the Independent Labour Party but also for a time the avowedly Marxist Social Democratic Federation and other groups. such as the Fabians. On 1 December 1899 Anderson Dawson of the Australian Labour Party became the Premier of Queensland. Australia. forming the world's first parliamentary socialist government. The Dawson government. however. lasted only one week. being defeated at the first sitting of parliament.

The British Labour Party first won seats in the House of Commons in 1902. It won the majority of the working class away from the Liberal Party after World War I. In Australia. the Labour Party achieved rapid success. forming its first national government in 1904. Labour parties were also formed in South Africa and New Zealand but had less success. The British Labour Party adopted a specifically socialist constitution ('Clause four. Part four') in 1918.

The strongest opposition to revisionism came from socialists in countries such as the Russian Empire where parliamentary democracy did not exist. Chief among these was the Russian Vladimir Lenin. whose works such as *Our Programme* (1899) set out the views of those who rejected revisionist ideas. In 1903. there was the beginnings of what eventually became a formal split in the Russian Social Democratic Labour Party into revolutionary Bolshevik and reformist Menshevik factions.

In 1914. the outbreak of World War I led to a crisis in European socialism. The parliamentary leaderships of the socialist parties of Germany. France. Belgium and Britain each voted to support the war aims of their country's governments. although some leaders. like Ramsay MacDonald in Britain and Karl Liebknecht in Germany. opposed the war from the start. Lenin. in exile in

Switzerland. called for revolutions in all the combatant states as the only way to end the war and achieve socialism. Lenin. Leon Trotsky. Karl Liebknecht and Rosa Luxemburg. together with a small number of other Marxists opposed to the war. came together in the Zimmerwald Conference in September 1915. This conference saw the beginning of the end of the uneasy coexistence of revolutionary socialists with the social democrats. and by 1917 war-weariness led to splits in several socialist parties. notably the German Social Democrats.

The Russian Revolution of October 1917 led to a withdrawal from World War I. one of the principal demands of the Russian revolution. as the Soviet government immediately sued for peace. Germany and the former allies invaded the new Soviet Russia. which had repudiated the former Romanov regime's national debts and nationalized the banks and major industry. Russia was the only country in the world where socialists had taken power. and it appeared to many socialists to confirm the ideas. strategy and tactics of Lenin and Trotsky.

THE INTER-WAR ERA AND WORLD WAR II

The Russian Revolution of October 1917 brought about the definitive ideological division between Communists as denoted with a capital "C" on the one hand and other communist and socialist trends such as anarcho-communists and social democrats. on the other. The Left Opposition in the Soviet Union gave rise to Trotskyism which was to remain isolated and insignificant for another fifty years. except in Sri Lanka where Trotskyism gained the majority and the pro-Moscow wing was expelled from the Communist Party.

In 1922. the fourth congress of the Communist International took up the policy of the United Front. urging Communists to work with rank and file Social Democrats while remaining critical of their leaders. who they criticised for "betraying" the working class by supporting the war efforts of their respective capitalist classes. For their part. the social democrats pointed to the dislocation caused by revolution. and later. the growing authoritarianism of the Communist Parties. When the Communist Party of Great Britain applied to affiliate to the Labour Party in 1920 it was turned down.

REVOLUTIONARY SOCIALISM AND THE SOVIET UNION (1917-39)

After three years. the First World War. at first greeted with enthusiastic patriotism. produced an upsurge of radicalism in most of Europe and also as far afield as the United States and Australia. In the Russian revolution of February 1917. workers' councils (in Russian. *soviets*) had been formed. and Lenin and the Bolsheviks called for "All power to the Soviets". After the October 1917 Russian revolution. led by Lenin and Trotsky. consolidated power in the Soviets. Lenin declared "Long live the world socialist revolution!" Briefly in Soviet Russia socialism was not just a vision of a future society. but a description of an existing one. The Soviet regime began to bring all the means of production (except agricultural production) under state control. and implemented a system of government through the workers' councils or soviets.

The initial success of the Russian Revolution inspired other revolutionary parties to attempt the same thing unleashing the Revolutions of 1917-23. In the chaotic circumstances of postwar Europe. with the socialist parties divided and discredited. Communist revolutions across Europe seemed a possibility. Communist parties were formed. often from minority or majority factions in most of the world's socialist parties. which broke away in support of the Leninist model.

The German Revolution of 1918 overthrew the old absolutism and. like Russia. set up Workers' and Soldiers' Councils almost entirely made up of SPD and Independent Social Democrats (USPD) members. The Weimar republic was established and placed the SPD in power. under the leadership of Friedrich Ebert. Ebert agreed with Max von Baden that a social revolution was to be prevented and the state order must be upheld at any cost. In 1919 the Spartacist uprising challenged the power of the SPD government. but it was put down in blood and the German Communist leaders Karl Liebknecht and Rosa Luxemburg were assassinated. Communist regimes briefly held power under Béla Kun in Hungary and under Kurt Eisner in Bavaria. There were further revolutionary movements in Germany until 1923. as well as in Vienna. and also in the industrial centres of northern Italy.

In this period few Communists doubted. least of all Lenin and Trotsky. that successful socialist revolutions carried out by the working classes of the most developed capitalist counties were essential to the success of the socialism. and therefore to the success of socialism in Russia in particular. In March 1918. Lenin said. "we are doomed if the German revolution does not break out". In 1919. the Communist Parties came together to form a 'Third International'. termed the Communist International or Comintern. But the prolonged revolutionary period in Germany did not bring a socialist revolution.

A marxist current critical of the bolcheviks emerged and as such "Luxemburg's workerism and spontaneism are exemplary of positions later taken up by the far-left of the period – Pannekoek. Roland Holst. and Gorter in the Netherlands. Sylvia Pankhurst in Britain. Gramsci in Italy. Lukacs in Hungary. In these formulations. the dictatorship of the proletariat was to be the dictatorship of a class. "not of a party or of a clique"." However within this line of thought "The tension between anti-vanguardism and vanguardism has frequently resolved itself in two diametrically opposed ways: the first involved a drift towards the party; the second saw a move towards the idea of complete proletarian spontaneity...The first course is exemplified most clearly in Gramsci and Lukacs...The second course is illustrated in the tendency. developing from the Dutch and German far-lefts. which inclined towards the complete eradication of the party form." In the emerging Soviet state there appeared Left-wing uprisings against the Bolsheviks which were a series of rebellions and uprisings against the Bolsheviks led or supported by left wing groups including Socialist Revolutionaries. Left Socialist Revolutionaries. Mensheviks. and anarchists. Some were in support of the White Movement while some tried to be an independent force. The uprisings started in 1918 and continued through the Russian Civil War and after until 1922. In response the Bolsheviks increasingly abandoned attempts to get these groups to join the government and suppressed them with force.

Within a few years a bureaucracy developed in Russia as a result of the Russian Civil War. foreign invasion. and Russia's historic poverty and backwardness. The bureaucracy undermined the democratic and socialist ideals of the Bolshevik Party and elevated Stalin to their leadership after Lenin's death. In order to consolidate power. the bureaucracy conducted a brutal campaign of lies and violence against the Left Opposition led by Trotsky.

By the mid 1920s. the impetus had gone out of the revolutionary forces in Europe and the national reformist socialist parties had regained their dominance over the working-class movement in most countries. The German Social Democrats held office for much of the 1920s. the British Labour Party formed its first government in 1924. and the French Socialists were also influential. In the Soviet Union. from 1924 Stalin pursued a policy of "socialism in one country". Trotsky argued that this approach was a shift away from the theory of Marx and Lenin. while others argued that it was a practical compromise fit for the times.

The postwar revolutionary upsurge provoked a powerful reaction from the forces of conservatism. Winston Churchill declared that Bolshevism must be "strangled in its cradle". The invasion of Russia by the Allies. their trade embargo and backing for the White forces fighting against the Red Army in the civil war in the Soviet Union was cited by Aneurin Bevan. the leader of the left-wing in the Labour Party. as one of the causes of the Russian revolution's degeneration into dictatorship. A "Red scare" in the United States was raised against the American Socialist Party of Eugene V. Debs and the Communist Party of America which arose after the Russian revolution from members who had broken from Debs' party.

In Europe. fascist movements received significant funding. particularly from industrialists in heavy industry. and came to power in Italy in 1922 under Benito Mussolini. and later in Germany in 1933. in Spain (1937) and Portugal. while strong fascist movements also developed in Hungary and Romania. After 1929. with the Left Opposition legally banned and Trotsky exiled. Stalin led the Soviet Union into a what he termed a "higher stage of socialism." Agriculture was forciblycollectivised. at the cost of a massive famine and millions of deaths among the resistant peasantry. The surplus squeezed from the peasants was spent on a programme of crash industrialisation. guided by the Communist Party through the Five Year Plan. This programme produced some impressive results. though at enormous human costs. Russia raised itself from an economically backward country to that of a superpower. Later Soviet development. however. particularly after the Second World War. was no faster than it was in Japan or the United States under capitalism.

The use of resources. material and human. in the Soviet Union became very wasteful. Stalin's industrialization policy was geared towards the development of heavy industry. an emphasis that facilitated Soviet military action in its defence against Hitler's invasion during the Second World War in which the USSR stood on the side of the Allies of World War II. For "many Marxian libertarian socialists. the political bankruptcy of socialist orthodoxy necessitated a theoretical break. This break took a number of forms. The Bordigists and the SPGB championed a super-Marxian intransigence in theoretical matters. Other socialists made a return "behind Marx" to the anti-positivist programme of German idealism. Libertarian socialism has frequently linked its anti-authoritarian political aspirations with this theoretical differentiation from orthodoxy... Karl Korsch... remained a libertarian socialist for a large part of his life and because of the persistent urge towards theoretical openness in his work. Korsch rejected the eternal and static. and he was obsessed by the essential role of practice in a theory's truth. For Korsch. no theory could escape history. not even Marxism. In this vein. Korsch even credited the stimulus for Marx's Capital to the movement of the oppressed classes. "

The Soviet achievement in the 1930s seemed hugely impressive from the outside. and convinced many people. not necessarily Communists or even socialists. of the virtues of state planning and authoritarian models of social development. This was later to have important consequences in countries like China. India and Egypt. which tried to copy some aspects of the Soviet model. It also won large sections of the western intelligentsia over to a pro-Soviet view. to the extent that many were willing to ignore or excuse such events as Stalin's Great Purge of 1936-38. in which millions of people died.

The Great Depression. which began in 1929. seemed to socialists and Communists everywhere to be the final proof of the bankruptcy. literally as well as politically. of capitalism. But socialists were unable to take advantage of the Depression to either win elections or stage revolutions. Labour governments in Britain and Australia were disastrous failures. In the United States. the liberalism of President Franklin D. Roosevelt won mass support and deprived socialists of any chance of gaining ground. And in Germany it was the fascists of Adolf Hitler's Nazi Party who successfully exploited the Depression to win power. in January 1933. Hitler's regime swiftly destroyed both the German Communist Party and the Social Democratic Party. the worst blow the world socialist movement had ever suffered. This forced Stalin to reassess his strategy. and from 1935 the Comintern began urging a Popular Front against fascism. The socialist parties were at first suspicious. given the bitter hostility of the 1920s. but eventually effective Popular Fronts were formed in both France and Spain. After the election of a Popular Front government in Spain in 1936 a fascist military revolt led to the Spanish Civil War. The crisis in Spain also brought down the Popular Front government in France under Léon Blum. Ultimately the Popular Fronts were not able to prevent the spread of fascism or the aggressive plans of the fascist powers. Trotskyists considered Popular Fronts a "strike breaking conspiracy" and considered them an impediment to successful resistance to fascism.

When Stalin consolidated his power in the Soviet Union in the late 1920s. Trotsky was forced into exile. eventually residing in Mexico. He maintained active in organizing the Left Opposition internationally. which worked within the Comintern to gain new members. Some leaders of the Communist Parties sided with Trotsky. such as James P. Cannon in the United States. They found themselves expelled by the Stalinist Parties and persecuted by both GPU agents and the political police in Britain. France. the United States. China. and all over the world. Trotskyist parties had a large influence in Sri Lanka and Bolivia.

In 1938. Trotsky and his supporters founded a new international organisation of dissident communists. the Fourth International. In his *Results and Prospects* and *Permanent Revolution* Trotsky developed a theory of revolution uninterrupted by the stagism of Stalinist orthodoxy. He argued that Russia was a bureaucratically degenerated workers statein his work *The Revolution Betrayed*. where he predicted that if a political revolution of the working class did not overthrow Stalinism. the Stalinist bureaucracy would resurrect capitalism. Trotsky's monumental *History of the Russian Revolution* is considered a work of primary importance by Trotsky's followers.

BRITAIN

Once the world's most powerful nation. Britain avoided a revolution during the period of 1917–1923 but was significantly affected by revolt. The Prime Minister. David Lloyd George. had promised the troops in the 1918 election that his Conservative-led coalition would make post-war Britain "a fit land for heroes to live in". But many demobbed troops complained of chronic unemployment and suffered low pay. disease and poor housing.

In 1918. the Labour Party adopted as its aim to secure for the workers. "the common ownership of the means of production. distribution and exchange". In 1919. the Miners Federation. whose Members of Parliament pre-dated the formation of the Labour Party and were since 1906 a part of that body. demanded the withdrawal of British troops from Soviet Russia. The 1919 Labour Party conference voted to discuss the question of affiliation to the Third (Communist) International. "to the distress of its leaders". A vote was won committing the

Labour Party committee of the Trades Union Congress to arrange "direct industrial action" to "stop capitalist attacks upon the Socialist Republics of Russia and Hungary." The threat of immediate strike action forced the Conservative-led coalition government to abandon its intervention in Russia.

In 1914 the unions of the transport workers. the mine workers and the railway workers had formed a Triple Alliance. In 1919. Lloyd George sent for the leaders of the Triple Alliance. one of whom was miner's leader Robert Smillie. a founder member of the Independent Labour Party in 1889 who was to become a Labour Party MP in the first 1924 Labour government. According to Smillie. Lloyd George said:

" Gentlemen. you have fashioned. in the Triple Alliance of the unions represented by you. a most powerful instrument. I feel bound to tell you that in our opinion we are at your mercy. The Army is disaffected and cannot be relied upon. Trouble has occurred already in a number of camps. We have just emerged from a great war and the people are eager for the reward of their sacrifices. and we are in no position to satisfy them. In these circumstances. if you carry out your threat and strike. then you will defeat us.But if you do so. have you weighed the consequences? The strike will be in defiance of the government of the country and by its very success will precipitate a constitutional crisis of the first importance. For. if a force arises in the state which is stronger than the state itself. then it must be ready to take on the functions of the state. or withdraw and accept the authority of the state. Gentlemen. have you considered. and if you have. are you ready? "

— Aneurin Bevan. *In Place of Fear*

"From that moment on". Smillie conceded to Aneurin Bevan. "we were beaten and we knew we were". When the UK General Strike of 1926 broke out. the trade union leaders. "had never worked out the revolutionary implications of direct action on such a scale". Bevan says. Bevan was a member of the Independent Labour Party and one of the leaders of the South Wales miners during the strike. The TUC called off the strike after nine days. In the North East of England and elsewhere. "councils of action" were set up. with many rank and file Communist Party members often playing a critical role. The councils of action took control of essential transport and other duties. When the strike ended. the miners were locked out and remained locked out for six months. Bevan became a Labour MP in 1929.

In January 1924. the Labour Party formed a minority government for the first time with Ramsay MacDonald as prime minister. The Labour Party intended to ratify an Anglo-Russian trade agreement. which would break the trade embargo on Russia. This was attacked by the Conservatives and new elections took place in October 1924. Four days before polling day the *Daily Mail* published the Zinoviev letter. a forgery that claimed the Labour Party had links with Soviet Communists and was secretly fomenting revolution. The fears instilled by the press of a Labour Party in secret Communist manoeuvres. together with the half-hearted "respectable" policies pursued by MacDonald. led to Labour losing the October 1924 general election. The victorious Conservatives repudiated the Anglo-Soviet treaty.

The leadership of the Labour Party. like social democratic parties almost everywhere. (with the exception of Sweden and Belgium). tried to pursue a policy of moderation and economic orthodoxy. At times of depression this policy was not popular with the Labour Party's working class supporters. The influence of Marxism grew in the Labour Party during the inter-war years. Anthony Crosland argued in 1956 that under the impact of the 1931 slump and the growth of fascism. the younger generation of left-wing intellectuals for the most part "took to Marxism" including the "best-known leaders" of the Fabian tradition. Sidney and Beatrice Webb. The Marxist Professor Harold Laski. who was to be chairman of the Labour Party in 1945-6. was the "outstanding influence" in the political field.

The Marxists within the Labour Party differed in their attitude to the Communists. Some were uncitical and some were expelled as "fellow travellers". while in the 1930s others were Trotskyists and sympathisers working inside the Labour Party. especially in its youth wing where they were influential.

In the general election of 1929 the Labour Party won 288 seats out of 615 and formed another minority government. The depression of that period brought high unemployment and Prime Minister MacDonald sought to make cuts in order to balance the budget. The trade unions opposed MacDonald's proposed cuts and he split the Labour government to form the National Government of 1931. This experience moved the Labour Party leftward. and at the start of the Second World War an official Labour Party pamphlet written by Harold Laski argued that. "the rise of Hitler and the methods by which he seeks to maintain and expand his power are deeply rooted in the economic and social system of Europe... economic nationalism. the fight for markets. the destruction of political democracy. the use of war as an instrument of national policy":

- The war will leave its meed of great problems. problems of internal social organisation... Business men and aristocrats. the old ruling classes of Europe. had their chance from 1919 to 1939; they failed to take advantage of it. They rebuilt the world in the image of their own vested interests... The ruling class has failed; this war is the proof of it. The time has come to give the common people the right to become the master of their own destiny... Capitalism has been tried; the results of its power are before us today. Imperialism has been tried; it is the foster-parent of this great agony.Given power [the Labour Party] will seek. as no other Party will seek. the basic transformation of our society. It will replace the profit-seeking motive

by the motive of public service... there is now no prospect of domestic well-being or of international peace except in Socialism. "
— Harold Laski. *The Labour Party. the War and the Future* (1939)

NITED STATES

After embracing anarchism Albert Parsons turned his activity to the growing movement to establish the 8-hour day. In January 1880. the Eight-Hour League of Chicago sent Parsons to a national conference in Washington. DC. a gathering which launched a national lobbying movement aimed at coordinating efforts of labour organizations to win and enforce the 8-hour workday. In the fall of 1884. Parsons launched a weekly anarchist newspaper in Chicago. *The Alarm.* The first issue was dated October 4. 1884. and was produced in a press run of 15.000 copies.

The publication was a 4-page broadsheet with a cover price of 5 cents. *The Alarm* listed the International Working People's Association as its publisher and touted itself as "A Socialistic Weekly" on its page 2 masthead. On May 1. 1886. Parsons. with his wife Lucy Parsons and two children. led 80.000 people down Michigan Avenue. in what is regarded as the first-ever May Day Parade. in support of the eight-hour work day. Over the next few days 340.000 laborers joined the strike. Parsons. amidst the May Day Strike. found himself called to Cincinnati. where 300.000 workers had struck that Saturday afternoon. On that Sunday he addressed the rally in Cincinnati of the news from the "storm centre" of the strike and participated in a second huge parade. led by 200 members of The Cincinnati Rifle Union. with certainty that victory was at hand. In 1886. the Federation of Organized Trades and Labour Unions (FOTLU) of the United States and Canada unanimously set 1 May 1886. as the date by which the eight-hour work day would become standard.

In response. unions across the United States prepared a general strike in support of the event. On 3 May. in Chicago. a fight broke out when strikebreakers attempted to cross the picket line. and two workers died when police opened fire upon the crowd. The next day. 4 May. anarchists staged a rally at Chicago's Haymarket Square. A bomb was thrown by an unknown party near the conclusion of the rally. killing an officer. In the ensuing panic. police opened fire on the crowd and each other. Seven police officers and at least four workers were killed. Eight anarchists directly and indirectly related to the organisers of the rally were arrested and charged with the murder of the deceased officer. The men became international political celebrities among the labour movement. Four of the men were executed and a fifth committed suicide prior to his own execution. The incident became known as the Haymarket affair. and was a setback for the labour movement and the struggle for the eight-hour day. In 1890 a second attempt. this time international in scope. to organise for the eight-hour day was made. The event also had the secondary purpose of memorializing workers killed as a result of the Haymarket affair. Although it had initially been conceived as a once-off event. by the following year the celebration of International Workers' Day on May Day had become firmly established as an international worker's holiday. Albert Parsons is best remembered as one of four Chicago radical leaders convicted of conspiracy and hanged following a bomb attack on police remembered as the Haymarket affair. Emma Goldman. the activist and political theorist. was attracted to anarchism after reading about the incident and the executions. which she later described as "the events that had inspired my spiritual birth and growth."

She considered the Haymarket martyrs to be "the most decisive influence in my existence". Her associate. Alexander Berkman also described the Haymarket anarchists as "a potent and vital inspiration." Others whose commitment to anarchism crystallized as a result of the Haymarket affair included Voltairine de Cleyre and "Big Bill" Haywood. a founding member of the Industrial Workers of the World. Goldman wrote to historian. Max Nettlau. that the Haymarket affair had awakened the social consciousness of "hundreds. perhaps thousands. of people".

In the Presidential election of 1912. Eugene V. Debs received 5.99per cent of the popular vote (a total of 901.551 votes). while his total of 913.693 votes in the 1920 campaign. although smaller percentage-wise. remains the all-time high for a Socialist Party candidate in the United States.

In the United States. the Communist Party USA was formed in 1919 from former adherents of the Socialist Party of America. One of the founders. James Cannon. later became the leader of Trotskyist forces outside the Soviet Union. The Great Depression began in the US on Black Tuesday. October 29. 1929. Unemployment rates passed 25per cent. prices and incomes fell 20–50per cent. but the debts remained at the same dollar amount. 9.000 banks failed during the decade of the 30s. By 1933. depositors saw $140 billion of their deposits disappear due to uninsured bank failures.

Workers organized against their deteriorating conditions and socialists played a critical role. In 1934 the Minneapolis Teamsters Strike led by the Trotskyist Communist League of America. the West Coast Longshore Strike led by the Communist Party USA. and the Toledo Auto-Lite Strike led by the American Workers Party. played an important role in the formation of the Congress of Industrial Organizations (CIO) in the USA.

In Minnesota. the General Drivers Local 574 of the International Brotherhood of Teamsters struck. despite an attempt to block the vote by AFL officials. demanding union recognition. increased wages. shorter hours. overtime rates. improved working conditions and job protection through seniority. In the battles that followed. which captured country-wide media attention. three strikes took place. martial law was declared and the National Guard was sent in. Two strikers were killed. Protest rallies of 40.000 were held. Farrell Dobbs.

who became the leader of the local. had at the outset joined the "small and poverty-stricken" Communist League of America. founded by James P. Cannon and others in 1928 after their expulsion from the Communist Party USA for Trotskyism.

Success for the CIO quickly followed its formation. In 1937. one of the founding unions of the CIO. the United Auto Workers. won union recognition at General Motors Corporation after a tumultuous forty-four day sit-down strike. while the Steel Workers Organizing Committee. which was formed by the CIO. won a collective bargaining agreement with U.S. Steel. The CIO merged with the American Federation of Labour (AFL) in 1955 becoming the AFL-CIO.

GERMANY

In 1928. the Communist International. now fully under the leadership of Stalin. turned from the united front policy to an ultra-left policy of the Third Period. a policy of aggressive confrontation of social democracy. This divided the working class at a critical time.Like the Labour Party in the UK. the Social Democratic Party in Germany. which was in power in 1928. followed an orthodox deflationary policy and pressed for reductions in unemployment benefits in order to save taxes and reduce budget deficits. These policies did not halt the recession and the government resigned.

The Communists described the Social Democratic leaders as "social fascists" and in the Prussian Landtag they voted with the Nazis to bring down the Social Democratic government. Fascism continued to grow. with powerful backing from industrialists. especially in heavy industry. and Hitler was invited into power in 1933.Hitler's regime swiftly destroyed both the German Communist Party and the Social Democratic Party. the worst blow the world socialist movement had ever suffered. This forced Stalin to reassess his strategy. and from 1935 the Comintern began urging the formation of Popular Fronts. which were to include not just the Social Democratic parties but critically also "progressive capitalist" parties which were wedded to a capitalist policy.

After the election of a Popular Front government in Spain in 1936 a fascist military revolt led to the Spanish Civil War. The crisis in Spain brought down the Popular Front government in France under Léon Blum. Ultimately the Popular Fronts were not able to prevent the spread of fascism or the aggressive plans of the fascist powers. Trotskyists considered Popular Fronts a "strike breaking conspiracy". an impediment to successful resistance to fascism due to their inclusion of pro-capitalist parties which demanded policies of opposition to strikes and workers' actions against the capitalist class.

SWEDEN

The Swedish Socialists formed a government in 1932. They broke with economic orthodoxy during the depression and carried out extensive public works financed from government borrowing. They emphasised large-scale intervention and the high unemployment they had inherited was eliminated by 1938. Their success encouraged the adoption of Keynesian policies of deficit financing pursued by almost all Western countries after World War II.

SPAIN

During the Spanish Civil War. anarchists set up different forms of cooperative and communal arrangements. especially in the rural areas of Aragon and Catalonia. However. these communes were disbanded by the Popular Front government.

ISRAEL

Jewish Zionists established utopian socialist communities in Palestine. which were known as kibbutzim. a small number of which still survive.

THE POST-WAR ERA (1945-85)

In the 1930s. the Social Democratic Party of Germany (SPD). a reformist socialist political party that was up to then based upon revisionist Marxism. began a transition away from Marxism towards liberal socialism beginning in the 1930s. After the party was banned by the Nazi regime in 1933. the SPD acted in exile through the Sopade. In 1934 the Sopade began to publish material that indicated that the SPD was turning towards liberal socialism. Sopade member Curt Geyer was a prominent proponent of liberal socialism within the Sopade. and declared that Sopade represented the tradition of Weimar Republic social democracy — liberal democratic socialism. and declared that Sopade's held true to its mandate of traditional liberal principles combined with the political realism of socialism. After the restoration of democracy in West Germany. The SPD's Godesberg Programme in 1959 eliminated the party's remaining Marxist-aligned policies. The SPD then became officially based upon *freiheitlicher Sozialismus* (liberal socialism). West German Chancellor Willy Brandt has been identified as a liberal socialist.

In 1945. the world's three great powers met at the Yalta Conference to negotiate an amicable and stable peace. UK Prime Minister Winston Churchill joined USA President Franklin D. Roosevelt and Joseph Stalin. General Secretary of the Communist Party of the Soviet Union's Central Committee. With the relative decline of Britain compared to the two superpowers. the USA and the Soviet Union. however. many viewed the world as "bi-polar" – a world with two irreconcilable and antagonistic political and economic systems.

As a result of the failure of the Popular Fronts and the inability of Britain and France to conclude a defensive alliance against Hitler. Stalin again changed his policy in August 1939 and signed a non-aggression pact. the Molotov-Ribbentrop Pact. with Nazi Germany. Shortly afterwards World War II broke out. and within two years Hitler had occupied most of Europe. and by 1942 both democracy and social democracy in central Europe fell under the threat of fascism. The only socialist parties of any significance able to operate freely were those in Britain. Sweden. Switzerland. Canada. Australia and New Zealand. But the entry of the Soviet Union into the war in 1941 marked the turning of the tide against fascism. and as the German armies retreated another great upsurge in left-wing sentiment swelled up in their wake. The resistance movements against German occupation were mostly led by socialists and communists. and by the end of the war the parties of the left were greatly strengthened.

One of the great postwar victories of democratic socialism was the election victory of the British Labour Party led by Clement Attlee in June 1945. Socialist (and in some places Stalinist) parties also dominated postwar governments in France. Italy. Czechoslovakia. Belgium. Norway and other European countries. The Social Democratic Party had been in power in Sweden since 1932. and Labour parties also held power in Australia and New Zealand. In Germany. on the other hand. the Social Democrats emerged from the war much weakened. and were defeated in Germany's first democratic elections in 1949. The united front between democrats and the Stalinist parties which had been established in the wartime resistance movements continued in the immediate postwar years. The democratic socialist parties of Eastern Europe. however. were destroyed when Stalin imposed so-called "Communist" regimes in these countries.

The Second International. which had been based in Amsterdam. ceased to operate during the war. It was refounded as the Socialist International at a congress in Frankfurt in 1951. Since Stalin had dissolved the Comintern in 1943. as part of a deal with the imperialist powers. this was now the only effective international socialist organisation. The Frankfurt Declaration took a stand against both capitalism and the Communism of Stalin:

" Socialism aims to liberate the peoples from dependence on a minority which owns or controls the means of production. It aims to put economic power in the hands of the people as a whole. and to create a community in which free men work together as equals... Socialism has become a major force in world affairs. It has passed from propaganda into practice. In some countries the foundations of a Socialist society have already been laid. Here the evils of capitalism are disappearing...Since the Bolshevik revolution in Russia. Communism has split the International Labour Movement and has set back the realisation of socialism in many countries for decades. Communism falsely claims a share in the Socialist tradition. In fact it has distorted that tradition beyond recognition. It has built up a rigid theology which is incompatible with the critical spirit of Marxism... Wherever it has gained power it has destroyed freedom or the chance of gaining freedom...— The Frankfurt Declaration. 1951

Anarcho-pacifism became influential in the Anti-nuclear movement and anti war movements of the time as can be seen in the activism and writings of the English anarchist member of Campaign for Nuclear Disarmament Alex Comfort or the similar activism of the American catholic anarcho-pacifists Ammon Hennacy and Dorothy Day. Anarcho-pacifism became a "basis for a critique of militarism on both sides of the Cold War." The resurgence of anarchist ideas during this period is well documented in Robert Graham's Anarchism: A Documentary History of Libertarian Ideas. *Volume Two: The Emergence of the New Anarchism (1939–1977).*

THE FIRST SOCIALIST GOVERNMENT IN A NORTH AMERICAN COUNTRY

The first socialist government of North America and one of the most influential came to power in the Canadian province of Saskatchewan in 1944. The Co-operative Commonwealth Federation of Tommy Douglas won an overwhelming victory toppling the age old Liberal regime which had dominated Saskatchewan politics since the founding of the province in 1905. Douglas and the CCF won five consecutive electoral victories.

During his time in office he created the Saskatchewan Power Corp. which extended electricity services to the many rural villages and farms who before did without. created Canada's first public automobile insurance agency. created a substantial number ofCrown Corporations (government and public owned businesses) many of which still exist today in Saskatchewan. allowed the unionization of the public service. created the first system of Universal Health Care in Canada (which would later be adopted nationally in 1965). and created Saskatchewan's Bill of Rights. the first such charter in Canada. This preceded the Canadian Charter of Rights and Freedoms as well as the previous Canadian Bill of Rights.

The New Democratic Party (as the CCF became known in 1962) went on to dominate the politics of Saskatchewan and form governments in British Columbia. Manitoba.Ontario. and the Yukon Territory. Nationally the NDP would become very influential during four minority governments. and is today by far Canada's most successful left-wing political party. In 2004 Canadians voted Tommy Douglas in as *The Greatest Canadian* as part of a nation-wide contest organized by the Canadian Broadcasting Corporation(CBC).

SOCIAL DEMOCRACY IN GOVERNMENT

The social democratic governments in the post war period introduced measures of social reform and wealth redistribution through state welfare and taxation policy. For instance the newly elected UK Labour government carried out nationalisations of major utilities such as mines. gas. coal. electricity. rail. iron and steel. and the Bank of England.France claimed to be the most state controlled capitalist country in the world. carrying through many nationalisations. In the UK the National Health Service was established bringing free health care to all for the first time. Social housing for working-class families was provided in council housing estates and university education was made available for working-class people through a grant system.

However the parliamentary leadership of the social democracies in general had no intention of ending capitalism. and their national outlook and their dedication to the maintenance of the post-war 'order' prevented the social democracies from making any significant changes to the economy. They were termed 'socialist' by all in 1945. but in the UK. for instance. where Social Democracy had a large majority in Parliament. "The government had not the smallest intention of bringing in the 'common ownership of the means of production. distribution and exchange'" as written in Clause 4 of the Labour Party constitution. In Germany. the Social Democratic Party of Germany adopted theGodesberg Programme in 1959. which rejected class struggle and Marxism. In the UK. cabinet minister Herbert Morrison famously argued that. "Socialism is what the Labour government does". and Anthony Crosland argued that capitalism had been ended.

However many socialists within the social democracy. at rank and file level as well as in a minority in the leadership such as Aneurin Bevan. feared the 'return of the 1930s' unless capitalism was ended. either directly or over a definite period of time. They criticised the government for not going further to take over the commanding heights of the economy.

Bevan demanded that the "main streams of economic activity are brought under public direction" with economic planning. and criticised the Labour Party's implementation of nationalisation for not empowering the workers in the nationalised industries with democratic control over their operation. In the post war period. many Trotskyists expected at first the pattern of financial instability and recession to return. Instead the capitalist world. now led by the United States. embarked on a prolonged boom which lasted until 1973. Rising living standards across Europe and North America alongside low unemployment. was achieved. in the view of the socialists. by the efforts of trade union struggle. social reform by social democracy. and the ushering in of what was termed a "mixed economy".

Social democracy at first took the view that they had begun a "serious assault" on the five "Giant Evils" afflicting the working class. identified for instance by the British social reformer William Beveridge: "Want. Disease. Ignorance. Squalor. and Idleness".

At the same time. the wartime alliance between the Soviet Union and the west broke down from 1946 onwards. and relations between the Communist parties and the democratic socialist parties broke down in parallel. Once the Stalinists helped stabilize the capitalist governments in the immediate upheavals of 1945. as per the agreements betweens Stalin. Roosevelt. and Churchill. the capitalist politicians had no more use for them. The French. Italian and Belgian Communists withdrew or were expelled from post-war coalition governments. and civil war broke out in Greece. The imposition of Stalinist regimes in Poland. Hungary and Czechoslovakia not only destroyed the socialist parties in those countries. it also produced a reaction against socialism in general.

The Australian and New Zealand Labour governments were defeated in 1949. and the British Labour government in 1951. As the Cold War deepened. conservative rule in Britain. Germany and Italy became more strongly entrenched. Only in the Scandinavian countries and to some extent in France did the socialist parties retain their positions. But in 1958 Charles de Gaulle seized power in France and the French socialists (SFIO) found themselves cast into opposition.In the 1960s and 1970s the new social forces. introduced. the social democrats argued. by their 'mixed economy' and their many reforms of capitalism. began to change the political landscape in the western world.

The long postwar boom and the rapid expansion of higher education produced. as well as rising living standards for the industrial working class. a mass university-educated white collar workforce. nevertheless began to break down the old socialist-versus-conservative polarity of European politics. This new white-collar workforce. some claimed. was less interested in traditional socialist policies such as state ownership and more interested expanded personal freedom and liberal social policies. The proportion of women in the paid workforce increased and many supported the struggle for equal pay. which. some argued. changed both the composition and the political outlook of the working class. Some socialist parties reacted more flexibly and successfully to these changes than others. but eventually the leaderships of all social democracies in Europe moved to an explicitly pro-capitalist stance. Symbolically in the UK. the socialist clause. Clause four. was removed from the Labour Party constitution. in 1995. A similar change took place in the German SDP.

However. particularly after the coming to power of British Premier Margaret Thatcher in 1979 and US President Ronald Reagan in 1981. and the fall of the Berlin Wall in 1989. many social democratic party leaders were won to the ideological offensive which argued that capitalism had "won" and that. in the words of Francis Fukuyama's essay. capitalism had reached "the end point of mankind's ideological evolution and the universalization of Western liberal democracy as the final form of human government.".Some parties reacted to these changes by engaging in a new round of revisionist re-assessment of socialist ideology. and adopting a neo-liberal outlook. Some critics argue that in practice the Social Democratic parties. and the Labour Party in particular. can no longer be described as socialist. On Prime Minister Tony Blair's departure in June 2007. left wing trade union leader Bob Crow. general secretary of the Rail. Maritime and Transport workers union (RMT). argued that Blair will be remembered for "seamlessly continuing the neo-liberal economic and social policies of Margaret Thatcher".

MASS DISCONTENT AND RADICALIZATION

Another manifestation of this changing social landscape was the rise of mass discontent. including the radical student movement. both in the United States – where it was driven mainly by opposition to the Vietnam War. and in Europe. Aside from the Civil Rights Movement. in which socialists participated. the anti-war movement was the first left-wing upsurge in the United States since the 1930s. but neither there nor in Europe did the traditional parties of the left lead the movement. In the mid-20th century some libertarian socialist groups emerged from disagreements with Trotskyism which presented itself as leninist anti-stalinism. As such the French group *Socialisme ou Barbarie* emerged from the Trotskyist Fourth International. where Castoriadis and Claude Lefort constituted a Chaulieu–Montal Tendency in the French Parti Communiste Internationaliste in 1946. In 1948. they experienced their "final disenchantment with Trotskyism".

leading them to break away to form Socialisme ou Barbarie. whose journal began appearing in March 1949. Castoriadis later said of this period that "the main audience of the group and of the journal was formed by groups of the old. radical left: Bordigists. council communists. some anarchists and some offspring of the German "left" of the 1920s". Instead Trotskyist. Maoist and anarchist groups arose. They became particularly influential in 1968. when riots amounting almost to an insurrection broke out in Paris in May 1968. Between eight and ten million workers struck. challenging the view becoming popular amongst socialists at the time that the working class were no longer a force for change. There were also major disturbances in Chicago namely the Columbia University protests of 1968. Berlin by the embryonic Red Army Faction and in other cities. In the short-term these movements provoked a conservative backlash. seen in De Gaulle's 1968 election victory and the election of Richard Nixon in the United States. But in the 1970s. as particularly the far left Trotskyist groups continued to grow. the socialist and Communist parties again sought to channel people's anger back into safe confines. as they did in 1945.

The British Labour Party had already returned to office under Harold Wilson in 1964. and in 1969 the German Social Democrats came to power for the first time since the 1920s under Willy Brandt. In France François Mitterrand buried the corpse of the old socialist party. the SFIO. and founded a new Socialist Party in 1971. although it would take him a decade to lead it to power. Labour governments were elected in both Australia and New Zealand in 1972. and the Austrian Socialists under Bruno Kreisky formed their first post-war government in 1970. The emergence of the New Left in the 1950s and 1960s led to a revival of interest in libertarian socialism. The New Left's critique of the Old Left's authoritarianism was associated with a strong interest in personal liberty. autonomy and led to a rediscovery of older socialist traditions. such as left communism. council communism. and the Industrial Workers of the World. The New Left also led to a revival of anarchism. Journals like *Radical America* and *Black Mask* in America. *Solidarity*. *Big Flame* and *Democracy and Nature*. succeeded by *The International Journal of Inclusive Democracy*. in the UK. introduced a range of left libertarian ideas to a new generation. Social ecology. autonomism and. more recently. participatory economics (parecon). and Inclusive Democracy emerged from this.

The New Left in the United States also included anarchist. countercultural and hippie-related radical groups such as the Yippies who were led by Abbie Hoffman. The Diggers and Up Against the Wall Motherfuckers. By late 1966. the Diggers opened free stores which simply gave away their stock. provided free food. distributed free drugs. gave away money. organised free music concerts. and performed works of political art. The Diggers took their name from the original English Diggers led by Gerrard Winstanley and sought to create a mini-society free of money and capitalism. On the other hand the Yippies employed theatrical gestures. such as advancing a pig ("Pigasusthe Immortal") as a candidate for President in 1968. to mock the social status quo.

They have been described as a highly theatrical. anti-authoritarian and anarchist youth movement of "symbolic politics". Since they were well known for street theater and politically themed pranks. many of the "old school" political left either ignored or denounced them. According to ABC News. "The group was known for street theater pranks and was once referred to as the 'Groucho Marxists'." Autonomist Marxism. Neo-Marxism and Situationist theoryare also regarded as being anti-authoritarian variants of Marxism that are firmly within the libertarian socialist tradition. For libcom.org "In the 1980's and 90's. a series of other groups developed. influenced also by much of the above work. The most notable are Kolinko. Kurasje and Wildcat in Germany. *Aufheben* in England.

Theorie Communiste in France. TPTG in Greece and Kamunist Kranti in India. They are also connected to other groups in other countries. merging autonomia. operaismo. Hegelian Marxism. the work of the JFT. Open Marxism. the ICO. the Situationist International. anarchism and post-68 German Marxism." Related to this were intellectuals who were influenced by Italian left communist Amadeo Bordiga but who disagreed with his leninist positions and so these included the French publication *Invariance* edited by Jacques Camatte. published since 1968 and Gilles Dauve who published *Troploin* with Karl Nesic.

After the Stonewall Rebellion. the New York Gay Liberation Front based their organization in part on a reading of Murray Bookchin's anarchist writings.". In 1968 in Carrara. Italy the International of Anarchist Federations was founded during an international anarchist conference held there in 1968 by the three existing European federations ofFrance. the Italian and the Iberian Anarchist Federation as well as the Bulgarian federation in French exile. During the events of May 68 the anarchist groups active in France were Fédération anarchiste. Mouvement communiste libertaire. Union fédérale des anarchistes. Alliance ouvrière anarchiste. Union des groupes anarchistes communistes. Noir et Rouge. Confédération nationale du travail. Union anarcho-syndicaliste. Organisation révolutionnaire anarchiste. *Cahiers socialistes libertaires*. *À contre-courant*. *La Révolution prolétarienne*. and the publications close to Émile Armand.

The early 1970s were a particularly stormy period for socialists. as capitalism had its first world wide slump of 1973-4. suffered from rising oil prices. and a crisis in confidence. In southern Europe. for example. the Portuguese Carnation Revolution of 1974 threatened the existence of capitalism for a while due to the insurrection and the occupations which followed. A *New York Times* editorial on February 17. 1975. stated "a communist takeover of Portugal might encourage a similar trend in Italy and France. create problems in Greece and Turkey. affect the succession in Spain and Yugoslavia and send tremors throughout Western Europe."

The Greek military dictatorship fell in Greece. PASOK arose at first with a strong socialist outlook. and in Spain. the Franco dictatorship fell in a period of rising struggle. In Italy there was continual unrest. and governments fell almost annually. The Italian workers won and defended the "scala mobile". the sliding scale of wages linked to inflation. However. as before. neither the Communists nor the social democracy had any plans to abolish capitalism. and the occupations in Portugal. variously estimated to have taken between 70 - 90per cent of the economy. were gradually rolled back. The UK saw a state of emergency and the three day week. with 22 million days lost in strike action in 1972. leading to the fall of the Heath government and appearance of the Trotskyist Militant tendency in the Labour Party. which became the "fifth most important political party" for a period in the mid 1980s.

In Indonesia within the Indonesian killings of 1965–66 a right wing military regime killed between 300.000 and one million people mainly to cruch the growing influence of theCommunist Party of Indonesia and other leftist sectors In Latin America in the 1960s a socialist tendency within the catholic church appeared which was calledLiberation theology

THE SOVIET UNION AND EASTERN EUROPE (1945–1985)

Immediately after the Second World War. a period known as the Cold War began. It represented a period of conflict. tension and competition between the United States and the Soviet Union and their respective allies. Throughout the period. the rivalry between the two superpowers was played out in multiple arenas: military coalitions; ideology. psychology. and espionage; military.

industrial. and technological developments. including the space race; costly defence spending; a massive conventional and nuclear arms race; and many proxy wars.

The term "Cold War" was introduced in 1947 by Americans Bernard Baruch and Walter Lippmann to describe emerging tensions between the two former wartime allies. There never was a direct military engagement between the U.S. and the Soviet Union. but there was a half-century of military buildup. and political battles for support around the world. including significant involvement of allied and satellite nations. Although the U.S. and the Soviet Union had been allied against Nazi Germany. the two sides differed on how to reconstruct the postwar world even before the end of World War II. Over the following decades. the Cold War spread outside Europe to every region of the world. as the U.S. sought the "containment" of communism and forged numerous alliances to this end. particularly in Western Europe. the Middle East. and Southeast Asia.

In 1946. speaking at Westminster College in Fulton. Missouri. former British prime minister Winston Churchill warned that. "From Stettinin the Baltic to Trieste in the Adriatic. an iron curtain has descended across the Continent."

In the months that followed. Josef Stalin continued to solidify a Soviet sphere of influence in eastern Europe. For example. Bulgaria received its new Communist premier. Georgi Dimitrov. in November 1946. a Communist government under Boles³aw Bierut had been established in Poland already in 1945. and by 1947. Hungary and Romania had also come under full communist rule. The last democratic government in the eastern bloc.Czechoslovakia. fell to a Communist coup in 1948. and in 1949 the Soviets raised their occupation zone in Germany to become the German Democratic Republic under Walter Ulbricht.

To coordinate their new empire. the Soviets established a number of international organizations. first the Cominform to coordinate the policies of the various Communist parties. then the Council for Mutual Economic Assistance (COMECON). in 1948. to control economic planning. and finally (in response to the entry of the Federal Republic of Germanyinto the North Atlantic Treaty Organization) the Warsaw Pact in 1955. which served as a military alliance against the west.

But one crack within that sphere of influence emerged after 1948. when Marshal Josip Broz Tito became the president of Yugoslavia. Initial disagreement was over the level of independence claimed by Tito as the only East European Communist ruler commanding a strong domestic majority. Later the gap widened when Tito's government initiated a system of decentralized profit-sharing workers' councils. in effect a self-governing. somewhat market-oriented socialism. which Stalin considered dangerously revisionist. Stalin died in 1953. In the power struggle that followed Stalin's death. Nikita Khrushchev emerged triumphant. In 1956. at the 20th Congress of the Communist Party of the Soviet Union. he denounced the "personality cult" that had surrounded Stalin in a speech entitled On the Personality Cult and its Consequences. In the de-Stalinization campaign that followed. all buildings and towns that had been named for him were renamed. pictures and statues were destroyed. Although in some respects Khrushchev was a reformer and allowed the emergence of a certain amount of intra-party dissent. his commitment to reform was thrown into doubt with the brutal use of military force on the civilian population of Hungary in 1956 during the Hungarian Revolution and the March 9 massacre in Tbilisi. 1956.

By the late 1960s. the people of several eastern bloc countries had become discontented with the human and economic costs of the Soviet system. Czechoslovakia especially so. As a result of the growing discontent. the Communist Party began to fear a popular uprising. They initiated reforms to attempt to save the regime. but eventually relied on help from the Stalinists in Russia. In 1968. Alexander Dubèek initiated what is known as the Prague Spring. ending censorship of the press and decentralizing production decisions. so that they were to be made not by central planners but by the workers and managers of the factories. People were to be allowed to travel abroad.

Brezhnev reacted by announcing and enforcing what became known as the Brezhnev doctrine:

- When forces that are hostile to socialism try to turn the development of some socialist country towards capitalism the suppression of these counter-revolutionary forces becomes not only a problem of the country concerned. but a common problem and concern of all socialist countries."

  — The 'Brezhnev doctrine'. 1968

In August 1968. pursuant to this announcement. Soviet troops occupied Czechoslovakia. The following year. the Ukrainians responded to a campaign of passive disobedience on the part of the Czech populace by arranging the replacement of Dubèek as first secretary. The new first secretary. Gustáv Husák. would prove more compliant. He presided over a 'cleansing' of the Czech Communist Party and the introduction of a new constitution.

The early 1970s saw a period of détente. The arms race between the United States and the Soviet Union slackened. Brezhnev worked with US President Richard Nixon to negotiate and implement the Strategic Arms Limitations Treaty of 1972. Brezhnev also scored some diplomatic advances with the non-aligned world. such as a 1971 friendship pact with India. and the close relations the Soviet Union enjoyed with several Arab countries after Soviet material support in the Yom Kippur War of 1973. After his death in 1982. Brezhnev was succeeded by Yuri Andropov. who died in 1984. and then Konstantin Chernenko. who died in 1985. Andropov's brief tenure as General Secretary indicated that he might have had reformist plans. and though Chernenko put them aside. Andropov had had time to groom a group of potential reformist successors. one of whom was Mikhail Gorbachev.

It was also during Andropov's tenure and this period of generational turmoil that the rule of Communists next door. in Poland. came under challenge from Solidarnoœæ. orSolidarity. a labour union under the leadership of Lech Wa³êsa. The union was sufficiently threatening to the government that on 13 December 1981. the head of state. Wojciech Jaruzelski declared martial law. suspended the union. and imprisoned most of its leaders.

FINAL YEARS FOR THE SOVIET UNION 1985-91

Mikhail Gorbachev (1931-). who took control in 1985. was the first Soviet leader to have been born after the October revolution. He is remembered for three initiatives: *glasnost.perestroika*. and the "Frank Sinatra doctrine".

Glasnost. or "openness". was Gorbachev's term for allowing public debate in the Soviet Union to an unprecedented degree.

Perestroika was his term for market-oriented economic reforms. in recognition of the stagnating effects of central planning. The "Frank Sinatra" doctrine was his reversal of the Brezhnev doctrine. Sinatra sang "My Way". and the doctrine named for him was that each Warsaw Pact country could find its own "way" of doing things. Gorbachev also. in 1989. withdrew Soviet troops from their engagement in Afghanistan. ten years after Brezhnev had sent them there. They had been fighting the anti-government Mujahideen forces which since 1979 as part of its cold war strategy had been covertly funded and trained by the United States government through the Pakistani secret service known as Inter Services Intelligence (ISI).

By August 1991. anti-reform Communists in both the Party and the military were sufficiently desperate to attempt a military coup. Coup leaders called themselves the Committee on the State of Emergency. They announced that Gorbachev had been removed from his position as president due to illness.

Although the coup rapidly collapsed and Gorbachev returned to Moscow. it was Boris Yeltsin who had played a leading role in the street resistance to that Committee. and the incident marked a shift of power away from Gorbachev Towards Yeltsin. By the end of that year. Yeltsin was the leader of Russia. and the Soviet Union was no more.

CHINA (1945–65)

Through the Second World War. the Chinese Communist Party (CCP) under the leadership of Mao Zedong and the Nationalistgovernment of Chiang Kai-shek lived in an uneasy truce in order to combat the common foe. the Japanese occupation. Upon the Surrender of Japan. the Chinese Civil War immediately resumed. Another truce. negotiated by American general George

C. Marshall early in 1946. collapsed after only three months. While war raged in China. two post-occupation governments established themselves next door. in Korea. In 1948. Syngman Rhee was proclaimed president of the Republic of Korea (South Korea). at Seoul. while the Communist Workers Party of North Korea in the north proclaimed the establishment of the Democratic People's Republic of Korea (North Korea).

In January 1949. the Chinese Nationalist armies suffered a devastating defeat by the Communists at Tientsin. By spring. Chiang Kai-shek. now losing whole divisions by desertion to the Communists. began the removal of remaining forces to Formosa (Taiwan). In August. U.S. aid to the Nationalists ended due to Chiang's regime. which was corruption. In October. Mao Zedong took office as the Chairman of the Central People's Administrative Council of the People's Republic of China in Beijing. Zhou Enlai was named premier and foreign minister of the new state.

The nascent People's Republic did not yet control all of the territory of the Republic of China. Mao declared it his goal in 1950 to "liberate"Hainan. Tibet. and Formosa. and while he accomplished that of the first two. the third was interrupted: On 25 June 1950. the forces of North Korea invaded the South unleashing the Korean War. The United States Seventh Fleet was summarily dispatched to protect Formosa from a mainland Red Chinese invasion. Although Mao was apparently unenthusiastic about that war. a Chinese volunteer force entered the Korean War in November.

Claiming a victory against colonialism in the Korean War stalemate. the Communist government in China settled down to the consolidation of domestic power. During the 1950s. they redistributed land. established the Anti-Rightist Movement. and attempted mass industrialization. with technical assistance from the Soviet Union. By the mid-1950s. after an armistice in Korea and the surrender of French forces in Indochina. China's borders were secure. Mao's internal power base was likewise secured by the imprisonment of those he called "left-wing oppositionists".

As the 1950s ended. however. Mao became discontented with the status quo. On the one hand. he saw the Soviet Union attempting "peaceful co-existence" with the imperialist Western powers of NATO. and he believed China could be the centre of worldwide revolution only by breaking with Moscow. (Mao viewed then-Soviet leader Nikita Khrushchevas a revisionist [*i.e.* not a true Communist] and a traitor to socialism.) On the other hand. he was dissatisfied with the economic consequences of the revolution thus far. and believed the country had to enter into a programme of planned rapid industrialization known as the Great Leap Forward. The economic planning of the Great Leap period focused on steel – because steel was considered emblematic of industry. The government arranged to have small backyard steel furnaces built in communes. in the hope that the mobilization of the entire populace would compensate for the absence of the usual economies of scale. During this period. Mao stepped down as head of state in favour of Liu Shaoqi. but Mao remained Chairman of the Communist Party of China. The rushed programme of industrialization was a disaster. It diverted labour and resources from agriculture to marginally productive cottage industry and so contributed to years of famine. It also caused a loss of Mao's influence upon the Communist Party and government apparatus. Modernizers such as Liu and Deng Xiaoping sought to relegate him to the status of figurehead.

Mao wasn't ready to be a figurehead. In the early 1960s he gathered around himself the so-called "Shanghai Mafia" consisting of his fourth wife. Jiang Qing (a.k.a. "Madame Mao"). as well as Lin Biao. Chen Boda. and Yao Wenyuan. unleashing the Cultural Revolution.

In the People's Republic of China (PRC) since 1967. the terms Ultra-Left and left communist refers to political theory and practice self-defined as further "left" than that of the central Maoist leaders at the height of the GPCR ("Great Proletarian Cultural Revolution"). The terms are also used retroactively to describe some early 20th century Chinese anarchist orientations. As a slur. the Communist Party of China (CPC) has used the term "ultra-left" more broadly to denounce any orientation it considers further "left" than theparty line. According to the latter usage. in 1978 the CPC Central Committee denounced as "ultra-left" the line of Mao Zedong from 1956 until his death in 1976.

"Ultra-Left" refers to those GPCR rebel positions that diverged from the central Maoist line by identifying an antagonistic contradiction between the CPC-PRC party-state itself and themasses of workers and "peasants" conceived as a single proletarian class divorced from any meaningful control over production or distribution. Whereas the central Maoist line maintained that the masses controlled the means of production through the Party's mediation. the Ultra-Left argued that the objective interests of bureaucrats were structurally determined by the centralist state-form in direct opposition to the objective interests of the masses. regardless of however "red" a given bureaucrat's "thought" might be. Whereas the central Maoist leaders encouraged the masses to criticize reactionary "ideas" and "habits" among the alleged 5per cent of bad cadres. giving them a chance to "turn over a new leaf" after they had undergone "thought reform." the Ultra-Left argued that "cultural revolution" had to give way to "political revolution" – "in which one class overthrows another class".

SOCIALISM IN CHINA SINCE THE CULTURAL REVOLUTION

In 1965. Wenyuan wrote a thinly veiled attack on the deputy mayor of Beijing. Wu Han. Over the six months that followed. on behalf of ideological purity. Mao and his supporters purged many public figures. Liu Shao-chi among them. By the middle of 1966. Mao had not only put himself back into the centre of things. he had initiated what is known as the Cultural Revolution. a mass (and army-supported) action against the Communist Party apparatus itself on behalf of a renovated conception of Communism.

Chaos continued throughout China for three years. particularly due to the agitations of the Red Guards until the CCP's ninth congress in 1969. when Lin Biao emerged as the primary military figure. and the presumptive heir to Mao in the party. In the months that followed. Lin Biao restored domestic order. while diplomatic efforts by Zhou Enlai cooled border tensions with the Soviet Union. Lin Biao died under mysterious circumstances in 1971. Mao's final years saw a notable thaw in the People's Republic's relations with the United States. the period of "Ping Pong Diplomacy".

Mao died in 1976. and almost immediately his ideological heirs. the Gang of Four lost a power struggle to more "pragmatic" figures such as Deng Xiaoping. The term "pragmatic" is often used in media accounts of these factional struggles but should not be confused with the philosophy of pragmatism proper. Deng launched the "Beijing Spring". allowing open criticism of the excesses and suffering that had occurred during the Cultural Revolution period. He also eliminated the class-background system. under which the communist regime had limited employment opportunities available to people deemed associated with the pre-revolutionary landlord class.

Although Deng's only official title in the early 1980s was chairman of the central military commission of the CP. he was widely regarded as the central figure in the nation's politics. In that period. Zhao Ziyang became premier and Hu Yaobang became head of the party. Near the end of that decade. the death of Hu Yaobang sparked a mass demonstration of mourning students in Tiananmen Square. Beijing. The mourning soon turned into a call for greater responsiveness and liberalization. and the demonstration was captured live on cameras to be broadcast around the world. On May 30. 1989 students erected the "Goddess of Democracy" statue. which looked a bit like Lady Liberty in New York Harbour.

On 4 June 1989 under the orders of Deng Xiaoping. troops and tanks of the People's Liberation Army ended the peaceful protest. Thousands were killed in the resultant massacre. By the start of the 21st century. though. the leadership of China was embarked upon a programme of market-based reform that was more sweeping than had been Soviet leader Gorbachev's perestroika programme of the late 1980s. which is tracable to Deng's Socialism with Chinese characteristics.

It is in this context that Leo Melamed. chairman emeritus and senior policy adviser to the Chicago Mercantile Exchange. spoke to the 2003 Beijing Forum on China and East Asian Prospects of Financial Cooperation on September 23. He said that the CME applauds the National People's Congress for recognizing their country's need for additional trading in futures contracts.

21ST CENTURY DEMOCRATIC SOCIALISM IN LATIN AMERICA

Since the 1998 election of Hugo Chávez as President in Venezuela and the beginnings of his "Bolivarian Revolution" aimed at creating greater equality. Latin American nations have seen a tide of democratically elected socialist and centre-left governments emerge. They have been elected in increasing numbers as the poor and middle classes of many countries have become increasingly disillusioned with the neoliberal economic policies still encouraged by the United States and as a very large gap continues to exist between rich and poor. denying millions of people basic opportunities and necessities.

A long and very controversial history of U.S. military and political intervention in the region dating back to the 19th century has severely tarnished the image of the United States in the eyes of many Latin Americans and shapes governments' policies to this day. A recent example of the influence of the aforementioned sentiment was the Latin American and Caribbean Congress in Solidarity with Puerto Rico's Independence. an international summit held at Panama City. Panama. in which fifteen incumbent political parties (in government) requested that the United States "relinquish its colonial rule over said island-nation and recognise Puerto Rico's independence".

Chavez is joined by the democratic socialist president of Bolivia. Evo Morales (that nation's first indigenous leader). who has adopted strong reformist agendas and attracted overwhelming majority electoral victories. The democratically elected president of Ecuador. Rafael Correa is also an ally of Chavez. Correa describes himself as a humanist.Christian of the left and proponent of socialism of the 21st century.

A number of centre-left/social democratic presidents have also come to power in Latin American countries recently promosing a greater redistribution of wealth within the framework of the free market. They include Cristina Fernández de Kirchner of Argentina. Lula da Silva of Brazil. Michelle Bachelet of Chile. Tabaré Vázquez of Uruguay. Alan García of Peru. Álvaro Colom in Guatemala and Fernando Lugo of Paraguay. The majority of these governments are still enjoying high approval ratings in their nation's public opinion polls. In Nicaragua's 2006 elections the former Sandinista President Daniel Ortega was re-elected President after having been out of office since 1990.

In Colombia's previous presidential elections. Carlos Gaviria Díaz of the socialist Alternative Democratic Pole came in second place to Álvaro Uribe of Colombia First. a conservative party. While in Peru's previous presidential election Alan García's main challenger was Ollanta Humala of the Union for Peru. a leftwing Peruvian nationalist with close ties to Venezuelan President Hugo Chávez. The results of the 2006 Peruvian election were close. In El Salvador. the FMLN a former left-wing guerrilla group which once fought against a military dictatorship is now the official opposition to the Salvadoran government.

Other parts of the developing world have also seen a rise in radical socialist parties and movements. In Nepal following the end of the Civil War. the formerly militant Communist Party of Nepal (Maoist) and the more moderate Communist Party of Nepal (Unified Marxist-Leninist) have emerged as the two most powerful opposition parties in the country. In Nepal's 2008 Constituent Assembly elections the Maoists emerged as the largest party allowing them to form an interim government. Their leader. Prachanda has vowed to respect multiparty democracy.

In some of the poorest parts of India. the Communist Party of India (Maoist) has also been fighting a violent insurgency against the Indian government; a similar rebellion is being waged by the Maoist. New People's Army in the Philippines.

THE EMERGENCE OF A "NEW LEFT" IN THE DEVELOPED WORLD

In many developed nations the adoption of Third Way policies by social democratic parties has led to the rise of many new socialist parties running on solid left-wing agendas. They include Sinn Féin in the Republic of Ireland and Northern Ireland (they also represent the Nationalist constituency of Northern Ireland). the The Left of Germany. Left Party of Sweden. New Zealand Progressive Party. Socialist Party of Ireland. Socialist Party of the Netherlands. Respect Party of the United Kingdom. Scottish Socialist Party andQuébec solidaire in the Canadian province of Quebec.

3

Socialism–Theory and Practice

In this context. we must restrict the notion of socialism to that of a social system whose characteristics have been moulded both by specific theoretical works and. in the course of time. by practical political. legal and economic institutions and measures in communist-ruled countries. In our capacity as economists. we must then limit our view of this social system a little further. and primarily focus our examination on the socialist economic system – and. of course. its connection with the political system. However. since the socialist economic system represents the crucial structure of the entire socialist society. and is also regarded as the basis of society by the theoreticians of this social order. our narrowed view simultaneously enables us to receive a deeper insight into the socio-economic aspects of the socialist social system.

THE DEVELOPMENT OF THE CONCEPT OF COMMUNIST-CONTROLLED SOCIALISM

The genesis of the socio-economic meaning of the communist-controlled term 'socialism' has its main source in the theoretical works of Marx. Engels and Lenin. the so-called classics of Marxism-Leninism. How this concept has satisfied the fundamental criteria of the development of socialism in the course of its practical realisation in the Soviet Union and other socialist countries must now be examined. and whether it has resulted in the socio-economic development expected by the above-mentioned theorists.

To begin with it must be made clear that the term 'socialism' generally describes the social system which Marx had referred to as the 'first and lower phase of communism'. Marx inferred the characterisation of this lower form from the historical necessity of the development of communism. and from the fact that communism would directly emerge from capitalism and would therefore be characterised by capitalism for a relatively long time – the 'first phase'. The notion of 'socialist phase' or more briefly. 'socialism' to denote Marx's 'lower phase'. has become common currency and I propose to use it in this sense.

Marx and Engels substantiated the historical necessity of the development of communist society by saying that capitalism would increasingly impede the further development of productive forces and – as always in history -only new economic and social conditions. that is 'socialist conditions'. would cause productive forces to evolve at a substantially faster rate than they could under capitalism. This historical view gave rise to the fundamental criterion for the development of the socialist economy also held by Lenin. He was convinced that the expropriation of capitalists would result in an immense extension of social productive forces and in the achievement of a higher degree of labour productivity.

According to the classics. the retardatory effect of capitalist production conditions on the development of productive forces would be the result of the contrast between private ownership of the means of production and the social character of production. Private appropriation of the results of production would lead to increasing exploitation of the workers. to their pauperisation. Production could not be oriented towards the development of social demand at the outset. but would be corrected after the event. in accordance with market price fluctuations.

The workers' income. which would always lag behind production growth in relative terms. and their consumption capacity would cause cyclically recurring crises. The growth of the organic composition of capital would result in constantly increasing unemployment and in decreasing profit rates. The growing concentration of capital would first lead to the development of monopolies. and finally to a predominance of monopolies in the economy. All this would impede the development of productive forces to an ever greater extent. while simultaneously creating the economic and political preconditions for the abolition of capitalist production conditions.

Socialism. therefore. was meant to obviate its fundamental opposite. capitalism. by substituting social ownership of the means of production for their private ownership. This would adapt ownership conditions to the social character of production. while private production control and private appropriation of the results of production would be replaced by their social equivalents. Market relations would have to be eliminated. and production as a whole would a priori have to be oriented towards future developments of demand with the help of economic planning. Direct social labour on the part of the working population would result in a faster growth of labour productivity than under capitalism.

It was Engels who first drew conclusions from incipient state ownership in capitalism to a socialist state ownership of the means of production. He assumed. however. that the socialist (proletarian) state would only effect the expropriation of the capitalists by means of the nationalisation of their companies. Subsequent to nationalisation of the means of production and the disappearance of the contrast between labour and capital. the state was meant to begin to wither away so that even during the first (socialist) phase. the policy characterised by overall state ownership would disappear. Lenin. however.

extended the existence of the socialist state to the entire socialist phase and developed the theory of the leading role of state ownership in socialism.

Lenin also pointed out Engels' notion according to which. in socialism. the economy is something like a giant enterprise owned by the people. who are represented by the socialist state. In this giant enterprise. the division of labour would remain unaffected by market forces and only be technical in nature; individual parts. that is. enterprises. would relate to each other like departments. plants. and so on. The activity of all the parts. the overall production by all enterprises. as well as the distribution of the means of production and the labour force among them. would have to be determined with the help of one single overall plan. Later. this idea of marketfree and natural economic planning was developed further by the so-called 'Trotskyist' economists. such as Prcobrazchenski. Kricman and others.

Although Lenin's shift towards the New Economic Policy (NEP) resulted in the reintroduction of market relations in the economy. it did not change the idea of substituting systematic planning for market mechanisms in socialism. Lenin justified the reintroduction of market relations on the strength of the existence of private producers. chiefly farmers. during the transition to socialism. Lenin did not indicate anywhere that after the farmers' 'voluntary forming of cooperatives' which he was aiming at. and after the emergence of socialism on the basis of social ownership in two forms – leading state ownership. and cooperative ownership – market relations should continue to exist. It was Stalin who enforced the farmers' collectivisation instead of keeping it voluntary and then proceeded to retain formal market relations although the means of production were no longer in private ownership. Trotskyists have to this very day charged Stalin with deviation from Marxist theory while regarding their idea of the socialist economy as a market-free and naturally planned economy in harmony not only with Marxist but also with Leninist theory.

Stalin. however. understood the retention of market relations only in terms of formal commodity – money relations. and eliminated market mechanisms. Prices should not be market prices. but fixed on an administrative basis. competition between enterprises should be abolished. and the workers' incomes should no longer depend on the market income. but oil the plans or the fulfilment of quotas. Production should no longer take its bearings from tile market. that is. from price and profit developments. but be directed by means of planning. With the exception of the formal calculation of production with the help of prices. Stalin retained the Marxist-Leninist idea of a comprehensive economic plan for the development of production and the distribution of goods.

Of course. such a planning endeavour calls for the setting up of a hierarchically organised system of command. in which mandatory tasks are issued by a planning centre and then passed down to the relevant enterprises through a host of institutions. Gradual disaggregation and concretisation of central aggregates will. in the last instance. be transformed into concrete micro-plans by the managements of individual works. More than anything else. such a planning system requires the enforcement of central political objectives. with the help of a disciplined subordination of all lower levels of authority to the central will. This finds its clearest expression with Trotsky. who wanted to organise the socialist economy like a military system of command. The material (monetary) incentives of the works collective. which underwent varying developments under Stalin. did not greatly change this command economy either. since all remuneration was subject to planning and the fulfilment of quotas.

During Stalin's rule. some characteristic features of the socialist economic system developed. whose theoretical reflections ossified into dogma. which in turn economists and other social scientists were not allowed to doubt. These fundamental dogmas consisted of the following theoretical postulates.

- The means of production must not be in private ownership. Rather. they must be in state ownership to a decisive extent. and in cooperation ownership only to a restricted extent. and under state leadership.
- The development of production must not be determined by market mechanisms. Rather. it must be fixed with the help of central plans. that is. with production and investment tasks. mandatory for each enterprise.
- Prices are only retained for the purposes of formal planning and calculation. They must. however. be fixed by a central state authority and must not be changed by enterprises in accordance with market conditions.
- There must no longer be any competition between enterprises. since this is a capitalist feature. For this reason. production must be organised in such a manner that every branch of industry is amalgamated into one single monopolistic giant with a standardised administration.
- The distribution and use of incomes accruing in the form of money is no longer within the competence of enterprises but is determined by state planning. This means that the development of incomes must not depend on market income. but must be fixed by plans.
- The board and management of any enterprise must not be elected by the works collectives. Rather. they must be appointed by state authorities. Only in this manner can the enforcement of a concerted. central will be ensured.

Such and further fundamental dogmas were meant to preclude the reappearance of capitalist ownership and the re-emergence of 'economic anarchy while simultaneously ensuring the fast. effective and proportionate development of socialist production determined by planning. This form of production was meant to safeguard the satisfaction of social demand. The communist parties began to label a system organised along such economic lines as 'real' socialist.

FUNDAMENTAL DEFECTS IN THE ECONOMIC PRACTICE OF 'REAL' SOCIALISM

The development of a socialist economy has been going on in the Soviet Union for about seventy years – a period sufficiently long to warrant an examination of how socialist theory relates to reality. Not one of the objectives ever aimed at by a socialist development process was reached. This was not chiefly a consequence of subjective mistakes made by party and state leadership with regard to economic policies. rather. it was the result of defects inherent in the system. which had already been embodied in Marxist-Leninist theory.

Such objectives as faster development of productive forces. a more proportionate and economical form of production. and satisfaction of individual and social requirements that are an improvement on the capitalist system. have not been achieved. I have published comparative calculations in my book. *Wirtschaftssysteme*(Economic Systems).

The vital proof brought forward to justify the necessity of the socialist system – the idea that in comparison with the socialist system. the capitalist system does not permit a faster development of productive forces could not he substantiated. Socialist product on is increasingly lagging behind capitalist production. particularly as regards qualitative development. the innovation of productive forces. and technological and scientific progress. As a consequence. the quantitative growth of production is also increasingly slowing down. or rather changing into fictitious (covertly inflationary) growth.

In comparison with capitalist production. socialist production has the following defects which cause it to lag behind:

- Production shows a lower degree of efficiency (production output-input ratio) than a free-market system. *i.e.* substantially more labour. materials. energy and investments are needed for a comparable production process.
- Production grows in a predominantly extensive manner (extension of the production factors). while its intensive growth (through technological progress and the qualitative development of the production factors) is absolutely inadequate.
- Production is not sufficiently geared to demand: on the one hand. it produces quantities of unrequired goods. while on the other. it does not satisfy concrete demand to any large extent.
- Production supplies few. high-quality and fashionable consumer goods. and the technological standards of capital goods are far behind those of western countries.

- Production is completely disinclined from innovative development. producing an insufficient number of new goods. The novelty of goods is frequently bogus. so that consumers will not enjoy a higher benefit from them.
- The proportion of consumer-goods in production as a whole is substantially smaller than in Western free-market economics. In other words. the proportion of capital-goods production is much too high.

If production continues along such lines. then the requirements of the population can only be inadequately satisfied. and the standard of living of the widest strata will increasingly lag behind that of the industrialised nations of the West. Quantitative and qualitative successes have been achieved in arms and space development. since those two industries are given preference in every respect. Even so. their efficiency is immensely low. and the growth of arms production is increasingly being advanced at the expense of consumption growth.

The official economic theory or. more accurately the ideological propaganda of the USSR. as well as of the other socialist countries. has ignored or concealed those economic defects for years. It only worked with the fast growth rates of production volumes in the initial years. overlooking the losses in efficiency which were increasing from the beginning. Many socialist reformers also make the mistake of asserting that the dirigist planning system had functioned well in the initial years of socialist development. *i.e.* in the years of extensive growth. In their view. it would only fall in a development phase in which intensive growth is required.

This does not correspond to reality. Only this much is true. that the planning system – with the help of extensive expansions of industrial production factors – achieved a relatively fast production growth in the initial Years. From the outset however. this system merely enabled a relatively slow qualitative improvement and innovation of commodities and therefore. with the exception of arms and space production. only inadequate technological progress. while capital productivity was strongly decreasing in the long term. As a consequence. uncommonly large and heavily increasing investment volumes were required for extensive production growth at the expense of consumption development.

Ever since its inception. the planning system has prevented a highly efficient investment development. not only because of slow technological progress. but also because it renders impossible a selection of the most profitable investment projects from among a great number of substitution options. which are very numerous in a free-market economy.

Central investment planning and the allocation of investment funds is effected by means of a primitive accounting of input and output. without the existence of as many substitution options as in a free-market economy and without an optimal profitability selection. Finally. the planning system has from the start prevented consumers from influencing the development of production through the market. and from assessing the performance of individual enterprises with the help of market selection. Only in conditions where buying involves a choice between differing products. with competition at work in all industries. are producers forced to make production more efficient and more flexible. Both in the free-market and in the planned economy systems. lack of balance between supply and demand is bound to occur with regard to certain commodities. In a free-market system. however. producers are compelled to overcome these imbalances as soon as possible if they are to achieve profits rather than sustaining losses.

In a planned economy system. the extent of imbalance is substantially greater and is overcome considerably more slowly – if at all. The constantly inadequate supply of many commodities in relation to the demand for them is accompanied by goods produced in excess. which is reflected in stocks that are three to four times the size of those in a capitalist system.

From the beginning. all these mammoth losses in efficiency have been incurred at the expense of consumption development. in parallel with an exorbitant and unnecessary increase in capital goods production. This was production for the sake of production rather than for an optimal development of consumption: the growth of production became an end in itself. It sounds like mockery when official propaganda characterises such production as a process meant to safeguard the maximal satisfaction of society's material and cultural requirements.

As long as this production development served to achieve an even faster increase in the immensely preferred arms production. it was retained despite all losses in efficiency. Once the Soviet arms race with the USA threatened to result in an enforced reduction of the miserable living standards of the Soviet population to an absolute low. however. those forces in the USSR (headed by Gorbachev. who had recognised the inefficiency and untenability of the Stalinist planning system) were enabled to act.

ERRORS IN THE THEORETICAL JUSTIFICATION OF SOCIALISM

Realist-socialist practice was founded on a false theoretical premise. It was assumed that socialist works-managements and collectives would always work 'in a manner equal to social interests. The new socialist man should subordinate both his partial and his individual interests to the interests of society as a whole. It therefore the central controlling bodies were not in a position to draw up concrete plans for the microstructure of production. for innovative production development. for an economic utilisation of production factors and so on. then their subordinate enterprises should themselves carry out concrete measures in order to guarantee optimal production development.

In reality however. socialism still has conditions in which the producers' immediate individual and partial interests have priority over the interest of society as a whole. As long as the old. rigid division of labour and the lack of consumer goods persist. both the individual workers' and the works collectives' immediate interest in a maximal increase in income. achieved with a minimal amount of work. will be of overriding concern. If the plans from above cannot be sufficiently concrete. if there is neither market interest nor competitive pressure. and if there is a constant excess of demand (seller's market). then enterprises will always exploit all avenues in order to push incomes as high as possible with as little work as possible. and this also at the cost of the consumers. or rather at the cost of a possibly improved satisfaction of demand.

Enterprises will neglect the qualitative and innovative development of production; they will manipulate production structures in such a way as to achieve the formal fulfilment of quotas. even at the consumers' expense; they will produce uneconomically. If real market interest. prevailed (real competitive pressure and a real buyer's market) then enterprises could not operate in this manner. In conditions where market mechanisms functioned. partial and individual interests would be subordinated to social interests with much greater consistency.

In quest of the starting point of all these defects of 'real' socialist theory and practice. it is necessary to go as far back as Marx's economic theory. It contained cases of bias. simplification and errors. which were then integrated into the theory of socialism. leading to concepts of a new economic system which have since proved to be unviable.

First of all. it must be said by way of summary that in his economic analysis. Marx basically disregarded the significance of the various economic interests and motivations in society as well as their effect on the development of economic activity. This has been reflected in the fact that three development factors have been ignored. giving rise to simplified ideas with respect to both the capitalist and the future socialist economic systems:

First. the importance of consumers' interests and their influence on producers' decisions through market mechanisms. Producers' and consumers' interests are not of the same nature and in certain conditions will undergo anarchic developments. The one-sided emphasis on capitalist producers' and profit interest. which finds expression in Marx's labour theory of value and production prices. has paid insufficient attention to the consumers' assessment of the use value of commodities.

Marx's persistence in the scientifically unprovable labour theory of value and production prices as the basis for his notion of the market price. as well as his disregard for the consumers' continually changing assessment of the use value of the huge number of commodities. was responsible for his underestimation of market-mechanisms. This is what led him to the conclusion that in a socialist economy the market would have to be eliminated and be replaced by a planned development in the distribution of production and goods in the economy as a whole. The resulting Marxist dogma of the incompatibility of socialism and market mechanisms has been a great burden for Marxists. as well as the greatest contributor towards immense economic losses.

The second Marxian simplification is his underestimation of entrepreneurial activity and its significance above all for the qualitative and flexible development of production. The one-sided emphasis on capitalist exploitation was at the root of this underestimation. and the Marxist movement completely overlooked the necessary knowledge. the initiative and the courage to take risks – criteria which in capitalism have found expression in the years of industrial expansion. in productive innovation. in technological progress. and so on. and which can never be replaced by an economically uncommitted bureaucracy. Economically interested managers of large-scale. independent enterprises working in conditions of functioning market mechanisms may be able to compensate for a lack of entrepreneurial activity in this field. but this will still not solve the problem of the flexible setting-up of new enterprises with a view to filling newly occurring market gaps in good time. The relevance of a capital market to the necessary flexible changes in production structures has also been ignored.

A third basic error in Marxist economic theory must be seen in the notion of decreasing growth impulses for capitalist production. With the concept of a constantly growing rate of surplus value (rate of exploitation) resulting in a proportionally decreasing consumption rate. and with the simultaneous tendency of a decreasing profit rate (yield). Marx created the idea that in capitalism the development of productive forces would he increasingly decelerated. Decreasing sales and reduced profits were meant to push capitalism to the limits of its development potential. In reality. capitalism has neither a constantly growing rate of surplus nor a constantly decreasing profit rate. The refutation of Marxian theory by the real development of productive forces in capitalism has not only undermined the fundamental Justification of socialist revolutions in capitalistically developed countries. but has unmasked so many political objectives set by socialist countries (such as Khrushchev's idea of overtaking the USA within about 20 years) as subjectivistic wishful thinking.

On summarizing all these defects and errors of socialist practice and theory I have come to the conclusion that socialism. in its basic principles according to Marxist-Leninist ideology has no future. And yet this conclusion need not mean that the only alternative to the present 'real' socialist development must be a return to the capitalist system. By the same token it does not mean that capitalism is faultless and not in need of reform.

Serious defects in the capitalist system persist to this day: long periods of mass unemployment. periodically recurring economic crises. unnecessarily great differences in income unrelated to efficiency a concentration of private means providing individuals with an influence of power devoid of democratic legitimisation. or the alienation of large parts of the population from capital and the economy and so on. Marxism-Leninism tried to remove them in the wrong way. This does not. however. mean that they cannot be removed at all. As a scientist I cannot reconcile myself with the idea that such system defects cannot be precluded.

On the basis of analysis of both socialist and capitalist theory and practice. I reached the idea of a 'Third Way'. which I have held to this day.

THE MODEL OF THE 'THIRD WAY'

Since my model of the Third Way has become general currency. I will restrict myself to a brief sketch of its principles. To begin with I will address myself to the question of whether this model should be labelled 'socialist'. This is not easy to answer. since it immediately raises the new question of what 'socialism' means. The socialist label must be vigorously rejected. however. if this term is associated with everything that developed under the influence of Marx. Engels. Lenin and Stalin. as characterised above by the principles of the socialist economic system – though so far I have not dealt with the Stalinist political system.

Since the term 'socialism' has been identified by large parts of the population in East and West with the 'real' socialism which emerged under Stalin and which has rightly been strongly proscribed. it would. after all. not be felicitous to call 'socialist' a new system which differs from both the 'real' socialist' and the capitalist systems. For this reason I described the proposed target model. which should be built on the basis of reforms along the lines of the Third Way as 'Humane Economic Democracy'.

It must he assumed. however. that reforms in socialist countries would. for political reasons. be depicted as a 'democratisation of the socialist system'. even if they moved in the direction of the fundamental principles of the Third Way. What happens to be politic at a given moment. need not always be scientifically correct. What is crucial. however. is not the political label used (such as 'Democratic Socialist System'). but the contents of the target model aimed for. which should overcome the defects of both the 'real' socialist and the capitalist systems. I will now provide a brief sketch of my idea of the basis principles of such a target model. concentrating on its realisation in the socialist countries. In doing so. I will of course have to exclude the difficult problems of the transition to the conditions aimed for. which in any case may show considerable differences from country to country.

The target model must display conditions in which market mechanisms can function as perfectly as possible. This primarily requires the existence of independent enterprises. whose concrete activities must not be interfered with by any differentiated state intervention. The state should restrict itself to issuing generally valid. basic legal conditions with regard to economic activities. or it should strive towards fixed economic and social targets with economico-political instruments. Differentiated subsidies should only be granted to individual enterprises and industries in generally recognised and justified exceptional cases.

Competition should function in an optimal a manner as possible. so that every company will feel the pressure exerted by buyers who are in a position to exercise a choice. in both the domestic and foreign markets. With this aim in view. the state should create measures for the reorganisation of enterprises during the transitional period; it should also implement an effective anti-monopolist policy in the immediate future as well as in the long term. I have formulated proposals for such anti-monopolist measures elsewhere.

Prices should develop as market prices which are freely fixed by sellers under pressure from buyers in conditions of functioning competition. State control should only serve the anti-monopolist policy that is. expose covert or overt monopolist price dictates. and bring about anti-monopolist measures. In order to provide such measures. as well as competition. with the necessary scope to become effective. existing seller's markets (great surplus demand with adequate purchasing power) would have to be transformed into buyer's markets during the transitional period.

The market should not only function as a commodity and labour market. but also as a capital market. This requires the existence of joint-stock companies. particularly in the field of large enterprises. At the same time. merchant banks with an orientation towards economic interest would have to take up operations. The necessary stock exchange system should also be made available.

A wide variety of forms of ownership should develop in the corporate sphere – there would have to be private. cooperative. mixed. joint-stock and state companies. However. in order to prevent the formation of large concentrations of private capital. combined with a simultaneous alienation from capital of wide sectors of society direct equity participation by employees in all market enterprises should be aspired to from the outset. Joint equity ownership. profit-sharing and co-determination by employees is what I describe as general participation. In one form or another. this general participation should exist in all enterprises. with the exception of small. private companies with a minimal amount of capital.

General participation is conceivable both in terms of collective equity ownership on the part of employees (cooperative enterprises. enterprises with neutralised capital) and in terms of individually expressed equity ownership on the part of employees (joint-stock companies). It would be of advantage if the large-scale enterprises. which were previously in state ownership. assumed the form of employee companies. that is. joint-stock companies of which employees are co-owners and on whose corporate policy they exercise a decisive influence. On the one hand. this would ensure the development of the requisite capital market. On the other. strong employee equity-holding interest). coupled with participation (share democratic rights to co-determination and the vote. would make it possible to create equal opportunities for the realisation of both capital and labour interests.

Private setting-up initiatives should be backed by the state (legal aid. tax relief. and so on). Once the profit rate has reached a certain level. however. profit-sharing should be implemented for employees. partly in the form of profit shares which remain available to the company as employee stock (neutralised or shave capital). partly in the form of profit shares to be paid out (shares in the equity participation fund or dividends in joint-stock companies respectively). This would also require the introduction of a tax system and of profit-sharing regulations which would promise private entrepreneurs profit-shares increasing in proportion with profit rates. so that they would he sufficiently motivated to enhance efficiency.

The Soviet decision that private enterprises are only allowed to employ next of kin and no strangers. since this would amount to capitalist exploitation of alien labour. is an expression of adherence to the Marxist theory of surplus value. which explains exploitation. I have already mentioned that I do not consider the Marxian labour theory of value and his theory of surplus value scientifically tenable. and that I count them among those dogmas which the communist movement takes particular care to keep alive. However. since it is not possible to evolve a discussion of this fundamental theory. I will restrict myself to pointing out one of Marx's own theoretical views. which would allow for more flexibility in the Soviet approach to the development of private production.

Marx also regarded private entrepreneurs' activities. their technical preparation of production. the management and organisation of production. the supervision of work. and so forth. as productive activities. which also created labour value. As a type of work requiring particularly high qualifications. it also creates a relatively high labour value within a given number of working hours. It is therefore possible to argue in accordance with Marx that. in the case of a relatively small number of employees. the private entrepreneur's profit is largely an expression of the labour value created by himself. and does not therefore represent exploitation.

If private production. even with the help of third-party employees. is permitted. and if private entrepreneurs may appropriate profit subject to the introduction of employee profit-sharing above a certain profit rate. then this need not be in contradiction with marxist theory at all. It means that above a certain profit rate. part of the profit is transformed into the employees' profit share. which is again divided into employee equity shares (profit shares turned into net investments. or capital increase). and into profit shares to be paid out. In this way the private entrepreneur's appropriation of the remaining profits would not represent exploitation. not even according to pure Marxian theory.

The USSR's dogmatists. who object to any employment of third-party labour by private enterprises. could not therefore cite the Marxist theory of exploitation to justify their position. They also ignore the importance of private enterprise. of expertise. of organisational ability of management skills. or market initiative. and so on. which is required by such activities. and with which the Soviet commodity supply could be improved at quite a fast rate.

The evolution of private enterprise. combined with a safeguard of employees' profit-sharing and equity participation. should be accompanied by the democratisation of the enterprises' management systems. This means that employees would be involved in the fundamental corporate decision-making process (corporate policies). with elected councils in private. non-joint-stock companies. and with elected representatives on the board of directors or the supervisory board in joint-stock companies; the private enterprise and the management. respectively would remain in operative charge.

Employees should also be involved in the decision-making process both in management bodies and in autonomous working groups. In these autonomous working groups. such systems as job rotation and job enrichment would also be practised. Working groups would furthermore be important in terms of their initiative in looking for work for members of staff who have lost their jobs as a result of technological progress and structural change.

The development of incomes should be economically determined by means of planned increases in average wages. Profit shares to be paid out and dividends would also be linked to actual profits with the help of fixed formulae. Incomes planning would be a substantial component of macrocconomic distribution plans and of income policy.

The main objective of such macrodistribution plans would be the implementation of economico-political measures in line with the market. with a view to achieving socio-economic development aims. On the occasion of political elections. the population should be given the chance to choose from among a number of alternative

plans which differ from each other in their combinations of the main target factors (growth of private and public consumption. protection and improvement of the environment. development of employment. shorter working hours. and so on). and which would be realised with the help of corresponding incomes. fiscal. price. credit. monetary and currency policies.

The regulation of the functional distribution of income. *i.e.* the regulation of income growth. of the profit-sharing coefficient. of the coefficient for the withdrawal of profits for entrepreneurial consumption. as well as a division of credit into 'investment and consumer loans. are expected to be capable of maintaining the equilibrium of investive and consumptive developments in the economy. The determination of resource allocation would be left exclusively to companies and to market mechanisms.

The linking of market and planning should preserve the advantages of the free-market economy in their entirety particularly as regards a highly efficient. demand-oriented and innovative production. At the same time. macrodistribution planning should help overcome disturbances in the macrodisequilibrium. the emergence of large surplus capacities. mass unemployment. the threatening destruction of the environment. as well as people's insecurity about the future.

By the way of summary it may be said that the 'Humane Economic Democracy represents an ideal type of a system model with the following characteristics:

- It contains conditions for market mechanisms that can function as optimally as possible. for a free foreign trade. as well as for a convertible currency.
- It enables the achievement of socio-economic and ecological objectives with the help of macrodistribution planning and a coordinated economic policy.
- It enables the prevention of macrocconomic disequilibria and mass unemployment by means of macrodistribution planning. its full-employment policy and its educational policy.
- It is capable of overcoming the alienation from capital of personnel employed by market enterprises. by means of equity participation. codetermination and autonomy.
- It fully admits private enterprise. while restricting the formation of excessive private capital and power concentration.
- It allows for democratic decisions on socio-economic planning objectives from a variety of alternative plans.
- It preserves non-market activities and state control to areas where (a) social security. equality of opportunity and ecological aims are more important than efficiency. (b) there are insurmountable monopoly conditions. and (c) state control ensures that the efficiency of an enterprise is higher than in competitive split-up (*e.g.* water supply).

These are the main concepts of a model of Humane Economic Democracy which could emerge from socialist reform efforts. Would such a development contribute towards a convergence of the systems?

THE REVIVAL OF THE THEORY OF CONVERGENCE

At the beginning of the 1960s. Jan Tinbergen advocated his theory of convergence which attracted worldwide attention. Tinbergen's conviction that the two existing systems. the capitalist and the socialist. are developing towards each other in a process of mutual convergence. is not fundamentally wrong; at the time. however. Tinbergen based it on a number of simplifications which prevented his forecast from becoming reality in the course of time. I would like to point out these simplifications. so that once they are overcome it will be possible to achieve a further development of the theory of convergence which would be closer to reality.

There were. above all. three simplifications:

- An inadequate differentiation between the two courses of development preventing the emergence of a homogeneous basic system.
- An inadequately critical attitude towards public or state ownership. which was regarded as a convergence objective to be aimed for.
- The underestimation of the role of the politics and interests of powerful social groups in the prevention of system changes aiming at convergence.

AN INADEQUATE DIFFERENTIATION BETWEEN THE TWO COURSES OF DEVELOPMENT

In Tinbergen's theory it looked as if in both systems. only such processes would increase as are characteristic of the other system. Conversely. certain system-specific processes would tend to decrease. In this way. both sides would develop system characteristics that should lead to the formation of a homogeneous system. This idea conceives of the pressure on system changes in both systems as being more or less the same. In reality. however. there is a great difference between the demand for a change in the system on both sides. The demand for a system change will always be higher in the system which lags behind the other in its quantitative and qualitative development.

It is the socialist economic system which is quite generally lagging behind the development of the capitalist system in major development results. Particularly *in terms o f production efficiency the socialist planned economy has been inferior to the capitalist free market economy from the outset*. Also. socialist production efficiency is dropping back further year after year. which makes it increasingly difficult for socialist planned economies to guarantee that social objectives can be achieved. These shortcomings result in the necessity of a fundamental reform of the socialist planned economy system. with whose aid the causes of this development lag are to be eliminated.

A *lack of market mechanisms and the non-existence* of *private enterprise* are crucial causes of the low level of production efficiency in socialism. As mentioned before. centralised. dirigist planning is no substitute for market mechanisms. and bureaucratic administration has never been able to replace private initiative to its full extent either when it comes to the setting-up of new enterprises. technological progress. the flexible filling of market gaps. and so forth. Such enormous and increasing disadvantages result in the necessity of reintroducing market mechanisms and private enterprise in socialist countries to some extent or other. This is one side of the convergence development. which was indicated by Jan Tinbergen but not expressed with sufficient clarity to say that a *return to market mechanisms* by overcoming the state bureaucratic form of property is necessary in socialist countries.

Now for the other side of the coin – the capitalist system. The developments in the capitalist system are also pointing in the direction of a Third Way but not in the direction of the old socialist system.

TINBERGEN'S INADEQUATELY CRITICAL ATTITUDE TOWARDS PUBLIC OR STATE OWNERSHIP

Tinbergen saw the other side of the convergence process in the expansion of both the state ownership sector and state investment activity in capitalist countries. This attitude towards the nationalisation of the economy as a remedy for the defects of private-capitalist economic development. harks back to one of the fundamental postulates of the Marxist. socialist concept of the economy.

In the capitalist economy -various significant state ownership developments were also in evidence. It must be pointed out however. that such state developments had partially taken place even before the emergence of socialist ideologies: to be exact. whenever and wherever a social demand for commodities and services arose which. for one reason or another. failed to attract private interest or for which there was not enough private capital (railways. postal services. electric power stations. and so on). Wherever it was however. in socialist or in capitalist countries. such state administration gave rise to bureaucratisation and thus to immense losses in efficiency.

The bureaucratic form of economic administration is. above all. an administration by people who have no immediate. income-related interest in the efficiency of the economic development they administer and direct. People whose personal incomes will neither increase nor decrease if the economy they direct makes gains or sustains losses. will not face the consequences of their economic decisions with adequate interest. Conversely. if the personal income gains or losses experienced by people with a certain economic responsibility is linked to the gains and losses of the system they are part of economic decisions will be accompanied by a high degree of efficiency.

The difference in directive efficiency between bureaucratic administration on the one hand. and economically interested management on the other. are so serious that it cannot really come as a surprise that not only capitalism. but also socialism is turning its back on state ownership and the bureaucratic management associated with it. moving instead towards free-market independence for enterprises. coupled with a style of management characterised by economic interest and responsibility. Tinbergen's expectation of convergence. according to which the systems would move closer together as a result of an expansion of the state sector and of state planning and dirigism in the capitalist system. could therefore not become reality on account of changes in perception to be observed in both camps. However. this does not mean (especially in the sphere of ownership) that capitalism might not undergo certain changes that would lead to a different kind of convergence of the two systems.

A case in point is the process of increasing equity. profit and decision-making participation (general participation) of personnel employed by free-market enterprises. which in the last decade has experienced an extraordinary growth in almost all industrialised nations. An American analysis. for instance. shows that in the USA. the number of corporations with employee equity participation rose from 1600 to 8100 between 1974 and 1985. while during the same period the number of personnel holding shares in their corporations increased from 250 000 to 8 million?' A similar. and accelerating. development can be observed in almost all other industrialised nations.

In the USA. special economico-political measures have made a vital contribution to this development. It was. above all. potent forms of tax relief for the benefit of so-called Employee Stock Ownership Plans (ESOPs) which boosted employee capital participation. as a result of which the equity of the companies concerned experienced a comparatively faster growth rate.

This development reflects the *discovery of the significance of economic interest.* this time extended to all employees – the discovery that personnel with a share in the capital. in profits and in the decision-making process will be substantially more interested 'in the development of their corporations' efficiency. Also. profits and incomes of firms with such a form of participation rise a great deal faster than those of companies without participation. This. too. was shown by the American analysis.

Doubtless this development was also stimulated by theoretical works which pointed out the economic significance of general equity Participation as early as the late 1960s. The trail-blazer in this respect was a book by L. O. Kelso and P. Hetter. who demonstrate that it is realistically possible for low-income families with no savings to buy shares on borrowed money with the help of tax-privileged share sales through special trust companies and insurance institutes. The possibility computed and substantiated by the authors. of a second-income plan which could. in the foreseeable future. turn all Americans into owners of a considerable fortune in shares. makes a fascinating impression.

If employees of large enterprises own a sufficient share in their companies to he able to he represented in the boardrooms. and thus to take a closer interest in both the necessary market efficiency of the company and their own social interest. then this constitutes a new way of surmounting the old opposition between labour and capital in society. The generalisation of the ownership of the means of production by nationalising them subsequent to be expropriation of capital owners. proved to be a course which led to the loss of market efficiency while the standard of living increasingly lagged behind that of the free-market economics. There is. however. a modern solution to this old socio-economic problem: all members of society can be transformed into co-owners of the means of production used in line with the market. which means that market mechanisms will be retained. while everyone's standard of living will reach a social optimum.

Thus *popular capitalism* turns out to be a feasible utopia!

New technological developments and an accelerated transition to a modern information society will entail a very fast increase in general employee participation. In the new computerised service companies. a novel cooperative development. that is. my forecasted development of employee companies. will be gaining ground at an ever faster rate.

The high qualifications and high educational level of the personnel of such service companies will gradually assume greater importance than the actual capital required for entrepreneurial activity. Highly qualified experts will be less and less satisfied with the position of a simple wage earner. They will themselves set up such service companies in the form of cooperatives; a strong trend emerging in America's Silicon Valley. Employee interest and initiative in industrial companies. whose technological progress is growing increasingly faster. will also be of greater significance: this too will lead to a relatively rapid expansion of participation.

Considering that in the socialist countries a transformation of large-scale enterprises into independent free-market companies is proceeding in parallel with a gradual participation on the part of the employees of these enterprises. a completely new development in the field of convergence is represented.

In my view. a transition towards fundamental employee participation in the socialist countries could proceed in the following manner. Employees would receive an annual proportion of the company's profits in the form of inalienable personal shares. These profit shares would be used for the company's net investments. At the same time the company would issue. and sell to the third parties. normal shares with a view to faster capital expansion. Employees would receive the same dividends on their personal shares as external shareholders.

The peculiarities of such personal shares need not be looked at in any more detail: suffice it to say in general terms. that their allocation. maturity. personal nature. connection with dividend payments. voting rights and so on. should be provided with a legal frame work that would result in a fundamental change of the employees' position in the company and in their relationship to entrepreneurial activity – they would in fact be the basis of employee companies where labour and capital are equal. This method should above all boost employees' interest in the development of their company's efficiency – not. however. in the short-term maximization of their profits. but in an optimal long-term development of profits and equity. In this sense. dividend payments to previous employees during their retirement would also have a beneficial effect. At the same time. equity participation and democratic voting provisions should lead to a more effective protection of employees' social interests. that is. in terms of compensation for the pursuit of efficiency. Decisions with regard to requisite technological progress. changes in production structure. increases in capital intensity and so forth. can be combined with measures preventing unemployment and offsetting inescapable redundancies with the taking on of new labour in good time. All efforts at humanising work. such as the creation of autonomous working groups. job enlargement and job rotation. would come into their own to a greater extent through the creation of employee ownership structures.

In this way. the development of employee companies and the democratization of the economy could result in conditions in which the efficiency principle would not only be preserved. but reinforced – yet simultaneously associated with the humanisation of the working world. If this development should gain ground in the socialist countries. with the simultaneous re-emergence of small- and medium-sized private enterprises. then this would constitute a development in the direction of a democratic and humane economy. In the case of a concurrent. but in all probability much slower. development of general participation in the capitalist economics. this would represent a convergence of the two systems without the traditional state bureaucracy hostility to efficiency.

Such a development of participation in the sphere of enterprises would. for instance. both enable and support the macrodistribution planning that I have been advocating. Increases in income would no longer depend on short-sighted power struggles between trade unions and employer associations. but could specifically be linked to the development of productivity. An equal growth rate of the economic quotas of consumption and investment could be better ensured in this manner. In other words. the coordination of fiscal. credit. monetary and income policies could be improved. I am convinced that such a long-term planned coordination of economic policy will sooner or later have a breakthrough in the capitalist economies.

To sum up. this is a matter of the development of certain system features. different in nature in either system. which would represent reforms while at the same time giving rise to a convergence of the two systems. The reforms of the socialist system. however. are more fundamental and more extensive than those of the capitalist system. Moreover. they are being enforced by the increasingly obvious efficiency advantages of a free-market economy.

Capitalist systems are not under pressure to institute reforms which are demanded on the strength of advantages displayed by another system. Reforms in capitalist economics mainly derive from an awareness of efficiency gains to be achieved by means of general participation in the corporate sphere. Even with a long-term planned coordination of economic policy such reforms will only take place if they are seen to be advantageous in terms of efficiency. It may be argued. however. that the increasing pressure for a humane solution to unemployment and environmental problems will accelerate the development of both participation and macroplanning.

The introduction of general participation in capitalist systems will take a relatively long time. however. so the social difference between capital and labour interests will remain active for some time to come. Nonetheless one may speak of a change in the direction of an economic democracy in this system also. which is being accelerated by new technological developments.

THE UNDERESTIMATION OF THE NEXUS BETWEEN POLITICAL AND ECONOMIC DEVELOPMENT

Regrettably. the economy of all nations is linked with politics. and economic development is crucially dependent on whether conservative or progressive forces are at the helm. Precisely this nexus is what Jan Tinbergen underestimated most of all.

Now. it is – among other things – a function of economics to reveal certain connections in the economics which economically untrained. non-academic people. that is. the vast majority of the population. will not be able to recognise. All too often. however. economic discoveries of the causes of negative processes – of processes opposed to the interest of the great majority of the population – lead to reform demands opposed to the interest of frequently small but politically powerful social groups. As long as such groups retain political power. and as long as economists have no chance of convincing the vast majority of the population of the usefulness of certain reform processes. reforms will face enormous obstacles. even if they are supposed to serve the greater part of society.

Even in the conditions of a political democracy it is not always easy to acquaint the majority of the population with complex economic connections and certain reform requirements. In political dictatorships. where the groups in power enjoy large economic privileges and are therefore interested in maintaining the existing system unchanged. this ruling group is capable of almost totally preventing the population from being enlightened with regard to the long-term benefit of a reform.

This is one of the decisive reasons why in the socialist countries. the beginnings of a convergence correctly identified by Tinbergen – a trend towards market-oriented changes in production – could not gain ground with the consistency that would have been the result of real economic improvement. If market mechanisms are to bring about increases in efficiency then this calls for changes to the system which are also far-reaching and complex enough to undermine the foundations of the ruling social group's power and privilege.

And it is precisely these groups who have so far always managed to stifle such complex reforms. If the introduction of market mechanisms is merely partial – if say a works collective is granted a profit interest and an extension of its independence in production decisions. while prices remain centrally fixed. there is no competition in the market. production is organised monopolistically the seller's market is preserved. and governments tirelessly subsidised loss-making enterprises and practice a protectionist economic policy – then market mechanisms are more likely to produce losses than gains for society.

In all the countries where certain reforms have been implemented – in Yugoslavia. China. now in the USSR. in Czechoslovakia and so on – but where the changes were either not thought out in all their essential interconnections. or politically suppressed in their requisite complexity they have without fail increased losses. Reforms have become unpopular with the population and fallen into disrepute. All such partial reforms have been for the benefit of the conservative rather than tile progressive political forces. And ultimately it has always been the old dogmatic and bureaucratic forces which have contrived to nip reforms of socialism in the bud.

Tinbergen did not at the time discover this nexus between politics and the economy nor did he reveal the detrimental effect of merely half-hearted. inconsistent reforms in the direction of market mechanisms.

PROSPECTS

It must finally be emphasised that I find the emergence of a new economic system in the socialist countries realistic only if it is accompanied by the creation of pluralist. democratic conditions.

The transition to an economic system in which market mechanisms may return to full working order. and where both private and cooperative corporate initiative may have full scope for developing. but where the concentration of private capital power and the alienation of the workforce from capital should be prevented. is an immensely difficult process which may be painful for large parts of the population. Many inescapable developments which will at first involve distress to the public (price increases. higher standards of performance. structural change entailing the closure of many enterprises. and so forth are *de facto* consequences of previous. unreasonable economic activity; they must. however. be endured if market mechanisms should become effective again. if economic efficiency should increase. and if the standard of living should experience a rapid growth later oil. These difficulties encountered during the transition period will be illustrated in more concrete terms in the Appendix. where a reform problem serves as an example.

Such difficult reforms can only be implemented by a political leadership which is capable of winning the strong and lasting confidence of the population. Without a real democratisation of the political system. and without a completely free spread of information throughout society this will be impossible. People can only be sure that they are no longer at the mercy of bureaucratic powers. and are the real sovereign in control of the political representatives. if the causes of the monumental losses of the past are revealed. if the media may give unrestricted voice to discussion and criticism. if all relevant positions in society are filled with cadres that have been democratically selected and elected. if people may freely form groups and organisations. and if various proposals and programmes for solutions to social problems and future developments are drawn up and then compared.

The communist leaderships which reject such democratisation have not been able to understand that without the people's initiative. interest and sense of freedom. no highly efficient economic activity may be expected.

The Chinese communist leadership has not grasped that a pure command system of subordination and obedience. based on fear and discipline enforced through punishment and drill. may provide the foundation for a military organisation. but will not give rise to inventive. enterprising and economic activities that will also involve the courage to take risks. Even in China. the time has passed when it was sufficient to mobilise masses of people in large columns to do the same unchanging and primitive work in the country in factories. in road construction. etc.. and to control them with the help of an army of supervisors.

In this way labour and capital productivity and consequently. the masses' standard of living. will never be increased. It is the creativity of intellectuals. the spontaneity of the spirit of enterprise. and the innovatory initiative of million that are needed today. But all this cannot prosper in an atmosphere of fear. spying and denunciation.

At the time of writing. the Gorbachev leadership has so far rejected the necessity of a pluralist democracy for the Soviet Union. Even so it cannot be overlooked that with the implementation of glasnost. of the new election system and other measures. Gorbachev has made some important steps in the direction of democratisation. It is to be hoped that these have not been the last words of wisdom. Without a multi-party system. terrible relapses still remain possible. An excessive number of dogmatists in the monopolist parts. machine are sabotaging perestroika. provoking conflicts. and trying to undermine Gorbachev's position. Only with the support of newly organised undogmatic forces from the people will he be able to implement his policies.

The anti-reformist communist leadership of some other socialist countries cannot objectively refute the complete failure of the Stalinist planning system. To an even lesser extent are they able to legitimise their claim to exclusive. monopolist political leadership. even if they invoke the so-called 'scientific character of their theory. In their fear of democratisation. they are left with the attempt to maintain the old system with violence and repression. This is a short-sighted policy and doomed to failure. The later it fails. however. the greater the damage. and the greater the scale of human suffering in the countries concerned.

TYPES OF SOCIALISM

Democratic Socialism advocates Socialism as an economic principle (the means of production should be in the hands of ordinary working people). and democracy as a governing principle (political power should be in the hands of the people democratically through a co-operative commonwealth or republic). It attempts to bring about Socialism through peaceful democratic means as opposed to violent insurrection. and represents the reformist tradition of Socialism. It is similar. but not necessarily identical (although the two terms are sometimes used interchangeably). to Social Democracy. This refers to an ideology that is more centrist and supports a broadly Capitalist system. with some social reforms (such as the welfare state). intended to make it more equitable and humane. Democratic Socialism. by contrast. implies an ideology that is more left-wing and supportive of a fully socialist system. established either bygradually reforming Capitalism from within. or by some form of revolutionary transformation.

Revolutionary Socialism advocates the need for fundamental social change through revolution or insurrection(rather than gradual refom) as a strategy to achieve a socialist society. The Third International. which was founded following the Russian Revolution of 1917. defined itself in terms of Revolutionary Socialism but also became widely identified with Communism. Trotskyism is the theory of Revolutionary Socialism as advocated by Leon Trotsky (1879 - 1940). declaring the need for an international proletarian revolution (rather than Stalin's "socialism in one country") and unwavering support for a true dictatorship of the proletariat based on democratic principles. Luxemburgism is another Revolutionary Socialist tradition. based on the writings of Rosa Luxemburg (1970 - 1919). It is similar to Trotskyism in itsopposition to the Totalitarianism of Stalin. while simultaneously avoiding the reformist politics of modern Social Democracy.

Utopian Socialism is a term used to define the first currents of modern socialist thought in the first quarter of the 19th Century. In general. it was used by later socialist thinkers to describe early socialist. or quasi-socialist. intellectuals who created hypothetical visions of perfect egalitarian and communalist societies without actually concerning themselves with the manner in which these societies could be created or sustained. They rejected all political (and especially all revolutionary) action. and wished to attain their ends by peaceful means and small experiments. which more practical socialists like Karl Marx saw as necessarily doomed to failure. But the early theoretical work of people like Robert Owen (1771-1858). Charles Fourier (1772-1837) and Étienne

Cabet (1788–1856) gave much of the impetus to later socialist movements. Libertarian Socialism aims to create a society without political. economic or social hierarchies. in which every person would have free. equal access to tools of information and production. This would be achieved through the abolition of authoritarian institutions and private property. so that direct control of the means of production and resources will be gained by the working class and society as a whole. Most Libertarian Socialists advocate abolishing the statealtogether. in much the same way as Utopian Socialists and many varieties of Anarchism (including Social Anarchism. Anarcho-Communism. Anarcho-Collectivism and Anarcho-Syndicalism).

Market Socialism is a term used to define an economic system in which there is a market economy directed and guided by socialist planners. and where prices would be set through trial and error (making adjustments as shortages and surpluses occur) rather than relying on a free price mechanism. By contrast. a Socialist Market Economy. such as that practiced in the People's Republic of China. in one where major industries are owned by state entities. but compete with each other within a pricing system set by the market and the state does not routinely intervene in the setting of prices.

Eco-Socialism (or Green Socialism or Socialist Ecology) is an ideology merging aspects of Marxism. Socialism.Green politics. ecology and the anti-globalization movement. They advocate the non-violent dismantling ofCapitalism and the State. focusing on collective ownership of the means of production. in order to mitigate the social exclusion. poverty and environmental degradation brought about (as they see it) by the capitalist system. globalizationand imperialism.

Christian Socialism generally refers to those on the Christian left whose politics are both Christian and socialist. and who see these two things as being interconnected. Christian socialists draw parallels between what some have characterized as the egalitarian and anti-establishment message of Jesus. and the messages of modern Socialism.

MARX'S BASIC THEORY

Karl Marx and Friederich Engels wrote the Communist Manifesto 150 years ago. In this article we look at the basic theoretical position that Marx developed.

Any analysis of society and its problems must. according to Marx. start in an examination of its processes of production. All human societies have to be concerned. before anything else. with the production and distribution of the means of life. By using tools and instruments to effect changes in nature. humans are able to satisfy their material and other needs through productive labour. It is this activity which Marx saw as being at the base of all societies.

Before humans can do almost anything at all they must satisfy certain basic needs. they must feed. clothe and house themselves. Production is "the first premise of all human existence... men must be in a position to live in order to be able to 'make history'" (*The German Ideology*).This approach. called by Marx and Engels the Materialist Conception of History or historical materialism. was for Marx. as he put it in his *A Contribution to the Critique of Political Economy*. the "guiding thread" in his political studies.

Because humans produce their own means of life the means available to them to do so determines their level of existence. These are what Marx called the "productive forces" of society. The productive forces consist of means of production. and labour power. Means of production include tools. machinery. premises and infrastructure ("the means of labour"-what humans work with) and raw material ("the objects of labour"-what humans work on). Labour power (which enables them to work with means of production) includes strength. skill. knowledge and inventiveness.

It is the level of development of productive forces. and the way in which society organises their operation. which marks out the different stages of human development. It is "the multitude of productive forces accessible to men" which. Marx says. "determines the nature of society" (*The German Ideology*).

Marx took for granted that human beings are inventive and are continually improving the productive forces. and will not voluntarily give up advantages gained in the field of productive activity. This is the evidence of history. Productive advance is independent of the social form production takes. It is improvements in technology. improvements in the ability of human beings to win a living from nature. which cumulatively result in major changes in society. As an analogy we may take the invention of gunpowder making the reorganisation of armies necessary in the sixteenth and seventeenth centuries.

Marx had discovered that throughout history changes in the productive forces of society had made it necessary to radically change the organisation of human society. As a result of changes in the productive forces the economic structure of society (the "relations of production") had to change to accommodate the new situation. Because they were standing in the way of further development the old production relations had to make way for new ones.

PRODUCTION RELATIONS

Production relations are of two kinds. Firstly there are those pertaining to *ownership* by persons. either individually or collectively. of productive forces. These regulate and control access to. and use of. the means of production. Secondly. relationships that structure the labour process but which are not that process. These depend on which type of ownership relations dominate a given society. In turn they regulate and control what is produced and when. in what quantities. and for what purpose. The economic structure of feudal society. for example. had to be changed because it had developed within it means of production that were being hampered from further development by the way that that society produced and exchanged wealth. The feudal relations of property "became no longer compatible with the already developed productive forces; they became so many fetters. They had to be burst asunder; they were burst asunder" (*Communist Manifesto*). It was at this point that feudalism gave way to capitalism.

Marx believed capitalism had reached a similar stage in its expansion of the productive forces. They could not be further developed without plunging world society into periodic crises of overproduction. "The conditions of bourgeois society are too narrow to comprise the wealth created by them" (*Communist Manifesto*). The production relations of capitalism had to be replaced by new production relations. namely common ownership of the productive forces-communism (or socialism). Private ownership (that is property in the means of production) which still regulates and controls access to. and use of. the means of production has become "a fetter". They are operated in the interest of profit-making only. and not simply to satisfy human needs. In terms of technological knowledge the means to produce abundance now exists. Capitalism has solved the problem of production. but it cannot solve the problem of distribution. More and more can be produced with less and less labour. There is a "monstrous disproportion between the labour time applied. and its product". As has happened in the past social relations must change to accommodate expanding productive capability.

This was the conclusion reached by Marx and outlined in a passage in the Preface to his *A Contribution to the Critique of Political Economy* in 1859. It explained his views on the development of human society:

In the social production of their life. men enter into definite relations that are indispensable and independent of their will. relations of production which correspond to a definite stage of development of their material productive forces. The sum total of these relations of production constitutes the economic structure of society. the real foundation. on which rise legal and political superstructures and to which correspond definite forms of social consciousness. The mode of production of material life conditions the social. political and intellectual life process in general.

It appears from this passage that historical materialism is deterministic in at least the following senses:

1. Human beings cannot develop apart from society. and as material production is social they enter into social relations that are "given" by society.
2. That the society in which people live is the outcome of historical development and is by implication changeable.
3. The economic structure of society depends on the stage to which the productive forces have developed. and by implication cannot be changed by individual acts of will that ignore or try to circumvent these stages.

4. That the ideas of society are "conditioned" by the mode of production.
5. That changes in the economic structure that is the base (the "real foundation") of society give rise to changes in the "superstructure" and to changed ideas about how society should be structured.

FROM CAPITALISM TO SOCIALISM

Marx's analysis revealed that developments in the productive forces of society are working in favour of change. Marx showed that capitalism had outlived its social usefulness. It had fulfilled its historic role-that of developing the productive forces to such a point that it was both feasible and desirable to end class society and exploitation. It had compelled "all nations. on pain of extinction. to adopt the bourgeois mode of production... to become bourgeois themselves. In one word. it creates a world after its own image" (*Communist Manifesto*). Capitalism itself was producing the conditions for its own destruction by implementing changes that constantly increase productive capacities on a world scale. But it is unable to cope rationally with the productive resources of the planet and is constantly lurching from crisis to crisis. In other words the "material productive forces of society [are] in conflict with the existing relations of production" (Preface to *A Contribution to a Critique of Political Economy*).

Marx's analysis shows that the socialist revolution must be world-wide and cannot be achieved in one country alone. Because capitalism has become a world-wide system the society to replace it must also be world-wide. Class emancipation must mean the "freeing of the whole of society from exploitation. oppression and class struggle..." (Engels's Preface to 1883 German edition of *Communist Manifesto*). Capitalism has made abundance a possibility. and made workable the "Communistic abolition of buying and selling... the moment when labour can no longer be converted into capital. money or rent. into a social power capable of being monopolised" (*Communist Manifesto*). As we in the Socialist Party predicted at the time of the Bolshevik insurrection it was not possible to have a socialist revolution in those countries in which capitalism had not yet fully developed and then to wait for the rest of the world to join in. The Bolsheviks had no possibility of introducing socialism. There is no "short cut" that can be implemented by a minority "vanguard" on behalf of the working class.

The change from capitalism to socialism requires the deliberate actions of men and women-it is not an automatic or mechanistic process. The task must be carried out democratically by those whose interests are most involved and who have the most to gain: that is. the working class. Changes to the economic structure of society have to be brought about through action on the political field. The owners of the means of production must be dispossessed by those who must first "... win the battle of democracy" (*Communist Manifesto*). Before it is possible to have socialism a majority of the working class must understand what needs to be done. To be successful the socialist movement must be "the self-conscious. independent movement of the immense majority. in the interests of the immense majority" (*Communist Manifesto*). In addition to the struggle over wages and conditions at work. the working class has to contest with the owners of the means of production on the *political* field in order to change the economic structure. It must "thoroughly comprehend the historical conditions and thus the very nature of this act... and the meaning of the momentous act it is called upon to accomplish" (Engels. *Socialism: Utopian and Scientific*).

Marx's "guiding thread" had led him through his studies to the conclusion that capitalism had brought into being a class that would be able to free itself from exploitation without having to rely on leaders to do it for them. "We cannot therefore co-operate". said Marx. in a criticism of Leninism before its time "with people who openly state that the workers are too uneducated to emancipate themselves and must first be freed from above" (*Letters to Bebel. Liebknecht and others*. September 1879).

CLASS STRUCTURE AND POLITICAL AGENCY: THE IMPERATIVE OF A COALITION STRATEGY

Marx did not believe that workers' revolution would occur because of socialism's moral desirability or the wisdom of socialists. Rather. he posited that the increasingly interdependent nature of capitalist production would come into conflict with the private ownership and control of economic resources. For Marx. only the working class had a common interest in revolution and the structural power within the mode of production to carry it out. But it would take political organization for the working class to fulfill its potential as the social agent of revolution.

It turned out that Marx was overly optimistic about the development of class-consciousness and revolutionary activity on the part of the working class. Though Marx recognised that the working class was divided by functional tasks. ethnicity. and race. he believed that trade union struggle and political activity would engender a universal identity on the part of the working class committed to socialism. But the paradox of mature capitalism is its coexistence with universal suffrage. In no country has there yet been mobilized a conscious majority for socialism. This is not to deny the significant popular support for social democratic and labour parties that favour a mixed economy and greater socioeconomic equality. But even in Sweden there has yet to develop a conscious electoral majority for a cooperatively-run economy.

Why is it that in the 20th century there never emerged a conscious majority for socialism under liberal democracy? It is partially due to socialism's identification with authoritarian Communism. It may also be because prosperity after World War II enabled capitalist welfare states to satisfy the material needs of most of their populations. What's more. the "capital strike" by business. which has confronted ambitious Socialist governments such as the Allende regime in Chile and the Mitterrand regime in France. makes clear the risks governments take when they try to limit the rights of capital.

Marxists have often underestimated the functional differentiation among working people and the growth of a "middle strata" made up of those who are neither professionals nor blue-collar manual laborers. Today the number of working people who exercise some control over their labour and over others but who are not top-level managers is large (*e.g.*. legal. financial. and medical professions). Socialists must also address the changing nature of capitalist production. which has led to a proliferation of low-skilled workers in the clerical and service sectors. These workers have difficulty organizing into unions because of the decentralized nature of their workplaces. The trade union movement is only beginning to adjust to an increasingly female and minority workforce. with different needs than male blue-collar workers. Organizing this "new working class" is critical to the future of socialism.

One way of appealing both to the "middle strata" and the working class is to stress democratic control over consumption and social provision. in addition to Marxism's traditional focus on democratic control over production. In the United States today. large sectors of the middle class cannot afford decent Health care. housing. education. and childcare. The challenge for the left is to unite these sectors with the working class and poor in favour of universal. progressively financed. public provision. Providing these goods for the middle class through tax credits and private insurance will only insure the further impoverishment of social services for the bottom third of society.

]Thus. building a majority coalition between the middle strata and lower-income people becomes not only a moral imperative. but also a political necessity. The large number of workers in the helping professions and the public sector provides the structural basis for such a coalition. particularly if these sectors are increasingly unionized. But middle class opposition to an expanded public sector will decrease only if progressive taxation is restored and democracy and efficiency increasingly characterises social welfare provision.

Some Marxists have also overestimated the centrality of work to identity. Community. ethnic. and regional identities have often competed with class loyalties. Racial divisions and the initial organization of immigrants into ethnic-based political machines rather than class-conscious parties have weakened class identity in the United States. Democratic socialists recognise the pre-capitalist origins of racism and sexism.

While capitalism clearly structures these forms of oppression (for example. the use of racism and sexism to channel women and minorities into low-paying. service sector jobs). there is a relatively autonomous cultural and psychological dimension to these forms of domination. Socialist-feminists analyze how the sexual division of labour in child rearing produces different gendered attitudes towards nurturing and moral Judgement. Socialist analyses of racism examine the psychological underpinnings of racism in cultural fears of "the other" and anxieties about group identity and status.

Democratic socialists. influenced by the Black Liberation. Women's Liberation. and Gay and Lesbian Liberation movements. also recognise that "different" identities provide meaning for people. The orthodox Marxist desire to subsume all ethnic. racial. and cultural groups under the universal identity of "the working class" threatens the particular communities that provide sustenance to individuals. A democratic socialist society would facilitate the autonomy and enrichment of various cultural and ethnic traditions. But some "post-modern" theorists go too far in celebrating "particularity."

While particular identities and the autonomy of movements against oppression are central to a free. pluralist society. so is the development of a sense of common citizenship. Vibrant political life and a strong welfare society must be grounded in a strong sense of communal membership. Citizenship should not be viewed as a "homogenizing" category that reduces all to the pursuit of the same interests and needs. Rather. if human beings and the particular communities with which they identify are to be accorded equal respect they need to live in a society that guarantees that all members will be able to fulfill their unique potential.

STRATEGY: THE ROLE OF THE PARTY AND THE STATE

While Marx never adequately described how socialism would be achieved by crossing the terrain of a democratic capitalist society. V. I. Lenin claimed there was no choice but insurrection. Socialists could not use the capitalist state to abolish capitalism; they would have to overthrow the state and then "smash" its machinery. What institutions of government would take its place Lenin never made fully clear. except for vague references to the self-governance of workers' councils (soviets) in The State and Revolution. Obviously the Bolshevik party rapidly supplanted the councils as the main governing institution in Lenin's Soviet Union.

In *What Is To Be Done*. Lenin claimed that trade union activity would produce only a reformist desire for "more" economic goods rather than revolutionary consciousness. Lenin may not have inaccurately predicted the nature of predominant working class consciousness during "normal" periods of capitalist development. Workers under capitalism have more to lose than just their chains. But Lenin's belief in the privilege of the "vanguard" party—that it can do whatever it wants once it takes power because it represents the workers' "true" interests—contradicts Marx's belief in working-class self- emancipation. Though an effective strategy for clandestine organization in repressive societies. Leninism's track record in democratic capitalist societies is dismal. perhaps because self-described Leninist parties are usually thoroughly authoritarian.

Any possible transition to socialism would necessitate mass mobilization and the democratic legitimacy garnered by having demonstrated majority support. Only a strong majority movement that affected the consciousness of the army rank-and-file could forestall an armed coup by the right. Even when a repressive regime necessitates a minority road to revolution. democratic socialists stand with Rosa Luxemburg—revolutionary Marxist leader in Germany a century ago—in her advocacy of the restoration of civil rights and liberties once the authoritarian regime has been overthrown. There has yet to be a "Communist" revolution in which the "vanguard" party then allows itself to be voted out of office. The end of Communism in the former Soviet Union and Eastern Europe. and the inspiring struggles against "Communist capitalism" in China. will hopefully lead to movements for democratic socialism in these countries.

Leninists often argued the state under capitalism was nothing more than a tool of the capitalist class. What this "instrumentalist" view of the state cannot explain is why numerous reforms have been implemented under democratic capitalism against the fierce resistance of capitalists. Nor can it explain why some capitalist societies have stronger welfare states and greater democratic controls over capital than do others. Certainly structural dependence upon corporate investment to reproduce conditions of prosperity constrains democratic governments. The flight of capital has hindered liberal and social democratic reforms. But in times of depression. war. or mass political mobilization (*e.g.*. the 1930s. World War II. the 1960s). the state has implemented reforms that have curtailed the rights of capital and increased popular power. To preserve the legitimacy of democratic government (and. in the long run. democratic capitalism itself). the state must respond to popular mobilization.

In part. this is possible because the capitalist class does not directly rule under capitalism. While the demands of corporate and defence industry lobbyists heavily influence politicians and state bureaucrats. the major goal of politicians is to guarantee reelection through steady economic growth. Capitalist interests are often divided among themselves (importers versus exporters. finance versus manufacturing. etc.). thus providing state officials with a certain degree of autonomy. In times of economic crisis and/or popular mobilization. state managers and political elites will sometimes advocate programmes for economic recovery which are initially opposed by most capitalists. Politicians need to win elections and capitalists simply do not have enough votes to guarantee victory.

In the long run. however. if popular mobilization does not persist. reforms will often be restructured to shift the balance of power back towards capital (*e.g.*. the reintroduction of regressive taxation; cutting of benefits; deregulation; weaker enforcement of labour laws. and so on). State officials are always constrained by the need for business confidence and continued private investment. State policy results from class and political conflict. but the asymmetry of the capital-labour relationship stacks the deck against popular movements. Only by building strong trade unions. community organizations. and socialist parties can the left redress this imbalance of forces.

CLASS CONSCIOUSNESS AND STRUGGLE IN CIVIL SOCIETY

Marx believed that capitalist ideology would have a powerful sway over the working class ("The ruling ideas of the day are the ideas of the ruling class"). But Marx underestimated the predominance of ideas of individualism and competition in popular culture. In part. this is because such ideologies are not completely false. There is more political freedom and social mobility under Western capitalism than in all previous societies. The early 20th century Italian Marxist theoretician Antonio Gramsci better understood how bourgeois ideology underpinned the "common sense" of capitalist culture. The capitalist class not only disproportionately influences the state. but ideas of "consumer sovereignty." "freedom" and "choice" also dominate public opinion in the institutions of civil society. such as schools. religion. and the media.

Gramsci believed that the dominance of capitalist modes of thought could be countered by a conscious. "counter hegemonic." leftist cultural presence throughout civil society. The left would have to organize not only in the formal political arena. but also in the workplace. the neighborhood. the church. and the PTA. Though those who hold electoral state power set the boundaries within which political struggle occurs. organizing in civil society (at the grassroots) is critical for the growth of the left. Cultural. educational. and ideological work is as "political" as are elections.

In order to affect state power and to change the balance of forces in civil society. democratic socialists believe it is necessary to work both in electoral politics and in community and trade union organizing. In light of the peculiar structure of the American political system (the absence of proportional representation; the absence of coalition governments because of an executive rather than parliamentary system; open party membership and open primaries; single district. winner-take-all electoral districts). most progressive forces. when doing electoral work. pragmatically choose to work in the left wing of the Democratic Party. Hence. electoral class conflict runs through the Democratic Party. not around it.

Given the structure of the US government. any third party in the United States rapidly has to become a second or first party to survive. The critical question facing socialists in the United States today is not whether to form a nation-wide third party. Rather. it is how best to build those progressive constituencies which alone can push politicians—whatever their party affiliation—to the left. Forming a party is pointless if few will join it. If and when the mass constituencies of the American democratic left decide to leave the Democratic Party. only then will a credible national third party be on the political agenda.

THE TRANSITION TO SOCIALISM

Hopes for a rapid democratic transition to socialism were shattered by the horrors of Stalinism and the failure of social democratic governments to discern a socialist road out of the Great Depression. After World War II. "democratic socialism" increasingly became identified with the "Keynesian" welfare state. Post-war growth and the concomitant expansion of welfare provision enabled governing working class parties to put socialization of ownership on the back burner. As British Labour Party leader Tony Crosland argued in 1956 in his book *The Future of Socialism*. a state-regulated capitalism could respond to the needs of the people if income was equitably distributed. But even if the stronger welfare states of Northern Europe did significantly redistribute income across classes. with the crisis of the welfare state due to the end of post-WWII growth in the 1970s. the mainstream left again faced a crisis of vision and programme.

While expanded public provision and a strong infrastructure increases long-run productivity. it is impossible to achieve this when not only capital. but also significant populist movements (based both among the middle class and skilled unionized workers) demand that taxation and public provision be curtailed. Again. the left's task is both moral and programmatic. It must reintroduce the values of equality and solidarity which support universal public provision through progressive taxation. And it must also advance a compelling vision of economic growth through greater democratic control over capital.

A strategy of gradually encroaching upon the prerogatives of capital will involve creative experiments in workers' buy-outs. democratic control over pension funds. and mandated worker and consumer representation on corporate boards. But these can only occur through the growth of trade union and socialist political power. Socialism will be the achievement of an epoch in which the power of labour vis-à-vis capital will be constantly contested. If the relative power of labour grows. this terrain will take on increasingly favorable contours.

TRANSITIONAL STRATEGY: STRENGTHENING PUBLIC PROVISION AND DEMOCRATIC CONTROL OVER PRODUCTION

The strategy outlined above is borne out by sociologist John Stephens' historical argument that the stronger the "counter- hegemonic" strength of unions and left parties. the stronger the welfare state and the more egalitarian the distribution of economic and political power. There is a reason why health and safety regulations are much stricter in the Scandinavian countries than in the United States; why Sweden and West Germany. under social democratic governments. funneled almost half of their respective GNPs through the public sector while the United States only transfers 25 percent; why social democratic welfare states are financed through progressive taxation while others (the United States and Japan) are financed by regressive taxation. The structure of the welfare state is profoundly affected by relative trade union and political party strength. As the fight for reforms usually involves struggle "from below." in liberal democratic capitalist societies there is no radical divergence between strategies for reforms or revolution. Welfare state reforms that redistribute income and radical structural reforms that increase workers' control both necessitate stronger political and union organization.

Young radicals today often act as though street protest and direct-action tactics—even confrontation with the police—could bring about revolution. While direct action has its place in left politics. achieving serious social reform—let alone "full" socialism—requires movement-building and mass action. To refrain from struggles for reform (living wages. union organizing rights. police accountability. defence of reproductive rights and affirmative action) is to ensure marginality.

Socialists must take part in concrete struggles to improve peoples' living conditions—and do so in ways that increase their self-organization. political consciousness and capacity for collective action.

TOWARDS A VISION OF DEMOCRATIC PRODUCTION AND SOCIAL PROVISION

When socialists argue for "decommodifying"—taking out of private market provision—such basic human needs as Health care. childcare. education. transport. and housing. we have in mind a decentralized and more fully accountable welfare state than exists in Western democracies. While state financing of such goods is necessary to insure equity. decentralized social provision through community-based institutions must make welfare provision more human-scale and accessible. Democratic control of consumption should be as central to the socialist vision as democratic control over production. particularly given popular mistrust that socialism would be a bureaucratic nightmare which treated people as clients rather than citizens.

While the exact details of a socialist economy are open to debate. it will most likely be a mixture of democratic planning of major investments (*e.g.*. expenditure on infrastructure. investment in natural monopolies such as telecommunications. utilities. transport) and market exchange of consumer goods. Large. concentrated industries such as energy and steel would be publicly owned and managed by worker and consumer representatives. Many consumer-goods industries would be run as cooperatives. Workers would design the division of labour within their workplaces and thus overcome the authoritarianism of the traditional capitalist firm. Economic planning would set a guiding strategy by means of fiscal and monetary policy. with the daily coordination of supply and demand left to the market. But this market would be socialized by rendering it transparent. Enterprises would be obliged to divulge information about the design. production processes. price formation. wage conditions. and environmental consequences of the goods that they make. Publicly supported collectives—consumers' unions—would analyze this data and propose norms to govern various aspects of these practices. Information about actual production processes and proposed norms would then be disseminated via universal. publicly supported communication networks such as the Internet. This would encourage dialogue between producers and consumers over what is socially needed.

Again. there is no final blueprint for socialism. But only under socialism will fully democratic debate over the use of society's wealth be possible and the satisfaction of people's basic needs assured. Productive activity will become not merely a way to acquire money. but a means to develop the whole creative potential of all working women and men.

SOCIALIST INTERNATIONALISM VERSUS CAPITALIST GLOBALIZATION

Marx may have underestimated the capitalist state's ability to regulate the business cycle. but the stagnation and restructuring of capitalism since the 1970s demonstrates that the system is less stable than its apologists contend. The growing internationalization of capital (which Marx envisioned) erodes the ability of nation-states to control their economic destiny. Thus. if socialism is to be a viable movement in the twenty-first century it must become as international as is capital. How to maintain living standards in the First World while promoting equitable development in the (former) Third World poses a major challenge for democratic socialists.

Lenin's theory of imperialism was dominant on the socialist left until the 1960s. His theory held that the advanced capitalist nations would export their surplus capital to the less developed world. While the developed capitalist nations would control this capital. Lenin envisioned rapid development in the colonized nations and the eventual rebellion of their emerging working classes. In fact. few Third World countries experienced vigorous industrial growth until the 1960s and most overseas capital investment went to other First World nations. In the post-war period. as radical economists acknowledged the relative stagnation of less developed economies and the overall flow of capital out of the developing countries to the First World. the theory of "the development of underdevelopment" (or "dependency theory") emerged. Rather than industrializing the Third World. First World imperialism. according to dependency theory. relegated developing countries to producers of cheap raw materials and agricultural products. If industrialization occurred it was limited to "export platforms" producing relatively cheap goods for export to the imperial country. While dependency theory partly explained the evolution of the poorest Third World nations (though it ascribed too much causal power to the world market and too little to internal class relations). it could not explain the emergence of significant industrial producers in East Asia and parts of Latin America. Nor could it explain how abject poverty could coexist with advanced industrial production.

"Post-dependency" analysis explained how a strong state bureaucracy could ally with foreign and domestic capital to foster industrial growth. But such development rarely served the needs of the local economy for light industry and agricultural development. In addition. as it was heavily financed by foreign borrowing. this industrialization's "success" was often based on low-wage production guaranteed by state repression of labour unions. In "newly industrializing countries" such as Brazil. Mexico. and South Korea. industrialization is no longer the question. The question is whether this industrialization can benefit domestic workers rather than domestic elites and foreign consumers.

Democratic socialists favour an industrialization that will not repeat the social and ecological horrors of recent industrial experiences. We want ecologically sound growth of "qualitative gross national product." not simply quantitative product. Expending funds on environmentally sound technology is one way of increasing the qualitative product. Improvements in human services and growth in leisure time would also enhance the quality of life. There may well be ecological limits to strictly "quantitative" growth. but socialism will prove attractive to the world's population only if it both quantitatively and qualitatively enhances the standard of living of people in the less developed world.

Over twenty-five years of a "deregulated" world economy. imposed by conservative and "Third Way" centre-left governments in the developed world and by the International Monetary Fund throughout the rest of the planet. has severely increased global inequality. Masked in the rhetoric of "comparative advantage" and economic efficiency. "free market" policies impose the gutting of living standards and labour rights.

By demanding that all nation-states remove regulatory constraints on corporations. cut social welfare programmes. enact fiscal austerity. and declare war on unions. the World Trade Organization ensures that capital will be able to move labour-intensive forms of production to the "lowest cost producers" in the developing world. While more knowledge-intensive production remains in advanced industrial nations. such as software design and computerized tool production. the disproportionate share of the benefits of productivity increases goes to the top twenty percent of the population. the "symbolic manipulators" who organize production itself. Contrary to mainstream propaganda. nation-states can still influence corporate behaviour. To do so they must engage in regional and international cooperation aimed at instituting a new global social contract that would level up living standards. impose labour and environmental regulations upon transnational corporations. and regulate global financial actors in the interests of equitable and sustainable development. A rebuilt international socialist movement must work towards international cooperation among states to re-institute capital controls and reverse the unfavorable economic conditions of developing nations. If the social democratic welfare state can no longer be sustained strictly on a national level. it must be created on an international level. Absent a worldwide New Deal. even the "privileged" workers of the advanced industrial nations may join the global majority in poverty and hunger. If global social democratic capitalism proves impossible. there will be no chance for an international movement towards the full socialization of the world economy.

4

Socialist Economics

Socialist economics refers to the economic theories. practices. and norms of hypothetical and existing socialist economic systems.

A socialist economic system is based on some form of social ownership of the means of production. which may mean autonomous cooperatives or direct public ownership; wherein production is carried out directly for use. Where markets are utilised for allocating inputs and capital goods among economic units. the designation market socialism is used. When planning is utilised. the economic system is designated a planned socialist economy. Non-market forms of socialism usually include a system of accounting based oncalculation-in-kind or a direct measure of labour-time as a means to value resources and goods.

The term *socialist economics* may also be applied to analysis of former and existing economic systems that call themselves "socialist". such as the works of Hungarian economist János Kornai.

Socialist economics has been associated with different schools of economic thought. Marxian economics provided a foundation for socialism based on analysis of capitalism. while neoclassical economics and evolutionary economics provided comprehensive models of socialism. During the 20th century. proposals and models for both planned economies and market socialism were based heavily on neoclassical economics or a synthesis of neoclassical economics with Marxian or institutional economics.

HISTORY OF SOCIALIST ECONOMIC THOUGHT

Values of *socialism* have roots in pre-capitalist institutions such as the religious communes. reciprocal obligations. and communal charity of Mediaeval Europe. the development of its economic theory primarily reflects and responds to the monumental changes brought about by the dissolution of feudalism and the emergence of specifically capitalist social relations. As such it is commonly regarded as a movement belonging to the modern era. Many socialists have considered their advocacy as the preservation and extension of the radical humanist ideas expressed in Enlightenment doctrine such as Jean-Jacques Rousseau's *Discourse on Inequality*. Wilhelm von Humboldt's *Limits of State*

Action. or Immanuel Kant's insistent defence of the French Revolution. Capitalism appeared in mature form as a result of the problems raised when an industrial factory system requiring long-term investment and entailing corresponding risks was introduced into an internationalized commercial (mercantilist) framework. Historically speaking. the most pressing needs of this new system were an assured supply of the elements of industry – land. elaborate machinery. and labour – and these imperatives led to the commodification of these elements.

According to influential socialist economic historian Karl Polanyi's classic account. the forceful transformation of land. money and especially labour into commodities to be allocated by an autonomous market mechanism was an alien and inhuman rupture of the pre-existing social fabric. Marx had viewed the process in a similar light. referring to it as part of the process of "primitive accumulation" whereby enough initial capital is amassed to begin capitalist production. The dislocation that Polyani and others describe. triggered natural counter-movements in efforts to re-embed the economy in society. These counter-movements. that included. for example. the Luddite rebellions. are the incipient socialist movements. Over time such movements gave birth to or acquired an array of intellectual defenders who attempted to develop their ideas in theory.

As Polanyi noted. these counter-movements were mostly reactive and therefore not full-fledged socialist movements. Some demands went no further than a wish to mitigate the capitalist market's worst effects. Later. a full socialist programme developed. arguing for systemic transformation. Its theorists believed that even if markets and private property could be tamed so as not to be excessively "exploitative". or crises could be effectively mitigated. capitalist social relations would remain significantly unjust and anti-democratic. suppressing universal human needs for fulfilling. empowering and creative work. diversity and solidarity.

Within this context socialism has undergone four periods: the first in the 19th century was a period of utopian visions (1780s-1850s); then occurred the rise of revolutionary socialist and Communist movements in the 19th century as the primary opposition to the rise of corporations and industrialization (1830–1916); the polarisation of socialism around the question of the Soviet Union. and adoption of socialist or social democratic policies in response (1916–1989); and the response of socialism in the neo-liberal era (1990-). As socialism developed. so did the socialist system of economics.

UTOPIAN SOCIALISM

The first theories which came to hold the term "socialism" began to be formulated in the late 18th century. and were termed "socialism" early in the 19th century. The central beliefs of the socialism of this period rested on the exploitation of those who labored by those who owned capital or rented land and housing. The abject misery. poverty and disease to which laboring classes seemed destined was the inspiration for a series of schools of thought which argued that life under a class of masters. or "capitalists" as they were then becoming to be called. would consist of working classes being driven down to subsistence wages.

Socialist ideas found expression in utopian movements. which often formed agricultural communes aimed at being self-sufficient on the land. These included many religious movements. such as the Shakers in America.

Utopian socialism had little to offer in terms of a systematic theory of economic phenomena. In theory. economic problems were dissolved by a utopian society which had transcended material scarcity. In practice. small communities with a common spirit could sometimes resolve allocation problems.

SOCIALISM AND CLASSICAL POLITICAL ECONOMY

The first organised theories of socialist economics were significantly impacted by classical economic theory. including elements in Adam Smith. Robert Malthus and David Ricardo. In Smith there is a conception of a common good not provided by the market. a class analysis. a concern for the dehumanizing aspects of the factory system. and the concept of rent as being unproductive. Ricardo argued that the renting class was parasitic. This. and the possibility of a "general glut". an over accumulation of capital to produce goods for sale rather than for use. became the foundation of a rising critique of the concept that free markets with competition would be sufficient to prevent disastrous downturns in the economy. and whether the need for expansion would inevitably lead to war.

SOCIALIST POLITICAL ECONOMY BEFORE MARX

A key early socialist theorist of political economy was Pierre-Joseph Proudhon. He was the most well-known of nineteenth century mutualisttheorists and the first thinker to refer to himself as an anarchist. Others were: Technocrats like Henri de Saint Simon. agrarian radicals likeThomas Spence. William Ogilvie and William Cobbett; anti-capitalists like Thomas Hodgskin; communitarian and utopian socialists likeRobert Owen. William Thompson and Charles Fourier; anti-market socialists like John Gray and John Francis Bray; the Christian mutualistWilliam Batchelder Greene; as well as the theorists of the Chartist movement and early proponents of syndicalism.

The first advocates of socialism promoted social leveling in order to create a meritocratic or technocratic society based upon individual talent. Count Henri de Saint-Simon was the first individual to coin the term "socialism". Simon was fascinated by the enormous potential of science and technology. which led him to advocate a socialist society that would eliminate the disorderly aspects of capitalism and which would be based upon equal opportunities. Simon advocated a society in which each person was ranked according to his or her capacities and rewarded according to his or her work. This was accompanied by a desire to implement a rationally organised economy based on planning and geared towards large-scale scientific and material progress. which embodied a desire for a semi-planned economy.

Other early socialist thinkers were influenced by the classical economists. The Ricardian socialists. such as Thomas Hodgskin and Charles Hall. were based on the work of David Ricardo and reasoned that the equilibrium value of commodities approximated producer prices when those commodities were in elastic supply. and that these producer prices corresponded to the embodied labour. The Ricardian socialists viewed profit. interest and rent as deductions from this exchange-value.

KARL MARX AND *DAS KAPITAL*

Karl Marx employed systematic analysis in an attempt to elucidate capitalism's contradictory laws of motion. as well as to expose the specific mechanisms by which it exploits and alienates. He radically modified classical political economic theories. Marx transformed the labour theory of value. which had been worked upon by Adam Smith and David Ricardo. into his "law of value". and used it for the purpose of revealing how commodity fetishism obscures the reality of capitalist society.

His approach. which Friedrich Engels would call "scientific socialism". would stand as the branching point in economic theory. In one direction went those who rejected the capitalist system as fundamentally anti-social. arguing that it could never be harnessed to effectively realize the fullest development of human potentialities wherein "the free development of each is the condition for the free development of all.".

Marx's *Das Kapital* is an incomplete work of economic theory; he had planned four volumes but completed two and left his collaborator Engels to complete the third. In many ways. the work is modelled on Smith's *Wealth of Nations*. seeking to be a comprehensive logical description of production. consumption and finance in relation to morality and the state.

The work of philosophy. anthropology. sociology and economics includes the following topics:

- *The Law of Value:* Capitalist production is the production of "an immense multitude of commodities" or generalised commodity production. A commodity has two essential qualities firstly. they are useful. they satisfy some human want. "the nature of such wants. whether. for instance. they spring from the stomach or from fancy. makes no difference." and secondly they are sold on a market or exchanged. Critically the exchange value of a commodity "is independent of the amount of labour required to appropriate its useful qualities." But rather depends on the amount of socially necessary labour required to produce it. All commodities are sold at their value. so the origin of the capitalist profit is not in cheating or theft but in the fact that the cost of reproduction of labour power. or the worker's wage. is less than the value created during their time at work. enabling the capitalists to yield a surplus value or profit on their investments.

- *Historical Property Relations:* Historical capitalism represents a process of momentous social upheaval where rural masses were separated from the land and ownership of the means of production by force. deprivation. and legal manipulation. creating an urban proletariat based on the institution of wage-labour. Moreover. capitalist property relations aggravated the artificial separation between city and country. which is a key factor in accounting for the metabolic rift between human beings in capitalism and their natural environment. which is at the root of our current ecological dilemmas.
- *Commodity Fetishism:* Marx adapted previous value-theory to show that in capitalism phenomena involved with the price system (markets. competition. supply and demand) constitute a powerful ideology that obscures the underlying social relations of capitalist society. "Commodity fetishism" refers to this distortion of appearance. The underlying social reality is one of economic exploitation.
- *Economic Exploitation:* Workers are the fundamental creative source of new value. Property relations affording the right of usufruct and despotic control of the workplace to capitalists are the devices by which the surplus value created by workers is appropriated by the capitalists.
- *Capital accumulation:* Inherent to capitalism is the incessant drive to accumulate as a response to the competitive forces acting upon all capitalists. In such a context the accumulated wealth which is the source of the capitalist's social power derives itself from being able to repeat the circuit of Money—>Commodity—>Money'. where the capitalist receives an increment or "surplus value" higher than their initial investment. as rapidly and efficiently as possible. Moreover this driving imperative leads capitalism to its expansion on a worldwide scale.
- *Crises:* Marx identified natural and historically specific (*i.e.* structural) barriers to accumulation that were interrelated and interpenetrated one another in times of crises. Different types of crises. such as realization crises and overproduction crises. are expressions of capitalism's inability to constructively overcome such barriers.

Moreover. the upshot of crises is increased centralization. the expropriation of the many capitalists by the few.

- *Centralization:* The interacting forces of competition. endemic crises. intensive and extensive expansion of the scale of production. and a growing interdependency with the state apparatus. all promote a strong developmental tendency towards the centralization of capital.
- *Material Development:* As a result of its constant drive to optimize profitability by increasing the productivity of labour. typically by revolutionizing technology and production techniques. capitalism develops so as to progressively reduce the objective need for work. suggesting the potential for a new era of creative forms of work and expanded scope for leisure.
- *Socialization. and the pre-conditions for Revolution:* By socializing the labour process. concentrating workers into urban settings in large-scale production processes and linking them in a worldwide market. the agents of a potential revolutionary change are created. Thus Marx felt that in the course of its development capitalism was at the same time developing the preconditions for its own negation. However. although the objective conditions for change are generated by the capitalist system itself. the subjective conditions for social revolution can only come about through the apprehension of the objective circumstances by the agents themselves and the transformation of such understanding into an effective revolutionary programme.

ANARCHIST ECONOMICS

Anarchist economics is the set of theories and practices of economics and economic activity within the political philosophy of anarchism.

Pierre Joseph Proudhon was involved with the Lyons mutualists and later adopted the name to describe his own teachings. Mutualism is an anarchist school of thought that originates in the writings of Pierre-Joseph Proudhon. who envisioned a society where each person might possess a means of production. either individually or collectively. with trade representing equivalent amounts of labour in the free market. Integral to the scheme was the establishment of a mutual-credit bank that would lend to producers at a minimal interest rate. just high enough to cover administration. Mutualism is based on a labour theory of value that holds that when labour or its product is sold. in exchange. it ought to receive goods or services embodying "the amount of labour necessary to produce an article of exactly similar and equal utility". Receiving anything less would be considered exploitation. theft of labour. or usury.

Collectivist anarchism (also known as anarcho-collectivism) is a revolutionary doctrine that advocates the abolition of the state and private ownership of the means of production. Instead. it envisions the means of production being owned collectively and controlled and managed by the producers themselves. Once collectivization takes place. workers' salaries would be determined in democratic organizations based on the amount of time they contributed to production. These salaries would be used to purchase goods in a communal market. Collectivist anarchism is most commonly associated with Mikhail Bakunin. the anti-authoritarian sections of the First International. and the early Spanish anarchist movement.

Anarchist communism is a theory of anarchism which advocates the abolition of the state. private property. and capitalism in favour of common ownership of the means of production. direct democracy and a horizontal network of voluntary associations and workers' councils with production and consumption based on the guiding principle: "from each according to ability. to each according to need". Unlike mutualism. collectivist anarchism and marxism. anarcho-communism as defended by Peter Kropotkin and Errico Malatesta rejected the labour theory of value altogether. instead advocating a gift economy and to base distribution on need.

Anarchist communism as a coherent. modern economic-political philosophy was first formulated in the Italian section of the First Internationalby Carlo Cafiero. Emilio Covelli. Errico Malatesta. Andrea Costa and other ex-Mazzinian Republicans. Out of respect for Mikhail Bakunin. they did not make their differences with collectivist anarchism explicit until after Bakunin's death. By the early 1880s. most of the European anarchist movement had adopted an anarchist communist position. advocating the abolition of wage labour and distribution according to need. Ironically. the "collectivist" label then became more commonly associated with Marxist state socialists who advocated the retention of some sort of wage system during the transition to full communism.

AFTER MARX

Non-revolutionary socialists were inspired by the writings of John Stuart Mill. and later John Maynard Keynes and the Keynesians. who provided theoretical justification for state involvement in existing market economies. According to the Keynesians. if business cycles could be smoothed out by national ownership of key industries and state direction of their investment. class antagonism would be effectively tamed. They argue that a compact would form between labour and the capitalist class and that there would be no need for revolution. Joan Robinson and Michael Kalecki formed the basis of a critical post-Keynesian economics that at times went well beyond liberal reformism.

Marxist economists developed different tendencies based on conflicting interpretations of Marx's ideas. such as the 'Law of Value' and crisis theory. The monopoly capitalist school saw Paul A. Baran and Paul Sweezy attempt to modify Marx's theory of capitalist development — which was based upon the assumption of price competition — to reflect evolution to a stage where both economy and state were subject to the dominating influence of giant corporations. World-systems analysis restated Marx's ideas about the worldwide division of labour and the drive to accumulate from the holistic perspective of capitalism's historical development as a global system. Immanuel Wallerstein. wrote in 1979:

There are today no socialist systems in the world-economy any more than there are feudal systems because there is only *one* world-system. It is a world-economy and it is by definition capitalist in form. Socialism involves the creation of a new kind of world-system. neither a redistributive world-empire nor a capitalist world-economy but a socialist world-government. I don't see this projection as being in the least utopian but I also don't feel its institution is imminent. It will be the outcome of a long social struggle in forms that may be familiar and perhaps in very few forms. that will take place in *all* the areas of the world-economy.

Piero Sraffa attempted to construct a value theory that was an explanation of the normal distribution of prices in an economy. as well that of income and economic growth. He found that the net product or surplus in the sphere of production was determined by the balance of bargaining power between workers and capitalists. which was subject to the influence of non-economic. presumably social and political. factors.

The mutualist tendency associated with Pierre-Joseph Proudhon also continued. influencing the development of libertarian socialism. anarchist communism. syndicalism anddistributivism.

CHARACTERISTICS

A socialist economy is a system of production where goods and services are produced directly for use. in contrast to a capitalist economic system. where goods and services are produced to generate profit (and therefore indirectly for use). "Production under socialism would be directly and solely for use. With the natural and technical resources of the world held in common and controlled democratically. the sole object of production would be to meet human needs." Goods and services would be produced for their usefulness. or for their use-value. eliminating the need for market-induced needs to ensure a sufficient amount of demand for products to be sold at a profit.

Production in a socialist economy is therefore "planned" or "coordinated". and does not suffer from the business cycle inherent to capitalism. In most socialist theories. economic planning only applies to the factors of production and not to the allocation of goods and services produced for consumption. which would be distributed through a market. Karl Marx stated that "lower-stage communism" would consist of compensation based on the amount of labour one contributes to the social product. The ownership of the means of production varies in different socialist theories. It can either be based on public ownership by a state apparatus; direct ownership by the users of the productive property through worker cooperative; or commonly owned by all of society with management and control delegated to those who operate/use the means of production.

Management and control over the activities of enterprises is based on self-management and self-governance. with equal power-relations in the workplace to maximize occupational autonomy. A socialist form of organization would eliminate controlling hierarchies so that only a hierarchy based on technical knowledge in the workplace remains. Every member would have decision-making power in the firm and would be able to participate in establishing its overall policy objectives. The policies/goals would be carried out by the technical specialists that form the coordinating hierarchy of the firm. who would establish plans or directives for the work community to accomplish these goals.

However. the economies of the former Socialist states. excluding SFR Yugoslavia. were based on bureaucratic. top-down administration of economic directives and micromanagement of the worker in the workplace inspired by capitalist models of scientific management. As a result. socialists have argued that they were not socialist due to the lack of equal power-relations in the workplace. the presence of a new "elite". and because of the commodity production that took place in these economies. These economic and social systems have been classified as being either *Bureaucratic collectivist*. *State capitalist* or *Deformed workers' states*. the exact nature of the USSR *et al* remains unresolved within the socialist movement

"I am convinced there is only one way to eliminate (the) grave evils (of capitalism). namely through the establishment of a socialist economy. accompanied by an educational system which would be oriented Towards social goals. In such an economy. the means of production are owned by society itself and are utilised in a planned fashion. A planned economy. which adjusts production to the needs of the community. would distribute the work to be done among all those able to work and would guarantee a livelihood to every man. woman. and child. The education of the individual. in addition to promoting his own innate abilities. would attempt to develop in him a sense of responsibility for his fellow-men in place of the glorification of power and success in our present society."

— Albert Einstein. *Why Socialism?*. 1949

ECONOMIC PLANNING

Economic planning is a mechanism for the allocation of economic inputs and decision-making based on direct allocation. in contrast to the market mechanism. which is based on indirect allocation. An economy based on economic planning appropriates its resources as needed. so that allocation comes in the form of internal transfers rather than market transactions involving the purchasing of assets by one government agency or firm by another. Decision-making is carried out by workers and consumers on the enterprise-level. Economic planning is not synonymous with the concept of a *command economy*. which existed in the Soviet Union. and was based on a highly bureaucratic administration of the entire economy in accordance to a comprehensive plan formulated by a central planning agency. which specified output requirements for productive units and tried to micromanage the decisions and policies of enterprises. The command economy is based on the organizational model of a capitalist firm. but applies it to the entire economy.

Various advocates of economic planning have been staunch critics of command economies and centralized planning. For example. Leon Trotsky believed that central planners. regardless of their intellectual capacity. operated without the input and participation of the millions of people who participate in the economy and understand the local conditions and rapid changes in the economy. Therefore. central planners would be unable to effectively coordinate all economic activity because they lacked this informal information.

Economic planning in socialism takes a different form than economic planning in capitalist mixed economies (such as Dirigisme. Central banking and Indicative planning); in the former case planning refers to production of use-value directly (planning of production). while in the latter case planning refers to the planning of capital accumulation in order to stabilize or increase the efficiency of this process.

ANTI-CAPITALISM

The goal of socialist economics is to neutralize capital (or. in the case of market socialism. to subject investment and capital to social planning). to coordinate the production of goods and services to directly satisfy demand (as opposed to market-induced needs). and to eliminate the business cycle and crisis of overproduction that occur as a result of an economy based on capital accumulation and private property in the means of production.

Socialists generally aim to achieve greater equality in decision-making and economic affairs. grant workers greater control of the means of production and their workplace. and to eliminate exploitation by directing the surplus value to employees. Free access to the means of subsistence is a requisite for liberty. because it ensures that all work is voluntary and no class or individual has the power to coerce others into performing alienating work.

The ultimate goal for Marxist socialists is the emancipation of labour from alienating work. and therefore freedom from having to perform such labour to receive access to the material necessities for life. It is argued that freedom from necessity would maximize individual liberty. as individuals would be able to pursue their own interests and develop their own talents without being coerced into performing labour for others (the power-elite or ruling class in this case) via mechanisms of social control. such as the labour marketand the state. The stage of economic development in which this is possible is contingent upon advances in the productive capabilities of society. This advanced stage of social relations and economic organization is called *pure communism*.

ECONOMIC VALUE THEORIES

Socialist economic theories base the value of a good or service on its use value. rather than its cost of production (labour theory of value) or its exchange value (Marginal Utility). Other socialist theories. such as mutualism and market socialism. attempt to apply the labour theory of value to socialism. so that the price of a good or service is adjusted to equal the amount of labour time expended in its production. The labour-time expended by each worker would correspond to labour credits. which would be used as a currency to acquire goods and services. Market socialists that base their models on neoclassical economics. and thus marginal utility. such as Oskar Lange and Abba Lerner. have proposed that publicly owned enterprises set their price to equal marginal cost. thereby achieving pareto efficiency. Anarcho-communism as defended by Peter Kropotkinand Errico Malatesta rejected the labour theory of value and exchange value itself. advocated a gift economy and to base distribution on need.

ECONOMIC MODELS AND SYSTEMS

Robin Hahnel and Michael Albert identify five different economic models within socialist economics:

- Public Enterprise Centrally Planned Economy in which all property is owned by the State and all key economic decisions are made centrally by the State. *e.g.* the former Soviet Union.
- Public Enterprise State-Managed Market Economy. one form of market socialism which attempts to use the price mechanism to increase economic efficiency. while all decisive productive assets remain in the ownership of the state. *e.g.* socialist market economy in China after reform.
- A mixed economy. also a capitalist economy where public and private ownership are mixed. and where industrial planning is ultimately subordinate to market allocation. the model generally adopted by social democrats *e.g.* in twentieth century Sweden. Many different proposals for socialist economic systems call for a type of mixed economy. where multiple forms of ownership over the means of production co-exist with one another.
- Public Enterprise Employee Managed Market Economies. another form of market socialism in which publicly owned. employee-managed production units engage in free market exchange of goods and services with one another as well as with final consumers. *e.g.* mid twentieth

century Yugoslavia. Two more theoretical models are Prabhat Ranjan Sarkar's Progressive Utilization Theory and Economic democracy.

- Public Enterprise Participatory Planning. an economy featuring social ownership of the means of production with allocation based on an integration of decentralized democratic planning. *e.g.* stateless communism. libertarian socialism. An incipient historical forebear is that of Catalonia during the Spanish revolution. More developed theoretical models include those of Karl Polanyi. Participatory Economics. Inclusive Democracy and the negotiated coordination model of Pat Devine. as well as in Cornelius Castoriadis's pamphlet "Workers' Councils and the Economics of a Self-Managed Society".

János Kornai identifies five distinct types of socialism:

- Classical/ Marxist conception. where socialism is a stage of economic development in which wage labour. private property in the means of production and monetary relations have been made redundant through the development of the productive forces. so that capital accumulation has been superseded by economic planning. Economic planning in this definition means conscious allocation of economic inputs and the means of production by the associated producers to directly maximise use-values as opposed to exchange-values. in contrast to the "anarchy of production" of capitalism.
- Walrasian/ Market Socialist which defines socialism as public-ownership or cooperative-enterprises in a market economy. with prices for producer goods set through a trial-and-error method by a central planning board. In this view. socialism is defined in terms of de jure public property rights over major enterprises.
- Leninist conception. which includes a form of political organisation based on control of the means of production and government by a single political party apparatus that claims to act in the interest of the working class. and an ideology hostile Towards markets and political dissent. with coordination of economic activity through centralised economic planning (a "command economy").
- Social Democratic concept. based on the capitalist mode of production. which defines socialism as a set of values rather than a specific type of social and economic organisation. It includes unconditional support for parliamentary democracy. gradual and reformist attempts to establish socialism. and support for socially progressive causes. Social democrats are not opposed to the market or private property; instead they try to ameliorate the effects of capitalism through a welfare state. which relies on the market as the fundamental coordinating entity in the economy and a degree of public ownership/public provision of public goods in an economy otherwise dominated by private enterprise.

- East Asian model. or socialist market economy. based on a largely free-market. capital accumulation for profit and substantial private ownership along with state-ownership of strategic industries monopolised by a single political party. János Kornai ultimately leaves the classification of this model (as either socialist or capitalist) to the reader.

Socialism can be divided into market socialism and planned socialism based on their dominant mechanism of resource allocation. Another distinction can be made between the type of property structures of different socialist systems (public. cooperative or common) and on the dominant form of economic management within the economy (hierarchical or self-managed).

ECONOMIC DEMOCRACY

Economic democracy is a model of market socialism primarily developed by the American economist David Schweickart. In Schweickart's model. enterprises and natural resources are owned by society in the form of public banking. and management is elected by the workers within each firm. Profits would be distributed among the workers of the respective enterprise.

LANGE-LERNER MODEL

The Lange-Lerner model involves public ownership of the means of production and the utilization of a trial-and-error approach to achieving equilibrium prices by a central planning board. The Central Planning Board would be responsible for setting prices through a trial-and-error approach to establish equilibrium prices. effectively acting as the abstract *Walrasian auctioneer* in Walrasian economics. Managers of the state-owned firms would be instructed to set prices to equal marginal cost (P=MC). so that economic equilibrium and Pareto efficiency would be achieved. The Lange model was expanded upon by the American economist Abba Lerner and became known as the Lange-Lerner theorem. particularly the role of the social dividend. Forerunners of the Lange model include the Neo-classical economists Enrico Barone and Fred M. Taylor.

SELF-MANAGED ECONOMY

The self-managed economy is a form of socialism where enterprises are owned and managed by their employees. effectively negating the employer-employee (or wage labour) dynamic of capitalism and emphasizing the opposition to alienation. self-managing and cooperative aspect of socialism. Members of cooperative firms are relatively free to manage their own affairs and work schedules. This model was developed most extensively by the Yugoslav economists Branko Horvat. Jaroslav Vanek and the American economist Benjamin Ward.

WORKER SELF-DIRECTED ENTERPRISE

Worker Self-Directed Enterprise (WSDE) is a recent proposal advocated by the American Marxian economist Richard D. Wolff. This model shares many similarities with the model of socialist self-management in that employees own and direct their enterprises. but places a greater role on democratically elected management within a market economy.

DEMOCRATIC PLANNED SOCIALISM

Democratic planned socialism is a form of decentralized planned economy.

FEASIBLE SOCIALISM

Feasible socialism was the name Alec Nove gave his outline for socialism in his work *The Economics of Feasible Socialism*. According to Nove. this model of socialism is "feasible" because it can be realized within the lifetime of anyone living today. It involves a combination of publicly owned and centrally directed enterprises for large-scale industries. autonomous publicly owned enterprises. consumer and worker-owned cooperatives for the majority of the economy. and private ownership for small businesses. It is a market-based mixed economy that includes a substantial role for macroeconomic interventionism and indicative economic planning.

PRAGMATIC MARKET SOCIALISM

The American economist James Yunker detailed a model where social ownership of the means of production is achieved the same way private ownership is achieved in modern capitalism through the shareholder system that separates management functions from ownership. Yunker posits that social ownership can be achieved by having a public body. designated the Bureau of Public Ownership (BPO). owning the shares of publicly listed firms without affecting market-based allocation of capital inputs.

Yunker termed this model*Pragmatic market socialism* because it does not require massive changes to society and would leave the existing management system intact. and would be at least as efficient as modern-day capitalism while providing superior social outcomes as public ownership of large and established enterprises would enable profits to be distributed among the entire population in a social dividend rather than going largely to a class of inheriting rentiers.

PARTICIPATORY ECONOMY

Participatory economics utilises participatory decision making as an economic mechanism to guide the production. consumption and allocation of resources in a given society.

COMPUTER-MANAGED ALLOCATION

Proposals for utilizing computer-based coordination and information technology for the coordination and optimization of resource allocation (also known as cybernetics) within an economy have been outlined by various socialists. economists and computer scientists. including Oskar Lange. the Soviet engineer Viktor Glushkov. and more recently the Paul Cockshott and Allin Cottrell.

PEER-TO-PEER ECONOMY AND OPEN SOURCE

The "networked information age" has enabled the development and emergence of new forms of organizing the production of value in non-market arrangements that have been termed commons-based peer production along with the negation of ownership and the concept of property in the development of software in the form of open source and open design.

NEGOTIATED COORDINATION

Economist Pat Devine has created a model of coordination called "negotiated coordination". which is based upon social ownership by those affected by the use of the assets involved. with decisions made by those at the most localised level of production.

ELEMENTS OF SOCIALISM IN PRACTICE

Although a number of economic systems have existed with various socialist attributes. or have been deemed socialist by their proponents. almost all of the economic systems listed below have largely retained elements of capitalism such as wage labour. the accumulation of capital. and commodity production. Non-etheless. various elements of a socialist economy have been implemented or experimented with in various economies throughout history.

Various forms of socialist organizational attributes have existed as minor modes of production within the context of a capitalist economy throughout history — examples of this include cooperative enterprises in a capitalist economy. and the emerging free-software movement based on social peer-to-peer production.

CENTRALLY PLANNED ECONOMIES

A centrally planned economy combines public ownership of the means of production with centralised state planning. This model is usually associated with the Soviet-style command economy. In a centrally planned economy. decisions regarding the quantity of goods and services to be produced are planned in advance by a planning agency. In the early years of Soviet central planning. the planning process was based upon a selected number of physical flows with inputs mobilized to meet explicit production targets measured in natural or technical units. This material balances method of achieving plan coherence was later complemented and replaced by value planning. with money provided to enterprises so that they could recruit labour and procure materials and intermediate production goods and services. The Soviet economy was brought to balance by the interlocking of three sets of calculation. namely the setting up of a model incorporating balances of production. manpower and finance.

The exercise was undertaken annually and involved a process of iteration (the "method of successive approximation"). Although nominally a "centrally planned" economy. in reality formulation of the plan took place on a more local level of the production process as information was relayed from enterprises to planning ministries. Aside from the USSR and Eastern bloc economies. this economic model was also utilised by the People's Republic of China. Socialist Republic of Vietnam. Republic of Cuba and North Korea.

SOVIET UNION

The Soviet Union and some of its European satellites aimed for a fully centrally planned economy. They dispensed almost entirely with private ownership over the means of production. Workers were still. however. effectively paid a wage for their labour. Some believe that according to Marxist theory this should have been a step towards a genuine workers' state. However. some Marxists consider this a misunderstanding of Marx's views of historical materialism. and his views of the process of socialization.

The characteristics of this model of economy were:

- Production quotas for every productive unit. A farm. mine or factory was judged on the basis of whether its production met the quota. It would be provided with a quota of the inputs it needed to start production. and then its quota of output would be taken away and given to downstream production units or distributed to consumers. Criticsof both left and right persuasions have argued that the economy was plagued by incentive-related problems; claiming. for instance. that the system incentivized enterprise managers to underreport their unit's productive capacities so that their quotas would be easier to achieve. especially since the manager's bonuses were linked to the fulfillment of quotas.
- Allocation through political control. In contrast with systems where prices *determined* allocation of resources. in the Soviet Union. allocation. particularly of means of production was determined by the bureaucracy. The prices that were constructed were done so *after* the formulation of the economy plan. and such prices did not factor into choices about what was produced and how it was produced in the first place.
- Full employment. Every worker was ensured employment. However workers were generally not directed to jobs. The central planning

administration adjusted relative wages rates to influence job choice in accordance with the outlines of the current plan.

- Clearing goods by planning: if a surplus of a product was accumulated. then the central planning authority would either reduce the quota for its production or increase the quota for its use.
- Five Year Plans for the long-term development of key industries.

The planning system in the USSR was introduced under Stalin between 1928 and 1934. Following the Second World War. in the seven countries with communist governments in Central and Eastern Europe. central planning with five- (or six-) year plans on the Soviet model had been introduced by 1951. The common features were the nationalization of industry. transport and trade. compulsory procurement in farming (but not collectivization) and a monopoly on foreign trade. Prices were largely determined on the basis of the costs of inputs. a method derived from the labour theory of value. Prices did not therefore incentivize production enterprises whose inputs were instead purposely rationed by the central plan. This "taut planning" began around 1930 in the USSR and was only attenuated after the economic reforms in 1966-68 when enterprises were encouraged to make profits.

The stated purpose of planning according to the communist party was to enable the people through the party and state institutions to undertake activities that would have been frustrated by a market economy (for example. the rapid expansion of universal education and health care. urban development with mass good quality housing and industrial development of all regions of the country). Nevertheless. markets continued to exist in socialist planned economies. Even after the collectivization of agriculture in the USSR in the 1930s. members of the collective farm and anyone with a private garden plot were free to sell their own produce (farm workers were often paid in kind).

Licensed markets operated in every town and city borough where non-state-owned enterprises (such as cooperatives and collective farms) were able to offer their products and services. From 1956/59 onwards all wartime controls over manpower were removed and people could apply and quit jobs freely in the USSR. The use of market mechanisms went furthest in Yugoslavia. Czechoslovakia and Hungary. From 1975 Soviet citizens had the right to engage in private handicraft and in 1981 collective farmers could raise and sell livestock privately. It should also be noted that households were free to dispose of their income as they chose and incomes were lightly taxed.

DISPUTE THAT THE SOVIET MODEL IS SOCIALISM

Various scholars and political economists have criticized the claim that the centrally planned economy. and specifically. the Soviet model of economic development. constitutes a form of socialism. They argue that the Soviet economy was structured upon the accumulation of capital and the extraction of surplus value from the working class by the planning agency in order to reinvest this surplus into the economy — and to distribute to managers and senior officials. indicating the Soviet Union (and other Soviet-style economies) were state capitalist economies. More fundamentally. these economies are still structured around the dynamic of capitalism: the accumulation of capital and production for profit (as opposed to being based on production for use — the defining criterion for socialism). and have not yet transcended the system of capitalism but are in fact a variation of capitalism based on a process of state-directed accumulation.

On the other side of the argument are those who contend that no surplus value was generated from labour activity or from commodity markets in the socialist planned economies and therefore claim that there was no exploiting class. even if inequalities existed. Since prices were controlled and set below market clearing levels there was no element of 'value added' at the point of sale as occurs in capitalist market economies. Prices were built up from the average cost of inputs. including wages. taxes. interest on stocks and working capital. and allowances to cover the recoupment of investment and for depreciation. so there was no 'profit margin' in the price charged to customers.

Wages did not reflect the purchase price of labour since labour was not a commodity traded in a market and the employing organizations did not own the means of production. Wages were set at a level that permitted a decent standard of living and rewarded specialist skills and educational qualifications. In macroeconomic terms. the plan allocated the whole national product to workers in the form of wages for the workers' own use. with a fraction withheld for investment and imports from abroad. The difference between the average value of wages and the value of national output per worker did not imply the existence of surplus value since it was part of a consciously formulated plan for the development of society.

Furthermore. the presence of inequality in the socialist planned economies did not imply that an exploiting class existed. In the USSR communist party members were able to buy scarce goods in special shops and the leadership elite took advantage of state property to live in more spacious accommodation and sometimes luxury. Although they received privileges not commonly available and thus some additional income in kind there was no difference in their official remuneration in comparison to their non-party peers. Enterprise managers and workers received only the wages and bonuses related to the production targets that had been set by the planning authorities. Outside of the cooperative sector. which enjoyed greater economic freedoms and whose profits were shared among all members of the cooperative. there was no profit-taking class.

Other socialist critics point to the lack of socialist social relations in these economies — specifically the lack of self-management. a bureaucratic elite based on hierarchical and centralized powers of authority. and the lack of genuine worker control over the means of production — leading them to conclude that they were not socialist but eitherbureaucratic collectivism or state capitalism. Trotskyists argue they are neither socialist nor capitalist — but are deformed workers' states.

This analysis is consistent with Lenin's April Theses. which stated that the goal of the Bolshevik revolution was *not* the introduction of socialism. which could only be established on a worldwide scale. but was intended to bring production and the state under the control of the Soviets of Workers' Deputies. Furthermore. these "Communist states" often do not claim to have achieved socialism in their countries; on the contrary. they claim to be *building* and working Towards the establishment of socialism in their countries. For example. the preamble to the Socialist Republic of Vietnam's constitution states that Vietnam only entered a transition stage between capitalism and socialism after the country was re-unified under the Communist party in 1976. and the 1992 Constitution of the Republic of Cuba states that the role of the Communist Party is to "guide the common effort Towards the goals and construction of socialism".

This view is challenged by Stalinists and their followers. who claim that socialism was established in the Soviet Union after Joseph Stalin came to power and instituted the system of five year plans. The 1936 Constitution of the USSR. known as the Fundamental Law of Victorious Socialism. embodied the claim that the foundations for socialism had been laid. Joseph Stalin introduced the theory of Socialism in one country. which argued that socialism can be built in a single country. despite existing in a global capitalist economic system. Nevertheless. it was recognized that the stage during which developed socialism would be built would be a lengthy one and would not be achieved by the USSR on its own. According to the official textbooks. the first stage of the transition period from capitalism to socialism had been completed by the 1970s in the European socialist countries (except Poland and Yugoslavia). and in Mongolia and Cuba. The next stage of developed socialism would not be reached until "the economic integration of the socialist states becomes a major factor of their economic progress" and social relations had been reconstructed on "collectivist principles".

Communist writers accepted that during these earlier stages in constructing socialism. the exchange of commodities on the basis of the average socially necessary labour embodied within them occurred and involved the mediation of money. Socialist planned economies were systems of commodity production but this was directed in a conscious way towards meeting the needs of the people and not left to the "anarchy of the market". At the stage of developed socialism "the state of dictatorship of the proletariat changes into a state of all people reflecting the increasing homogeneity of society" and the "evening out of economic development levels" within and between socialist countries. It would provide the foundations for a further stage of perfected socialist society. where an abundance of goods permitted their distribution according to need. Only then could the world socialist system progress towards the higher phase of communism.

WORLD SOCIALIST ECONOMIC SYSTEM

By the 1980s the world economic socialist system embraced one-third of the world's population but generated no more than 15 percent of global economic output. At its height in the mid-1980s the world socialist system could be said to comprise the following countries with a "socialist orientation". though not all were allies of the Soviet Union: Afghanistan. Albania. Angola. Bulgaria. Cambodia. China. Cuba. Czechoslovakia. Eastern Germany. Ethiopia. Hungary. Mozambique. Nicaragua. North Korea. Laos. Mongolia. Poland. Romania. Vietnam. South Yemen. Yugoslavia and the USSR. The system co-existed alongside the world capitalist system but was founded upon the principles of cooperation and mutual assistance rather than upon competition and rivalry The countries involved aimed to even-out the level of economic development and to play an equal part in the international division of labour.

An important role was played by the Council for Mutual Economic Assistance (CMEA) or Comecon. an international body set up to promote economic development. It involved joint planning activity. the establishment of international economic. scientific and technical bodies and methods of cooperation between state agencies and enterprises. including joint ventures and projects. Allied to the CMEA were the International Development Bank. established in 1971. and the International Bank for Economic Cooperation. founded in 1963. which had their parallel in the World Bank and the Bank for International Settlements and the International Monetary Fund in the non-socialist world.

The main tasks of the CMEA were plan coordination. production specialization and regional trade. In 1961 Nikita Khrushchev. the Soviet leader. put forward proposals for establishing an integrated. centrally planned socialist commonwealth in which each geographic region would specialize production in line with its set of natural and human resources. The resulting document. the "Basic Principles of the International Socialist Division of Labour" was adopted at the end of 1961. despite objections from Romania on certain aspects. The "Basic Principles" were never implemented fully and were replaced in 1971 by the adoption of the "Comprehensive Programme for Further Extension and Improvement of Cooperation and Development of Socialist Economic Integration". As a result many specialization agreements were made between CMEA member states for investment programmes and projects. The importing country pledged to rely on the exporting country for its consumption of the product in question. Production specialization occurred in engineering. automotive. chemicals. computers and automation. telecommunications and biotechnology. Scientific and technical cooperation between CMEA member states was facilitated by the establishment in 1969 of the International Centre for Scientific and Technical Information in Moscow.

Trade between CMEA member states was divided into 'hard' goods and 'soft' goods. The former could be sold on world markets and the latter could not. Commodities such as food. energy products and raw materials tended to be 'hard' goods and were traded within the CMEA area at world market prices. Manufactures tended to be 'soft' goods and their prices were negotiable and often adjusted to make bilateral payment flows balance.

Other countries with privileged affiliation with the CMEA were Algeria. Benin. Burma. Congo. Finland. Madagascar. Mali. Mexico. Nigeria. Seychelles. Syria. Tanzania and Zimbabwe. The USSR also provided substantial economic aid and technical assistance to developing countries including Egypt. India. Iraq. Iran. Somalia and Turkey. It supported developing countries in calling for a New International Economic Order and backed the UN Charter of Economic Rights and Obligations of States adopted by the General Assembly in 1974.

ACHIEVEMENTS OF THE SOCIALIST PLANNED ECONOMIES

In the officially sanctioned textbooks describing the socialist planned economies as they existed in the 1980s it was claimed that:

- Class and national oppression had been totally eradicated.
- Unemployment. hunger. poverty. illiteracy and uncertainty about the future had been eliminated.
- Every citizen had a guaranteed right to work. rest. education. health care. abode and security in old age and maintenance in the event of disability.
- Material standards of living were rising steadily and everyone had free access to knowledge and to the values of world and national culture.
- Every citizen had a right in practice to take part in discussing and solving any problems in the life of the enterprise. region. republic and the country they lived in. including the rights to free speech. of assembly and to demonstrate.

Data collected by the United Nations of indicators of human development in the early 1990s show that a high level of social development was achieved in the former socialist planned economies of Central and Eastern Europe and the Commonwealth of Independent States (CEE/CIS). Life expectancy in the CEE/CIS area in the period 1985-1990 was 68 years. while for the countries of the Organization for Economic Cooperation and Development (OECD) it was 75 years. Infant mortality in the CEE/CIS area was 25 for every 1.000 live births in 1990. compared to 13 in the OECD area. In terms of education. the two areas enjoyed universal adult literacy and full enrolment of children in primary and secondary schools. For tertiary education. the CEE/CIS had 2.600 university students per 100.000 population. while in the OECD the comparable figure was 3.550 students. Overall enrolment at primary. secondary and tertiary levels was 75 percent in the CEE/CIS region and 82 percent in the OECD countries.

On housing the main problem was over-crowding rather than homelessness in the socialist planned economies. In the USSR the area of residential accommodation was 15.5 square meters per person by 1990 in urban areas but 15 percent of the population were without their own separate accommodation and had to live in communal apartments according to the 1989 census. Housing was generally of good quality in both the CEE/CIS region and in the OECD countries: 98 and 99 percent of the population in the OECD countries had access to safe drinking water and improved sanitation respectively. compared to 93 and 85 percent in the CEE/CIS area by 1990.

Unemployment did not exist officially in the socialist planned economies. though there were people between jobs and a fraction of unemployable people as a result of illness. disability or other problems. such as alcoholism. The proportion of people changing jobs was between 6 and 13 percent of the labour force a year according to employment data during the 1970s and 1980s in Central and Eastern Europe and the USSR. Labour exchanges were established in the USSR in 1967 to help enterprises re-allocate workers and provide information on job vacancies. Compulsory unemployment insurance schemes operated in Bulgaria. Eastern Germany and Hungary but the numbers claiming support as a result of losing their job through no fault of their own numbered a few hundred a year.

By 1988 GDP per person. measured at purchasing power parity in US dollars. was $7.519 in Russia and $6.304 for the USSR. The highest income was to be found in Slovenia ($10.663) and Estonia ($9.078) and the lowest in Albania ($1.386) and Tajikistan ($2.730). Across the whole CEE/CIS area. GDP per person was estimated at $6.162. This compared to the USA with $20.651 and $16.006 for Germany in the same year. For the OECD area as a whole estimated GDP per person was $14.385. Thus. on the basis of IMF estimates. national income (GDP) per person in the CEE/CIS area was 43 percent of that in the OECD area.

ECONOMIC PROBLEMS OF THE SOCIALIST PLANNED ECONOMIES

From the 1960s onwards. CMEA countries. beginning with Eastern Germany. attempted "intensive" growth strategies. aiming to raise the productivity of labour and capital. However. in practice this meant that investment was shifted towards new branches of industry. including the electronics. computing. automotive and nuclear power sectors. leaving the traditional heavy industries dependent upon older technologies. Despite the rhetoric about modernization. innovation remained weak as enterprise managers preferred routine production that was easier to plan and brought them predictable bonuses. Embargoes on high technology exports organised through the US-supported CoComarrangement hampered technology transfer. Enterprise managers also ignored inducements to introduce labour-saving measures as they wished to retain a reserve of personnel to be available to meet their production target by working at top speed when supplies were delayed.

Under conditions of "taut planning". the economy was expected to produce a volume of output higher than the reported capacity of enterprises and there was no "slack" in the system. Enterprises faced a resource constraint and hoarded labour and other inputs and avoided sub-contracting intermediate production activities. preferring to retain the work in-house.

The enterprise. according to the theory promulgated by János Kornai. was constrained by its resources not by the demand for its goods and services; nor was it constrained by its finances since the government was not likely to shut it down if it failed to meet its financial targets. Enterprises in socialist planned economies operated within a "soft" budget constraint. unlike enterprises in capitalist market economies which are demand-constrained and operate within "hard" budget constraints. as they face bankruptcy if their costs exceed their sales. As all producers were working in a resource-constrained economy they were perpetually in short supply and the shortages could never be eliminated. leading to chronic disruption of production schedules. The effect of this was to preserve a high level of employment.

As the supply of consumer goods failed to match rising incomes (because workers still received their pay even if they were not fully productive). household savings accumulated. indicating. in the official terminology. "postponed demand". Western economists called this "monetary overhang" or "repressed inflation". Prices on the black market were several times higher than in the official price-controlled outlets. reflecting the scarcity and possible illegality of the sale of these items. Therefore although consumer welfare was reduced by shortages. the prices households paid for their regular consumption were lower than would have been the case had prices been set at market-clearing levels.

Over the course of the 1980s it became clear that the CMEA area was "in crisis". although it remained viable economically and was not expected to collapse. The "extensive" growth model was retarding growth in the CMEA as a whole. with member countries dependent upon supplies of raw materials from the USSR and upon the Soviet market for sales of goods. The decline in growth rates reflected a combination of diminishing returns to capital accumulation and low innovation as well as micro-economic inefficiencies. which a high rate of saving and investment was unable to counter.

The CMEA was supposed to ensure coordination of national plans but it failed even to develop a common methodology for planning which could be adopted by its member states. As each member state was reluctant to give up national self-sufficiency the CMEA's efforts to encourage specialization was thwarted. There were very few joint ventures and therefore little intra-enterprise technology transfer and trade. which in the capitalist world was often undertaken by trans-national corporations.

The International Bank for Economic Cooperation had no means of converting a country's trade surplus into an option to buy goods and services from other CMEA members.

TRANSITION TO MARKET ECONOMIES

After the dissolution of the Soviet Union and the Eastern bloc. many of the remaining socialist states presiding over centrally planned economies began introducing reforms that shifted their economies away from centralized planning. In Central and Eastern Europe and the USSR the transition from a planned economy to a market economy was accompanied by the transformation of the socialist mode of production to a capitalist mode of production. In Asia (China. Laos. North Korea and Vietnam) and in Cuba market mechanisms were introduced by the ruling communist parties and the planning system was reformed without systemic transformation.The transformation from socialism to capitalism involved a political shift: from a people's democracy with a constitutionally entrenched "leading role" for the communist and workers' parties in society to a liberal representative democracy with a separation of legislative. executive and judicial authorities and centres of private power that can act as a brake on the state's activity.

Vietnam adopted an economic model it formally titled the *socialist-oriented market economy*. This economic system is a form of mixed-economy consisting of state. private. co-operative and individual enterprises coordinated by the market mechanism. This system is intended to be transitional stage in the development of socialism.

TRANSITION ECONOMIES

The transformation of an economic system from a socialist planned economy to a capitalist market economy in Central and Eastern Europe. the former Soviet Union and Mongolia in the 1990s involved a series of institutional changes.

These included:

- Control over the means of production was removed from the state through privatization and private property rights were re-established.

In several countries property was restored to its former owners or their legal successors. If the actual property could not be returned the former owners received compensation. This occurred in Eastern Germany. Czechoslovakia. Hungary and Estonia. In all the countries of the Commonwealth of Independent States. the government decided against restoration or compensation on the grounds that too much time had elapsed and in many cases compensation had already been made through bilateral treaties between the USSR and foreign governments representing the former owners. Voucher privatization in which citizens and workers in the enterprises received free or cheap shares was undertaken in most of the transition economies.

- The decision-making system was de-centralized through the ending of central planning and the privatization of enterprises. Work collectives and trade unions lost much of their influence in enterprise decision-making.
- Markets became the dominant coordination mechanism following price liberalization and the de-control of foreign trade that permitted more or less unrestricted importation of goods in 1990/92. Queues at retail outlets disappeared as did hoarded inventories at factories. Stock exchanges were established between 1990 and 1995. Anti-monopoly legislation was introduced. As workers lost their jobs or found their wages unpaid. informal labour markets sprang up along certain streets. particularly for construction trades.
- The incentive system was modified by the legalization of private enterprise and alteration to employment laws. A large informal sphere developed estimated at comprising 21 to 30 percent of official calculations of GDP.
- The organizational forms prevailing in the socialist planned economies were restructured by breaking up vertically-integrated industrial and agricultural concerns and closing non-viable undertakings. The hardening of enterprise budget constraints was more significant in driving industrial restructuring than privatization according to some studies.
- The distribution system became more unequal as price controls on necessities were removed fuelling the growth of poverty among people on fixed incomes such as pensioners and the unemployed. Redistributive measures through taxation and social safety nets proved unable to counteract the growth of poverty and. at the other end of the income scale. the emergence of a rich business elite.
- The public choice mechanism was overhauled to rescind the communist party's leading role and introduce a liberal constitution entrenching civil rights and representative democracy in almost all transition economies except Belarus. Turkmenistan and Uzbekistan.

PEOPLE'S REPUBLIC OF CHINA

China embraced a socialist planned economy after the Communist victory in its Civil War. Private property and private ownership of capital were abolished. and various forms of wealth made subject to state control or to workers' councils.

The Chinese economy broadly adopted a similar system of production quotas and full employment by fiat to the Russian model. The Great Leap Forward saw a remarkably large-scale experiment with rapid collectivisation of agriculture. and other ambitious goals. Results were less than expected. (*e.g.*. there were food shortages and mass starvation) and the programme was abandoned after three years.

In recent decades China has opened its economy to foreign investment and to market-based trade. and has continued to experience strong economic growth. It has carefully managed the transition from a socialist planned economy to a market economy. officially referred to as the *socialist commodity market economy*. which has been likened to capitalism by some outside observers. As a result. centralized economic planning has little relevance in China today.

The current Chinese economic system is characterised by state ownership combined with a strong private sector that privately owned enterprises that generate about 33per cent(People's Daily Online 2005) to over 50per cent of GDP in 2005. with a BusinessWeek article estimating 70per cent of GDP. a figure that might be even greater considering theChengbao system. Some western observers note that the private sector is likely underestimated by state officials in calculation of GDP due to its propensity to ignore small private enterprises that are not registered.

Most of the state and private sectors of economy are governed by free market practices. including a stock exchange for trading equity. The free-market is the arbitrator for most economic activity. which is left to the management of both state and private firms. A significant amount of privately owned firms exist. especially in the consumer service sector.

The state sector is concentrated in the 'commanding heights' of the economy with a growing private sector engaged primarily in commodity production and light industry. Centralized directive planning based on mandatory output requirements and production quotas has been superseded by the free-market mechanism for most of the economy and directive planning is utilised in some large state industries.

A major difference from the old planned economy is the privatization of state institutions. 150 state-owned enterprises remain and report directly to the central government. most having a number of subsidiaries. By 2008. these state-owned corporations have became increasingly dynamic largely contributing to the increase in revenue for the state. The state-sector led the economic recovery process and increased economic growth in 2009 after the financial crises.

This type of economic system is defended from a Marxist perspective which states that a socialist planned economy can only be possible after first establishing the necessary comprehensive commodity market economy. letting it fully develop until it exhausts its historical stage and gradually transforms itself into a planned economy. Proponents of this model distinguish themselves from market socialists who believe that economic planning is unattainable. undesirable or ineffective at distributing goods. viewing the market as the solution rather than a temporary phase in development of a socialist planned economy.

OTHER SOCIALIST STATES

The Socialist Republic of Vietnam has pursued similar economic reforms. though less extensive. which have resulted in a socialist-oriented market economy. a mixed economy in which the state plays a dominant role intended to be a transitional phase in establishment of a socialist economy.

The Republic of Cuba. under the leadership of Raul Castro. has begun to encourage co-operatives and self-employment in a move to reduce the central role of state enterprise and state management over the economy. with the goal of building a co-operative form of socialism.

SOCIAL DEMOCRATIC MIXED ECONOMIES

Many of the industrialized. open countries of Western Europe experimented with one form of social democratic mixed economies or another during the 20th century. These include Britain (mixed economy and welfare state) from 1945 to 1979. France (state capitalism and indicative planning) from 1945 to 1982 under dirigisme. Sweden (social democratic welfare state) and Norway (state capitalist mixed economy) to the present. They can be regarded as social democratic experiments. because they universally retained a wage-based economy and private ownership and control of the decisive means of production.

Nevertheless. these western European countries tried to restructure their economies away from a purely private capitalist model. Variations range from social democratic welfare states. such as in Sweden. to mixed economies where a major percentage of GDP comes from the state sector. such as in Norway. which ranks among the highest countries in quality of life and equality of opportunity for its citizens. Elements of these efforts persist throughout Europe. even if they have repealed some aspects of public control and ownership.

They are typically characterised by:

- Nationalization of key industries. such as mining. oil. steel. energy and transportation. A common model is for a sector to be taken over by the state and then one or morepublicly owned corporations set up for its day-to-day running. Advantages of nationalization include: the ability of the state to direct investment in key industries. the distribution of state profits from nationalized industries for the overall national good. the ability to direct producers to social rather than market goals. greater control of the industries by and for the workers. and the benefits and burdens of publicly funded research and development are extended to the wider populace.

- Redistribution of wealth. through both tax and spending policies that aim to reduce economic inequalities. Social democracies typically employ various forms ofprogressive taxation regarding wage and business income. wealth. inheritance. capital gains and property. On the spending side. a set of social policies typically provides free access to public services such as education. health care and child care. while subsidized access to housing. food. pharmaceutical goods. water supply. waste management and electricity is also common.
- Social security schemes where workers contribute to a mandatory public insurance programme. The insurance typically include monetary provisions for retirement pensions and survivor benefits. permanent and temporary disabilities. unemployment and parental leave. Unlike private insurance. governmental schemes are based on public statutes and not contracts. so that contributions and benefits may change in time and are based on solidarity among participants. Its funding is done on an ongoing basis. without direct relationship with future liabilities.
- Minimum wages. employment protection and trade union recognition rights for the benefit of workers. The objectives of these policies are to guarantee living wages and help produce full employment. There are a number of different models of trade union protection which evolved. but they all guarantee the right of workers to form unions. negotiate benefits and participate in strikes. Germany. for instance. appointed union representatives at high levels in all corporations and had much less industrial strife than the UK. whose laws encouraged strikes rather than negotiation.
- National planning for industrial development.
- Demand management in a Keynesian fashion to help ensure economic growth and employment.

STATE CAPITALISM

Various state capitalist economies. which consist of large commercial state enterprises that operate according to the laws of capitalism and pursue profits. have evolved in countries that have been influenced by various elected socialist political parties and their economic reforms. While these policies and reforms did not change the fundamental aspect of capitalism. and non-socialist elements within these countries supported or often implemented many of these reforms themselves. the result has been a set of economic institutions that were at least partly influenced by socialist ideology.

SINGAPORE

Singapore pursued a state-led model of economic development under the People's Action Party. which initially adopted a Leninist approach to politics and a broad socialist model of economic development. The PAP was initially a member of the Socialist International. Singapore's economy is dominated by state-owned enterprises and government-linked companies through Temasek Holdings. which generate 60per cent of Singapore's GDP. Temasek Holdings operates like any other company in a market economy. Managers of the holding are rewarded according to profits with the explicit intention to cultivate an ownership mind-set.

The state also provides substantial public housing. free education. health and recreational services. as well as comprehensive public transportation. Today Singapore is often characterised as having a state capitalist economy that combines economic planning with the free-market. While government-linked companies generate a majority of Singapore's GDP. moderate state planning in the economy has been reduced in recent decades.

INDIA

After gaining independence from Britain. India adopted a broadly socialist-inspired approach to economic growth. Like other countries with a democratic transition to a mixed economy. it did not abolish private property in capital. India proceeded by nationalizing various large privately run firms. creating state-owned enterprises and redistributingincome through progressive taxation in a manner similar to social democratic Western European nations than to planned economies such as the USSR or China. Today India is often characterised as having a free-market economy that combines economic planning with the free-market. It did however adopt a very firm focus on national planning with a series of broad Five-Year Plans.

PARIS COMMUNE

The Paris Commune was considered to be a prototype mode of economic and political organization for a future socialist society by Karl Marx. Private property in the means of production was abolished so that individuals and co-operative associations of producers owned productive property and introduced democratic measures where elected officials received no more in compensation than the average worker and could be recalled at any time. Anarchists also participated actively in the establishment of the Paris Commune. George Woodcock manifests that "a notable contribution to the activities of the

Commune and particularly to the organization of public services was made by members of various anarchist factions. including the mutualists Courbet. Longuet. and Vermorel. the libertarian collectivists Varlin. Malon. and Lefrangais. and the bakuninistsElie and Elisée Reclus and Louise Michel.

SOCIAL OWNERSHIP AND PEER-TO-PEER PRODUCTION

Various forms of socialist organization based on co-operative decision making. workplace democracy and in some cases. production directly for use. have existed within the broader context of the capitalist mode of production since the Paris Commune. New forms of socialist institutional arrangements began to take form at the end of the 20th century with the advancement and proliferation of the internet and other tools that allow for collaborative decision-making.

Michel Bauwens identifies the emergence of the open software movement and peer-to-peer production as an emergent alternative mode of production to the capitalist economy that is based on collaborative self-management. common ownership of resources. and the (direct) production of use-values through the free cooperation of producers who have access to distributed capital.

Commons-based peer production generally involves developers who produce goods and services with no aim to profit directly. but freely contribute to a project relying upon an open common pool of resources and software code. In both cases. production is carried out directly for use — software is produced solely for their use-value.

Wikipedia. being based on collaboration and cooperation and a freely associated individuals. has been cited as a template for how socialism might operate. This is a modern example of what the Paris Commune — a template for possible future organization — was to Marx in his time.

SOCIALIST FEDERAL REPUBLIC OF YUGOSLAVIA

Yugoslavia pursued a socialist economy based on autogestion or worker-self management. Rather than implementing a centrally planned economy. Yugoslavia developed a market socialist system where enterprises and firms were socially owned rather than publicly owned by the state. In these organizations. the management was elected directly by the workers in each firm. and were later organised according to Edvard Kardelj's theory of associated labour.

SELF-MANAGED ENTERPRISES

The Mondragon Corporation. a federation of cooperatives in the Basque region of Spain. organises itself as an employee-owned. employee-managed enterprise. Similar styles of decentralised management. which embrace cooperation and collaboration in place of traditional hierarchical management structures. have been adopted by various private corporations such as Cisco Systems. inc. But unlike Mondragon. Cisco remains firmly under private ownership. More fundamentally. employee-owned. self-managed enterprises still operate within the broader context of capitalism and are subject to the accumulation of capital and profit-loss mechanism.

ANARCHIST SPAIN

In Spain. the national anarcho-syndicalist trade union Confederación Nacional del Trabajo initially refused to join a popular front electoral alliance. and abstention by CNT supporters led to a right wing election victory. But in 1936. the CNT changed its policy and anarchist votes helped bring the popular front back to power. Months later. the former ruling class responded with an attempted coup causing the Spanish Civil War (1936–1939). In response to the army rebellion. an anarchist-inspired movement of peasants and workers. supported by armed militias. took control of Barcelona and of large areas of rural Spain where they collectivised the land. But even before the fascist victory in 1939. the anarchists were losing ground in a bitter struggle with the Stalinists. who controlled the distribution of military aid to the Republican cause from the Soviet Union.

The events known as the Spanish Revolution was a workers' social revolution that began during the outbreak of the Spanish Civil War in 1936 and resulted in the widespread implementation of anarchist and more broadly libertarian socialist organizational principles throughout various portions of the country for two to three years. primarily Catalonia. Aragon. Andalusia. and parts of the Levante. Much of Spain's economy was put under worker control; in anarchist strongholds like Catalonia. the figure was as high as 75per cent. but lower in areas with heavy Communist Party of Spain influence. as the Soviet-allied party actively resisted attempts at collectivization enactment. Factories were run through worker committees. agrarian areas became collectivised and run as libertarian communes. Anarchist historian Sam Dolgoff estimated that about eight million people participated directly or at least indirectly in the Spanish Revolution. which he claimed "came closer to realizing the ideal of the free stateless society on a vast scale than any other revolution in history."

CRITICISMS

Criticism of socialist economics comes from market economists. including the classicals. Neo-classicals and Austrians. as well as from some anarchist economists. Besides this. some socialist economic theories are criticized by other socialists. Libertarian socialist. mutualist. and market socialist economists. for example. criticize centralized economic planning and propose participatory economics and decentralized socialism. Market economists generally criticise socialism for eliminating the free market and its price signals. which they consider necessary for rational economic calculation. They also consider that it causes lack of incentive. They believe that these problems lead to a slower rate of technological advance and a slower rate of growth of GDP.

Austrian school economists. such as Friedrich Hayek and Ludwig Von Mises. have argued that the elimination of private ownership of the means of production would inevitably create worse economic conditions for the general populace than those that would be found in market economies. They argue that without the price signals of the market. it is impossible to calculate rationally how to allocate resources. Mises called this the economic calculation problem. Polish economist Oskar Lange and Abba Lerner responded to Mises' argument by developing the Lange Model during the Economic calculation debate. The Lange model argues that an economy in which all production is performed by the state. where there is a functioning price mechanism. has similar properties to a market economy under perfect competition. in that it achieves Pareto efficiency.

The Neo-classical view is that there is a lack of incentive. not a lack of information in a planned economy. They argue that within a socialist planned economy there is a lack of incentive to act on information. Therefore. the crucial missing element is not so much information as the Austrian school argued. as it is the motivation to act on information.

PLANNED ECONOMY

A planned economy is the economic system in which decisions regarding production and investment are embodied in a plan formulated by a central authority. usually by a public body such as a government agency. Thus it may be termed a "command economy". Although a planned economy may be based on either centralized or decentralized forms of economic planning. it usually refers to a centrally planned economy. Central planning aims to improve productivity and coordination by enabling planners to take advantage of better information achieved through the consolidation of economic resources when making decisions regarding investment and the allocation of economic inputs.

Planned economies are usually categorized as a particular variant of socialism. and have historically been supported by and implemented by Marxist-Leninist socialist states. Analysts argue that Soviet-type central planning did not actually constitute a planned economy in that a comprehensive and binding plan did not guide production and investment; therefore the termadministrative command economy emerged as a more accurate designation for the economic system that existed in the formerSoviet Union and Eastern bloc. highlighting the role of centralized hierarchical administrative decision-making in the absence of popular and democratic local market-based oversight as the essential coordinating feature of these economies. A planned economy may consist of state-owned enterprises. private enterprises directed by the state. or a combination of both. Though "planned economy" and "command economy" are often used as synonyms. some make the distinction that under a command economy. the means of production are publicly owned. That is. a planned economy is "an economic system in which the government controls and regulates production. distribution. prices. etc." but a command economy. while also having this type of regulation. necessarily has substantial public ownership of industry. Therefore. command economies are planned economies. but not necessarily the reverse.

Planned economies are held in contrast to unplanned economies. such as the market economy and proposed self-managed economy. where production. distribution. pricing. and investment decisions are made by autonomous firms based upon their individual interests rather than upon a macroeconomic plan. Less extensive forms of planned economies include those that useindicative planning as components of a market-based or mixed economy. in which the state employs "influence. subsidies. grants. and taxes. but does not compel." This latter is sometimes referred to as a "planned market economy". In some instances. the term planned economy has been used to refer to national economic development plans and state-directed investment in market economies.

Beginning in the 1980s and 1990s. many governments presiding over planned economies began a process of marketization. moving Towards market-based economies by allowing individual enterprises to make the decisions regarding management and pricing. granting autonomy to state enterprises. and ultimately expanding the scope of the private sector through privatization. Limited free market activity gradually entered the Eastern Bloc during the 1980s. on January 1. 1992 the newly independentRussian Federation abolished the Soviet price controls.

Although most economies today are market-based mixed economies (which are partially planned). fully planned economies of the Soviet-type continue to exist (as of 2013) in Cuba. North Korea and Laos.

The possibility of a digital planned economy was explored by Chile with the creation of Project Cybersyn.

ECONOMIC PLANNING VERSUS COMMAND ECONOMIES

Economic planning in general is defined as a mechanism for the allocation of inputs based on a direct allocation. held in contrast with the market mechanism. which is based on indirect allocation. Economic planning may be carried out in a decentralized. distributed or centralized manner depending on the specific organization of economic institutions. An economy based on economic planning (either through the state. an association of worker cooperatives or another economic entity that has jurisdiction over the means of production) appropriates its resources as needed. so that allocation comes in the form of internal transfers rather than market transactions involving the purchasing of assets by one government agency or firm by another. In a traditional model of planning. decision-making would be carried out by workers and consumers on the enterprise-level.

This is contrasted with the concept of a centrally planned. or a *command* economy. where most of the economy is planned by a central authority and organised in a top-down administrative model. where decisions regarding investment and production output requirements are decided upon by planners at the top in the chain of command. with little input from lower levels of the chain of command. Advocates of economic planning have sometimes been staunch critics of command economies and centralised planning. For example. Leon Trotsky believed that central planners. regardless of their intellectual capacity. operated without the input and participation of the millions of people who participate in the economy and understand/respond to local conditions and changes in the economy. and therefore would be unable to effectively coordinate all economic activity.

Another key difference is that command economies are usually authoritarian in nature. whereas economic planning in general can be either participatory and democratic or authoritarian. Indicative planning is a form of planning in market economies that directs the economy through incentive-based methods. Economic planning can be practiced in a decentralized manner through different government authorities. For example. in some predominately market-oriented and mixed economies. the state utilises economic planning in strategic industries such as the aerospace industry. Mixed economies usually employ macroeconomic planning. while micro-economic affairs are left to the market and price system.

Another example of this is the utilization of dirigisme. both of which were practiced in France and Great Britain after the Second World War. Swedish public housing models were planned by the government in a similar fashion as urban planning.

A planned economy may consist of state enterprises. cooperative enterprises. or private enterprises. or a combination of different enterprise types coordinated through some form of planning. Some make the distinction that in a "command economy". enterprises need not follow a comprehensive plan or be coordinated through planning - the dominant coordinating mechanism comes in the form of a command from higher authorities. That is. a planned economy is "an economic system in which the government controls and regulates production. distribution. prices. etc." but a command economy. while also having this type of regulation. necessarily has substantial public ownership of industry.Therefore. command economies are planned economies. but not necessarily the reverse.

RELATIONSHIP WITH SOCIALIST ECONOMICS

While socialism is not equivalent to economic planning or to the concept of a planned economy. an influential conception of socialism involves the replacement of capital markets with some form of economic planning in order to achieve *ex ante* coordination of the economy. The goal of such an economic system would be to achieve conscious control over the economy by the population. specifically. so that the use of the surplus product is controlled by the producers. The specific forms of planning proposed for socialism and their feasibility are the subject of debate within the broader socialist calculation debate.

TRANSITION FROM A PLANNED ECONOMY TO A MARKET ECONOMY

The shift from a command economy to a market economy has proven to be difficult; in particular. there were no theoretical guides for doing so before the 1990s. One transition from a command economy to a market economy that manyconsider successful is that of the People's Republic of China.

By contrast. the Soviet Union's transition was much more problematic. and its successor republics faced a sharp decline in GDP during the early 1990s. One of the suggested causes is that under Soviet planning. price ceilings created major problems (shortages. queuing for bread. households hoarding money). which made the transition to an unplanned economy more difficult. While the transition to a market economy proved difficult. many of the post-Soviet states have been experiencing strong. resource-based economic growth in recent years. though the levels vary substantially. However. a majority of the former Soviet Republics have not yet reached pre-collapse levels of economic development.

Still. most of the economic hardship that struck many of the former East Bloc countries and the post-Soviet states comes from the programme of shock therapy. The idea behind this programme is to convert from a centrally planned economy to a market economy in a short space of time. This means mass-scale privatization. budget cuts and liberalization of economy and finance regulations. This shock therapy programme was implemented in several former communist states like Poland and Russia. Wealth inequality continues to be extremely severe in the rapidly privatized post-soviet countries. People in poverty have seen an approximately 50per cent reduction in their income. compared to late soviet era income statistics. Much of the acquired wealth is attributed to the political nature of the respective privatization processes.

ADVANTAGES OF ECONOMIC PLANNING

The government can harness land. labour. and capital to serve the economic objectives of the state. Consumer demand can be restrained in favour of greater capital investment for economic development in a desired pattern. The state can begin building a heavy industry at once in an underdeveloped economy without waiting years for capital to accumulate through the expansion of light industry. and without reliance on external financing. This is what happened in the Soviet Union during the 1930s when the government forced the share of GNP dedicated to private consumption from eighty percent to fifty percent. As a result. the Soviet Union experienced massive growth in heavy industry.

DISADVANTAGES OF ECONOMIC PLANNING

INEFFICIENT RESOURCE DISTRIBUTION: SURPLUS AND SHORTAGE

Critics of planned economies argue that planners cannot detect consumer preferences. shortages. and surpluses with sufficient accuracy and therefore cannot efficiently co-ordinate production (in a market economy. a free price system is intended to serve this purpose). This difficulty was notably written about by economists Ludwig von Mises andFriedrich Hayek. both of whom called it the "economic calculation problem". These opponents of central planning argue that the only way to satisfy individuals who have a constantly changing hierarchy of needs. and are the only ones to possess their particular individual's circumstances. is by allowing those with the most knowledge of their needs to have it in their power to use their resources in a competing marketplace to meet the needs of the most amount of consumers. most efficiently. This phenomenon is recognised as spontaneous order. Additionally. misallocation of resources would naturally ensue by redirecting capital away from individuals with direct knowledge and circumventing it into markets where a coercive monopoly influences behaviour. ignoring market signals. According to Tibor R. Machan. "Without a market in which allocations can be made in obedience to the law of supply and demand. it is difficult or impossible to funnel resources with respect to actual human preferences and goals."

SUPPRESSION OF ECONOMIC DEMOCRACY AND SELF-MANAGEMENT

Economist Robin Hahnel notes that. even if central planning overcame its inherent inhibitions of incentives and innovation. it would nevertheless be unable to maximize economic democracy and self-management. which he believes are concepts that are more intellectually coherent. consistent and just than mainstream notions of economic freedom. Says Hahnel. "Combined with a more democratic political system. and redone to closer approximate a best case version. centrally planned economies no doubt would have performed better. But they could never have delivered economic self-management. they would always have been slow to innovate as apathy and frustration took their inevitable toll. and they would always have been susceptible to growing inequities and inefficiencies as the effects of differential economic power grew. Under central planning neither planners. managers. nor workers had incentives to promote the social economic interest. Nor did impeding markets for final goods to the planning system enfranchise consumers in meaningful ways. But central planning would have been incompatible with economic democracy even if it had overcome its information and incentive liabilities. And the truth is that it survived as long as it did only because it was propped up by unprecedented totalitarian political power."

ECONOMIC INSTABILITY

Studies of Eastern European planned economies in the 1950s and 1960s by both American and Eastern European economists found that. contrary to expectations. they showed greater fluctuations in output than market economies during the same period.

FICTIONAL PORTRAYALS OF PLANNED ECONOMIES

The 1888 novel *Looking Backward* by Edward Bellamy depicts a fictional planned economy in a United States around the year 2000 which has become a socialist utopia.

The World State in Aldous Huxley's *Brave New World* and Airstrip One in George Orwell's *Nineteen Eighty Four* are both fictional examples of command economies. albeit with diametrically opposed aims: The former is a consumer economy designed to engender productivity while the latter is a shortage economy designed as an agent of totalitarian social control. Airstrip One is organised by the intentionally sarcastically named Ministry of Plenty. Other literary portrayals of planned economies were Yevgeny Zamyatin's *We*. which was an influence on Orwell's work. Like *Nineteen Eighty Four*. Ayn Rand's dystopian story *Anthem* was also an artistic portrayal of a command economy that was influenced by *We*. The difference is that it was a primitivist planned economy. as opposed to the advanced technology of *We* or *Brave New World*.

DECENTRALIZED PLANNING (ECONOMICS)

A decentralized-planned economy or decentrally-planned economy (occasionally horizontally-planned economy) is a type of economic system based on decentralized economic planning. in which decision-making is distributed amongst various economic agents or localized within production units. Decentralized planning is held in contrast to centralized planning where economic information is aggregated and used to formulate a plan for production. investment and resource allocation by a central authority. Decentralised planning can take shape both in the context of a mixed economy as well as in a post-capitalist economic system. Usually this implies some form of democratic decision-making within the economy or within firms. in the form of economic democracy or industrial democracy. Alternatively. computer-based or computer-managed forms of decentralized coordination between economic enterprises have been proposed by various economists and computer scientists.

Recent proposals for decentralized-economic planning have used the term participatory planning to highlight the cooperative and democratic character of this system and to contrast it with centralized planning associated with the former Soviet Union. Proponents present decentralized and participatory economic planning as an alternative to market socialism for a post-capitalist society. Decentralized-planning has been proposed as a basis for socialism. and has been advocated by democratic socialists andanarchists who advocate a non-market form of socialism while rejecting Soviet-type central planning.

MODELS

CYBERNETICS

The use of computers to coordinate production in an optimal fashion has been proposed for socialist economies. The economistOskar Lange argued that the computer is more efficient than the market process at solving the multitude of simultaneous equations required for allocating economic inputs efficiently (either in terms of physical quantities or monetary prices).

The 1970 Chilean computer-controlled planned economy cybersyn was pioneered by Salvador Allende's socialist government. in an attempt to move towards decentralised planning with the experimental cyberfolk component.

NEGOTIATED COORDINATION

Economist Pat Devine has created a model of coordination called "negotiated coordination". which is based upon social ownership by those affected by the use of the assets involved. with decisions made by those at the most localised level of production.

PARTICIPATORY PLANNING

The planning structure of a decentralized planned economy is generally based on a consumers council and producer council (or jointly. a distributive cooperative). which is sometimes called a consumers' cooperative. Producers and consumers. or their representatives. negotiate the quality and quantity of what is to be produced. This structure is central to participatory economics. guild socialism. and economic theories related to anarchism.

SIMILAR CONCEPTS IN PRACTICE

DECENTRALISED PLANNING IN KERALA AND INDIA

Some decentralised participation in economic planning has been implemented in various regions and states in India. most notably in Kerala. Local level planning agencies assess the needs of people who are able to give their direct input through the Gram Sabhas (village-based institutions) and the planners subsequently seek to plan accordingly.

COMMUNITY PARTICIPATORY PLANNING

The United Nations has developed local projects that promote participatory planning on a community level. Members of communities take decisions regarding community development directly.

POLITICAL ADVOCACY

Decentralised planning has been a feature of socialist and anarchist economics. Variations of decentralized planning include participatory economics. economic democracy andindustrial democracy. and have been promoted by various political groups. most notably libertarian socialists. guild socialists. Marxists. anarchists and democratic socialists.

During the Spanish Revolution some areas. where anarchist and libertarian socialist influence through the CNT and UGT was extensive. particularly rural regions. were run on the basis of decentralised planning resembling the principles laid out by Diego Abad de Santillan in the book *After the Revolution*.

ECONOMIC DEMOCRACY

Economic democracy or stakeholder democracy is a socioeconomic philosophy that proposes to shift decision-making power from corporate managers and corporate shareholders to a larger group of public stakeholders that includes workers.

Customers. suppliers. neighbors and the broader public. No single definition or approach encompasses economic democracy. but most proponents claim that modern property relations externalize costs. subordinate the general well-being to private profit. and deny the polity a democratic voice in economic policy decisions. In addition to these moral concerns. economic democracy makes practical claims. such as that it can compensate for capitalism's inherent effective demand gap.

Classical liberals argue that ownership and control over the means of production belongs to private firms and can only be sustained by means of consumer choice. exercised daily in the marketplace. "The capitalistic social order". they claim. therefore. "is an economic democracy in the strictest sense of the word". Critics of this claim point out that consumers only vote on the value of the*product* when they make a purchase; they are not participating in the management of firms. voting on decisions relating to investment and how the profits are to be used. Proponents of economic democracy generally argue that modern capitalism periodically results in economic crises characterized by deficiency of effective demand. as society is unable to earn enough income to purchase its output production.

Corporate monopoly of common resources typically creates artificial scarcity. resulting in socio-economic imbalances that restrict workers from access to economic opportunity and diminish consumer purchasing power. Economic democracy has been proposed as a component of larger socioeconomic ideologies. as a stand-alone theory. and as a variety of reform agendas. For example. as a means to securing full economic rights. it opens a path to full political rights. defined as including the former. Both market and non-market theories of economic democracy have been proposed. As a reform agenda. supporting theories and real-world examples range from decentralization and economic liberalization to democratic cooperatives. public banking. fair trade. and the regionalization offood production and currency.

DEFICIENCY OF EFFECTIVE DEMAND

According to many analysts. deficiency of effective demand is the most fundamental economic problem. That is. modern society does not earn enough income to purchase its output. For example. geographer David Harvey claims. "Workers spending their wages is one source of effective demand. but the total wage bill is always less than the total capital in circulation (otherwise there would be no profit). so the purchase of wage goods that sustain daily life (even with a suburban lifestyle) is never sufficient for the profitable sale of the total output." While balanced mixed economies have existed briefly throughout history. veteran Project Manager for the U.S. Treasury Department. Richard C. Cook. and other critics claim that command economies are predominate. citing state capitalism and imperialism as related. As common resources are monopolized by imperial centers of wealth and power. conditions of scarcity are imposed artificially upon the majority. resulting in large-scale socio-economic imbalance.

In the Georgist view of any economic system. "wealth" includes all material things produced by labour for the satisfaction of human desires and having exchange value. Land.labour and capital are generally considered the essential factors in producing wealth. Land includes all natural opportunities and forces. Labour includes all human exertion. Capitalincludes the portion of wealth devoted to producing more wealth. While the income of any individual might include proceeds from any combination of these three sources—land. labour. and capital are generally considered mutually exclusive factors in economic models of the production and distribution of wealth. According to Henry George. "People seek to satisfy their desires with the least exertion". Human beings interact with nature to produce goods and services that other human beings need or desire. The laws andcustoms that govern the relationships among these entities constitute the economic structure of a given society.

Alternately. David Schweickart asserts in his book. After Capitalism: "The structure of a capitalist society consists of three basic components:

- "The bulk of the means of production are privately owned. either directly by individuals or by corporations that are themselves owned by private individuals.
- "Products are exchanged in a market — that is to say. goods and services are bought and sold at prices determined for the most part by competition and not by some governmental pricing authority. Individual enterprises compete with one another in providing goods and services to consumers. each enterprise trying to make a profit. This competition is the primary determinant of prices.
- "Most of the people who work for pay in this society work for other people. who own the means of production. Most working people are 'wage labourers'."

Supply and demand are generally accepted as market functions for establishing prices. Organisations typically endeavor to 1) minimize the cost of production; 2) increase sales; in order to 3) maximize profits. But. according to David Schweickart. if "those who produce the goods and services of society are paid less than their productive contribution". then as consumers they cannot buy all the goods produced. and investor confidence tends to decline. triggering declines in production and employment. Such economic instability stems from a central contradiction: Wages are both a cost of production and an essential source of effective demand (needs or desires backed with purchasing power). resulting in deficiency of effective demand along with a growing interest in economic democracy.

Theory and Practice". Douglas P. Biklen discusses a variety of perspectives on "The Making of Social Problems". One of those views suggests that "writers and organizers who define social problems in terms of social and economic democracy see problems not as the experiences of poor people. but as the relationship of poverty to wealth and exploitation". Biklen states that. according to this viewpoint:

"[C]orporate power. upper class power. uneven distribution of wealth and prejudice cause social problems... [T]he problem is not one of poverty. but of enormous wealth. The problem is not one of gaps or cracks in an otherwise fine system but of a system which perpetuates prejudicial views concerning race. sex. age. and disability. The problem is not one of incompetence but of barriers to education. jobs. and power. Accordingly. as long as there is a deep gulf between social classes. both in terms of wealth. power. and outlook. traditional social programmes will act merely as palliatives to oppression and not as a way of ending large scale human misery. This perspective is. above all. eclectic. It embraces Marx's criticism of social class inequality but is not only a social class analysis. It is anti-racist. but it is not only a theory of race equality. It favors democratic distribution of power but is also an economic theory. It can be called a social and economic democracy perspective."

SAVINGS. INVESTMENT. AND UNEMPLOYMENT

In his 1879 book *Progress and Poverty*. Henry George argued that a majority of wealth created in a "free market" economy was appropriated by land owners and monopoliststhrough economic rents. and that concentration of such unearned wealth was the root cause of poverty. "Behind the abstraction known as 'the market' lurks a set of institutions designed to maximize the wealth and power of the most privileged group of people in the world—the creditor-rentier class of the first world and their junior partners in the third". Schweickart claimed that private savings are not only unnecessary for economic growth. they are often harmful to the overall economy.

In an advanced industrial society. business credit is necessary for a healthy economy. A business that wants to expand production needs to command the labour of others. and money is the default mechanism for exercising this authority. It is often cheaper for a business to borrow capital from a bank than to stockpile cash.

If private savings are loaned out to entrepreneurs who use them to buy raw materials and hire workers. then aggregate demand is not reduced. However. when private savings are not reinvested. the whole economy suffers recession. unemployment. and disappearance of savings which characterize deficiency of effective demand.

In this view. unemployment is not an aberration. indicating any sort of systemic malfunction. Rather. unemployment is a necessary structural feature of capitalism. intended to discipline the workforce. If unemployment is too low. workers make wage demands that either cut into profits to an extent that jeopardizes future investment. or are passed on to consumers. thus generating inflationary instability. Schweickart suggested. "Capitalism cannot be a full-employment economy. except in the very short term. For unemployment is the "invisible hand"—carrying a stick—that keeps the workforce in line." In this view. Adam Smith's "invisible hand" does not seem reliable to guide economic forces on a large scale.

Assuming business credit could come from public sources rather than from private savers. Schweickart and other analysts consider interest payments to private savers both undeserved and unnecessary for economic growth. Moreover. the personal decision to save rather than consume decreases aggregate demand. increases the likelihood of unemployment. and exacerbates the tendency Towards economic stagnation. Since wealthy people tend to save more than poor people. the propensity of an economy to slump because of excess saving becomes ever more acute as a society becomes more affluent. Richard Wilkinson and Kate Pickett suggested that health and social problems are significantly worse in more unequal wealthy nations. They argue that there are "pernicious effects that inequality has on societies: eroding trust. increasing anxiety and illness. (and) encouraging excessive consumption"

MONOPOLY POWER VERSUS PURCHASING POWER

Regarding a social and economic democracy perspective on social problems. Douglas P. Biklen states:

"The theme of profit superseding individual well-being flows through this antimonopoly view of social problems. On the one hand. poor and middle income people find their lives deformed by their Meagre or nonexistent ability to pay for goods and services. Wealthy people. on the other hand. find that their relative position. in terms of wealth and power. grows with their ability to maintain the gulf between social classes. Thus monopolies or concentrated wealth plays a large part in creating social problems. Indeed. one might say. monopolies and policies which promote the former or concentrations of wealth are the problem."

The discipline of economics is largely a study of scarcity management; "the science which studies human behaviour as a relationship between ends and scarce means which have alternative uses". Absent scarcity and alternative uses of available resources. many analysts claim there is no economic problem". For example. Richard C. Cook asserts that conditions of scarcity are artificially maintained by corporate structures that confine abundance to an exclusively entitled minority. In this view. socio-economic imbalance stems not from a failure to manage limited resources in a world of scarcity. but from mismanagement of virtually unlimited abundance and prosperity. American businessman Edward Kellogg (1790–1858) supports this perspective in his 1849 book. *Labour and Other Capital*. where he states:

Money power is not only the most governing and influential. but it is also the most unjust and deceitful of all earthly powers. It entails upon millions excessive toil. poverty and want. while it keeps them ignorant of the cause of their sufferings; for. with their tacit consent. it silently transfers a large share of their earnings into the hands of others. who have never lifted a finger to perform any productive labour.

While he considers these functions a public wrong. Kellogg also asserted the responsibility of the public to find and implement a remedy. Generally considered monopoly power. some view this "public wrong" as the most influential factor in artificial scarcity. For example. Henry George further suggested:

There is in reality no conflict between labour and capital; the true conflict is between labour and monopoly... Abolish the monopoly that forbids men to employ themselves and capital could not possibly oppress labour... [R]emove the cause of that injustice which deprives the laborer of the capital his toil creates and the sharp distinction between capitalist and laborer would. in fact.

cease to exist". For example. many analysts consider invention a "more or less costless store of knowledge. captured by monopoly capital and protected in order to make it secret and a 'rare and scarce commodity'. for sale at monopoly prices. So far as invention is concerned. a price is put on them not because they are scarce but in order to make them scarce to those who want to use them." Patent monopolies raise share prices above tangible labour value. The difference between labour-value and monopoly-value raises goods prices. and is collected as "profit" by intermediaries who have contributed nothing to earn it.

Analysts generally agree that such conditions typically result in a deficiency of effective demand. Labour does not earn enough to buy what enterprises produce. For example. Richard C. Cook maintains that the difference between earnings and prices is typically appropriated by industrial and banking centers of capital through monopoly control of finance and other market resources. Such exclusive entitlement tends to artificially impose conditions of economic scarcity upon the majority of the population. While the accelerating advance of technology. developed and maintained by labour. tends to generate abundance. this process depresses wages as workers are replaced by machines. ironically minimizing the purchasing power of workers in the market. According to Jack Rasmus. author of *The Trillion Dollar Income Shift*. in June 2006. investment bank Goldman Sachs reported: "The most important contribution to the higher profit margins over the past five years has been a decline in Labour's share of national income."

ENCLOSURE OF THE COMMONS

The term "land" typically denotes the "universe of natural opportunities" or "public utilities". generally known as the commons. Artificially restricted access of labour to common resources is generally considered monopoly or enclosure of the commons. Due to the economic imbalance inherently imposed. such monopoly structures tend to be centrally dictated by law. and must be maintained by military force. trade agreements. or both.

In 1911. American journalist Ambrose Bierce defined "land" as:

A part of the earth's surface. considered as property. The theory that land is property subject to private ownership and control is the foundation of modern society.... Carried to its logical conclusion. it means that some have the right to prevent others from living; for the right to own implies the right exclusively to occupy; and in fact laws of trespass are enacted wherever property in land is recognized. It follows that if the whole area of terra firma is owned by A. B and C. there will be no place for D. E. F and G to be born. or. born as trespassers. to exist". In *The Servile State* (1912). Hilaire Belloc referred to the Enclosures Movement when he said. "England was already captured by a wealthy oligarchy before the series of greatindustrial discoveries began". If you sought the accumulated wealth preliminary to launching new industry. "you had to turn to the class which had already monopolized the bulk of the means of production in England. The rich men alone could furnish you with those supplies".

According to Peter Barnes. author of *Capitalism 3.0*. when Adam Smith wrote *The Wealth of Nations* in 1776. the dominant form of business was partnership. in which regional groups of co-workers ran co-owned businesses. From this perspective. many considered the corporate model—stock sold to strangers—inherently prone to fraud. While numerous scandals historically support this dim view of corporate policy. small partnerships could not possibly compete with the aggregate capital generated by corporateeconomies of scale. The greatest advantage of corporations over any other business model is their ability to raise capital from strangers. The corporate model benefits from laws that limit stockholders' liability to the amounts they have invested.

In *A Preface To Economic Democracy*. Robert A. Dahl suggests that agrarian economy and society in the early United States "underwent a revolutionary transformation into a new system of commercial and industrial capitalism that automatically generated vast inequalities of wealth. income. status. and power." Dahl claims that such inequalities result from the "liberty to accumulate unlimited economic resources and to organise economic activity into hierarchically governed enterprises."

THE RISE OF CORPORATIONS AND ENDING LABOUR SHORTAGE

According to author Greg MacLeod. the concept of the corporation originated in Roman times. However. "the modern business corporation evolved radically from its ancient roots into a form with little relation to the purpose as understood by historians of law." John Davis. a legal historian. noted that the precursor of the business corporation was the first monastery. established in the sixth century. the purpose of which was to serve society. Most business corporations before 1900 developed in Great Britain. where they were established by royal charter. with the expectation of contributions to society. Incorporation was a privilege granted in return for service to the crown or the nation. MacLeod goes on to say:

A corporation is considered by the law to exist as a legal person. In the Middle Ages it was called a "persona ficta". This is a very useful way of looking at a business corporation. because it suggests correctly that the corporate person has a certain personality. It has duties and responsibilities vested unto it by the legitimate government or society that fostered it. The corporate person receives great benefits from society – and. in return. it must exercise great responsibilities. One of the most basic responsibilities is job creation. a fundamental need in any society." By the mid-nineteenth century. corporations could live forever. engage in any legal activity. and merge with or acquire other corporations. In 1886. the U.S. Supreme Courtlegally recognised corporations as "persons". entitled under the Fourteenth Amendment to the same protections as living citizens. Unlike average citizens. large corporations had large flows of money at their disposal. With this money they can hire lobbyists. donate copiously to politicians. and sway public opinion.

But. despite Supreme Court rulings. the modern corporation is not a real person. Rather. the publicly traded stock corporation is what Barnes terms an "automaton". explicitly designed to maximize return to its owners. A corporation never sleeps or slows down. It externalizes as many costs as possible. and never reaches an upper limit of profitability. because no such limit has yet been established. As a result. corporations keep getting larger. In 1955. sales of the Fortune 500 accounted for one-third of U.S. gross domestic product. By 2004 they commanded two-thirds. In other words. these few hundred corporations replaced smaller firms organised as partnerships or proprietorships.

Corporations have established a homogeneous global playing field around which they can freely move raw materials. labour. capital. finished products. tax-paying obligations. and profits. Thus. corporate franchise has become a perpetual grant of sovereignty. including immortality. self-government. and limited liability. By the end of the twentieth century. corporate power—both economic and political—stretched worldwide. International agreements not only lowered tariffs but extended corporate property rights and reduced the ability of sovereign nations to regulate corporations.

David Schweickart submits that such "hypermobility of capital" generates economic and political insecurity. "If the search for lower wages comes to dominate the movement of capital. the result will be not only a lowering of worldwide wage disparities (the good to which some economists point) but also a lowering of total global income (a straight-out utilitarian bad)." Jack Rasmus. author of *The War At Home* and *The Trillion Dollar Income Shift*. argues that increasing concentration of corporate power is a cause of the large-scale debt. unemployment. and poverty characteristics of economic recession and depression.

According to Rasmus. income inequality in contemporary America increased as the relative share of income for corporations and the wealthiest one per cent of households rose while income shares declined for 80-percent of the United States workforce. After rising steadily for three decades after World War II. the standard of living for most American workers has sharply declined between the mid-1970s to the present. Rasmus likens the widening income gap in contemporary American society to the decade leading up to the Great Depression. estimating "well over $1 trillion in income is transferred annually from the roughly 90 million working class families in America to corporations and the wealthiest non-working-class households. While a hundred new billionaires were created since 2001. real weekly earnings for 100 million workers are less in 2007 than in 1980 when Ronald Reagan took office". According to economist Richard D. Wolff. the 1970s brought an end to the labour shortage which had facilitated more than a century of rising average real wages in the United States. Wolff says Americans responded to the resulting deficiency of effective demand by working more hours and excessive borrowing; the latter paving the way for thefinancial crisis of 2007–08.

IMPERIALISM

According to David Harvey. "the export of capital and the cultivation of new markets around the world" is a solution "as old as capitalism itself" for the deficiency of effective demand. Imperialism. as defined by *Dictionary of Human Geography*. is "the creation and/or maintenance of an unequal economic. cultural. and territorial relationship. usually between states and often in the form of an empire. based on domination and subordination." "These geographic shifts". according to David Harvey. "are the heart of uneven geographic development".

Vladimir Lenin viewed imperialism as the highest stage of capitalism. He asserted that the merging of banks and industrial cartels gave rise to finance capital. which was then exported (rather than goods) in pursuit of greater profits than the home market could offer. Political and financial power became divided among international monopolist firms and European states. colonizing large parts of the world in support of their businesses. According to analyst Michael Parenti. imperialism is "the process whereby the dominant politico-economic interests of one nation expropriate for their own enrichment the land. labour. raw materials. and markets of another people." Parenti says imperialism is older than capitalism. Given its expansionist nature. capitalism has little inclination to stay home. While he conceded imperialism is not typically recognised as a legitimate allegation about the United States. Parenti argued:

"Emperors and conquistadors were interested mostly in plunder and tribute. gold and glory. Capitalist imperialism differs from these earlier forms in the way it systematically accumulates capital through the organised exploitation of labour and the penetration of overseas markets. Capitalist imperialism invests in other countries. transforming and dominating their economies. cultures. and political life. integrating their financial and productive structures into an international system of capital accumulation."

In his book. *The Political Struggle for the 21st century*. J.W. Smith examines the economic basis for the history of imperial civilization. On a global scale. he says developed nations tended to impede or prohibit the economic and technological advancement of weaker developing countries through the military force. martial law. and inequitable practices of trade that typically characterise colonialism. Rhetorically termed as "survival of the fittest". or "might makes right". such economic crises stem from the imbalances imposed by corporate imperialism. Just as cities in the Middle Ages monopolized the means of production by conquering and controlling the sources of raw materials and countryside markets. Smith claims that contemporary centers of capital now control our present world through private monopoly of public resources sometimes known as "the commons". Through inequalities of trade. developing countries are overcharged for import of manufactured goods and underpaid for raw material exports. as wealth is siphoned from the periphery of empire and hoarded at the imperial-centers-of-capital:

"Over eight-hundred years ago the powerful of the city-states of Europe learned to control the resources and markets of the countryside by raiding and destroying others' primitive industrial capital. thus openly monopolizing that capital and establishing and maintaining extreme inequality of pay. This low pay siphoned the wealth of the countryside to the imperial-centers-of-capital. The powerful had learned to plunder-by-trade and have been refining those skills ever since."

Smith goes on to say that. like other financial empires in history. the contemporary model forms alliances necessary to develop and control wealth. keeping peripheral nations impoverished providers of cheap resources for the imperial capital centers. Belloc estimated that. during the British Enclosures. "perhaps half of the whole population wasproletarian". while roughly the other "half" owned and controlled the means of production. Under modern Capitalism. J.W. Smith claimed that fewer than 500 individuals possess more wealth than half of the earth's population. The wealth of 1/2 of 1-percent of the United States population roughly equals that of the lower 90-percent.

Richard Cook claimed that the United States maintained stability by economically dominating the world as a means of filling the gap between production and consumption. Beginning with loans to European combatants during World War I. and continuing through the lend-lease programme of World War II. U.S. domination of trade peaked through economic recovery measures following those wars. Though forming the basis for U.S. prosperity during the 1950s and 1960s. U.S trade domination was exhausted by the mid-1970s. when the United States implemented a policy known as dollar hegemony. intended to stabilize the economy.

ALTERNATIVE MODELS

Advocating for an "alternative economic system free of capitalism's structural flaws". economist Richard D. Wolff says reform agendas are fundamentally inadequate. given that capitalist corporations. the dominant institutions of the existing system. retain the incentives and the resources to undo any sort of reform policy. For example. Wolff goes on to say: "The New Deal–era taxes on business and the rich and regulations of enterprise behaviour proved vulnerable and unsustainable. The enemies of the New Deal had the incentives (profit maximization) and the resources (their returns on investments) to undo many of its reforms after World War II. with ever-greater effect in the period since the 1970s.

They systematically evaded. then weakened. the taxes and regulations of the New Deal. and eventually. when politically possible. eliminated them altogether. Business profits funded the parties. politicians. public relations campaigns. and professional think tanks that together shaped the real social effects and historical decline of government economic regulation. Examples include the destruction of the Glass-Steagall Act. the current assault on Social Security. the shift in the federal tax burden from business to individuals and from upper- to middle-income individuals. and so on."

According to David Schweickart. a serious critique of any problem cannot be content to merely note the negative features of the existing model. Instead. we must specify precisely the structural features of an alternative: "But if we want to do more than simply denounce the evils of capitalism. we must confront the claim that 'there is no alternative'—by proposing one." Schweickart argued that both full employment and guaranteed basic income are impossible under the restrictions of the U.S. economic system for two primary reasons: a) unemployment is an essential feature of capitalism. not an indication of systemic failure; and b) while capitalism thrives under polyarchy. it is not compatible with genuine democracy. Assuming these "democratic deficits" significantly impact the management of both the workplace and new investment. many proponents of economic democracy tend to favour the creation and implementation of a new economic model over reform of the existing one.

For example. Dr. Martin Luther King Jr. claimed "Communism forgets that life is individual. Capitalism forgets that life is social. and the Kingdom of Brotherhood is found neither in the thesis of Communism nor the antithesis of Capitalism but in a higher synthesis. It is found in a higher synthesis that combines the truths of both". Regarding the gap between productivity and purchasing power. Dr. King maintained:

"The problem indicates that our emphasis must be two-fold. We must create full employment or we must create incomes. People must be made consumers by one method or the other. Once they are placed in this position. we need to be concerned that the potential of the individual is not wasted. New forms of work that enhance the social good will have to be devised for those for whom traditional jobs are not available."

According to historian and political economist. Gar Alperovitz: "King's final Judgement stands as instructive evidence of his understanding of the nature of systemic challenge — and also as a reminder that given the failures of both traditional socialism and corporate capitalism. it is time to get serious about clarifying not only the question of strategy. but what. in fact. the meaning of changing the system in a truly democratic direction might one day entail."

Trade unionist and social activist Allan Engler argued further that economic democracy was the working-class alternative to capitalism.

In his book. "Economic Democracy". Engler stated:

- When economic democracy – a world of human equality. democracy and cooperation – is the alternative. capitalism will no longer be seen as a lesser evil. When the working class. not a revolutionary party. is the agency of social transformation. change will be based on workplace organization. community mobilizations and democratic political action. The goal will be to transform capitalism into economic democracy through gains and reforms that improve living conditions while methodically replacing wealth-holders' entitlement with human entitlement. capitalist ownership with community ownership and master-servant relations with workplace democracy."

Assuming that "democracy is not just a political value. but one with profound economic implications. the problem is not to choose between plan and market. but to integrate these institutions into a democratic framework".

Like capitalism. economic democracy can be defined in terms of three basic features:

- Worker self-management: Each productive enterprise is controlled democratically by its workers.
- Social control of investment: Funds for new investment are returned to the economy through a network of public investment banks."
- The market: Enterprises interact with one another and with consumers in an environment largely free of governmental price controls. Raw materials. instruments of production and consumer goods are all bought and sold at prices largely determined by the forces of supply and demand.

In real-world practice. Schweickart concedes economic democracy will be more complicated and less "pure" than his model. However. to grasp the nature of the system and to understand its essential dynamic. it is important to have a clear picture of the basic structure. Capitalism is characterised by private ownership of productive resources. the market. and wage labour. The Soviet economic model subordinated private ownership of productive resources to public ownership by collectivizing farms and factories. It further subordinated the market to central planning — but retained institution of wage labour.

Most proposed models for economic democracy generally begin with democratizing the workplace and the ownership of capital. Other proposals advocate replacing the market with some form of planning. as well.

WORKER SELF-MANAGEMENT

In worker self-management. each productive enterprise is controlled by those who work there. Workers are responsible for the operation of the facility.

including organization. discipline. production techniques. and the nature. price. and distribution of products. Decisions concerning distribution are made democratically. Problems of authority delegation are solved by democratic representation. Management is chosen by the worker. not appointed by the State. not elected by the community at large and not selected by a board of directors elected by stockholders. Ultimate authority rests with the enterprise's workers. following the one-person. one-vote principle.

According to veteran World Bank economic adviser David P. Ellerman it's the employment contract that needs to be abolished. not private property. In other words. "a firm can be socialized and yet remain 'private' in the sense of not being government-owned." In his book. "The Democratic Firm". Ellerman stated:

In the world today. the main form of enterprise is based on renting human beings (privately or publicly). Our task is to construct the alternative. In the alternative type of firm. employment by the firm is replaced with membership in the firm. Economic democracy requires the abolition of the employment relation. not the abolition of private property. Democracy can be married with private property in the workplace; the result of the union is the democratic worker-owned firm."

Alternately. in Schweickart's model. workers control the workplace. but they do not "own" the means of production. Productive resources are regarded as the collective property of the society. Workers run the enterprise. use its capital assets as they see fit. and distribute the profits among themselves. Here. societal "ownership" of the enterprise manifests itself in two ways: 1) All firms pay tax on their capital assets. which goes into society's investment fund. In effect. workers rent capital assets from society. 2) Firms are required to preserve the value of the capital stock entrusted to them. This means that a depreciation fund must be maintained to repair or replace existing capital stock. This money may be spent on capital replacements or improvements. but not to supplement workers' incomes.

Italy's Legacoop and Spain's Mondragon multi-sectoral worker-cooperatives have both been able to reach significant scale and demonstrate long-term sustainability. According to a study conducted by Massachusetts Institute of Technology. the greatest lesson to be learned from these European experiences is the importance of developing an economically integrated network of cooperatives rather than a single cooperative. The report goes on to say:

In a market based economy the cooperative business form suffers from several strategic challenges when operating independently. One worker cooperative on its own is most likely doomed to fail in a highly competitive global economy. However. an ecosystem of several worker cooperatives and support organizations can create an infrastructure that leads to sustained growth and expansion. In Mondragon the cooperative network expanded from a single cooperative polytechnic school to a network of 256 industrial. retail. finance. educational. and research and development firms.

SOCIAL CONTROL OF INVESTMENT

While there is no single approach or 'blueprint' for social control of investment. many strategies have been proposed. For example. Gar Alperovitz claims many real-world strategies have already emerged to democratise and decentralize the ownership of wealth and capital. In addition to worker cooperatives. Alperovitz highlights ESOPs. credit unions and other cooperative forms. social enterprises. municipally-owned utilities and public banks as starting points for what he has termed a "Pluralist Commonwealth".

Alternately. David Schweickart proposes a flat-rate tax on capital assets to replace all other business taxes. This "capital assets tax" is collected and invested by the central government. Funds are dispersed throughout society. first to regions and communities on a per capita basis. then to public banks in accordance with past performance. then to those firms with profitable project proposals. Profitable projects that promise increased employment are favored over those that do not. At each level. national. regional and local. legislatures decide what portion of their funds is to be used for public capital expenditures. then send the remainder to the next lower level. Associated with most banks are entrepreneurial divisions. which promote firm expansion and new firm creation. For large (regional or national) enterprises. local investment banks are complemented by regional and national investment banks. These too would be public institutions that receive their funds from the national investment fund.

Banks are public. not private. institutions that make grants. not loans. to business enterprises. According to Schweickart. these grants do not represent "free money". since an investment grant counts as an addition to the capital assets of the enterprise. upon which the capital-asset tax must be paid. Thus the capital assets tax functions as an interest rate. A bank grant is essentially a loan requiring interest payments but no repayment of principal.

While an economy of worker-self-managed enterprises might tend Towards lower unemployment than under capitalism. Schweickart says it does not guarantee full employment. Social control of investment serves to increase employment. If the market provides insufficient employment. the public sector becomes the employer of last resort. The original formulation of the U.S. Humphrey-Hawkins Act of 1978 assumed that only in this way could full employment be assured in a market economy. Economic Democracy adopts this approach. Social control of investment then blocks the cyclical unemployment typical of capitalism.

THE MARKET

Hungarian historian Karl Polanyi suggested that market economies should subordinate themselves to larger societal needs. He states that human-beings. the source of labour. do not reproduce for the sole purpose of providing the market with workers. In The Great Transformation Polanyi says that. while modern states and market economies tend to grow under capitalism. both are mutually interdependent for functional development. In order for market economies to be truly prosperous. he claims social constructs must play an essential role. With the term "fictitious commodities". Polanyi claimed that land. labour. and money are all commodified under capitalism. though the inherent purpose of these items was never intended "for sale". He says natural resources are "God-given". money is a bookkeeping entry validated by law. and labour is a human prerogative. not a personal obligation to market economies.

Schweickart's economic democracy is a form of market economy. at least insofar as the allocation of consumer and capital goods is concerned. Firms buy raw materials and machinery from other firms and sell their products to other enterprises or consumers. "Prices are largely unregulated except by supply and demand. although in some cases price controls or price supports might be in order – as they are deemed in order in most real-world forms of capitalism."

Without a price mechanism sensitive to supply and demand. it is extremely difficult for a producer or planner to know what and how much to produce. and which production and marketing methods are the most efficient. Otherwise. it is difficult to motivate producers to be both efficient and innovative. Market competition resolves these problems. to a significant if incomplete degree. in a non-authoritarian. non-bureaucratic fashion.

Schweikart claims that centralized planning is inherently flawed. and schemes for decentralized non-market planning are unworkable. He argues that the historical record confirms that central planning is both inefficient and conducive to an authoritarian concentration of power. a lessons he says is to be drawn from the Soviet experience.

Enterprises still strive to make a profit. However. "profit" in a worker-run firm is calculated differently than under capitalism. For a capitalist firm. labour is counted as a cost. For a worker-run enterprise it is not. Labour is not another "factor of production" on par with land and capital. Labour is the residual claimant. Workers get all that remains. once other costs. including depreciation set asides and the capital assets tax. have been paid.

Because of the way workplaces and the investment mechanism are structured. Schweickart's model aims to facilitate fair trade. not free trade. between nations. Under Economic Democracy. there would be virtually no cross-border capital flows. Enterprises themselves would not relocate abroad. since they are democratically controlled by their own workers. Finance capital stays mostly at home. since funds for investment are publicly generated and are mandated by law to be reinvested domestically. "Capital doesn't flow into the country. either. since there are no stocks nor corporate bonds nor businesses to buy. The capital assets of the country are collectively owned – and hence not for sale."

According to Michael Howard. "in preserving commodity exchange. a market socialism has greater continuity with the society it displaces than does Non-market socialism. and thus it is more likely to emerge from capitalism as a result of tendencies generated within it." But Howard also suggested. "one argument against the market in socialist society has been that it blocks progress Towards full communism or even leads back to capitalism". From this perspective. Non-market models of economic democracy have also been proposed.

ECONOMIC DEMOCRACY AS PART OF AN INCLUSIVE DEMOCRACY

Economic democracy is described as an integral component of an inclusive democracy. in Takis Fotopoulos' *Towards An Inclusive Democracy* as a stateless. moneyless and marketless economy that precludes private accumulation of wealth and the institutionalization of privileges for some sections of society. without relying on a mythical post-scarcity state of abundance. or sacrificing freedom of choice.

The proposed system aims to meet the basic needs of all citizens (macroeconomic decisions). and secure freedom of choice (microeconomic decisions). Therefore. the system consists of two basic elements: (1) democratic planning. which involves a feedback process between *workplace* assemblies. *demotic* assemblies and a *confederal* assembly. and (2) an artificial market using personal vouchers. which ensures freedom of choice but avoids the adverse effects of real markets. Although David Pepper called this system "a form of money based on the labour theory of value". it is not a money model since vouchers cannot be used as a general medium of exchange and store of wealth.

Another distinguishing feature of inclusive democracy is its distinction between basic and non-basic needs. Remuneration is determined separately according to the cost of basic needs. and according to degree of effort for non-basic needs. Inclusive democracy is based on the principle that meeting basic needs is a fundamental human right which is guaranteed to all who are in a physical condition to offer a minimal amount of work. By contrast. participatory economics guarantees that basic needs are satisfied only for public goods or are covered by compassion and by a guaranteed basic income for the unemployed and those who cannot work. Many advocates of participatory economics andParticipism have contested this. As part of inclusive democracy. economic democracy is the authority of demos (community) in the economic sphere—which requires equal distribution of economic power. Therefore. all macroeconomic decisions (overall level of production. consumption and investment. amounts of work and leisure implied. technologies to be used. etc.) are made by the collectively and without representation. However. microeconomic decisions are made by the individual production or consumption unit through a proposed system of vouchers.

As with the case of direct democracy. economic democracy is only feasible if the participants can easily cooperate.

REFORM AGENDAS

Assuming the most basic requirement for societal prosperity is a healthy. educated. and enterprising population. Economic Democracy seeks to close the gap betweenpurchasing power and productive output. While reform agendas tend to critique the existing system and recommend corrective measures. they do not necessarily suggest alternative models to replace the fundamental structures of capitalism; private ownership of productive resources. the market. and wage labour.

SOCIAL CREDIT

Rather than an economic shortfall. many analysts consider the gap between production and purchasing power a social dividend. In this view. credit is a public utility rather than debt to financial centers. Once reinvested in human productive potential. the surplus of societal output could actually increase Gross Domestic Product rather than throttling it. resulting in a more efficient economy. overall. Social Credit is an economic reform movement that originates from theories developed by Scottish engineer Major C. H. Douglas. His aim to make societal improvement the goal of economic systems is reflected in the term "Social Credit". and published in his book. entitled *Economic Democracy*. In this view. the term "economic democracy" does not mean worker control of industry.

While technological advancement tends to increase unemployment along with productivity.

Douglas suggests that our perspective will determine whether this problem is a "catastrophe" or a "magnificent achievement":

- The so-called unemployment problem is really a problem of leisure. The problem really is a problem. first of the distribution of purchasing power to those who are not required. and will decreasingly be required. in the industrial system. and secondly. of ensuring that the total purchasing distributed shall always be enough to pay for the goods and services for sale."

A national dividend and a compensated price mechanism are the two most essential components of the Social Credit programme. While these measure have never been implemented in their purest form. they have provided a foundation for Social Credit political parties in many countries and for reform agendas that retain the title. "economic democracy".

CREDIT AS A PUBLIC UTILITY

Following Douglas and a reform programme based on direct government spending set forth by groups such as the American Monetary Institute. veteran Project Manager for theU.S. Treasury Department. Richard C. Cook proposes two general measures. which together he terms. "economic democracy":

- *Credit as a public utility:* "We should spend sufficient credit into existence to supply the basic operating expenses of government at all levels without recourse to either taxes or borrowing. At least ninety percent of all taxes could be eliminated. The only taxes that should be retained would be those in the form of user fees for infrastructure operations and maintenance and those levied only for dire emergencies. Capital expenses for infrastructure construction at the federal. state. and local levels should be financed through a self-capitalized national infrastructure bank lending at zero-interest. Operating on a national scale. such a bank could begin to rebuild our job base starting at the state and local levels. A public programme of direct government expenditures as described herein would be as effective. as timely. far less inflationary. and much cheaper than creating new public debt by borrowing credit created 'out of thin air' by the banking system."
- *A national dividend:* "The endemic gap between prices and purchasing power in an advanced economic system in reality is the "leisure dividend" that we never received from our amazing producing economy. That gap should now be filled by a non-taxable national dividend of two types. One would be a cash stipend paid to all citizens which would also serve the purpose of eliminating poverty by providing everyone with a basic income guarantee. The remainder of the national dividend would consist of an overall pricing subsidy. whereby a designated proportion of all purchases. including home building expenses. would be rebated to consumers. The average national dividend per person would probably exceed $12.000 per year under today's economic conditions. It would be a calculated value charged against a government ledger but would be off-budget. with no need to finance it with taxation or borrowing

While Smith and others suggest an economic crisis might be necessary to drive a movement Towards large-scale economic democracy.

Cook argues that "most economic reform programmes address symptoms. not causes":

- Monetary reform embraces the enormous productivity of modern industrial methods with approval and hope. But it identifies factors in the nature of industrial production at the level of the corporation as creating a chronic state of instability". "The top priority of the reform programme would be to use public credit to rebuild the producing economy which has been wrecked by the phony ideology of 'market' economics and the inept and self-serving manipulation of the money supply by the Federal Reserve and the banks."

Cook avoided collectivist solutions. Rather. he affirmed the value of "democratic capitalism." combined with a shift to more public control of credit. and suggested a new approach to achieving worldwide prosperity. starting with economic recovery in the United States. Cook's argument stemmed from prior success in the United States treating credit as a public utility. including colonial paper currencies which allowed an emerging American society to monetize the value of its goods and services. the Greenbacks issued by President Abraham Lincoln during the American civil war. and the Reconstruction Finance Corporation (RFC) which moved to recapitalize failing state banks in rural areas and small towns during the Great Depression. While President Herbert Hoover's efforts failed. Cook credits RFC programmes with providing low interest loans to the railroad industry. farmers. exporters. state and local governments. and wartime industries over a period of at least 20 years.

NATIONAL DIVIDEND

Cook also proposed a national dividend. sometimes known as a Basic Income Guarantee or "BIG". was advocated in the United States by economists. politicians and reformers. including Thomas Paine. Milton Friedman. Dr. Martin Luther King Jr.. and John Kenneth Galbraith. Friedman originally proposed a negative income tax to support this system. but then opposed the bill because its revised implementation would have merely supplemented rather than replacing existing tax-structures. Cook suggested that racism might have been at the root of BIG's demise in the late 1960s. as "many beneficiaries of the programme would have been African-American". In 2006. State Representative Bob Filner(D-CA) as H.R. 5257. proposed a basic income guarantee. According to the U.S. Basic Income Guarantee Network:

"The basic income guarantee (BIG) is a government insured guarantee that no citizen's income will fall below some minimal level for any reason. All citizens would receive a BIG without means test or work requirement. BIG is an efficient and effective solution to poverty that preserves individual autonomy and work incentives while simplifying government social policy. Some researchers estimate that a small BIG. sufficient to cut the poverty rate in half could be financed without an increase in taxes by redirecting funds from spending programmes and tax deductions aimed at maintaining incomes."

Cook suggests existing U.S. (GDP) could support such a system. GDP of \$12.98-trillion minus \$9.21-trillion in purchasing power ("wages") equals a difference of \$3.77-trillion. Distributed equally amongst United States citizens. Cook estimates a "National Dividend" of approximately \$12.600 could be provided annually to every U.S. citizen. A primary function of monetary reform is to "provide sufficient individual income"—not merely "create jobs"—for American workers displaced by technological advancement. outsourcing. and other economic influences beyond their control.

Funding of the National Dividend would be drawn from a national credit account. which would include all factors that generate production costs and create new capital assets. The national credit account could also be used for price subsidies to discourage manufacturers from cutting costs by shipping jobs overseas. Rather than Federal Reserve Notes. circulated only through debt payable to a bank with interest. the National Dividend would be "real money". based on the productive capacity of the economy expressed as GDP. Cook says. "it's important to realize that Social Credit is not a socialist system. Rather it is 'democratic capitalism.' in contrast to the 'finance capitalism' that has become so damaging". Rooted in the ideals of Social Credit. proposed by Douglas in the 1920s. Cook explains:

"The difference between a National Dividend and a basic income guarantee is that the dividend is tied to production and consumption data and may vary from year to year. During years that the dividend falls below a designated threshold. the balance of a basic income guarantee could be provided from tax revenues. But in a highly automated economy such as that of the U.S.. the National Dividend would normally be sufficient".

In his book. *Capitalism 3.0*. Peter Barnes likens a "National Dividend" to the game of Monopoly. where all players start with a fair distribution of financial opportunity to succeed. and try to privatize as much as they can as they move around "the commons". Distinguishing the board game from real-world business. Barnes claims that "the top 5 percent of the population owns more property than the remaining 95 percent". providing the smaller minority with an unfair advantage of approximately "$5-trillion" annually. at the beginning of the game. Contrasting "redistribution" of income (or property) with "predistribution". Barnes argues for "propertizing" (without corporately privatizing) "the commons" to spread ownership universally. without taking wealth from some and giving it to others. His suggested mechanism to this end is the establishment of a "Commons Sector". ensuring payment from the Corporate Sector for "the commons" they utilize. and equitably distributing the proceeds for the benefit of contemporary and future generations of society.

One real-world example of such reform is in the U.S. State of Alaska. where each citizen receives an annual share of the part of the state's oil revenues via the "Alaska Permanent Fund Dividend". Barnes suggests this model could extend to other states and nations because "we jointly own many valuable assets". As corporate pollution of common assets increased. the permits for such pollution would become more scarce. driving prices for those permits up. "Less pollution would equal more revenue". and over time. "trillions of dollars could flow into an American Permanent Fund". However. none of these proposals aspire to the mandates recommended by Dr. Martin Luther King Jr.:

Two conditions are indispensable if we are to ensure that the guaranteed income operates as a consistently progressive measure. First. it must be pegged to the median income of society. not the lowest levels of income. To guarantee an income at the floor would simply perpetuate welfare standards and freeze into the society poverty conditions. Second. the guaranteed income must be dynamic; it must automatically increase as the total social income grows. Were it permitted to remain static under growth conditions. the recipients would suffer a relative decline. If periodic reviews disclose that the whole national income has risen. then the guaranteed income would have to be adjusted upward by the same percentage. Without these safeguards a creeping retrogression would occur. nullifying the gains of security and stability.

Barnes deem any such reform unlikely. Thomas Paine originally recommended a National Dividend to compensate for the brutality of British Enclosures. but his idea was never adopted.

MONOPOLY POWER VERSUS PUBLIC UTILITY

Rather than superficially compensating for legalized inequities. Smith recommends abolishing or redefining property rights laws with particular respect for "the commons".According to Smith exclusive title to natural resources and technologies should be converted to inclusive conditional titles—the condition being that society should collect rental values on all natural resources.

Smith suggests the basic principles of monopolization under feudalism were never abandoned. and residues of exclusive feudal property rights restrict the potential efficiency of capitalism in Western cultures. He estimated that roughly 60 percent of American capital is little more than capitalized values of unearned wealth. He proposed that elimination of these monopoly values would double economic efficiency. maintain quality of life. and reduce working hours by half. Wasteful monetary flows could be stopped only by eliminating all methods of monopolization typical in Western economies.

Smith divided "primary (feudal) monopoly" into four general categories: banking; land; technology and communications. He listed three general categories of "secondary (modern) monopoly"; insurance. law. health care. Smith further claimed that converting these exclusive entitlements to inclusive human rights would minimize battles formarket share. thereby eliminating most offices and staff needed to maintain monopoly structures. and stop the wars generated to protect them. Dissolving roughly half the economic activity of a monopoly system would reduce the costs of common resources by roughly half. and significantly minimize the most influential factors of poverty. In Smith's view. most taxes should be eliminated. and productive enterprise should be privately owned and managed. Inventors should be paid well and all technology placed in the public domain.

Crucial services currently monopolized through licensing should be legislated as human rights. Smith envisioned a balanced economy under a socially owned banking commons within an inclusive society with full and equal rights for all. Federated regions collectresource rents on land and technology to a social fund to operate governments and care for social needs. Socially owned banks provide finance capital by creating debt-free money for social infrastructure and industry.

Rental values return to society through expenditure on public infrastructures. Local labour is trained and employed to build and maintain water systems. sewers. roads. communication systems. railroads. ports. airports. post offices. and education systems. Purchasing power circulates regionally. as labour spends wages in consumption and governments spend resource rent and banking profits to maintain essential services.

According to Smith. all monetary systems. including money markets. should function within fractional-reserve banking. Financial capital should be the total savings of all citizens. balanced by primary-created money to fill any shortfall. or its destruction through increased reserve requirements to eliminate any surplus. Adjustments of required reserves should facilitate the balance between building with socially created money or savings. Any shortage of savings within a socially owned banking system should be alleviated by simply printing it.

DEMOCRATIC COOPERATIVES

A cooperative is a limited liability entity. organised either for-profit or not-for-profit. that differs from a corporation in that its producing members. rather than investors. comprise the decision-making authority. By various names. cooperatives play an essential role in all forms of Economic Democracy. Classified as either consumer cooperatives or worker cooperatives. the cooperative business model is fundamental to the interests of economic democracy.

According to the International Cooperative Alliance's Statement on the Cooperative Identity. "cooperatives are democratic organizations controlled by their members. who actively participate in setting policies and making decisions. Men and women serving as elected representatives are accountable to the membership. In primary cooperatives members have equal voting rights (one member. one vote) and cooperatives at other levels are also organised in a democratic manner."

WORKER COOPERATIVES

According to the United States Federation of Worker Cooperatives:

"Worker cooperatives are business entities that are owned and controlled by their members. the people who work in them. The two central characteristics of worker cooperatives are: 1) workers invest in and own the business and (2) decision-making is democratic. generally adhering to the principle of one worker-one vote." Worker cooperatives occupy multiple sectors and industries in the United States. mostly in the Northeast. the West Coast and the Upper Midwest. totaling 300 democratic workplaces in the United States. employing over 3.500 people and generating over $400 million in annual revenues. While a few are larger enterprises. most are small. Growing steadily between 1990 and 2010. technology and home health care experienced most of the recent increase.

Worker cooperatives generally employ an industrial model called workplace democracy. which rejects the "master-servant relationship" implicit in the traditional employment contract. According to Wilkinson and Pickett. neither ownership or participation alone are sufficient to establish democracy in the workplace. "[M]any share-ownership schemes amount to little more than incentive schemes. intended to make employees more compliant with management and sometimes to provide a nest-egg for retirement... To make a reliable difference to company performance. share-ownership has to be combined with more participative management methods." Dahl further argued that self-governing enterprises should not be confused with other systems they might resemble:

"Self-governing enterprises only remotely resemble pseudodemocratic schemes of employee consultation by management; schemes of limited employee participation that leave all critical decisions with a management elected by stockholders; or Employee Stock Ownership Plans (ESOPs) that are created only or primarily to provide corporations with low-interest loans. lower corporate income taxes. greater cash flow. employee pension plans. or a market for their stock. without. however. any significant changes in control."

In worker cooperatives. net income is called surplus instead of profit and is distributed among the members based on hours worked. seniority. or other criteria. In a worker cooperative. workers own their jobs. and therefore have a direct stake in the local environment and the power to conduct business in ways that benefit the community rather than destroying it. Some worker cooperatives maintain what is known as a "multiple bottom line". evaluating success not merely in terms of net income. but also by factors like their sustainability as a business. their contribution to the community. and the happiness and longevity of their workers.

Worker-control can take many forms depending on the size and type of the business. Approaches to decision-making include: an elected board of directors. elected managers. management job roles. no management at all. consensus. majority vote. or combinations of the above. Participation in decision-making becomes the responsibility and privilege of each member. In one variation. workers usually invest money when they begin working. Each member owns one share. which provides its owner with one vote in company decision-making. While membership is not a requirement of employment. only employees can become members. According to Kenneth W. Stikkers. the Mondragon cooperatives in the Basque region of Spain have achieved a previously unknown level of economic democracy. Established in 1956. Mondragon has since become an economic model that transcends the capitalist-socialist dichotomy and thereby helps us to imagine creative solutions to current economic problems.

Economist Richard D. Wolff argues that Mondragon is an example of "a stunningly successful alternative to the capitalist organization of production."

CONSUMER COOPERATIVES

A consumers' cooperative is owned by its customers for their mutual benefit. Oriented towards service rather than profit. consumers often provide capital to launch or purchase the enterprise. In practice. consumer cooperatives price goods and services at competitive market rates. The co-op returns profits to the consumer/owner according to a formula instead of paying a separate investor group. In his book. *From Mondragon To America*. Greg MacLeod argues that "in consumer cooperatives where the customer-members own the capital and the employees are subject to capital. the normal dynamic is the adversarial relationship of labour to capital. Sometimes the result is strikes of labour against management." In some cooperatives. however. consumer/owners are workers as well. For example. Mondragon has developed a large "hybrid" cooperative which sells groceries and furniture in Spain. In this regard. MacLeod states:

"It is not necessary to opt for either the consumer or the producer but to link them both in one complex organization. The [Mondragon] founders have thereby shown that it is possible to devise a system that respects the rights of both producer and consumer. both sides of the economic question." Consumer cooperatives vary in organization and operations. but typically follow the Rochdale Principles.

Consumer cooperatives may also form Co-operative Federations. These may take the form of co-operative wholesale societies. through which they collectively purchase goods at wholesale prices and. in some cases. cooperatively own factories. Alternatively. they may be members of Co-operative unions. Consumer cooperatives are very different from "discount clubs." which charge annual fees in exchange for a discount on purchases. The club is not owned or governed by the members and profits go to investors. not to members.

FOOD COOPERATIVES

Most food co-ops are consumer cooperatives that specialize in grocery products. Members patronize the store and vote in elections. The members elect a board of directors to make high-level decisions and recruit managers. Food cooperatives were originally established to provide fresh. organic produce as a viable alternative to packaged imports. The ideas of local and slow food production can help local farmers prosper. in addition to providing consumers with fresher products. But the growing ubiquity of organic food products in corporate stores testifies to broadening consumer awareness. and to the dynamics of global marketing.

Associated with national and international cooperative communities. Portland Oregon cooperatives manage to survive market competition with corporate franchise. As Lee Lancaster. financial manager for Food Front. states. "cooperatives are potentially one democratic economic model that could help guide business decisions Towards meeting human needs while honoring the needs of society and nature". He admits. however. it is difficult to maintain collaboration among cooperatives while also avoiding integration that typically results in centralized authority. Tim Calvert believes that dollars are the most important vote to make. and others tend to agree. Citing members of People's Co-op and Alberta Cooperative Grocery.Romona DeNies of *The Portland Alliance* states. "Co-ops are the antidote to the centralization of power. People forget they have power as consumers to make choices. We can't be completely disentangled from the corporate world. but we can try to provide a local model of living further from it. No one is getting rich off your money at a co-op. But that's the economic value of shopping here. In return. you support a viable alternative to the vicious cycle of bottom lines and end profits".

As World Trade Organization representatives negotiate issues of competition. agricultural subsidies. and protectionism among developed nations. the American farmer resembles third-world farmers who must compete with subsidized agricultural giants like Monsanto Company. Lee Lancaster says. "Underneath our unique aspects. we have the same structure and principles. Welfare of our respective neighborhoods is of vital concern to us. Food co-ops were started to provide local. organic produce.

Now with those things more mainstream. the demand is going up. and our share of that market is declining. We have to reevaluate." Further. Lancaster claims that the traditional independence and decentralization of U.S. cooperatives have restricted their impact on the food industry through economies of scale.

Proposing more collaboration. he asks:

- What if we could work with other co-ops to nurture and establish other cooperatives? In essence. this is an extension of neighborhood organizing. We're all driven by competition from national chains. but in looking at national issues and realizing there's a lot to address. what's needed is a bigger movement. not a big corporation."

REGIONAL TRADING CURRENCIES

According to Thomas H. Greco. Jr.. author of New Money for Healthy Communities "The pinnacle of power in today's world is the power to issue money. If that power can be democratized and focused in a direction which gives social and ecological concerns top priority. then there may yet be hope for saving the world". In this regard. he recommended the regionalization of currencies. Cook suggested that "under the Bretton Woods system. the Federal Reserve acted as the world's central bank. This gave America enormous leverage over economic policies of its principal trading partners". Cook claimed that developing nations were susceptible to exploitation mainly because they have no independent monetary system. using the U.S. dollar instead. This fed the fractional reserve banking system. operated by the U.S.. Canada. Europe. and Japan. Developing nations paid heavily for this service through market interest rates and because banking profits and property ownership emigrate to financial centers elsewhere.

According to Smith. "Currency is only the representation of wealth produced by combining land (resources). labour. and industrial capital". He claimed that no country was free when another country has such leverage over its entire economy. But by combining their resources. Smith claimed that developing nations have all three of these foundations of wealth:

By peripheral nations using the currency of an imperial centre as its trading currency. the imperial centre can actually print money to own industry within those periphery countries. By forming regional trading blocs and printing their own trading currency. the developing world has all four requirements for production. resources. labour. industrial capital. and finance capital. The wealth produced provides the value to back the created and circulating money.

Smith further explained that developed countries need resources from the developing world as much as developing countries need finance capital and technology from the developed world. Aside from the superior military power of the imperial centers. the undeveloped world actually has superior bargaining leverage. With independent trading currencies. developing countries could barter their resources to the developed world for the latest industrial technologies. Barter avoids "hard money monopolization" and the unequal trade between weak and strong nations that result. Smith suggested that barter was how Germany resolved many financial difficulties "put in place to strangle her". and that "World Wars I and II settled that trade dispute". He claimed that their intentions of exclusive entitlement were clearly exposed when the imperial centers resorted to military force to prevent such barter and maintain monopoly control of others' resources.

5

Market Socialism

Market socialism is a type of economic system where the means of production are either publicly owned or socially owned ascooperatives and operated in a market economy. This differs from non-market socialism in that a market exists for allocating capital goods and the means of production. There are many models of market socialism. Depending on the specific model. profits generated by socially-owned firms may variously be used to directly remunerate employees. accrue to society at large as the source of public finance. or be distributed amongst the population in a social dividend. Although models of socialism involvingfactor markets have existed since the early 19th century. the term "market socialism" only emerged in the 1920s during the Socialist calculation debate.

Market socialism is distinguished from the concept of the mixed economy. because unlike the mixed economy. models of market socialism are complete and self-regulating systems. Market socialism is also contrasted with social democratic policies implemented within capitalist market economies: while social democracy aims to achieve greater economic stability and equality through policy measures such as taxes. subsidies and social welfare programmes; market socialism aims to achieve similar goals through changing patterns of enterprise ownership and management.

Early models of market socialism trace their roots to the works of Adam Smith and the theories of classical economics. These consisted of proposals for cooperative enterprises operating in a free-market economy with the aim of eliminating exploitation by allowing individuals to receive the full product of their labour. while removing the market-distorting effects of concentrating ownership and wealth in the hands of private owners. Among early advocates of market socialism were Ricardian socialist economists andmutualist philosophers.

Beginning in the early twentieth century. neoclassical economic theory provided the theoretical basis for more comprehensive models of market socialism. Early Neo-classical models of socialism included a role for a central planning board (CPB) in setting prices equal marginal cost to achieve Pareto efficiency. Even though these early models did not rely on genuine markets. they were labeled "market socialist" for their utilization of financial prices and calculation. Alternative outlines for market socialism involve models where socially owned enterprises or producer co-operatives operate within free markets under the criterion of profitability. In recent models proposed by American Neo-classical economists. public ownership of the means of production is achieved through public ownership of equity and social control of investment.

Market socialism has also been used to refer to reformed economic systems in Marxist-Leninist states. most notably in reference to the contemporary economy of the People's Republic of China. where a free price system is used for the allocation of capital goods in both the state and private sectors. However. Chinese political and economic proponents of the "socialist market economy" do not consider it to be a form of market socialism in the Neo-classical sense. and many Western economists and political scientists question the degree to which this model constitutes a form of market socialism. often preferring to describe it as "state capitalism".

THEORETICAL HISTORY

CLASSICAL ECONOMICS

The key theoretical basis for market socialism is the negation of the underlying expropriation of surplus value present in other. exploitative. modes of production. Socialist theories that favored the market date back to the Ricardian socialists and anarchist economists. who advocated a free-market combined with public ownership or mutual ownership of the means of production.Proponents of early market socialism include the Ricardian socialist economists. the classical liberal philosopher John Stuart Mill. and the anarchist philosopher Pierre-Joseph Proudhon. These models of socialism entailed "perfecting" or improving the market-mechanism and free-price system by removing distortions caused by exploitation. private property. and alienated labour.This form of market socialism has been termed "free-market socialism" because it does not involve planners.

Mutualism

Pierre-Joseph Proudhon developed a theoretical system called mutualism. which attacks the legitimacy of existing property rights.subsidies. corporations. banking. and rent. Proudhon envisioned a decentralized market where people would enter the market with equal power. negating wage slavery. Proponents believe that cooperatives. credit unions. and other forms of worker ownership would become viable without being subject to the state. Market socialism has also been used to describe some individualist anarchist works which argue that free markets help workers and weaken capitalists.

American anarchism

For American anarchist historian Eunice Minette Schuster "It is apparent... that Proudhonian Anarchism was to be found in the United States at least as early as 1848 and that it was not conscious of its affinity to the Individualist Anarchism of Josiah Warrenand Stephen Pearl Andrews... William B. Greene presented this Proudhonian Mutualism in its purest and most systematic form.".Josiah Warren is widely regarded as the first American anarchist. and the four-page weekly paper he edited during 1833. *The Peaceful Revolutionist*. was the first anarchist periodical published. an enterprise for which he built his own printing press. cast his own type. and made his own printing plates. Warren was a follower of Robert Owen and joined Owen's community at New Harmony. Indiana. Josiah Warren termed the phrase "Cost the limit of price." with "cost" here referring not to monetary price paid but the labour one exerted to produce an item. Therefore. "[m]e proposed a system to pay people with certificates indicating how many hours of work they did.

They could exchange the notes at local time stores for goods that took the same amount of time to produce.". He put his theories to the test by establishing an experimental "labour for labour store" called the Cincinnati Time Storewhere trade was facilitated by notes backed by a promise to perform labour. The store proved successful and operated for three years after which it was closed so that Warren could pursue establishing colonies based on mutualism. These included "Utopia" and "Modern Times." Warren said that Stephen Pearl Andrews' *The Science of Society*. published in 1852. was the most lucid and complete exposition of Warren's own theories. Later Benjamin Tucker fused the economics of Warren and Proudhon and published these ideas in *Liberty* calling them "Anarchistic-Socialism". Tucker said. *"the fact that one class of men are dependent for their living upon the sale of their labour. while another class of men are relieved of the necessity of labour by being legally privileged to sell something that is not labour.... And to such a state of things I am as much opposed as any one. But the minute you remove privilege... every man will be a labourer exchanging with fellow-labourers... What Anarchistic-Socialism aims to abolish is usury... it wants to deprive capital of its reward."*.

NEO-CLASSICAL ECONOMICS

Early 20th Century

The earliest models of Neo-classical socialism were developed by Leon Walras. Enrico Barone (1908) and Oskar R. Lange (c. 1936). Lange and Fred M. Taylor (1929) proposed that central planning boards set prices through "trial and error". making adjustments as shortages and surpluses occurred rather than relying on a free price mechanism. If there were shortages. prices would be raised; if there were surpluses. prices would be lowered. Raising the prices would encourage businesses to increase production. driven by their desire to increase their profits. and in doing so eliminate the shortage. Lowering the prices would encourage businesses to curtail production to prevent losses. which would eliminate the surplus. Therefore. it would be a simulation of the market mechanism. which Lange thought would be capable of effectively managing supply and demand.

Although the Lange-Lerner model was often labelled as "market socialism". it is better described as "market simulation" because factor markets did not exist for the allocation of capital goods. The objective of the Lange-Lerner model was explicitly to replace markets with a non-market system of resource allocation.

H. D. Dickinson published two articles proposing a form of market socialism: "Price Formation in a Socialist Community" (*The Economic Journal* 1933) and "The Problems of a Socialist Economy" (*The Economic Journal* 1934). Dickinson proposed a mathematical solution whereby the problems of a socialist economy could be solved by a central planning agency. The central agency would have the necessary statistics on the economy. as well as the capability of using statistics to direct production. The economy could be represented as a system of equations. Solution values for these equations could be used to price all goods at marginal cost and direct production. Hayek (1935) argued against the proposal to simulate markets with equations. Dickinson (1939) adopted the Lange-Taylor proposal to simulate markets through trial and error.

The Lange-Dickinson version of market socialism kept capital investment out of the market. Lange (1926 p65) insisted that a central planning board would have to set capital accumulation rates arbitrarily. Lange and Dickinson saw potential problems with bureaucratization in market socialism. According to Dickinson "the attempt to check irresponsibility will tie up managers of socialist enterprises with so much red tape and bureaucratic regulation that they will lose all initiative and independence" Dickinson 1938 p214). In the Economics of Control (1944) Abba Lerner admitted that capital investment would be politicized in market socialism.

Late 20th Century

Economists active in the former Yugoslavia. including Czech-born Jaroslav Vanek and Croat-born Branko Horvat. promoted a model of market socialism dubbed the *Illyrian model*. where firms were socially owned by their employees and structured on workers' self-management. and competed with each other in open and free markets.

American economists in the latter half of the 20th century developed models based such as "Coupon Socialism" (by the economist John Roemer) and "Economic Democracy" (by the philosopher David Schweickart). Pranab Bardham and John Roemer proposed a form of Market Socialism where there was a "stock market" that distributed shares of the capital stock equally among citizens. In this stock market. there is no buying or selling of stocks. which leads to negative externalities associated with a concentration of capital ownership.

The Bardham and Roemer model satisfied the main requirements of both Socialism (workers own all the factors of production – not just labour) and market economies (prices determine efficient allocation of resources).

A New Zealand Economist. Steven O'Donnell. expanded on the Bardham and Roemer model and decomposed the capital function in a general equilibrium system to take account of entrepreneurial activity in market socialist economies. O'Donnell (2003) set up a model that could be used as a blueprint for transition economies. and the results suggested that although market socialist models were inherently unstable in the long term. in the short term they would provide the economic infrastructure necessary for a successful transition from planned to market economies.

In the early 21st century. the Marxian economist Richard D. Wolff has promoted a variation of market socialism based on autonomous employee-owned and self-managed enterprises.

ANTI-EQUILIBRIUM ECONOMICS

Another form of market socialism was promoted by critics of central planning and Neo-classical general equilibrium theory. the most notable economists being Alec Nove andJanos Kornai. In particular. Alec Nove proposed what he called *feasible socialism*. a mixed economy consisting of state-run enterprises. autonomous publicly owned firms. cooperatives. and small-scale private enterprise operating in an economy consisting of both markets and indirect macroeconomic planning.

IMPLEMENTATION

The economy of the former Socialist Federal Republic of Yugoslavia is widely considered to be a model of market-based socialism.

The Mondragon Cooperative Corporation in the Basque Country is widely cited as a highly successful co-operative enterprise based on worker-ownership and democratic management. Peter Drucker described the U.S. system of regulated pension funds providing capital to financial markets as "pension fund socialism". William H. Simon characterised pension fund socialism as "a form of market socialism". concluding that it was promising but perhaps with prospects more limited than those envisioned by its enthusiasts.

Similar policies to the market socialist proposal of a social dividend and basic income scheme have been implemented on the basis of public ownership of natural resources in Alaska (Alaska Permanent Fund) and in Norway (The Government Pension Fund of Norway).

RELATION TO POLITICAL IDEOLOGIES

MARXISM-LENINISM

The phrase "market socialism" has occasionally been used in reference to any attempt by a Soviet-type planned economy to introduce market elements into its economic system. In this sense. "market socialism" was first attempted during the 1920s in the Soviet Union as theNew Economic Policy (NEP) before being abandoned. Later. elements of "market socialism" were introduced in Hungary (where it was nicknamed "goulash communism"). Czechoslovakia and Yugoslavia in the 1970s and 1980s. The Economy of Belarus has been described as a "market socialist" system. The Soviet Union attempted to introduce a market system with its perestroika reforms underMikhail Gorbachev. During the later stages there was talk within top circles that the USSR should move Towards a market-based socialist system.

Historically. these kinds of "market socialist" systems attempt to retain state ownership of the *commanding heights of the economy*. such as heavy industry. energy. and infrastructure. while introducing decentralised decision making and giving local managers more freedom to make decisions and respond to market demands. Market socialist systems also allow private ownership and entrepreneurship in the service and other secondary economic sectors. The market is allowed to determine prices for consumer goods and agricultural products. and farmers are allowed to sell all or some of their products on the open market and keep some or all of the profit as an incentive to increase and improve production.

SOCIALISM WITH CHINESE CHARACTERISTICS

Although similar in name. market socialism differs markedly from the "socialist market economy" and "Socialist-oriented market economy" models practiced in the contemporary People's Republic of China and Socialist Republic of Vietnam. respectively. Officially these economic systems represent market economies that are in the long-term process of transition Towards socialism. Key differences between models of market socialism and the Chinese and Vietnamese models include the role of private investment in enterprises. the lack of a social dividend or basic income system to equitably distribute state profits among the population. and the existence and role of financial markets in the Chinese model - markets which are absent in the market socialist literature.

The Chinese experience with socialism with Chinese characteristics is frequently referred to as a "socialist market economy" where the "commanding heights" are state-owned. but a substantial portion of both the state and private sectors of economy are governed by free market practices. including a stock exchange for trading equity. and the utilization of indirect macroeconomic market mechanisms (*i.e.*: fiscal. monetary and Industrial policies) to influence the economy in the same manner governments affect the economy in capitalist economies. The free-market is the arbitrator for most economic activity. with economic planning being relegated to macro-economic government indicative planning that does not encompass the microeconomic decision-making that is left to the individual organizations and state-owned enterprises. This model includes a significant amount of privately owned firms that operate as a business for profit. but only for consumer goods and services.

In the Chinese system. directive planning based on mandatory output requirements and quotas were displaced by free-market mechanisms for most of the economy. including both the state and private sectors. although the government engages in indicative planning for large state enterprises. In comparison with the Soviet-type planned economy. the Chinese socialist market model is based on the corporatization of state institutions. transforming them into joint-stock companies. As of 2008. there were 150 state-owned corporations directly under the central government. These state-owned corporations have been reformed and become increasingly dynamic and a major source of revenue for the state in 2008. leading the economic recovery in 2009 during the wake of the global financial crises.

This economic model is defended from a Marxist perspective. which states that a planned socialist economy can only emerge after first developing the basis for socialism through the establishment of a market economy and commodity-exchange economy. and that socialism will only emerge after this stage has exhausted its historical necessity and gradually transforms itself into socialism. Proponents of this model argue that the economic system of the former USSR and its satellite states attempted to go from a natural economy to a planned economy by decree. without passing through the necessary market economy phase of development.

ANARCHISM

The French philosopher Pierre Joseph Proudhon is the first person to call himself an "anarchist". and considered among its most influential theorists. He is considered by many to be the "father of anarchism". He became a member of the French Parliament after the revolution of 1848. whereon he referred to himself as a "federalist". His best-known assertion is that *Property is Theft!*. contained in his first major work. *What is Property? Or. an Inquiry into the Principle of Right and Government* (*Qu'est-ce que la propriété? Recherche sur le principe du droit et du gouvernement*). published in 1840. The book's publication attracted the attention of the French authorities. It also attracted the scrutiny of Karl Marx. who started a correspondence with its author. The two influenced each other: they met in Paris while Marx was exiled there. Their friendship finally ended when Marx responded to Proudhon's *The System of Economic Contradictions. or The Philosophy of Poverty* with the provocatively titled *The*

Poverty of Philosophy. The dispute became one of the sources of the split between the anarchist and Marxian wings of the International Working Men's Association.

Mutualism is an economic theory and anarchist school of thought that advocates a society where each person might possess a means of production. either individually or collectively. with trade representing equivalent amounts of labour in the free market. Integral to the scheme was the establishment of a mutual-credit bank that would lend to producers at a minimal interest rate. just high enough to cover administration.Mutualism is based on a labour theory of value that holds that when labour or its product is sold. in exchange. it ought to receive goods or services embodying "the amount of labour necessary to produce an article of exactly similar and equal utility". Mutualism originated from the writings of philosopher Pierre-Joseph Proudhon. Mutualists oppose the idea of individuals receiving an income through loans. investments. and rent. as they believe these individuals are not laboring.

Though Proudhon opposed this type of income. he expressed that he had never intended *"...to forbid or suppress. by sovereign decree. ground rent and interest on capital. I think that all these manifestations of human activity should remain free and voluntary for all: I ask for them no modifications. restrictions or suppressions. other than those which result naturally and of necessity from the universalization of the principle of reciprocity which I propose."* Insofar as they ensure the worker's right to the full product of their labour. mutualists support markets (or artificial markets) and property in the product of labour. However. they argue for conditional titles to land. whose ownership is legitimate only so long as it remains in use or occupation (which Proudhon called "possession"); thus advocating personal property. but not private property.

Left-wing market anarchism. a form of left-libertarianism and individualist anarchism is associated with scholars such as Kevin Carson. Roderick T. Long. Charles Johnson. Brad Spangler. Samuel Edward Konkin III. Sheldon Richman. Chris Matthew Sciabarra. and Gary Chartier. who stress the value of radically free markets. termed *freed markets* to distinguish them from the common conception which these libertarians believe to be riddled with statist and capitalist privileges. Referred to as left-wing market anarchists or market-oriented left-libertarians. proponents of this approach strongly affirm the classical liberal ideas of self-ownership and free markets. while maintaining that. taken to their logical conclusions. these ideas support anti-capitalist. anti-corporatist. anti-hierarchical. pro-labour positions in economics; anti-imperialism in foreign policy; and thoroughly liberal or radical views regarding such cultural issues as gender. sexuality. and race.

The genealogy of contemporary market-oriented left-libertarianism—sometimes labeled "left-wing market anarchism"—overlaps to a significant degree with that of Steiner–Vallentyne left-libertarianism as the roots of that tradition are sketched in the book *The Origins of Left-Libertarianism*. Carson–

Long-style left-libertarianism is rooted in 19th-century mutualism and in the work of figures such as Thomas Hodgskin and the individualist anarchists Benjamin Tucker and Lysander Spooner. While. with notable exceptions. market-oriented libertarians after Tucker tended to ally with the political right. relationships between such libertarians and the New Left thrived in the 1960s. laying the groundwork for modern left-wing market anarchism.

Left wing market anarchism identifies with Left-libertarianism (or left-wing libertarianism) which names several related but distinct approaches to politics. society. culture. and political and social theory. which stress both individual freedom and social justice. Unlike right-libertarians. they believe that neither claiming nor mixing one's labour with natural resources is enough to generate full private property rights. and maintain that natural resources (land. oil. gold. trees) ought to be held in some egalitarian manner. either unowned or owned collectively. Those left-libertarians who support private property do so under the condition that recompense is offered to the local community.

SOCIALIST MARKET ECONOMY

The socialist market economy is the economic model employed by the People's Republic of China. It is based on the dominance of the state-owned sector and an open-market economy. and has its origins in the Chinese economic reforms introduced underDeng Xiaoping. The ideological rationale is that China is in the primary stage of socialism. an early stage within the socialist mode of production. and therefore has to adapt capitalist techniques to thrive. Despite this. the system has widely been cited as a form ofstate capitalism.

DESCRIPTION

After the Great Leap Forward (1958–1961) and the ousting of the Gang of Four from power. Chairman Deng Xiaoping was willing to consider market-based methods of economic growth so as to revitalise China's economy and find an economic system compatible with China's specific conditions. However. in doing so. he remained committed to the centralized control and the one-party state central to Leninism.

The socialist market economy was a concept first proposed by Deng Xiaoping in order to incorporate the market into the planned economy in the People's Republic of China. and later. to the in Vietnam. Following its implementation. this economic system has supplemented the centrally planned economy in the People's Republic of China. with high growth rates in GDP during the past decades having been attributed to it. Within this model. privately owned enterprises have become a major component of the economic system alongside the central state-owned enterprises and collective/ township village enterprises. There are some similarities to Western mixed economies. with some fundamental differences. The fundamental distinction between the

Chinese and Western mixed-market economy models lies less in the implementation of the mixed economic model but rather in the degree of state-ownership and underlying authoritarian political philosophy. which eschews Western notions of democracy. individual rights. and the rule of law.

This type of economic system is defended from a Stalinist perspective which states that a fully developed socialist planned economy can only come into existence after first establishing the necessary and comprehensive commodity market economy and letting it fully develop until it exhausts its historical stage and gradually transforms itself into a planned economy (the Stalinist Two-Stage theory of revolution). Proponents of this economic model distinguish it from Market socialism: Market socialists believe thateconomic planning is unattainable. undesirable or ineffective. and thus view the market as an integral part of socialism. whereas proponents of the socialist market economy view markets as a temporary phase in development of a fully planned economy.

Analysis

Despite the official designation of "socialism". analysts often describe the Chinese economy as a form of state capitalism. One analysis carried out by the Global Studies Association at the DePaul University reports that the Chinese economy does not constitute a form of socialism when "socialism" is defined variously as a planned economy where production for use has replaced production for profit; when it is defined as a system where the working-class is the dominant class (controls the surplus value produced by the economy); and when it is defined as self-management or workplace democracy. The study also found that as of 2006 capitalism was not the dominant mode of organization in the Chinese economy. suggesting that China is still a partially pre-capitalist agrarian system with almost 50per cent of its population engaged in agricultural work.

Analysis of the "Chinese model" by the economists Julan Du and Chenggang Xu finds that the contemporary economic system of the People's Republic of China represents a state capitalist system as opposed to a market socialist system. The reason for this categorization is that financial markets exist in the Chinese economic system. which are absent in classic models of market socialism and in the market socialist literature; and that state profits are retained by enterprises rather than being equitably distributed among the population in a social dividend or similar scheme (which are central features in most models of market socialism). They conclude that China is neither a form of market socialism nor a stable form of capitalism.

Other Marxist analyses point out that the current Chinese system contains capitalist commodity relations in production. dis-empowers the working class. and has contributed to a sharp increase in social inequality while growing the size and political power of a small capitalist class. Classical Marxists believe a "socialist commodity economy" (or a "socialist market economy") is contradictory. Other socialists believe the Chinese have embraced many elements of market capitalism. specifically commodity production and privatization. resulting in a full-blown capitalist economic system. Although many enterprises are nominally publicly owned. the profits are retained by the enterprises and used to pay managers excessively high salaries rather than being distributed amongst the population.

Proponents of the socialist market economy compare it to the New Economic Policy in Soviet Russia that introduced market-oriented reforms while maintaining state-ownership of the 'commanding heights' of the economy. The reforms are justified through the belief that changing conditions necessitate new strategies for socialist development.According to Li Rongrong in 2003. chairman of the State-Owned Assets Supervision and Administration Commission of the State Council.

Public ownership. as the foundation of the socialist economic system. is a basic force of the state to guide and promote economic and social development and a major guarantee for realising the fundamental interests and the common prosperity of the majority of the people... The state owned economy has taken a dominant place in major trades that have a close bearing on the country's economic lifeline and key areas. and has propped-up. guided and brought along the development of the entire socio-economy. The influence and control capacity of SOEs have further increased. State owned economy has played an irreplaceable role in China's socialist modernisation drive.

The state sector

By 2005 the market-oriented reforms. including privatisation. were virtually halted and partially reversed. In 2006. the Chinese government announced that the armaments. power generation and distribution. oil and petrochemicals. telecommunications. coal. aviation and shipping industries had to remain under "absolute state control" and public ownership by law. The state retains indirect control in directing the non-state economy through the financial system. which lends according to state priorities. Liberalization continues to be rolled back in the state-sector by the consolidation of state enterprises into large "national champions" with the goal of consolidating efforts and creating internationally competitive national industries.

The state sector is concentrated in the 'commanding heights' of the economy with a growing private sector engaged primarily in commodity production and light industry. Centralized directive planning based on mandatory output requirements and production quotas has been superseded by the free-market mechanism for most of the economy and directive planning in large state industries. A major difference from the old planned economy is the restructuring of state companies along a commercial basis. with the exception of 150 large state-owned enterprises that remain and report directly to the central government. most having a number of subsidiaries.

By 2008. these state-owned corporations have become increasingly dynamic largely contributing to the increase in revenue for the state. By 2009 the government considered a state insurance scheme to expand Health care coverage. The state-sector led the economic recovery process and increased economic growth in 2009 after the financial crises. partially because most of the Chinese stimulus package was directed towards these state-owned firms. The state-sector make out 40 to 50 percent of China's GDP.

Enterprise forms

The socialist market economy consists of a wide range of state enterprises and mixed-enterprises. Following the 1978 reforms. most state enterprises were reorganised into Western-style corporations and joint-stock companies. with the government retaining control through owning controlling shares in these corporations.

- *State-owned enterprise:* Commercial enterprises established by either the central government or a local government. where managers are appointed by the government or public bodies. This category only includes wholly state-funded and managed firms. Most state-owned enterprises are not entities of the central government. Central government state-owned enterprises are subunits of the State-owned Assets Supervision and Administration Commission (SASAC).
- *State-holding enterprise:* State-holding. or state-controlled enterprises. are publicly listed firms where the state owns a large share or a controlling share within the firms. thereby exerting influence on the management of the firm. These include firms that receive foreign direct investment.
- *Privately owned enterprise:* This category includes private limited liability corporations. private shareholding corporations. private partnership enterprises and private sole investment enterprises.
- *Urban Collectives*
- *Township-Village Enterprise*

HISTORY

The transition to a socialist market economy began in 1978 when Deng Xiaoping introduced his programme of "Socialism with Chinese characteristics". Initial reforms in decollectivising agriculture and allowing private businesses and foreign investment in the late 1970s and early 1980s later led to large-scale radical reforms. consisting of partial privatisation of the state sector. liberalisation of trade and prices. and dismantling of the "iron rice bowl" system of job security in the late 1990s. Since the beginning of Deng Xiaoping's reforms. China's GDP rose from some 150 billion USD to more than 1.6 trillion USD. with an annual increase of 9.4 percent.

The private sector's share of the GDP rose from less than 1per cent in 1978 to 70per cent by 2005. a figure that is still increasing. Due to the poor performance of traditional state enterprises in the market economy. China embarked on a massive restructuring programme of corporatization. Under this scheme. the state retains ownership and control of large enterprises but the central government has little direct control over the operations of state-owned enterprises. Recently the Conservative Hu-Wen Administration rolled back many of Deng's reforms. leaving observers dubbing 2008 the "third anniversary of the end of reform.

PRODUCTION FOR USE

Production for use is a phrase referring to the principle of economic organization and production taken as a defining criterion for asocialist economy. It is held in contrast to production for profit. This criterion is used to distinguish socialism from capitalism. and was one of the fundamental defining characteristics of socialism initially shared by Marxian socialists. evolutionary socialists.anarchists and Christian socialists.

This principle is broad and can refer to an array of different configurations that vary based on the underlying theory of economics employed. In its classic definition. production for use implied an economic system whereby the law of value and law of accumulationno longer directed economic activity. whereby a direct measure of utility and value is used in place of the abstractions of the price system. money and capital. Alternative conceptions of socialism that don't utilise the profit system such as the Lange modelinvolve the use of a price system and monetary calculation.

The central critique of the *profits system* by socialists is that the accumulation of capital ("making money") becomes increasingly detached from the process of producing economic value. leading to waste. inefficiency. and social issues. Essentially it is a distortion of proper accounting based on the assertion of the law of value instead of the "real" costs of the factors of production.objectively determined outside of social relations.

EXPOSITION

Production for *use* refers to an arrangement whereby the production of goods and services is carried out ex *ante* (directly) for their utility (also called Use-value). The implication is that the value of economic output would be based on use-value or a direct measure of utility as opposed to exchange-value; because economic activity would be undertaken to directly satisfy economic demands and human needs. the productive apparatus would directly serve individual and social needs. This is contrasted with production for exchange of the produced good or service in order to *profit*. where production is subjected to the perpetual accumulation of capital. a condition where production is only undertaken if it generates profit. implying an ex *post* or indirect means of satisfying economic demand.

The profits system is oriented Towards generating a profit to be reinvested into the economy (and the constant continuation of this process). the result being that society is structured around the need for a perpetual accumulation of capital. In contrast.*production for use* means that the accumulation of capital is not a compulsory driving force in the economy. and by extension. the core process which society and culture revolves around. Production for profit. in contrast. is the dominant mode of production in the modern world system. equivocates "profitability" and "productivity" and presumes that the former always equates to the latter.

Some thinkers. including the Austrian philosopher and political economist Otto Neurath. have used the phrase socialization to refer to the same concept of "production for use". In Neurath's phraseology. "total socialization" involves calculation in kind in place of financial calculation and a system of planning in place of market-based allocation of economic goods. Alternative conceptions exist in the form of market socialism.

USAGE

Norman Thomas. a presidential candidate in the United States for the Socialist Party of America. contrasted socialism with capitalism by stating that socialism is based on production for use and an end to the profit system.

Eugene V. Debs popularly used the phrase when running for president of the United States in 1912. stating that capitalism is founded upon production for profit. and in contrast. socialism is postulated upon production for use.

Karl Marx referred to the "production of use-values" as a feature of any economic mode of production. but characterised capitalism as a mode of production that subjugated the production of use-value for the self-expansion of capital (*i.e.*: capital accumulation or production for profit). In contrast. socialism was vaguely defined as a system based on the direct production of use-value free of the process of continuous capital accumulation.

Friedrich Hayek defined socialism as "...the common ownership of the means of production and their 'employment for use. not for profit.'". associating the rise of the welfare state by social democrats in post-World War II Europe as a rejection of socialism in the technical sense.

DESCRIPTION

Proponents of socialism argue that production for profit (*i.e.*. capitalism) does not always satisfy the economic needs of people. especially the working-class. because capital only invests in production when it is profitable. This fails to satisfy demand (the needs) of people who lack basic necessities but have insufficient purchasing power to acquire these needs in a manner that would be profitable for businesses. This results in a number of inefficiencies: unsold items are rarely given away to people who need but can't afford them. unemployed workers are not utilised to produce such services. and resources are expended on occupations that serve no other purpose than to support the accumulation of profit instead of being utilised to provide useful goods and services. For example. the United States housing bubble resulted in an overproduction of housing units that could not be sold at a profit. despite there being sufficient demand and need for housing units.

Production for use in some form was the historically dominant modality until the initial primitive accumulation of capital.

Production for use is not in conflict with market allocation. For example. final output (goods and services for consumption) would still be distributed to consumers through a market. Only in a sufficiently developed stage of socialism whereby the forces of production are advanced enough to allow for superabundances of goods and services can distribution be based on free-access/ according to needs. Economic planning is not synonymous with *production for use*. Planning is essential in modern globalised production both within enterprises and within nation states. Planning to maximize profitability (*i.e.*. within industries and private corporations) or to improve the efficiency of capital accumulation in the capitalist macro-economy (*i.e.*. monetary policy.fiscal policy. industrial policy) does not change the fundamental criteria and need to generate a financial profit to be reinvested into the economy. lest it go into a crisis. A more recent critique of production for profit is that it fails spectacularly to address issues such as externalities which the board and management of a for profit enterprise are often under a fiduciary responsibility to ignore if they harm or conflict with the shareholders' profit motives.

Criticisms of production for profit

A number of irrational outcomes occur from capitalism and the need to accumulate capital when capitalist economies reach a point in development whereby investment accumulates at a greater rate than growth of profitable investment opportunities. The central critique of the profits system maintained by socialists is that the accumulation of capital ("making money") becomes further detached from the process of producing economic value. leading to waste. inefficiency and underlying social issues. Advertisement and planned obsolescence are strategies used by businesses to generate demand for the perpetual consumption required for capitalism to sustain itself so that instead of satisfying social and individual needs. capitalism first and foremost serves the artificial need for the perpetual accumulation of capital.

The creation of industries. projects and services for no other purpose than generating profit. economic growth or maintaining employment. The drive to create such industries arises from the need to absorb the savings in the economy (and thus. to maintain the accumulation of capital). This can take the form of corporatization and commercialization of public services (*i.e.*. transforming them into profit-generating industries to absorb investment). or the creation and expansion of sectors of the economy that don't produce any economic value by themselves (that deal only with exchange-related activities) such as financial services. contributing to the formation of economic bubbles. crises and ultimately recessions.

For socialists. the solution to these problems entails a reorientation of the economic system from production for profit and the need to accumulate capital to a system where production is adjusted to meet individual and social demands directly.

Criticisms of central planning

Socialist and non-socialist critics of the Soviet model of economic planning have criticized the Soviet model of a planned economy on similar grounds to the critique leveled against capitalism: production was often undertaken in order to fulfill plan targets as opposed to being produced for use.

Contrasted with state capitalism

As an objective criterion for socialism. *production for use* can be used to evaluate the socialistic content of the composition of former and existing economic systems. For example. an economic system that is dominated by nationalized firms organised around the production of profit – whether this profit is retained by the firm or paid to the government as a dividend payment – would be a state capitalist economy.

In such a system. the organizational structure of the firm remains similar to a private-sector firm; non-financial costs are externalized because profitability is the criterion for production. so that the majority of the economy remains essentially capitalist despite the formal title of "public ownership". This has led many socialists to categorize the current Chinese economic system as a capitalist or state-capitalist economy.

The economy of the Soviet Union was based upon capital accumulation for reinvestment and production for profit; the difference between Western capitalism was that the Soviet Union achieved this through nationalized industry and state-directed investment with the eventual goal of building a socialist society based upon production for use and self-management.

Vladimir Lenin described the Soviet economy as "state-monopoly capitalism" and did not consider it to be socialism. During the 1965 Liberman Reforms. the Soviet Union re-introduced profitability as a criterion for industrial enterprises. Other views argue the Soviet Union evolved into a non-capitalist and non-socialist system characterized by control and subordination of society by the party apparatus or those who coordinate the economy (bureaucratic collectivism).

Contrary socialist theories

The concept of production for use has been rejected by some socialists. most notably proponents of market socialism. who argue that cooperative and public enterprises can compete with each other to generate profit in a market economy. and that these profits would accrue to society at large (*i.e.*. a Social dividend). Neo-classical economists argue that. under conditions of pareto optimality. the pursuit of profit leads to a satisfaction of economic demands - the provision of use-values - and that market socialism would be able to achieve this outcome while retaining profitability as the operational criteria for socialist enterprises.

In particular. some market socialists justify their position by claiming that society as a whole would control the surplus product (the profit generated by publicly owned firms). which could be used to finance public goods or public investment as opposed to accumulating in the hands of capitalists/shareholders.

Social democrats have rejected this concept altogether. and wish to retain the capitalist economic system by promoting a welfare state and economic interventions in order to make capitalism more "equitable" without questioning the legitimacy of the profits system.

SOCIAL PRODUCTION AND PEER-TO-PEER PROCESSES

Michel Bauwens identifies the emergence of the open software movement and peer-to-peer production as an emergent alternative mode of production to the capitalist economy that is based on collaborative self-management. common ownership of resources. and the (direct) production of use-values through the free cooperation of producers who have access to distributed capital.

Commons-based peer production generally involves developers who produce goods and services with no aim to profit directly. but freely contribute to a project relying upon an open common pool of resources and software code. In both cases. production is carried out directly for use - software is produced solely for their use-value.

VALUATION AND CALCULATION

Multiple forms of valuation have been proposed to govern production in a socialist economy. to serve as a unit of account and to quantify the usefulness of an object in socialism. These include valuations based on labour-time. the expenditure of energy in production. or disaggregated units of physical quantities.

Physical quantities

The classic formulation of socialism involved replacing the criteria of value from money (exchange-value) to physical utility (use-value). to be quantified in terms of physical quantities (Calculation in kind and Input-Output analysis) or some natural unit of accounting. such as energy accounting.

Input-output model analysis is based upon directly determining the physical quantities of goods and services to be produced and allocating economic inputs accordingly; thus production targets are pre-planned. Soviet economic planning was overwhelmingly focused on material balances - balancing the supply of economic inputs with planned output targets.

Marginal cost

Oskar Lange formulated a mechanism for the direct allocation of capital goods in a socialist economy that was based on the marginal cost of production. Under a capitalist economy. managers of firms are ordered and legally required to base production around profitability. and in theory. competitive pressure creates a downward pressure on profits and forces private businesses to be responsive to demands of consumers. indirectly approximating production for use. In the Lange Model. the firms would be publicly owned and the managers would be tasked with setting the price of output to its marginal cost. thereby achieving pareto efficiency through direct allocation.

Cybernetics

Cybernetics. the use of computers to coordinate production in an optimal fashion. has been suggested for socialist economies. Oskar Lange. rejecting his earlier proposals formarket socialism. argued that the computer is more efficient than the market process at solving the multitude of simultaneous equations required for allocating economic inputs efficiently (either in terms of physical quantities or monetary prices).

Salvador Allende's socialist-led government developed Project Cybersyn; a system whereby economic decisions and feedback could be relayed in real-time through a network of telex machines fusing the information received/given by state enterprises and government departments. The project was disbanded after the 1973 Chilean coup d'état.

Free market

Based on the perspective that the law of value would continue to operate in a socialist economy. it is argued that a market economy purged of parasitical and wasteful elements in the form of private ownership of the means of production and the distortions that arise from the concentration of power and wealth in a class of capitalists would enable the market to operate efficiently without distortions. Simply replacing the antagonistic interests between capitalists and workers in enterprises would alter the orientation of the economy from private profit to meeting the demands of the community. as firms would seek to maximize the benefits to the member-workers - who would. as a whole. comprise society. Cooperative economist Jaroslav Vanek suggests that worker self-management and cooperative ownership of enterprises operating in a free-market would allow for a genuine free-market economy free of the market-distorting. monopolistic tendencies and antagonistic interests that emerge from private ownership over production.

Chapter 6: State socialism

State socialism is a classification for any socialist political or economic ideology that advocates state ownership of the means of production either as a temporary measure during the transition from capitalism to socialism. or as characteristic of socialism itself. It is often used in reference to the economic systems of Marxist-Leninist communist states to highlight the central role of state planning in these economies. State socialism only has a limited number of socialist characteristics. including public ownership of major industries. remedial measures to benefit the working class. and a gradual process of developing socialism through government action.

The ideology of state socialism is held in contrast with libertarian socialism and socialist anarchism. both of which reject the view that socialism can be constructed by using existing state institutions or by governmental policies.

The philosophy of state socialism was first explicitly expounded by Ferdinand Lassalle. In contrast to Karl Marx's perspective. Lassalle rejected the concept of the state as a class-based power structure whose main function was to preserve existing class structures; therefore Lassalle also rejected the Marxist view that the state was destined to "wither away". Lassalle considered the state to be an entity independent of class allegiances and as an instrument of justice that would therefore be essential for the achievement of socialism.

Early concepts of state socialism were articulated by anarchist and libertarian philosophers who opposed the concept of the state. In*Statism and Anarchy*. Mikhail Bakunin identified a "statist" tendency within the socialist movement. which he contrasted to anarchist socialism and attributed to Karl Marx's philosophy. Bakunin believed that Marx's theory of transition from capitalism to socialism involving the working class seizing state power in a dictatorship of the proletariat would eventually lead to an usurpation of power by the state apparatus acting in its own self-interest.

The American individualist anarcho-socialist Benjamin Tucker. wrote of state socialism in his 1886 essay entitled *State Socialism and Anarchism*. defining it as a tendency that advocates for governmental control over the means of production as a precondition for establishing socialism.

As a political ideology. state socialism rose to prominence during the 20th century Bolshevik. Leninist and later Marxist-Leninist revolutions where single-party control over the state. and by extension. over the political and economic spheres of society was justified as a means to safeguard the revolution against counter-revolutionary insurrection and foreign invasion. The Stalinist theory of socialism in one country further legitimized state-directed activity in an effort to rapidly mobilize the Soviet Union's resources to industrialize its internal economy.

Proponents of state socialism claim the state. through practical considerations of governing. must play at least a temporary part in building socialism. It is possible to conceive of a democratic state that owns the means of production but is internally organised in a participatory. cooperative fashion. thereby achieving both common ownership of productive property and workplace democracy in day-to-day operations.

DESCRIPTION AND THEORY

State socialism. as a political ideology. is one of the dividing lines within the broader socialist movement. It is often contrasted non-state or anti-state forms of socialism. such as those that advocate direct self-management. adhocracy and direct cooperative ownership and management of the means of production. Political philosophies contrasted to state socialism include libertarian socialism. anarchist socialism. anarchist communism. syndicalism. free-market socialism. De Leonism and economic democracy. These forms of socialism are opposed to hierarchical technocratic socialism. scientific management. and state-directed economic planning.

The modern concept of state socialism. when used in in reference to Soviet-style economic and political systems. emerged from a deviation in Marxist theory starting with Vladimir Lenin. In Marxist theory. socialism is projected to emerge in the most developed capitalist economies where capitalism suffers the greatest amount of internal contradictions and class conflict. "State socialism". on the other hand. became a revolutionary theory for the poorest. often quasi-feudal. countries of the world. In such systems. the state apparatus is used as an instrument of capital accumulation. forcibly extracting surplus from the working class and peasantry for the purposes of modernizing and industrializing poor countries. Such systems are described as state capitalism because the state engages in capital accumulation.

THE ROLE OF THE STATE IN SOCIALISM

In the traditional view of socialism. thinkers including Fredrick Engels and Saint-Simon took the position that the state will change in nature in a socialist society. with the function of the state changing from one of "political rule" over people into a scientific administration of the processes of production. Specifically. the state would become a coordinating economic entity consisting of interdependent inclusive associations rather than a mechanism of class and political control. and in the process it would cease to be a state in the traditional definition. In Marxist theory socialism would eventually give way to a stateless communist society.

Preceding the Bolshevik-led revolution in Russia. many socialist groups including reformists. orthodox Marxist currents such as council communism and the Mensheviks. Anarchists and Libertarian socialists criticised the idea of using the state to conduct central planning and nationalization of the means of production as a way to establish socialism.

POLITICAL PERSPECTIVES

State socialism was traditionally advocated as a means for achieving public ownership of the means of production through nationalization of industry. This was intended to be a transitional phase in the process of building a socialist economy. The goals of nationalization were to dispossess large capitalists and consolidate industry so that profit would go Towards public finance rather than private fortune. Nationalization would be the first step in a long-term process of socializing production: introducing employee management and reorganizing production to directly produce for use rather than profit.

Traditional social democrats and non-revolutionary democratic socialists argued for a gradual. peaceful transition from capitalism to socialism. They wish to abolish capitalism. but through political reform rather than revolution. This method of gradualism implies utilization of the existing state apparatus and machinery of government to gradually move society Towards socialism. and is sometimes derided by other socialists as a form of "socialism from above" or political "elitism" for relying on electoral means to achieve socialism.

In contrast. Marxist socialism and revolutionary socialism holds that a socialist revolution is the only practical way to implement fundamental changes in the structure of society. Marxists maintain that after a certain period of time under socialism. the state will "wither away" because class distinctions cease to exist and representative democracy would be replaced by direct democracy in the remaining public associations comprising the former state. Political power would be decentralised and distributed evenly among the population. producing a communist society.

STATE SOCIALISM IN COMMUNIST STATES

The economic model adopted in the former Soviet Union. Eastern Europe and other Communist states is often described as a form of state socialism. The ideological basis for this system was the Marxist-Leninist theory of Socialism in One Country. The system that emerged in the 1930s in the Soviet Union was based on state ownership of the means of production and centralised planning. along with bureaucratic management of the workplace by state officials that were ultimately subordinate to the all-encompassing communist party.

Rather than the producers controlling and managing production. the party controlled both the government machinery which directed the national economy on behalf of the communist party. and planned the production and distribution of capital goods.

Because of this. classical and orthodox Marxists as well as Trotskyist groups denounced the "Communist" states as being Stalinist and their economies as being state capitalist or representing degenerated workers' states. respectfully.

Trotskyism argues that the leadership of the Communist states was corrupt and that it abandoned Marxism in all but name. In particular. some Trotskyist schools call those countries degenerated workers' states to contrast them with proper socialism (*i.e.* workers' states); other Trotskyist schools call them *state capitalist*. to emphasise the lack of true socialism and presence of defining capitalist characteristics (wage labour. commodity production. bureaucratic control over workers).

BISMARCK'S SOCIAL POLICY

Otto von Bismarck implemented a set of social programmes between 1883–1889. following his anti-socialist laws. partly as remedial measures to appease the working class and detract support for the Social Democratic Party of Germany. Bismarck's biographer A. J. P. Taylor said: "It would be unfair to say that Bismarck took up social welfare solely to weaken the Social Democrats; he had had it in mind for a long time. and believed in it deeply. But as usual he acted on his beliefs at the exact moment when they served a practical need". When a reference was made to his friendship with Ferdinand Lassalle (a nationalist and state-oriented socialist). Bismarck said that he was a more practical "socialist" than the Social Democrats. These policies were informally referred to as "State Socialism" by liberal and conservative opponents; the term was later adopted by supporters of the programmes in a further attempt to detract the working class from the SPD. with the goal of making the working class content with a nationalist-oriented capitalistwelfare state.

Otto von Bismarck made the following statement on his social welfare programmes: "Whoever has pensions for his old age is far more easier to handle than one who has no such prospect. Look at the difference between a private servant in the chancellery or at court; the latter will put up with much more. because he has a pension to look forward to".

CRITICISMS

Many libertarian socialists. Syndicalists. Mutualists and anarchists go further in their critique. deriding even Marxism as *state socialism* for its support of a temporary. proletarian state instead of abolishing the state apparatus outright. They use the term in contrast with their own form of socialism. which involves either collective ownership (in the form ofworker cooperatives) or common ownership of the means of production without state economic planning. Libertarian socialists and anarchists believe there is no need for a state in a socialist system because there would be no class to suppress and no need for an institution based on coercion. and thus regard the state being a remnant of capitalism.

Most also hold that statism is itself antithetical to true socialism. the goal of which is the eyes of libertarian socialists such as William Morris; "to destroy the state and put free society in its place". State socialism is often referred to by detractors simply as "socialism". Austrian economists such as Ludwig Von Mises and Friedrich Hayek for example continually used the word "socialism" as a synonym for state socialism and central planning. The attributive "state" is usually added by socialists with a non-state based method for achieving socialism to criticize *state* socialism. Some socialists may deny that it even *is* socialism. calling it instead "state capitalism". Those socialists who oppose any system of state control whatsoever believe in a more decentralized approach which puts the means of production directly into the hands of the workers rather than indirectly through state bureaucracies—which they claim represent a new elite.

Trotskyists believe that central planners. regardless of their intellectual capacity. operate without the input and participation of the millions of people who participate in the economy who understand/respond to local conditions and changes in the economy. and because of this criticize central state planning as being unable to effectively coordinate all economic activity.

Orthodox Marxists view state socialism as an oxymoron; while an association for managing production and economic affairs would exist in socialism. it would no longer be a state in the Marxist definition (which is based on domination by one class). This leads some socialists to consider "state socialism" a form of state capitalism (an economy based on wage labour and capital accumulation but with the state owning the means of production) - which Fredrick Engels states would be the final form of capitalism.

Today. many political parties on the political centre-left advocate a mild version of what may be considered "mixed economies" or "regulated capitalism" in the form of modernsocial democracy. in which regulation is used in place of ownership.

These social reformers do not advocate the overthrow of capitalism in a social revolution. and they support the continuing existence of the government. private property and the capitalist economic system. only turned to more social purposes. Modern social democracy can also be considered "state capitalism" because the means of production are almost universally the private property of business owners. and production is carried out for exchange rather than directly for use.

COMMUNIST STATE

"Communist state" is a Western term for a state with a form of government characterised by single-party rule or dominant-party system by a party which claims to follow communism. usually with a professed allegiance to Marxism-Leninism as the guiding ideology of the state. None of these states achieved communism. and the term is used no matter to what degree that state or the movement associated with it actually follows communism. if at all. The label is the source of controversy. especially among the left; according to many communist and Marxist tendencies. the system in use in the Soviet Union and the states modeled after it (*i.e.*. "communist states") - which claimed to have reached socialism. not communism - was not socialism but rather state capitalism. The term "Communist state" is an oxymoron (a contradiction on itself) as a communist society is stateless. Usually. the term Marxist-Leninist state is more appropriate.

In the theories of German philosopher Karl Marx. a state in any society is an instrument of oppression by one social class over another. historically a minority exploiter class ruling over a majority exploited class. Marx saw that in his contemporary time. the newnation states were characterised by increasingly intensified class contradiction between the capitalist class and the working class it ruled over. He predicted that if the class contradictions of the capitalist system continue to intensify. that the working class will ultimately become conscious of itself as an exploited collective and will overthrow the capitalists and establish collective ownership over the means of production. therein arriving at a new phase of development called Socialism. The state ruled by the working class during the transition into classless society is called the Dictatorship of the Proletariat. Russian theoretician Vladimir Lenin further expounded upon this concept with the understanding of the revolutionary vanguard. Lenin saw that science is something that is initially practicable by only a minority of society who happen to be in a position free from distraction so that they may contemplate it. and believed that scientific socialism was no exception. He therefore advocated that the Communist party should be structured as a vanguard of those who have achieved full class consciousness to be at the forefront of the class struggle and lead the workers to expand class consciousness and replace the capitalist class as the ruling class. therein establishing the Communist state.

In a Communist state. the Communist party is the nucleus of society. Other parties may function alongside the Communist party occasionally. but parties advocating the restoration of capitalism are typically prohibited. Using Marxism-Leninism as a method of understanding the material and social conditions of society. the Communist party governs according to what the society's historical and national characteristics demand in order to unleash the productive forces and further advance towards communism. This has been done through a variety of methods in conforming to local circumstances. For example. in Russiaand the Soviet Union in the 1920s. a regulated market economy was initially implemented due to the country's lack of infrastructural development and to overcome the devastation of civil war. But into the 1930s. the economy of the Soviet Union was characterised by assessment planning. heavy industrialization. and a centralized bureaucracy headquartered inMoscow. Similarly. the People's Republic of China operated almost entirely along plans of development until the 1980s when it opened its economy to foreign investment. allowing for market development alongside planned development. Reliance on markets and planning have varied in different Communist states. but most such states are characterised by state monopoly over land ownership. full union representation in the workforce. and social security systems to provide for those unable to work.

During the 20th century. the world's first constitutionally socialist state was in Russia in 1917. In 1922. it joined other former territories of the empire to become the Union of Soviet Socialist Republics. After the Second World War. the Soviet Armyoccupied much of Eastern Europe and thus helped establish Communist states in these countries. Most Communist states in Eastern Europe were allied with the USSR. except for Yugoslavia which declared itself non-aligned. In 1949. after a war against Japanese occupation and a civil war resulting in a Communist victory. the People's Republic of China was established. Communist states were also established in Cuba. Vietnam. Laos. and Cambodia. A Communist state was established in North Korea. although it later withdrew from the Communist movement. In 1989. the Communist states in Eastern Europe collapsed under public pressure during a wave of non-violent movements which led to the dissolution of the Soviet Union in 1991. Today. the existing Communist states in the world are in China. Laos.Vietnam. and Cuba.

TYPES OF SOCIALIST STATES

While historically almost all claim lineage to Marxist thought. there are many varieties of socialist states. with indigenous adaptions.

These Socialist states often do not claim to have achieved socialism or communism in their countries; rather. they claim to be*building* and working Towards the establishment of socialism in their countries. For example. the preamble to the Socialist Republic of Vietnam's constitution states that Vietnam only entered a transition stage between capitalism and socialism after the country was re-unified under the Communist party in 1976. and the 1992 Constitution of the Republic of Cuba states that the role of the Communist Party is to "guide the common effort Towards the goals and construction of socialism". Alternative names that states adhering to an officially communist ideology may assign themselves is socialist state. socialist republic or "people's republic". This is because these nations have not yet transcended capitalism or state capitalism and progressed towardpure communism in the Marxist sense. which can only be achieved once capitalism exhausts itself.

STATE INSTITUTIONS

Marxist-Leninist states share similar institutions. which are organised on the premise that the communist party is a vanguard of the proletariat and represents the long-term interests of the people. The doctrine of democratic centralism. which was developed byVladimir Lenin as a set of principles to be used in the internal affairs of the communist party. is extended to society at large.

According to democratic centralism. all leaders must be elected by the people and all proposals must be debated openly. but. once a decision has been reached. all people have a duty to obey that decision and all debate should end. When used within a political party. democratic centralism is meant to prevent factionalism and splits. When applied to an entire state. democratic centralism creates a one-party system.

The constitutions of most socialist states describe their political system as a form of democracy. Thus. they recognise the sovereignty of the people as embodied in a series of representative parliamentary institutions. Such states do not have a separation of powers; instead. they have one national legislative body (such as the Supreme Soviet in the Soviet Union) which is considered the highest organ of state power and which is legally superior to the executive and judicial branches of government.

Such national legislative politics in socialist states often have a similar structure to the parliaments that exist in liberal republics. with two significant differences: first. the deputies elected to these national legislative bodies are not expected to represent the interests of any particular constituency. but the long-term interests of the people as a whole; second. against Marx's advice. the legislative bodies of socialist states are not in permanent session. Rather. they convene once or several times per year in sessions which usually last only a few days.

When the national legislative body is not in session. its powers are transferred to a smaller council (often called a presidium) which combines legislative and executive power. and. in some socialist states (such as the Soviet Union before 1990). acts as a collective head of state. In some systems. the presidium is composed of important communist party members who vote the resolutions of the communist party into law.

State social institutions

Another feature of socialist states is the existence of numerous state-sponsored social organizations (trade unions. youth organizations. women's organizations. associations of teachers. writers. journalists and other professionals. consumer cooperatives. sports clubs. etc.) which are integrated into the political system.In some socialist states. representatives of these organizations are guaranteed a certain number of seats on the national legislative bodies. In socialist states. the social organizations are expected to promote social unity and cohesion. to serve as a link between the government and society. and to provide a forum for recruitment of new communist party members.

Political power

Historically. the political organization of many socialist states has been dominated by a single-party monopoly. Some communist governments. such as North Korea. East Germany or the Czechoslovak Socialist Republic have or had more than one political party. but all minor parties are or were required to follow the leadership of the communist party. In socialist states. the government may not tolerate criticism of policies that have already been implemented in the past or are being implemented in the present.

Nevertheless. communist parties have won elections and governed in the context of multi-party democracies. without seeking to establish a one-party state. Examples includeSan Marino. Republic of Nicaragua. Moldova. Nepal (presently). Cyprus. and the Indian states of Kerala. West Bengal and Tripura. However. for the purposes of this article. these entities do not fall under the definition of socialist state.

STATE SOCIALISM (GERMANY)

State Socialism was a term introduced to describe Otto von Bismarck's social welfare policies. The term was actually coined by Bismarck's liberal opposition but later accepted by Bismarck. They refer to a set of social programmes implemented between 1884 to 1889 as remedial measures to appease the working class and detract support for socialismand the Social Democratic Party of Germany following earlier attempts to achieve the same objective through Bismarck's anti-socialist laws.

INTELLECTUAL PREDECESSORS AND HEIRS

The Prussian welfare state was developed by the German academic *Sozialpolitiker* (Social Policy Supporter) group. intellectually associated with the historical school of economics.

At the time. they influenced social liberalism in the United Kingdom and Progressivism in the United States. and the current (Post-World War II) German economy. the social market economy. is a continuation of similar policies.

TERMINOLOGY

According to William Harbutt Dawson. despite being labeled "socialist" by his opponents. Otto Von Bismarck's social legislation sought to preserve the existing economic order and state in Germany. This was in stark contrast to socialists. who sought to subvert the power of the existing state and eventually replace the capitalist order with a socialist economy.

BISMARCK'S SOCIAL LEGISLATION

„[...] the actual complaint of the worker is the insecurity of his existence; he is unsure if he will always have work. he is unsure if he will always be healthy and he can predict that he will reach old age and be unable to work. If he falls into poverty. and be that only through prolonged illness. he will find himself totally helpless being on his own. and society currently does not accept any responsibility towards him beyond the usual provisions for the poor. even if he has been working all the time ever so diligently and faithfully. The ordinary provisions for the poor. however. leaves a lot to be desired [...]."

— Otto von Bismarck. 20.03.1884

The 1880s were a period when Germany started on its long road towards the welfare state it is today. The Social Democratic. National Liberal and Centre Parties were all involved in the beginnings of social legislation. but it was Bismarck who established the first practical aspects of this programme. The programme of the Social Democrats included all of the programmes that Bismarck eventually implemented. but also included programmes designed to Pre-empt the programmes championed by Karl Marx and Friedrich Engels. Bismarck's idea was to implement the minimum aspects of these programmes that were acceptable to the German government without any of the overtly socialistic aspects.

Bismarck opened debate on the subject on 17 November 1881 in the Imperial Message to the Reichstag. using the term *practical Christianity* to describe his programme. In 1881 Bismarck had also referred to this programme as *Staatssozialismus*. when he made the following accurate prediction to a colleague:

"It is possible that all our politics will come to nothing when I am dead but state socialism will drub[force] itself in. (Der Staatssozialismus paukt sich durch.)"

Bismarck's programme centered squarely on insurance programmes designed to increase productivity and focus the political attentions of German workers on supporting the Junker's government. The programme included Health insurance. accident insurance (workman's compensation); disability insurance; and an old-age retirement Pension. none of which then in existence to any great degree.

Based on Bismarck's message. the Reichstag filed three bills designed to deal with the concept of Accident insurance. and one for Health Insurance. Retirement pensions and disability insurance were placed on the back burner for the time being.

Health Insurance Bill of 1883

The first bill that had success was the Health Insurance bill. which was passed in 1883. The programme was considered the least important from Bismarck's point of view and the least politically troublesome. The programme was established to provide health care for the largest segment of the German workers. The health service was established on a local basis. with the cost divided between employers and the employed.

The employers contributed one-third. the workers the rest. The minimum payments for medical treatment and sick pay for up to 13 weeks were legally fixed. The individual local health bureaus were administered by a committee elected by the members of each bureau. and this move had the unintended effect of establishing a majority representation for the workers on account of their large financial contribution. This worked to the advantage of the Social Democrats who. through heavy worker membership. achieved their first small foothold in public administration.

Accident Insurance Bill of 1884

Bismarck's government had to submit three draft bills before it could get one passed by the Reichstag in 1884. Bismarck had originally proposed that the Federal Government should pay a portion of the accident insurance contribution to show the willingness of the German government to lessen the hardship experienced by the German workers as a means of weaning them away from the various left-wing parties. most importantly the Social Democrats. The National Liberals took this programme to be an expression of State Socialism. which they were strongly against.

The Centre Party was afraid of the expansion of federal power at the expense of states' rights. As a result. the only way the programme could be passed at all was for the entire expense to be underwritten by the employers. To facilitate this. Bismarck arranged for the administration of this programme to be placed in the hands of "Der Arbeitgeberverband in den beruflichen Korporationen". "the organization of employers in occupational corporations". This organization established central and bureaucratic insurance offices on the federal. and in some cases the state. level to perform the actual administration. The programme kicked in to replace the health insurance programme as of the 14th week. It paid for medical treatment and a Pension of up to two-thirds of earned wages if the worker was fully disabled. This programme was expanded in 1886 to include agricultural workers.

Old Age and Disability Insurance Bill of 1889

The old-age pension programme. financed by a tax on workers. was designed to provide a pension annuity for workers who reached the age of 70. At the time. the life expectancyfor the average Prussian was 45. although this reflects the high infant mortality of the era. and retired workers could expect to live until 70 years. Unlike accident insurance and health insurance. this programme covered industrial. agrarian. artisans and servants from the start. Also. unlike the other two programmes. the principle that the federal government should contribute a portion of the underwriting cost. with the other two portions prorated accordingly. was accepted without question. The disability insurance programme was intended to be used by those permanently disabled. This time. the state supervised the programmes directly.

SOCIALIST STATE

The term socialist state (or socialist republic) usually refers to any state that is constitutionally dedicated to the construction of asocialist society. It is closely related to the political ideology of *state socialism*. the view that socialism can be established through the existing state or by government policies. Alternatively. the term Workers' State is used to describe a state where the working class controls the machinery of government but has not yet established a socialist economic system. Both of these concepts are distinguished from a socialist government. which generally refers to a liberal democratic state governed by an elected majoritysocialist party or social democratic party which need not pursue the development of socialism - in any case. the distinguishing feature between a socialist state and a socialist government is that in the latter the state apparatus is not constitutionally bound to the construction of a socialist system.

A variety of non-state socialist positions. such as social anarchism. libertarian socialism. and council communism reject the concept of a "socialist state" altogether. believing that the modern state is a byproduct of capitalism and cannot be used for the establishment of a socialist system. They reason that a "socialist state" is antithetical to socialism. and that socialism will emerge spontaneously from the grass-roots level in an evolutionary manner. developing its own unique political and economic institutions for a highly organised stateless society.

The phrase *Socialist state*. or *Communist state* in the West. is widely used by Leninists and Marxist–Leninists in reference to a state under the control of a vanguard party that is organizing the economic. social. and political affairs of said state Towards the construction of socialism. This often includes at least the "commanding heights" of the economy to be nationalised. usually operated according to a plan of production. at least in the major production and social spheres.

Under the Leninist definition. the socialist state presides over a state capitalist economy structured upon state-directed accumulation of capital. with the goal of building up the country's productive forces and promoting worldwide socialist revolution. with the eventual long-term goal of building a socialist economy. Most theories assume widespread democracy. and some assume workers' democratic participation at every level of economic and state administration. while varying in the degree to which economic planning decisions are delegated to public officials and administrative specialists. States where democracy is lacking. yet the economy is largely in the hands of the state. are termed by orthodox Trotskyist theories as "workers' states" but not socialist states. using the terms "degenerated" or "deformed" workers' states.

MARXIST CONCEPT OF A SOCIALIST STATE

Henri de Saint-Simon. a pre-Marxian socialist. understood that the nature of the state would change under socialism from that of political rule (via coercion) over people to a scientific administration of things and a direction of processes of production; specifically. the state would become a coordinating entity for production as opposed to a mechanism for political control.

Karl Marx understood the state to be an instrument of the class rule. dominated by the interests of the ruling class in any mode of production. Although Marx never referred to a "socialist state". he argued that the working-class would have to take control of the state apparatus and machinery of government in order to transition out of capitalism and to socialism. This transitional stage would involve working-class interests dominating the government policy (the "Dictatorship of the proletariat"). in the same manner that capitalist-class interests dominate government policy under capitalism. Fredrick Engels argued that the state under socialism is not a "government of people. but the administration of things". and thus would not be a state in the traditional sense of the term.

One of the most influential modern visions of a socialist state was based on the Paris Commune. in which the workers and poor took control of the city of Paris in 1871 in reaction to the Franco-Prussian War. Karl Marx described the Paris Commune as the prototype for a revolutionary government of the future. "the form at last discovered" for the emancipation of the proletariat.

Friedrich Engels noted that "all officials. high or low. were paid only the wages received by other workers... In this way an effective barrier to place-hunting and careerism was set up".

Commenting on the nature of the state. Engels continued: "From the outset the Commune was compelled to recognise that the working class. once come to power. could not manage with the old state machine".

In order not to be overthrown once having conquered power. Engels argues. the working class "must. on the one hand. do away with all the old repressive machinery previously used against it itself. and. on the other. safeguard itself against its own deputies and officials. by declaring them all. without exception. subject to recall at any moment." Such a state would be a temporary affair. Engels argued. A new generation. he suggested. brought up in "new and free social conditions". will be able to "throw the entire lumber of the state on the scrap-heap."

Leninist conception of a socialist state

The Leninist conception of a socialist state is tied to Vladimir Lenin's theory of the revolutionary party and democratic centralism. The objective of Marxism is to build a mass workers' movement which can smash the capitalist state. replace it with a revolutionary socialist workers' state based on workers councils. and bring production under control by the workers and peasants. According to Lenin's April Theses. the goal of the revolution and vanguard party is not the introduction of socialism. which could only be established on a worldwide scale. but to bring production and the state under the control of the Soviets of Workers' Deputies. Following the October revolution in Russia. the Bolsheviksconsolidated their power and sought to control and direct the social and economic affairs of the state and broader Russian society in order to safeguard against counterrevolutionary insurrection. foreign invasion. and to promote socialist consciousness among the Russian population.

These ideas were adopted by Vladimir Lenin in 1917 just prior to the October Revolution in Russia and published in *The State and Revolution*. a central text for many Marxists. With the failure of the worldwide revolution envisaged by Lenin and Trotsky. the Civil War. and finally Lenin's death. war measures that were deemed to be temporary. such as forced requisition of food and the lack of democratic control. became permanent and a tool to boost Stalin's power. leading to the emergence of Marxism–Leninismand Stalinism. as well as the notion that socialism can be created and exist in a single state.

Vladimir Lenin argued that as socialism is replaced by communism. the state would "wither away" as strong centralized control progressively reduces as local communities gain more empowerment. As he put succinctly: "So long as the state exists there is no freedom. When there is freedom. there will be no state."

Marxist–Leninist states

States run by Communist parties that adhere to Marxism–Leninism. or some variation thereof. refer to themselves as *socialist states*. TheSoviet Union was the first to proclaim itself a "socialist state" in its 1936 Constitution and a subsequent 1977 Constitution. Another well-known example is the People's Republic of China. which proclaims itself to be a "socialist state" in its 1982 Constitution of the People's Republic of China. In the West. such states are commonly known as "communist states" (though they do not use this term to refer to themselves). These "Communist states" often don't claim to have achieved socialism in their countries; rather. they claim to be *building* and working Towards the establishment of socialism (and the development towards communism thereafter) in their countries. For example. the preamble to the Socialist Republic of Vietnam's constitution states that Vietnam only entered a transition stage between capitalism and socialism after the country was re-unified under the Communist party in 1976. and the 1992 Constitution of the Republic of Cubastates that the role of the Communist Party is to "guide the common effort Towards the goals and construction of socialism (and the progress Towards a communist society)".

The Democratic People's Republic of Korea (North Korea) used to be a Marxist-Leninist state. In 1972. the country adopted a newconstitution. which changed the official state ideology to *"Juche"*. Today. although no longer a "communist state". the DPRK remains a constitutionally socialist state.

NON-LENINIST COUNTRIES

Countries such as Portugal (which states that one of the primary roles of the Constituent Assembly is to open the way to socialist society). India and Algeria have used the term "socialist" in their official name or constitution without claiming to follow Communism or any of its derivatives.

In such cases. the intended meaning of "socialism" can vary widely. and sometimes the constitutional references to socialism are left over from a previous period in the country's history. In the case of many Middle-Eastern states. "socialism" was often used in reference to an Arab-socialist/nationalist philosophy adopted by specific regimes. such as that of Gamal Abdel Nasser and that of the various Ba'ath Parties.

Examples of countries using the word "socialist" in a non-communist sense in their names include the *Democratic Socialist Republic of Sri Lanka*. Countries with non-Leninist/communist references to socialism in their constitutions include India and Portugal.

Post-war European countries

In the post-war period. when nationalisation of large industries was relatively widespread. it was not uncommon for commentators to describe some European countries as socialist states seeking to move their countries Towards a socialist economy. In 1956. for example. leading British Labour Party politician and author Anthony Crosland claimed that capitalism had been abolished in Britain. although others. such as Welshman Aneurin Bevan. Minister of Health in the first post-war Labour government. disputed the claim that Britain was a socialist state. For Crosland and others who supported his views. Britain was a socialist state. For Bevan. Britain had a socialist National Health Service which stood in opposition to the hedonism of Britain's capitalist society. He stated:

The National Health service and the Welfare State have come to be used as interchangeable terms. and in the mouths of some people as terms of reproach. Why this is so it is not difficult to understand. if you view everything from the angle of a strictly individualistic competitive society. A free health service is pure Socialism and as such it is opposed to the hedonism of capitalist society.

—Aneurin Bevan. *In Place of Fear. p. 106*

When the Socialist Party was in power in France in the post-war period. some commentators claimed that France was a socialist country. although. as in the rest of Europe. the laws of capitalism still operated fully and private enterprises dominated their economy. Mitterrand Government scheduled to nationalize all banks but this attempt faced opposition of the European Economic Community.

ESTABLISHING A SOCIALIST STATE BY REFORMISM OR REVOLUTION

Reformist socialists and Marxists. exemplified by Eduard Bernstein. take the view that a socialist state will evolve out of political reforms won by the struggle of the socialists. "The socialist movement is everything to me while what people commonly call the goal of Socialism is nothing." These views are considered a "revision" of Marxist thought.

Revolutionary Marxists. following Marx. take the view that. on the one hand. the working class grows stronger through its battle for reforms. (such as. in Marx's time. the ten-hours bill):

"Now and then the workers are victorious. but only for a time. The real fruit of their battles lies. not in the immediate result. but in the ever expanding union of the workers... it ever rises up again. stronger. firmer. mightier. It compels legislative recognition of particular interests of the workers. by taking advantage of the divisions among the bourgeoisie itself. Thus. the ten-hours' bill in England was carried."

—Marx and Engels. *Manifesto of the Communist Party. Chapter I. Bourgeois and Proletarians*

However. on the other hand. in the orthodox Marxist conception. these battles of the workers reach a point at which a revolutionary movement arises. A revolutionary movement is required. in the view of Marxists. to sweep away the capitalist state. which must be smashed. so as to begin to construct a socialist society:

"In depicting the most general phases of the development of the proletariat. we traced the more or less veiled civil war. raging within existing society. up to the point where that war breaks out into open revolution. and where the violent overthrow of the bourgeoisie lays the foundation for the sway of the proletariat."

—Marx and Engels. *Manifesto of the Communist Party. Chapter I. Bourgeois and Proletarians*

In this view. only in this way can a socialist state be established.

CONTROVERSY WITH THE TERM

Within the socialist movement. a number of criticisms are maintained towards the use of the term "socialist states" in relation to countries such as

China and previously of Soviet Union and Eastern and Central European states before what some term the 'collapse of Stalinism' in 1989. Democratic Socialists. left communists. Anarchists and someTrotskyists claim that the so-called "socialist states" or "people's states" actually presided over state capitalist economies and thus cannot be called "socialist".

Other Trotskyists. while agreeing that these states could not be described as socialist. deny that they were state capitalist. They support Trotsky's analysis of (pre-restoration) USSR as a workers' state that had degenerated into a "monstrous" bureaucratic dictatorship which rested on a largely nationalised industry run according to a plan of production. and claimed that the former "Stalinist" states of Central and Eastern Europe were deformed workers' states based on the same relations of production as USSR.

STATE CAPITALISM

State capitalism is usually described as an economic system in which commercial (*i.e.* for-profit) economic activity is undertaken by the state. with management and organization of the means of production in a capitalist manner. including the system of capital accumulation. wage labour. and centralized management. This designation applies to economies regardless of the political aims of the state. even if the state is nominally socialist. State capitalism is characterised by the dominance of state-owned business enterprises in the economy. Examples of state capitalism include corporatized government agencies (agencies organised along corporate and business management practices) and states that own controlling shares of publicly listed corporations (acting as a shareholder). State capitalism is usually used as criticism of states that named themselves socialist; for instance. many communist and Marxist tendencies argue that the Soviet Union did not establish socialism. but rather established state capitalism.

State capitalism has also come to refer to an economic system where the means of production are owned privately but the state has considerable control over the allocation of credit and investment. as in the case of France during the period ofdirigisme. Alternatively. state capitalism may be used (sometimes interchangeably with state monopoly capitalism) to describe a system where the state intervenes in the economy to protect and advance the interests of large-scale businesses. This practice is often claimed to be in contrast with the ideals of both socialism and *laissez-faire* capitalism.

There are various theories and critiques of state capitalism. some of which have existed before the 1917 October Revolution. The common themes among them are to identify that the workers do not meaningfully control the means of production and that commodity relations and production for profit still occur within state capitalism. Vladimir Lenin notably described the economy of Russia as state capitalism. Socialists of a libertarian or anarchist persuasion. such as

Noam Chomsky. use the term "state capitalism" to refer to economies that are nominally capitalist. such that the decisive research and development is performed by the public sector at public cost. but private owners reap the profits.

Marxist literature typically defines state capitalism as a social system combining capitalism—the wage system of producing and appropriating surplus value—with ownership or control by a state. By that definition. a state capitalist country is one where the government controls the economy and essentially acts like a single huge corporation. extracting the surplus value from the workforce in order to invest it in further production. Friedrich Engels. in *Socialism: Utopian and Scientific*. argued that state ownership does not do away with capitalism by itself. but rather would be the final stage of capitalism. consisting of ownership and management of large-scale production and communication by the bourgeois state. Yet. the tools for ending capitalism are found in state capitalism. he said.

Some even use the term to refer to capitalist economies such that the state provides substantial public services and regulation of business activity. This could refer to several ideologies ranging from social liberalism and social democracy to fascism. The term is also used by some in reference to a private capitalist economy controlled by a state. often meaning a privately owned economy that is subject to statist economic planning. In the 1930s. Italian Fascist leader Benito Mussolini said that were Fascism to conform itself to modern capitalism. it would end up as being "state socialism turned on its head". This term was often used to describe the controlled economies of the great powers in the First World War.

ORIGINS AND EARLY USES OF THE TERM

The term was first used by Wilhelm Liebknecht in 1896 who said: "Nobody has combatted State Socialism more than we German Socialists; nobody has shown more distinctively than I. that State Socialism is really State capitalism!" It has been suggested that the concept of state capitalism can be traced back to Mikhail Bakunin's critique during the First International of the potential for state exploitation under Marxist-inspired socialism. or to Jan Waclav Machajski's argument in *The Intellectual Worker* (1905) that socialism was a movement of the intelligentsia as a class. resulting in a new type of society he termed state capitalism. For anarchists. state socialism is equivalent to state capitalism. hence oppressive and merely a shift from private capitalists to the state being the sole employer and capitalist.

During World War I. using Vladimir Lenin's idea that Czarism was taking a "Prussian path" to capitalism. the Bolshevik Nikolai Bukharinidentified a new stage in the development of capitalism. in which all sectors of national production and all important social institutions had become managed by the state; he termed this new stage 'state capitalism.' After the October Revolution. Lenin used the term positively. In spring 1918. during a brief period of economic liberalism prior to the introduction of war communism. and again during the New Economic Policy (NEP) of 1921. Lenin justified the introduction of state capitalism controlled politically by the dictatorship of the proletariat to further central control and develop the productive forces:

Reality tells us that state capitalism would be a step forward. If in a small space of time we could achieve state capitalism. that would be a victory. (Lenin 1918) State capitalism would be a step forward as compared with the present state of affairs in our Soviet Republic. If in approximately six months' time state capitalism became established in our Republic. this would be a great success and a sure guarantee that within a year socialism will have gained a permanently firm hold.

Lenin argued the state should *temporarily* run the economy. which would eventually be taken over by workers. To Lenin "state capitalism" did not mean the state would run most of the economy. but that "state capitalism" would be one of five elements of the economy.

USE BY SOCIALISTS

State capitalism has been used by various socialists. including anarchists. Marxists and Leninists.

Use by anarchists

Perhaps the earliest critique of the USSR as state-capitalist was formulated by the Russian anarchists. as documented in Paul Avrich's work on Russian anarchism. This claim would become standard in anarchist works. For example. the prominent anarchist Emma Goldman in an article from 1935 titled "There Is No Communism in Russia" said of the USSR: "Such a condition of affairs may be called state capitalism. but it would be fantastic to consider it in any sense Communistic...Soviet Russia. it must now be obvious. is an absolute despotism politically and the crassest form of state capitalism economically".

Murray Bookchin. when speaking about Marxism said that "Marxism. in fact. becomes ideology. It is assimilated by the most advanced forms of state capitalist movement — notably Russia. By an incredible irony of history. Marxian "socialism" turns out to be in large part the very state capitalism that Marx failed to anticipate in the dialectic of capitalism.

The proletariat. instead of developing into a revolutionary class within the womb of capitalism. turns out to be an organ within the body of bourgeois society...Lenin sensed this and described "socialism" as "nothing but state capitalist monopoly made to benefit the whole people." This is an extraordinary statement if one thinks out its implications. and a mouthful of contradictions." The authors of An Anarchist FAQ. while speaking about leninism say that "Rather than present an effective and efficient means of achieving revolution.

the Leninist model is elitist. hierarchical and highly inefficient in achieving a socialist society. At best. these parties play a harmful role in the class struggle by alienating activists and militants with their organisational principles and manipulative tactics within popular structures and groups. At worse. these parties can seize power and create a new form of class society (a state capitalist one) in which the working class is oppressed by new bosses (namely. the party hierarchy and its appointees)."

USE BY THE RUSSIAN COMMUNIST LEFT

Another early analysis the USSR as state capitalist came from various groups advocating left communism. One major tendency of the 1918 Russian communist left criticised the re-employment of authoritarian capitalist relations and methods of production. As Ossinsky in particular argued. "one-man management" (rather than the democratic factory committees workers had established and Lenin abolished) and the other impositions of capitalist discipline would stifle the active participation of workers in the organisation of production; Taylorism converted workers into the appendages of machines. and piece work imposed individualist rather than collective rewards in production so instilling petty bourgeois values into workers.

In sum these measures were seen as the re-transformation of proletarians within production from collective subject back into the atomised objects of capital. The working class. it was argued. had to participate consciously in economic as well as political administration. This tendency within the 1918 left communists emphasized that the problem with capitalist production was that it treated workers as objects. Its transcendence lay in the workers' conscious creativity and participation. which is reminiscent of Marx's critique of alienation.

These criticisms were revived on the left of the Russian Communist Party after the 10th Congress in 1921. which introduced theNew Economic Policy. Many members of the Workers' Opposition and the Decists (both later banned) and two new underground Left Communist groups. Gavril Myasnikov's Workers' Group and the Workers' Truth group. developed the idea that Russia was becoming a state capitalist society governed by a new bureaucratic class. The most developed version of this idea was in a 1931 booklet by Myasnikov.

Use by Mensheviks and 'Orthodox' Marxists

Immediately after the Russian Revolution many western Marxists questioned whether socialism was possible in Russia. Specifically. Karl Kautsky:

It is only the old feudal large landed property which exists no longer. Conditions in Russia were ripe for its abolition but they were not ripe for the abolition of capitalism. Capitalism is now once again celebrating a resurrection. but in forms that are more oppressive and harrowing for the proletariat than of old. Instead of assuming higher industrialised forms. private capitalism has assumed the most wretched and shabby forms of black marketeering and money speculation. Industrial capitalism has developed to become state capitalism. Formerly state officials and officials from private capital were critical. often very hostile towards each other. Consequently the working man found that his advantage lay with one or the other in turn. Today the state bureaucracy and capitalist bureaucracy are merged into one—that is the upshot of the great socialist revolution brought about by the Bolsheviks. It constitutes the most oppressive of all despotisms that Russia has ever had to suffer.

After 1929. exiled Mensheviks such as Fyodor Dan began to argue that Stalin's Russia constituted a state capitalist society. In the United Kingdom. the orthodox Marxist group the Socialist Party of Great Britain independently developed a similar doctrine. Although initially beginning with the idea that Soviet capitalism differed little from western capitalism. they later began to argue that the bureaucracy held its productive property in common. much like the Catholic Church's. As John O'Neill notes:

Whatever other merits or problems their theories had. in arguing that the Russian revolution was from the outset a capitalist revolution they avoided the ad hoc and post hoc nature of more recent Maoist- and Trotskyist-inspired accounts of state capitalism. which start from the assumption that the Bolshevik revolution inaugurated a socialist economy that at some later stage degenerated into capitalism.

Use by Schachtmanite "Trotskyists"

Leon Trotsky said the term state capitalism "originally arose to designate the phenomena which arise when a bourgeois state takes direct charge of the means of transport or of industrial enterprises" and is therefore a "partial negation" of capitalism. However. Trotsky rejected that description of the USSR claiming instead that it was a degenerated workers' state. After World War II. most Trotskyists accepted an analysis of the Soviet bloc countries as being deformed workers' states. However. alternative opinions of the Trotskyist tradition have developed the theory of state capitalism as a New Class theory to explain what they regard as the essentially non-socialist nature of the USSR. Cuba. China. and other self-proclaimed socialist states.

The discussion goes back to internal debates in the Left Opposition during the late 1920s and early 1930s. Ante Ciliga. a member of the Left Opposition imprisoned at Verkhne-Uralsk in the 1930s. described the evolution of many Left Oppositionists to a theory of state capitalism influenced byGavril Myasnikov's Workers Group and other Left Communist factions. On release. and returning to activity in the International Left Opposition. Ciliga "was one of the first. after 1936. to raise the theory [of state capitalism] in Trotskyist circles". George Orwell. who was an anti-Stalinist leftistlike Ciliga. used the term in his *Homage to Catalonia* (1938). After 1940. dissident Trotskyists developed more theoretically sophisticated accounts of state capitalism. One influential formulation has been that of the Johnson-Forest Tendency of CLR James and Raya Dunayevskaya who formulated her theory in the early 1940s on the basis of a study of the first three Five Year Plans alongside readings of Marx's early humanist writings.

Their political evolution would lead them away from Trotskyism. Another is that of Tony Cliff. associated with the International Socialist Tendency and the British Socialist Workers Party (SWP). dating back to the late 1940s. Unlike Johnson-Forest. Cliff formulated a theory of state capitalism that would enable his group to remain Trotskyists. albeit heterodox ones. A relatively recent text by Stephen Resnick and Richard D. Wolff. *Class Theory and History*. explores what they term state capitalism in the former Soviet Union. continuing a theme that has been debated within Trotskyist theory for most of the past century.

Compare with other left-wing theories regarding Soviet-style societies: deformed workers' states. degenerated workers' states. new class. state socialism and bureaucratic collectivism.

Use by later left communists and council communists

The left communist/council communist traditions outside Russia consider the Soviet system as state capitalist. Otto Rühle. a major German left communist. developed this idea from the 1920s. and it was later articulated by Dutch council communist Anton Pannekoek. for instance in "State Capitalism and Dictatorship" (1936).

Use by Maoists and "anti-revisionists"

From 1956 to the early 1980s. the Communist Party of China and their Maoist or "anti-revisionist" adherents around the world often described the Soviet Union as state-capitalist. essentially using the accepted Marxist definition. albeit on a different basis and in reference to a different span of time from either the Trotskyists or the left-communists. Specifically. the Maoists and their descendants use the term state capitalism as part of their description of the style and politics of Nikita Khrushchev and his successors. as well as to similar leaders and policies in other self-styled "socialist" states. This was involved in the ideological Sino-Soviet Split.

After Mao's death. amidst the supporters of the Cultural Revolution and the exploits of the "Gang of Four". most extended the state capitalist formulation to China itself. and ceased to support the Communist Party of China. which likewise distanced itself from these former fraternal groups. The related theory of Hoxhaism was developed in 1978. largely by Albanian president Enver Hoxha. who insisted that Mao himself had pursued state capitalist and revisionist economic policies. Most current Communist groups descended from the Maoist ideological tradition still adopt the description of both China and the Soviet Union as being "state-capitalist" from a certain point in their history onwards—most commonly. the Soviet Union from 1956 to its collapse in 1991. and China from 1976 to the present. Maoists and "anti-revisionists" also sometimes use the term "Social-imperialism" to describe socialist states that they consider to be actually capitalist in essence—their phrase. *"socialist in words. imperialist in deeds"* denotes this.

USE BY LIBERAL ECONOMISTS

Murray Rothbard. a laissez-faire capitalist philosopher. uses the term interchangeably with the term state monopoly capitalism. and uses it to describe a partnership of government and big business in which the state intervenes on behalf of large capitalists against the interests of consumers. He distinguishes this from laissez-faire capitalism where big business is not protected from market forces. This usage dates from the 1960s. when Harry Elmer Barnes described the post-New Deal economy of the United States as "state capitalism." More recently. Andrei Illarionov. former economic advisor to Russian President Vladimir Putin. resigned in December 2005. protesting Russia's "embracement of state capitalism."

The term is not used by the classical liberals to describe the public ownership of the means of production. The Austrian School economistLudwig von Mises explained the reason: *"The socialist movement takes great pains to circulate frequently new labels for its ideally constructed state. Each worn-out label is replaced by another which raises hopes of an ultimate solution of the insoluble basic problem of Socialism—until it becomes obvious that nothing has been changed but the name. The most recent slogan is "State Capitalism." It is not commonly realized that this covers nothing more than what used to be called Planned Economy and State Socialism. and that State Capitalism. Planned Economy. and State Socialism diverge only in non-essentials from the "classic" ideal of egalitarian Socialism."*

USE BY ITALIAN FASCISTS

On economic issues. Italian Fascist leader Benito Mussolini claimed in 1933 that. were Fascism to follow the modern phase of capitalism. its path would "lead inexorably into state capitalism. which is nothing more nor less than state socialism turned on its head.

In either event. [whether the outcome be state capitalism or state socialism] the result is the bureaucratization of the economic activities of the nation." Mussolini claimed that capitalism had degenerated in three stages. starting with dynamic or heroic capitalism (1830–1870) followed by static capitalism (1870–1914) and then reaching its final form of decadent capitalism. also known as supercapitalism beginning in 1914.

Mussolini denounced supercapitalism for causing the "standardization of humankind" and for causing excessive consumption. Mussolini claimed that at this stage of supercapitalism "[it] is then that a capitalist enterprise. when difficulties arise. throws itself like a dead weight into the state's arms. It is then that state intervention begins and becomes more necessary. It is then that those who once ignored the state now seek it out anxiously." Due to the inability of businesses to operate properly when facing economic difficulties. Mussolini claimed that this proved that state intervention into the economy was necessary to stabilize the economy.

Mussolini claimed that dynamic or heroic capitalism and the bourgeoisie could be prevented from degenerating into static capitalism and then supercapitalism only if the concept of economic individualism were abandoned and if state supervision of the economy was introduced. Private enterprise would control production but it would be supervised by the state. Italian Fascism presented the economic system of corporatism as the solution that would preserve private enterprise and property while allowing the state to intervene in the economy when private enterprise failed.

IN WESTERN COUNTRIES

An alternate definition is that state capitalism is a close relationship between the government and private capitalism. such as one in which the private capitalists produce for a guaranteed market. An example of this would be the military-industrial complex in which autonomous entrepreneurial firms produce for lucrative government contracts and are not subject to the discipline of competitive markets. Many consider this as part of a continuum characterizing the modern world economy with "normal" capitalism at one extreme and complete state capitalism like that of the former USSR at the other.

Both the Trotskyist definition and this one derive from discussion among Marxists at the beginning of the 20th century. most notably Nikolai Bukharin who. in his book*Imperialism and the world economy* thought that advanced. 'imperialist' countries exhibited the latter definition and considered (and rejected) the possibility that they could arrive at the former.

State capitalism is practised by a variety of Western countries with respect to certain strategic resources important for national security. These may involve private investment as well. For example. a government may own or even monopolize oil production or transport infrastructure to ensure availability in the case of war. Examples include Neste. Statoiland OMV.

There are limits. according to arguments that state capitalism exists to ensure that wealth creation does not threaten the ruling elite's political power. which remains unthreatened by tight connections between the government and the industries while state capitalist fears of capitalism's "creative destruction." of the threat of revolution. and of any significant changes in the system result in the persistence of industries that have outlived their economic usefulness and an inefficient economic environment that is ill equipped to inspire innovation.

IN EUROPEAN STUDIES

Several European scholars and political economists have used the term to describe one of the three major varieties of capitalism that prevail in the modern context of the European Union. This approach is mainly influenced by Schmidt's (2002) article on *The Futures of European Capitalism*. in which he divides modern European capitalism in three groups: Market. Managed and State. Here. state capitalism refers to a system where high coordination between the state. large companies and labour unions ensures economic growth and development in a quasi-corporatist model. The author cites France and. to a lesser extent. Italy as the prime examples of modern European State capitalism. A general theory of Capitalist forms. whereby state capitalism is a particular case. was developed by Ernesto Screpanti. who argues that soviet type economies of the 20th century used state capitalism to sustain processes of primitive accumulation.

CURRENT FORMS IN 21ST CENTURY

State capitalism is distinguished from capitalist mixed economies where the state intervenes in markets to correct market failures or to establish social regulation or social welfare provisions in the following way: in a state capitalist system the state operates businesses for the purpose of accumulating capital and directing investment in the framework of either a free-market or a mixed-market economy. In such a system. governmental functions and public services are often organised as corporations. companies or business enterprises.

People's Republic of China

Many analysts assert that China is one of the main examples of state capitalism in the 21st century. In his book. *The End of the Free Market: Who Wins the War Between States and Corporations*. political scientist Ian Bremmer describes China as the primary driver for the rise of state capitalism as a challenge to the free market economies of the developed world. particularly in the aftermath of the 2008 financial crisis. Bremmer describes state capitalism thus:

In this system. governments use various kinds of state-owned companies to manage the exploitation of resources that they consider the state's crown jewels and to create and maintain large numbers of jobs. They use select privately owned companies to dominate certain economic sectors. They use so-called sovereign wealth funds to invest their extra cash in ways that maximize the state's profits. In all three cases. the state is using markets to create wealth that can be directed as political officials see fit. And in all three cases. the ultimate motive is not economic (maximizing growth) but political (maximizing the state's power and the leadership's chances of survival). This is a form of capitalism but one in which the state acts as the dominant economic player and uses markets primarily for political gain.

Following on Bremmer. Aligica and Tarko further develop the theory that state capitalism in countries like modern-day China and Russia is an example of a rent-seekingsociety. They argue that. following the realization that the centrally planned socialist systems could not effectively compete with capitalist economies. formerly Communist party political elites are trying to engineer a limited form of economic liberalization that increases efficiency while still allowing them to maintain political control and power.

Analysis of the "Chinese model" by the economists Julan Du and Chenggang Xu finds that the contemporary economic system of the People's Republic of China represents a state capitalist system as opposed to a market socialist system. The reason for this categorization is the existence of financial markets in the Chinese economic system. which are absent in the market socialist literature and in the classic models of market socialism; and that state profits are retained by enterprises rather than being equitably distributed among the population in a basic income/social dividend or similar scheme. which are major features in the market socialist literature. They conclude that China is neither a form of market socialism nor a stable form of capitalism.

Singapore's version of state capitalism

Singapore's government owns controlling shares in many government-linked companies and directs investment through sovereign wealth funds. Singapore has attracted some of the world's most powerful corporations through business friendly legislation and through the encouragement of western style corporatism. with close cooperation between the state and corporations.

Singapore's large holdings of government-linked companies and the state's close cooperation with business are defining aspects of Singapore's version of state capitalism.

State capitalism in Norway

The economy of Norway has ownership stakes in many of the country's largest publicly listed companies (owning 37per cent of the Oslo stock exchange) and operates the country's largest non-listed companies including Statoil and Statkraft. The government also operates a sovereign wealth fund. the Government Pension Fund of Norway - whose partial objective is to prepare Norway for a post-oil future. Modern Norwegian state capitalism has its origins in public ownership of the country's oil reserves and in the country's post-Second World War social democratic reforms.

6

Socialism and Marxism

In Marxist theory. socialism (also called lower-stage communism or the socialist mode of production) refers to a specific historical phase of economic development and its corresponding set of social relations that supersede capitalism in the schema ofhistorical materialism. Socialism is defined as a mode of production where the sole criterion for production is use-value and therefore the law of value no longer directs economic activity.

Production for use is coordinated through *conscious* economic planning. while distribution of economic output is based on the principle of *To each according to his contribution*.

The social relations of socialism are characterised by the working-class effectively owning the means of production and the means of their livelihood. either through cooperative enterprises or by public ownership and self management. so that the social surplus accrues to the working class and society as a whole.

This view is consistent with. and helped to inform. early conceptions of socialism where the law of value no longer directs economic activity. and thus monetary relations in the form of exchange-value. profit. interest and wage labour would not operate and apply to socialism.

The Marxian conception of socialism stands in contrast to other early conceptions of socialism. most notably early forms of market socialism based on classical economics such as Mutualism and Ricardian socialism. Unlike the Marxian conception. these conceptions of socialism retained commodity exchange (markets) for labour and the means of production. seeking to perfect the market process. The Marxist idea of socialism was also heavily opposed to Utopian socialism.

Although Karl Marx and Friedrich Engels wrote very little on socialism and neglected to provide any details on how it might be organised. numerous social scientists and Neo-classical economists have used Marx's theory as a basis for developing their own models of socialist economic systems. The Marxist view of socialism served as a point of reference during the socialist calculation debate.

MODE OF PRODUCTION

Socialism is a post-commodity economic system. meaning that production is carried out to directly produce use-value (to directly satisfy human needs. or economic demands) as opposed to being produced with a view to generating a profit. The stage in which the accumulation of capital was viable and effective is rendered insufficient at the socialist stage of social and economic development.

leading to a situation where production is carried out independently of capital accumulation in a supposedly *planned*fashion. Although Karl Marx and Friedrich Engels understood *planning* to involve the input and decisions of the individuals involved at localized levels of production and consumption. planning has been interpreted to mean centralized planning by Marxist-Leninistsduring the 20th century. However. there have been other conceptions of economic planning. including decentralized-planning andparticipatory planning.

In contrast to capitalism. which relies upon the coercive market forces to compel capitalists to produce use-values as a byproduct of the pursuit of profit. socialist production is to be based on the rational planning of use-values and coordinated investment decisions to attain economic goals. As a result. the cyclical fluctuations that occur in a capitalist market economy will not be present in a socialist economy. The value of a good in socialism is its physical utility rather than its embodied labour. cost of production and exchange value as in a capitalist system.

Socialism would make use of incentive-based systems. and inequality would still exist but to a diminishing extent as all members of society would be worker-owners. This eliminates the severity of previous tendencies towards inequality and conflicts arising ownership of the means of production and property income accruing to a small class of owners. The method of compensation and reward in a socialist society would be based on an authentic meritocracy. along the principle of "from each according to his ability. to each according to his contribution". The advanced stage of socialism. referred to as "upper-stage communism" in the *Critique of the Gotha Programme*. is based on the socialist mode of production but is differentiated from lower-stage socialism in a few fundamental ways. While socialism implies public ownership (by a state apparatus) or cooperative ownership (by a worker cooperative enterprise). communism would be based on common ownership of the means of production.

Class distinctions based on ownership of capital cease to exist. along with the need for a state. A superabundance of goods and services are made possible by automated production that allow for goods to be distributed based on need rather than merit.

INTERMEDIATE PHASES

The period in which capitalism becomes increasingly insufficient as an economic system and immediately after the proletarian conquest of the state. an economic system that features elements of both socialism and capitalism will probably exist until both the productive forces of the economy and the cultural and social attitudes develop to a point where they satisfy the requirements for a full socialist society (one that has lost the need for monetary value. wage labour and capital accumulation). Specifically. market relations will still exist but economic units are either nationalized or re-organized into cooperatives. This transitional phase is sometimes described as "state capitalism" or "market socialism". China is officially in the primary stage of socialism.

SOCIAL RELATIONS

The fundamental goal of socialism from the view of Marx and Engels was the realization of human freedom and individual autonomy. Specifically. this refers to freedom from the alienation imposed upon individuals in the form of coercive social relationships as well as material scarcity. whereby the individual is compelled to engage in activities merely to survive (to reproduce his or herself). The aim of socialism is to provide an environment whereby individuals are free to express their genuine interests. creative freedom. and desires unhindered by forms of social control that force individuals to work for a class of owners who expropriate and live off the surplus product.

As a set of social relationships. socialism is defined by the degree to which economic activity in society is planned by the associated producers. so that the surplus product produced by socialized assets is controlled by a majority of the population through democratic processes. The sale of labour power would be abolished so that every individual participates in running their institution as stakeholders or members with no one having coercive power over anyone else in a vertical social division of labour (which is to be distinguished from a non-social. technical division of labour which would still exist in socialism). The incentive structure changes in a socialist society given the change in the social environment. so that an individual laborers' work becomes increasingly autonomous and creative. creating a sense of responsibility for his or her institution as a stakeholder. The individual is no longer alienated from his or her work: work becomes a means by which the individual fulfills his or her humanity (pursues his or her interests).

ROLE OF THE STATE

In Marxist theory. the state is "the institution of organised violence which is used by the ruling class of a country to maintain the conditions of its rule. Thus. it is only in a society which is divided between hostile social classes that the state exists." The state is thus seen as a mechanism that is dominated by the interests of the ruling class and utilised to subjugate other classes in order to protect and legitimize the existing economic system.After a workers' revolution. the state would initially become the instrument of the working class. Conquest of the state apparatus by the working class must take place to establish a socialist system.

As socialism is built. the role and scope of the state changes as class distinctions (based on ownership of the means of production) gradually deteriorate due to the concentration of means of production in state hands. From the point where all means of production become state property. the nature and primary function of the state would change from one of political rule (via coercion) over men by the creation and enforcement of laws into a scientific administration of things and a direction of processes of production; that is the state would become a coordinating economic entity rather than a mechanism of class or political control. and would no longer be a state in the Marxian sense.

MARXISM

Marxism is a worldview and method of societal analysis that focuses on class relations and societal conflict. that uses a materialist interpretation of historical development. and a dialectical view of social transformation. Marxist methodology uses economic andsociopolitical inquiry and applies that to the critique and analysis of the development of capitalism and the role of class struggle in systemic economic change.

In the mid-to-late 19th century. the intellectual tenets of Marxism were inspired by two German philosophers: Karl Marx andFriedrich Engels. Marxist analyses and methodologies have influenced multiple political ideologies and social movements. Marxism encompasses an economic theory. a sociological theory. a philosophical method. and a revolutionary view of social change.

There is no single definitive Marxist theory; Marxist analysis has been applied to diverse subjects and has been misconceived and modified during the course of its development. resulting in numerous and sometimes contradictory theories that fall under the rubric of Marxism or Marxian analysis.

Marxism builds on a materialist understanding of societal development. taking as its starting point the necessary economic activities required by human society to provide for its material needs. The form of economic organization or mode of production is understood to be the basis from which the majority of other social phenomena – including social relations. political and legal systems. morality and ideology – arise (or at the least by which they are directly influenced).

These social relations form thesuperstructure. for which the economic system forms the base. As the forces of production (most notably technology) improve. existing forms of social organization become inefficient and stifle further progress. These inefficiencies manifest themselves as social contradictions in the form of class struggle. According to Marxist analysis. class conflict within capitalism arises due to intensifying contradictions between highly productive mechanized and socialized production performed by the proletariat. and private ownership and private appropriation of the surplus product in the form of surplus value (profit) by a small minority of private owners called the bourgeoisie. As the contradiction becomes apparent to the proletariat. social unrest between the two antagonistic classes intensifies. culminating in a social revolution. The eventual long-term outcome of this revolution would be the establishment of socialism – a socioeconomic system based on cooperative ownership of the means of production. distribution based on one's contribution. and production organised directly for use. Karl Marx hypothesized that. as the productive forces and technology continued to advance. socialism would eventually give way to a communist stage of social development. Communism would be a classless. stateless. humane society erected on common ownership and the principle of "From each according to his ability. to each according to his needs".

Marxism has developed into different branches and schools of thought. Different schools place a greater emphasis on certain aspects of classical Marxism while de-emphasizing or rejecting other aspects of Marxism. sometimes combining Marxist analysis with non-Marxian concepts. Some variants of Marxism primarily focus on one aspect of Marxism as the determining force in social development – such as the mode of production. class. power-relationships or property ownership – while arguing other aspects are less important or current research makes them irrelevant. Despite sharing similar premises. different schools of Marxism might reach contradictory conclusions from each other. For instance. different Marxian economists have contradictory explanations of economic crisis and different predictions for the outcome of such crises. Furthermore. different variants of Marxism apply Marxist analysis to study different aspects of society (*e.g.* mass culture. economic crises. or feminism).

These theoretical differences have led various socialist and communist parties and political movements to embrace different political strategies for attaining socialism and advocate different programmes and policies from each other. One example of this is the division between revolutionary socialists and reformists that emerged in the German Social Democratic Party (SPD) during the early 20th century. Marxist understandings of history and of society have been adopted by academics in the disciplines of archaeology andanthropology. media studies. political science. theater. history. sociology. art history and art theory. cultural studies. education.economics. geography. literary criticism. aesthetics. critical psychology. and philosophy.

OVERVIEW

The Marxian analysis begins with an analysis of material conditions. taking at its starting point the necessary economic activities required by human society to provide for its material needs. The form of economic organization. or mode of production. is understood to be the basis from which the majority of other social phenomena – including social relations. political and legal systems. morality and ideology – arise (or at the least by which they are directly influenced). These social relations base the economic system and the economic system forms the superstructure. As the forces of production. most notably technology. improve. existing forms of social organization become inefficient and stifle further progress.

As Karl Marx observed: "At a certain stage of development. the material productive forces of society come into conflict with the existing relations of production or_ this merely expresses the same thing in legal terms with the property relations within the framework of which they have operated hitherto. From forms of development of the productive forces these relations turn into their fetters. Then begins an era of social revolution."

These inefficiencies manifest themselves as social contradictions in society in the form of class struggle. Under the capitalist mode of production. this struggle materialises between the minority (the bourgeoisie) who own the means of production. and the vast majority of the population (the proletariat) who produce goods and services. Taking the idea that social change occurs because of the struggle between different classes within society who are under contradiction against each other. leads the Marxist analysis to the conclusion that capitalism exploits and oppresses the proletariat. which leads to a proletarian revolution.

Capitalism (according to Marxist theory) can no longer sustain the living standards of the population due to its need to compensate for falling rates of profit by driving down wages. cutting social benefits and pursuing military aggression. The socialist system would succeed capitalism as humanity's mode of production through workers' revolution. According to Marxism. especially arising from Crisis theory. Socialism is a historical necessity (but not an inevitability).

In a socialist society private property in the means of production would be superseded by co-operative ownership. A socialist economy would not base production on the creation of private profits. but would instead base production and economic activity on the criteria of satisfying human needs – that is. production would be carried out directly for use. As Engels observed: "Then the capitalist mode of appropriation in which the product enslaves first the producer. and then appropriator. is replaced by the mode of appropriation of the product that is based upon the nature of the modern means of production; upon the one hand. direct social appropriation. as means to the maintenance and extension of production_ on the other. direct individual appropriation. as means of subsistence and of enjoyment."'

CONCEPTS

Historical Materialism

"The discovery of the materialist conception of history. or rather. the consistent continuation and extension of materialism into the domain of social phenomenon. removed two chief defects of earlier historical theories. In the first place. they at best examined only the ideological motives of the historical activity of human beings. without grasping the objective laws governing the development of the system of social relations... in the second place. the earlier theories did not cover the activities of the*masses* of the population. whereas historical materialism made it possible for the first time to study with the accuracy of the natural sciences the social conditions of the life of the masses and the changes in these conditions."

Russian Marxist theoretician and revolutionary Vladimir Lenin. 1913.

"Society does not consist of individuals. but expresses the sum of interrelations. the relations within which these individuals stand."

— Karl Marx. *Grundrisse*. 1858

The historical materialist theory of history dialectically analyses the underlying causes of societal development and change in the collective ways humans make their living. All constituent features of a society (social classes. political pyramid. ideologies) stem from economic activity. an idea often conveyed with the metaphor of the base and superstructure.

The base and superstructure metaphor explains that the totality of social relations in and by which humans product and re-product their social existence. forms a society's economic *base*. From this base rises a *superstructure* of political and legal institutions. *i.e.*.ruling class. The base corresponds to the social consciousness (politics. religion. philosophy. etc.). and it conditions the superstructure and the dominant ideology. A conflict between the development of material productive forces and the relations of production provokes social revolutions. thus. the resultant changes to the economic base will lead to the transformation of the superstructure.

This relationship is reflexive; At first the base gives rise to the superstructure and remains the foundation of a form of social organization. Hence. that formed social organization can act again upon both parts of the base and superstructure. whose relationship is not unilinear but dialectic. namely a relationship driven by conflicts and contradictions. As Friedrich Engels clarified: "The history of all hitherto existing society is the history of class struggles. Freeman and slave. patrician and plebeian. lord and serf. guild-master and journeyman. in a word. oppressor and oppressed. stood in constant opposition to one another. carried on uninterrupted. now hidden. now open fight. a fight that each time ended. either in a revolutionary reconstitution of society at large. or in the common ruin of the contending classes.'"

Marx considered these socio-economic conflicts as the driving force of human history since these recurring conflicts have manifested themselves as distinct transitional stages of development in Western Europe. Accordingly Marx designates human history as encompassing four stages of development in relations of production.

1. *Primitive Communism:* as in co-operative tribal societies.
2. *Slave Society:* a development of tribal to city-state; aristocracy is born.
3. *Feudalism:* aristocrats are the ruling class; merchants evolve into capitalists.
4. *Capitalism:* capitalists are the ruling class. who create and employ the proletariat.

Criticism of capitalism

"We are. in Marx's terms. 'an ensemble of social relations' and we live our lives at the core of the intersection of a number of unequal social relations based on hierarchically interrelated structures which. together. define the historical specificity of the capitalist modes of production and reproduction and underlay their observable manifestations."

—Martha E. Gimenez. *Marxism and Class. Gender and Race: Rethinking the Trilogy*

According to the Marxist theoretician and revolutionary Vladimir Lenin. "the principal content of Marxism" was "Marx's economic doctrine". Marx believed that the capitalist bourgeois and their economists were promoting what he saw as the lie that "The interests of the capitalist and those of the worker are... one and the same"; he believed that they did this by purporting the concept that "the fastest possible growth of productive capital" was best not only for the wealthy capitalists but also for the workers because it provided them with employment.

Exploitation is a matter of surplus labour – the amount of labour one performs beyond what one receives in goods. Exploitation has been a socio-economic feature of every class society. and is one of the principal features distinguishing the social classes. The power of one social class to control the means of production enables its exploitation of the other classes.

In capitalism. the labour theory of value is the operative concern; the value of a commodity equals the socially necessary labour time required to produce it. Under that condition.surplus value (the difference between the value produced and the value received by a labourer) is synonymous with the term "surplus labour"; thus. capitalist exploitation is realised as deriving surplus value from the worker.

In pre-capitalist economies. exploitation of the worker was achieved via physical coercion. In the capitalist mode of production. that result is more subtly achieved; because the worker does not own the means of production. he or she must voluntarily enter into an exploitive work relationship with a capitalist in order to earn the necessities of life. The worker's entry into such employment is voluntary in that he or she chooses which capitalist to work for. However. the worker must work or starve. Thus. exploitation is inevitable. and the "voluntary" nature of a worker participating in a capitalist society is illusory.

Alienation is the estrangement of people from their humanity (German: *Gattungswesen*. "species-essence". "species-being"). which is a systematic result of capitalism. Under capitalism. the fruits of production belong to the employers. who expropriate the surplus created by others. and so generate alienated labourers. In Marx's view. alienation is an objective characterization of the worker's situation in capitalism – his or her self-awareness of this condition is not prerequisite.

Social classes

The identity of a social class derives from its relationship to the means of production; Marx describes the social classes in capitalist societies:

- *Proletariat:* "those individuals who has nothing to offer but their labour power. because in the capitalist mode of production. they do not own the means of production". As Andrei Platonov expressed "The working class is my home country and my future is linked with the proletariat." The capitalist mode of production establishes the conditions enabling the bourgeoisie to exploit the proletariat because the workers' labour generates a surplus value greater than the workers' wages.
- *Bourgeoisie:* those who "own the means of production" and buy labour power from the proletariat. thus exploiting the proletariat; they subdivide as bourgeoisie and the petit bourgeoisie.
- Petit bourgeoisie are those who work and can afford to buy little labour power *i.e.* small business owners. peasant landlords. trade workers et al. Marxism predicts that the continual reinvention of the means of production eventually would destroy the petit bourgeoisie. degrading them from the middle class to the proletariat.
- *Lumpenproletariat:* The outcasts of society such as criminals. vagabonds. beggars. prostitutes. et al.. who have no stake in the economy and no mind of their own and so are decoyed by every bidder.
- *Landlords:* an historically important social class who retain some wealth and power.
- *Peasantry and farmers:* a scattered class incapable of organizing and effecting socio-economic change. most of whom would enter the proletariat. and some become landlords.

Class consciousness denotes the awareness – of itself and the social world – that a social class possesses. and its capacity to rationally act in their best interests; hence. class consciousness is required *before* they can effect a successful revolution.Without defining ideology. Marx used the term to denote the production of images of social reality; according to Engels. "ideology is a process accomplished by the so-called thinker consciously. it is true. but with a false consciousness. The real motive forces impelling him remain unknown to him; otherwise it simply would not be an ideological process. Hence he imagines false or seeming motive forces". Because the ruling class controls the society's means of production. the superstructure of society. the ruling social ideas are determined by the best interests of the said ruling class. In *The German Ideology*. "the ideas of the ruling class are in every epoch the ruling ideas. *i.e.* the class which is the ruling material force of society. is. at the same time. its ruling intellectual force".

The term "political economy" originally denoted the study of the conditions under which economic production was organised in the capitalist system. In Marxism. political economy studies the means of production. specifically of capital. and how that manifests as economic activity.

"Marxism taught me what society was. I was like a blindfolded man in a forest. who doesn't even know where north or south is. If you don't eventually come to truly understand the history of the class struggle. or at least have a clear idea that society is divided between the rich and the poor. and that some people subjugate and exploit other people. you're lost in a forest. not knowing anything."

Cuban revolutionary and Marxist-Leninist politician Fidel Castro on discovering Marxism. 2009.

Revolution. socialism. and communism

Marxists believe that the transition from capitalism to socialism is an inevitable part of the development of human society; as Lenin stated. "it is evident that Marx deduces the inevitability of the transformation of capitalist society [into a socialist society] wholly and exclusively from the economic law of motion of contemporary society."

Marxists believe that a socialist society will be far better for the majority of the populace than its capitalist counterpart. for instance. prior to the Russian revolution of 1917. Lenin wrote that "The socialization of production is bound to lead to the conversion of the means of production into the property of society... This conversion will directly result in an immense increase in productivity of labour. a reduction of working hours. and the replacement of the remnants. the ruins of small-scale. primitive. disunited production by collective and improved labour."

CLASSICAL MARXISM

The term Classical Marxism denotes the collection of socio-eco-political theories expounded by Karl Marx and Friedrich Engels. "Marxism. as Ernest Mandel remarked. is always open. always critical. always self-critical." As such. Classical Marxism distinguishes between "Marxism" as broadly perceived. and "what Marx believed"; thus. in 1883. Marx wrote to the French labour leader Jules Guesde and to Paul Lafargue (Marx's son-in-law) – both of whom claimed to represent Marxist principles – accusing them of "revolutionary phrase-mongering" and of denying the value of reformist struggle; from Marx's letter derives the paraphrase: "If that is Marxism. then I am not a Marxist".American Marxist scholar Hal Draper responded to this comment by saying. "there are few thinkers in modern history whose thought has been so badly misrepresented. by Marxists and anti-Marxists alike".

Criticism

Some Marxists have criticised the academic institutionalisation of Marxism for being too shallow and detached from political action. For instance. Zimbabwean Trotskyist Alex Callinicos. himself a professional academic. stated that "Its practitioners remind one of Narcissus. who in the Greek legend fell in love with his own reflection... Sometimes it is necessary to devote time to clarifying and developing the concepts that we use. but indeed for Western Marxists this has become an end in itself. The result is a body of writings incomprehensible to all but a tiny minority of highly qualified scholars."

ACADEMIC MARXISM

Marxism has been adopted by a large number of academics and other scholars working in various disciplines.

The theoretical development of Marxist archaeology was first developed in the Soviet Union in 1929. when a young archaeologist named Vladislav I. Ravdonikas (1894–1976) published a report entitled "For a Soviet history of material culture". Within this work. the very discipline of archaeology as it then stood was criticised as being inherently bourgeoisie and therefore anti-socialist. and so. as a part of the academic reforms instituted in the Soviet Union under the administration of Premier Joseph Stalin. a great emphasis was placed on the adoption of Marxist archaeology throughout the country. These theoretical developments were subsequently adopted by archaeologists working in capitalist states outside of the Leninist bloc. most notably by the Australian academic V. Gordon Childe (1892–1957). who used Marxist theory in his understandings of the development of human society.

ETYMOLOGY

The term "Marxism" was popularized by Karl Kautsky who considered himself an "orthodox" Marxist during the dispute between the orthodox and revisionist followers of Marx. Kautsky's revisionist rival Eduard Bernstein also later adopted use of the term. Engels did not support the use of the term "Marxism" to describe either Marx's or his views. Engels claimed that the term was being abusively used as a rhetorical qualifier by those attempting to cast themselves as "real" followers of Marx while casting others in different terms. such as "Lassallians". In 1882. Engels claimed that Marx had criticized self-proclaimed "Marxist" Paul Lafargue. by saying that if Lafargue's views were considered "Marxist". then "One thing is certain and that is that I am not a Marxist".

HISTORY

Karl Marx and Friedrich Engels

Karl Heinrich Marx (5 May 1818 – 14 March 1883) was a German philosopher. political economist. and socialist revolutionary. who addressed the matters of alienation andexploitation of the working class. the capitalist mode of production. and historical materialism. He is famous for analysing history in terms of class struggle. summarised in the initial line introducing the *Communist Manifesto* (1848): "The history of all hitherto existing society is the history of class struggles". His ideas were influential in his time. and it was greatly expanded by the successful Bolshevik October Revolution of 1917 in Imperial Russia. As Joseph Schumpeter noted. however. "there [wa]s. between the true meaning of Marx's message and bolshevist practice and ideology. at least as great a gulf as there was between the religion of humble Galileans and the practice and ideology of the princes of the church or the warlords of the Middles Ages."

Friedrich Engels (28 November 1820 – 5 August 1895) was a German political philosopher and Karl Marx's co-developer of communist theory. Marx and Engels met in September 1844; discovering that they shared like views of philosophy and socialism. they collaborated and wrote works such as *Die heilige Familie* (*The Holy Family*). After the French deported Marx from France in January 1845. Engels and Marx moved to Belgium. which then permitted greater freedom of expression than other European countries; later. in January 1846. they returned to Brussels to establish the Communist Correspondence Committee.

In 1847. they began writing *The Communist Manifesto* (1848). based upon Engels' *The Principles of Communism*; six weeks later. they published the 12.000-word pamphlet in February 1848. In March. Belgium expelled them. and they moved to Cologne. where they published the *Neue Rheinische Zeitung*. a politically radical newspaper. Again. by 1849. they had to leave Cologne for London. The Prussian authorities pressured the British government to expel Marx and Engels. but Prime Minister Lord John Russell refused. After Karl Marx's death in 1883. Friedrich Engels became the editor and translator of

Marx's writings. With his *Origins of the Family. Private Property. and the State* (1884) – analysing monogamous marriage as guaranteeing male social domination of women. a concept analogous. in communist theory.

Tto the capitalist class's economic domination of the working class – Engels made intellectually significant contributions to feminist theory and Marxist feminism.

LATE 20TH CENTURY

Political Marxism

In 1959. the Cuban Revolution led to the victory of anti-imperialist Fidel Castro (1926–) and his July 26 Movement. Although the revolution had not been explicitly socialist. upon victory Castro ascended to the position of Prime Minister and eventually adopted the Leninist model of socialist development. forging an alliance with the Soviet Union.

One of the leaders of the revolution. the Argentine Marxist revolutionary Che Guevara (1928–1967). subsequently went on to aid revolutionary socialist movements in Congo-Kinshasaand Bolivia. eventually being killed by the Bolivian government. possibly on the orders of the CIA. though the CIA agent sent to search for Guevara. Felix Rodriguez expressed a desire to keep him alive as a possible bargaining tool with the Cuban government; he would posthumously go on to become an internationally recognised icon.

In the People's Republic of China. the Maoist government undertook the Cultural Revolution from 1966 through to 1976 in order to purge capitalist elements from Chinese society and entrench socialism.

However. upon Mao's death. his rivals seized political power and under the Premiership of Deng Xiaoping (1978–1992). many of Mao's Cultural Revolution era policies were revised or abandoned and much of the state sector privatised.

The late 1980s and early 1990s saw the collapse of most of those socialist states that had professed a Marxist–Leninist ideology. In the late 1970s and 1980s. the emergence of the New Right and Neo-liberal capitalism as the dominant ideological trends in western politics – championed by U.S. President Ronald Reagan and U.K. Prime Minister Margaret Thatcher – led the west to take a more aggressive stand against the Soviet Union and its Leninist allies. Meanwhile. in the Soviet Union. the reformist Mikhael Gorbachev(1931–) became Premier in March 1985. and began to move away from Leninist-based models of development towards social democracy.

Ultimately. Gorbachev's reforms. coupled with rising levels of popular ethnic nationalism in the Soviet Union. led to the state's dissolution in late 1991 into a series of constituent nations. all of which abandoned Marxist–Leninist models for socialism. with most converting to capitalist economies.

21ST CENTURY

Political Marxism

At the turn of the 21st century. China. Cuba. Laos and Vietnam remained the only officially Marxist–Leninist states remaining. although a Maoist government led by Prachanda(1954–) was elected into power in Nepal in 2008 following a long guerrilla struggle. The early 21st century also saw the election of socialist and anti-imperialist governments in several Latin American nations. in what has come to be known as the "Pink tide". Dominated by the Venezuelan government of Hugo Chávez. this trend also saw the election ofEvo Morales in Bolivia. Rafael Correa in Ecuador and Daniel Ortega in Nicaragua; forging political and economic alliances through international organisations like the Bolivarian Alliance for the Americas. these socialist governments allied themselves with Marxist–Leninist Cuba. and although none of them espoused a Leninist path directly. most admitted to being significantly influenced by Marxist theory. For Italian Marxist Gianni Vattimo in his 2011 book *Hermeneutic Communism* "this new weak communism differs substantially from its previous Soviet (and current Chinese) realization. because the South American countries follow democratic electoral procedures and also manage to decentralize the state bureaucratic system through the misiones (social missions for community projects). In sum. if weakened communism is felt as a specter in the West. it is not only because of media distortions but also for the alternative it represents through the same democratic procedures that the West constantly professes to cherish but is hesitant to apply"

CRITICISMS

Criticisms of Marxism have come from various political ideologies. Additionally. there are intellectual critiques of Marxism that contest certain assumptions prevalent in Marx's thought and Marxism after him. without exactly rejecting Marxist politics. Other. contemporary supporters of Marxism argue that many aspects of Marxist thought are viable. but that the corpus is incomplete or outdated in regards to certain aspects of economic. political or social theory. They may therefore combine some Marxist concepts with the ideas of other theorists such as Max Weber: the Frankfurt school is one example.

Socialist critiques

Democratic socialists and social democrats reject the idea that socialism can be accomplished only through extra-legal class conflict and a proletarian revolution. The relationship between Marx and other socialist thinkers and organizations. rooted in Marxism's "scientific" and anti-utopian socialism. among other factors. has divided Marxists from other socialists since Marx's life. After Marx's death. and with the emergence of Marxism. there have additionally been dissensions within Marxism itself- the splitting of theRussian Social Democratic Labour Party into Bolsheviks and Mensheviks a notable example. "Orthodox" Marxism became counterposed to a less dogmatic. more innovative. or even revisionist Marxism.

Anarchist critiques

Anarchism has had a strained relationship with Marxism since Marx's life. Anarchists reject the need for a transitory state phase. claiming that socialism cannot be established except through decentralized. Non-coercive organization. Individualist anarchists. who are often neither socialists nor capitalists. reject Marxism as a statist ideology.

Economic critiques

Other critiques come from an economic standpoint. Economists such as Friedrich Hayek have criticized Marxism for allocating resources inefficiently.

V. K. Dmitriev. writing in 1898. Ladislaus von Bortkiewicz. writing in 1906–07. and subsequent critics have alleged that Marx's value theory and law of the tendency of the rate of profit to fall are internally inconsistent. In other words. the critics allege that Marx drew conclusions that actually do not follow from his theoretical premises. Once these alleged errors are corrected. his conclusion that aggregate price and profit are determined by. and equal to. aggregate value and surplus value no longer holds true. This result calls into question his theory that the exploitation of workers is the sole source of profit.

Both Marxism and socialism have received considerable critical analysis from multiple generations of Austrian economists in terms of scientific methodology. economic theory. and political implications. During the marginal revolution. subjective value theory was rediscovered by Carl Menger. a development which undermined the British cost theories of value fundamentally. The restoration of subjectivism and praxeological methodology previously employed by classical economic scientists including Richard Cantillon.Anne-Robert-Jacques Turgot. Jean-Baptiste Say. and Frédéric Bastiat led Menger to criticise historicist methodology in general. Second-generation Austrian economist Eugen Böhm von Bawerk employed praxeological and subjectivist methodology attacking the law of value fundamentally. Non-Marxist economists have regarded his criticism as definitive with Gottfried Haberler arguing that Böhm-Bawerk's critique of Marx's economics was so thorough and devastating that as of the 1960s no Marxian scholar had conclusively refuted it. Third-generation Austrian Ludwig Von Mises sparked the economic calculation debate by identifying that without price signals in capital goods all other aspects of the market economy are irrational. This led him to declare "... that rational economic activity is impossible in a socialist commonwealth." Mises then elaborated on every form of socialism more completely in his 1922 book *Socialism. an*

Economic and Sociological Analysis. Contemporary Austrian critics include Murray Rothbard. David Gordon Yuri Maltsev. Gary North. and Joseph Salerno.

CLASSICAL MARXISM

KARL MARX

Karl Heinrich Marx (May 5. 1818. Trier. Germany – March 14. 1883. London) was an immensely influential German philosopher.political economist. and socialist revolutionary.

Marx addressed a wide range of issues. including alienation and exploitation of the worker. the capitalist mode of production and historical materialism. although he is most famous for his analysis of history in terms of class struggles. summed up in the opening line of the introduction to the Communist Manifesto: "The history of all hitherto existing society is the history of class struggles." The influence of his ideas. already popular during his life. was given added impetus by the victory of the Russian Bolsheviks in the 1917October Revolution. and there are few parts of the world which were not significantly touched by Marxian ideas in the course of the twentieth century.

As the American Marx scholar Hal Draper remarked. "there are few thinkers in modern history whose thought has been so badly misrepresented. by Marxists and anti-Marxists alike."

Early influences

The early influences on Marx are often grouped into 3 categories: German Philosophy. English/Scottish Political Economy and French socialism.

German philosophy

Main influences: Immanuel Kant. G. W. F. Hegel; Ludwig Feuerbach. Marx studied under one of Hegel's pupils. Bruno Bauer. a leader of the circle of Young Hegelians to whom Marx attached himself. However from 1841.

Marx and Engels came to disagree with Bruno Bauer and the rest of the Young Hegelians about socialism and also about the usage of Hegel's dialectic and progressively broke away from German idealism and the Young Hegelians. Marx's early writings are thus a response towards Hegel. German Idealism and a break with the rest of the Young Hegelians. Marx. "stood Hegel on his head." in his own view of his role. by turning the idealistic dialectic into a materialistic one. in proposing that material circumstances shape ideas. instead of the other way around. In this.

Marx was following the lead of Feuerbach. His theory of alienation. developed in the *Economic and Philosophical Manuscripts of 1844* (published in 1932). inspired itself from Feuerbach's critique of the alienation of Man in God through the objectivation of all his inherent characteristics (thus man projected on God all qualities which are in fact man's own quality which defines the "human nature"). But Marx also criticized Feuerbach for being insufficiently materialistic.

English and Scottish political economy

Main influences: Adam Smith and David Ricardo. Marx built on and critiqued the most well-known political economists of his day. the British classical political economists.

Marx critiqued Smith and Ricardo for not realizing that their economic concepts reflected specifically capitalist institutions. not innate natural properties of human society. and could not be applied unchanged to all societies. He proposed a systematic correlation between labour-values and money prices. He claimed that the source of profits under capitalism is value added by workers not paid out in wages. This mechanism operated through the distinction between "labour power". which workers freely exchanged for their wages. and "labour". over which asset-holding capitalists thereby gained control. This practical and theoretical distinction was Marx's primary insight. and allowed him to develop the concept of "surplus value". which distinguished his works from that of Smith and Ricardo.

French socialism

Main influences: Jean-Jacques Rousseau; Charles Fourier; Henri de Saint-Simon; Pierre-Joseph Proudhon; Louis Blanc.

Rousseau was one of the first modern writers to seriously attack the institution of private property. and therefore is sometimes considered a forebear of modern socialism andcommunism. though Marx rarely mentions Rousseau in his writings.

In 1833 France was experiencing a number of social problems arising out of the Industrial Revolution. A number of sweeping plans of reform were developed by thinkers on the left. Among the more grandiose were the plans of Charles Fourier and the followers of Saint-Simon. Fourier wanted to replace modern cities with utopian communities. while the Saint-Simonians advocated directing the economy by manipulating credit. Although these programmes didn't have much support. they did expand the political and social imagination of Marx.

Louis Blanc is perhaps best known for originating the social principle. later adopted by Marx. of how labour and income should be distributed: "From each according to his abilities. to each according to his needs".

Pierre-Joseph Proudhon participated in the February 1848 uprising and the composition of what he termed "the first republican proclamation" of the new republic. But he had misgivings about the new government because it was pursuing political reform at the expense of the socio-economic reform. which

Proudhon considered basic. Proudhon published his own perspective for reform. *Solution du problème social.* in which he laid out a programme of mutual financial cooperation among workers. He believed this would transfer control of economic relations from capitalists and financiers to workers. It was Proudhon's book *What is Property?* that convinced the young Karl Marx that private property should be abolished.

Other influences on Marx

Marx's revision of Hegelianism was also influenced by Engels' book. "The Condition of the Working Class" in England in 1844. which led Marx to conceive of the historical dialectic in terms of class conflict and to see the modern working class as the most progressive force for revolution.

Marx was influenced by Antique materialism. especially Epicurus (to whom Marx dedicated his thesis. "Difference of natural philosophy between Democritus and Epicurus". 1841) for his materialism and theory of clinamen which opened up a realm of liberty.

Giambattista Vico propounded a cyclical theory of history. according to which human societies progress through a series of stages from barbarism to civilization and then return to barbarism. In the first stage—called the Age of the Gods—religion. the family. and other basic institutions emerge; in the succeeding Age of Heroes. the common people are kept in subjection by a dominant class of nobles; in the final stage—the Age of Men—the people rebel and win equality. but in the process society begins to disintegrate. Vico's influence on Marx is obvious.

Marx drew on Lewis H. Morgan and his social evolution theory. He wrote a collection of notebooks from his reading of Lewis Morgan but they are regarded as being quite obscure and only available in scholarly editions. (However Engels is much more noticeably influenced by Morgan than Marx).

FRIEDRICH ENGELS

Friedrich Engels (November 28. 1820. Wuppertal – August 5. 1895. London) was a nineteenth-century German political philosopher. He developedcommunist theory alongside his better-known collaborator. Karl Marx.

In 1842 his father sent the young Engels to England to help manage his cotton factory in Manchester. Shocked by the widespread poverty. Engels began writing an account which he published in 1845 as *The Condition of the Working Class in England in 1844*.

In July 1845 Engels went to England. There he met an Irish working-class woman named Mary Burns (Crosby). with whom he lived until her death in 1863 (Carver 2003:19). Later he lived with her sister. Lizzie. marrying her the day before she died in 1877 (Carver 2003:42). These women may have introduced him to the Chartist movement. of whose leaders he met several. including George Harney. Engels actively participated in the Revolution of 1848. taking part in the uprising at Elberfeld. Engels fought in the Baden campaign against thePrussians (June/July 1849) as the aide-de-camp of August Willich. who commanded a Free Corps in the Baden-Palatinate uprising.

Marx and Engels

Marx and Engels first met in person in September 1844. They discovered that they had similar views on philosophy and on capitalism and decided to work together. producing a number of works including *Die heilige Familie* (*The Holy Family*). After the French authorities deported Marx fromFrance in January 1845. Engels and Marx decided to move to Belgium. which then permitted greater freedom of expression than some other countries in Europe. Engels and Marx returned to Brussels in January 1846. where they set up the Communist Correspondence Committee.

In 1847 Engels and Marx began writing a pamphlet together. based on Engels' *The Principles of Communism*. They completed the 12.000-word pamphlet in six weeks. writing it in such a manner as to make communism understandable to a wide audience. and published it as *The Communist Manifesto* in February 1848. In March. Belgium expelled both Engels and Marx. They moved to Cologne. where they began to publish a radical newspaper. the *Neue Rheinische Zeitung*. By 1849 both Engels and Marx had to leave Germany and moved to London. The Prussian authorities applied pressure on the British government to expel the two men. but Prime Minister Lord John Russell refused. With only the money that Engels could raise. the Marx family lived in extreme poverty. The contributions of Marx and Engels to the formation of Marxist theory have been described as inseparable.

After Marx's death

After Marx's death in 1883. Engels devoted much of the rest of his life to editing and translating Marx's writings. However. he also contributed significantly to feminist theory. seeing for instance the concept of monogamous marriage as having arisen because of the domination of men over women for the purpose of transferring (inheriting) property to their heir/ male children. In this sense. he ties communist theory to the family. arguing that men have dominated women just as the capitalist class has dominated workers. Engels died in London in 1895.

MAIN IDEAS

Marx's main ideas included:

- *Alienation:* Marx refers to the alienation of people from aspects of their "human nature" (*"Gattungswesen"*. usually translated as 'species-essence' or 'species-being'). He believed that alienation is a systematic result of capitalism. Under capitalism. the fruits of production belong to the employers. who expropriate the surplus created by others and in so doing generate alienated labour. Alienation describes objective features of a person's situation in capitalism - it isn't necessary for them to believe or feel that they are alienated.

- *Base and superstructure:* Marx and Engels use the "base-structure" concept to explain the idea that the totality of relations among people with regard to "the social production of their existence" forms the economic basis. on which arises a superstructure of political and legal institutions. To the base corresponds the social consciousness which includes religious. philosophical. and other main ideas. The base conditions both. the superstructure and the social consciousness. A conflict between the development of material productive forces and the relations of production causes social revolutions. and the resulting change in the economic basis will sooner or later lead to the transformation of the superstructure. For Marx. though. this relationship is not a one way process - it is reflexive; the base determines the superstructure in the first instance at the same time as it remains the foundation of a form of social organization which is itself transformed as an element in the overall dialectical process. The relationship between superstructure and base is considered to be a dialectical one. ineffable in a sense except as it unfolds in its material reality in the actual historical process (which scientific socialism aims to explain and. ultimately. to guide).
- *Class consciousness:* Class consciousness refers to the awareness. both of itself and of the social world around it. that a social class possesses. and its capacity to act in its own rational interests based on this awareness. Thus class consciousness must be attained before the class may mount a successful revolution. Other methods of revolutionary action have been developed however. such as vanguardism.
- *Exploitation:* Marx refers to the exploitation of an entire segment or class of society by another. He sees it as being an inherent feature and key element of capitalism and free markets. The profit gained by the capitalist is the difference between the value of the product made by the worker and the actual wage that the worker receives; in other words. capitalism functions on the basis of paying workers less than the full value of their labour. in order to enable the capitalist class to turn a profit.
- *Historical materialism:* Historical materialism was first articulated by Marx. although he himself never used the term. It looks for the causes of developments and changes in human societies in the way in which

humans collectively make the means to life. thus giving an emphasis. through economic analysis. to everything that co-exists with the economic base of society (*e.g.* social classes. political structures. ideologies).

- *Means of production:* The means of production are a combination of the means of labour and the subject of labour used by workers to make products. The *means of labor*include machines. tools. equipment. infrastructure. and "all those things with the aid of which man acts upon the subject of labour. and transforms it". The *subject of labor*includes raw materials and materials directly taken from nature. Means of production by themselves produce nothing — labour power is needed for production to take place.
- *Ideology:* Without offering a general definition for *ideology*. Marx on several instances has used the term to designate the production of images of social reality. According to Engels. "ideology is a process accomplished by the so-called thinker consciously. it is true. but with a false consciousness. The real motive forces impelling him remain unknown to him; otherwise it simply would not be an ideological process. Hence he imagines false or seeming motive forces". Because the ruling class controls the society's means of production. the superstructure of society. as well as its ruling ideas. will be determined according to what is in the ruling class's best interests. As Marx said famously in *The German Ideology*. "the ideas of the ruling class are in every epoch the ruling ideas. *i.e.* the class which is the ruling material force of society. is at the same time its ruling intellectual force". Therefore the ideology of a society is of enormous importance since it confuses the alienated groups and can create false consciousness such as commodity fetishism (perceiving labour as capital ~ a degradation of human life).
- *Mode of production:* The mode of production is a specific combination of productive forces (including human the means of production and labour power. tools. equipment. buildings and technologies. materials. and improved land) and social and technical relations of production (including the property. power and control relations governing society's productive assets. often codified in law. cooperative work relations and forms of association. relations between people and the objects of their work. and the relations between social classes).
- *Political economy:* The term "political economy" originally meant the study of the conditions under which production was organised in the nation-states of the new-born capitalist system. Political economy. then. studies the mechanism of human activity in organizing material. and the mechanism of distributing the surplus or deficit that is the

result of that activity. Political economy studies the means of production. specifically capital. and how this manifests itself in economic activity.

Marx's concept of class

Marx believed that class identity was configured in the relations with the mode of production. In other words. a class. is a collective of individuals who have a similar relationship with the means of production (as opposed to the more common-sense idea that class is determined by wealth alone. *i.e.* high class. middle class. poor class).

Marx describes several social classes in capitalist societies. including primarily:

- *The proletariat:* "those individuals who sell their labour power. (and therefore add value to the products). and who. in the capitalist mode of production. do not own the means of production". According to Marx. the capitalist mode of production establishes the conditions for the bourgeoisie to exploit the proletariat due to the fact that the worker'slabor power generates an added value greater than his salary.
- *The bourgeoisie:* those who "own the means of production" and buy labour power from the proletariat. who are recompensed by a salary. thus exploiting the proletariat.

The bourgeoisie may be further subdivided into the very wealthy bourgeoisie and the petty bourgeoisie. The petty bourgeoisie are those who employ labour. but may also work themselves. These may be small proprietors. land-holding peasants. or trade workers. Marx predicted that the petty bourgeoisie would eventually be destroyed by the constant reinvention of the means of production and the result of this would be the forced movement of the vast majority of the petty bourgeoisie to the proletariat. Marx also identified thelumpenproletariat. a stratum of society completely disconnected from the means of production.

Marx also describes the Communists as separate from the oppressed proletariat. The Communists were to be a unifying party among the proletariat; they were educated revolutionaries who could bring the proletariat to revolution and help them establish the democratic dictatorship of the proletariat. The Communists. according to Marx. would support any true revolution of the proletariat against the bourgeoisie. Thus. the Communists aide the proletariat in creating the inevitable classless society (Vladimir Lenin takes this concept a step further by stating that only "professional revolutionaries" can lead the revolution against the bourgeoisie).

Marx's theory of history

The Marxist theory of historical materialism understands society as fundamentally determined by the *material conditions* at any given time - this means the relationships which people enter into with one another in order to fulfill their basic needs. for instance to feed and clothe themselves and their families. In general Marx and Engels identified five successive stages of the development of these material conditions in Western Europe.

CRITICISMS OF MARXISM

GENERAL CRITICISMS

Democratic socialists and social democrats reject the idea that socialism can be accomplished only through class conflict and aproletarian revolution. Many anarchists reject the need for a transitory state phase. Some thinkers have rejected the fundamentals of Marxist theory. such as historical materialism and the labour theory of value. and gone on to criticize capitalism - and advocate socialism - using other arguments.

Some contemporary supporters of Marxism argue that many aspects of Marxist thought are viable. but that the corpus is incomplete or somewhat outdated in regards to certain aspects of economic. political or social theory. They may therefore combine some Marxist concepts with the ideas of other theorists such as Max Weber: the Frankfurt school is one example.

V. K. Dmitriev. writing in 1898. Ladislaus von Bortkiewicz. writing in 1906-07. and subsequent critics have alleged that Marx's value theory and law of the tendency of the rate of profit to fall are internally inconsistent. In other words. the critics allege that Marx drew conclusions that actually do not follow from his theoretical premises. Once these alleged errors are corrected. his conclusion that aggregate price and profit are determined by. and equal to. aggregate value and surplus value no longer holds true. This result calls into question his theory that the exploitation of workers is the sole source of profit.

Whether the rate of profit in capitalism has. as Marx predicted. tended to fall is a subject of debate. N. Okishio. in 1961. devised a theorem (Okishio's theorem) showing that if capitalists pursue cost-cutting techniques and if the real wage does not rise. the rate of profit must rise.

The inconsistency allegations have been a prominent feature of Marxian economics and the debate surrounding it since the 1970s. Andrew Kliman argues that. since internally inconsistent theories cannot possibly be right. the inconsistency charges serve to legitimate the suppression of Marx's critique of political economy and current-day research based upon it. as well as the correction of Marx's alleged inconsistencies.

Critics who have alleged that Marx has been proved internally inconsistent include former and current Marxian and/or Sraffian economists. such as Paul Sweezy. Nobuo Okishio. Ian Steedman. John Roemer. Gary Mongiovi. and David Laibman. who propose that the field be grounded in their correct versions of

Marxian economics instead of in Marx's critique of political economy in the original form in which he presented and developed it in *Capital*.Proponents of the Temporal Single System Interpretation (TSSI) of Marx's value theory claim that the supposed inconsistencies are actually the result of misinterpretation; they argue that when Marx's theory is understood as "temporal" and "single-system." the alleged internal inconsistencies disappear. In a recent survey of the debate. a proponent of the TSSI concludes that "the *proofs* of inconsistency are no longer defended; the entire case against Marx has been reduced to the *interpretive* issue."

HISTORICAL MATERIALISM

Historical materialism is normally considered the intellectual basis of Marxism. It proposes that technological advances in modes of production inevitably lead to changes in the social relations of production. This economic 'base' of society supports. is reflected by and influences the ideological 'superstructure' which encompasses culture. religion. politics and all other aspects of humanity's social consciousness. It thus looks for the causes of developments and changes in human history in economic. technological. and more broadly. material factors. as well as the clashes of material interests among tribes. social classes and nations. Law. politics. the arts. literature. morality. religion – are understood by Marx to make up the [superstructure]. as reflections of the economic base of society.

Many critics have argued that this is an oversimplification of the nature of society; they claim that the influence of ideas. culture and other aspects of what Marx called the superstructure are just as important as the economic base to the course of society. if not more so.

However. Marxism does not claim that the economic base of society is the only determining element in society as demonstrated by the following letter written by Friedrich Engels. Marx's long-time contributor:

According to the materialist conception of history. the *ultimately* determining element in history is the production and reproduction of real life. More than this neither Marx nor I ever asserted. Hence if somebody twists this into saying that the economic element is the *only* determining one he transforms that proposition into a meaningless. abstract. senseless phrase

However. this also creates another problem for Marxism. If the superstructure influences the base then there is no need for Marx's constant assertions that the history of society is one of economic class conflict. This then becomes a classic chicken or the egg argument as to whether the base or the superstructure comes first. Peter Singer proposes that the way to solve this problem is to understand that Marx saw the economic base as ultimately *real*. Marx believed that humanity's defining characteristic was its means of production and thus the only way for man to free himself from oppression was for him to take control of the means of production. According to Marx. this is the goal of history and the elements of the superstructure act as tools of history. Even if Singer's interpretation of Marx's intuitions on the "goal of history" is faithful to Marx's original intent. that still would not make this view point necessarily true. In fact. Karl Popper has argued that both the concept of Marx's historical method as well as its application are unfalsifiable. and thus it cannot be proven true or false:

The Marxist theory of history. in spite of the serious efforts of some of its founders and followers. ultimately adopted this soothsaying practice. In some of its earlier formulations (for example in Marx's analysis of the character of the 'coming social revolution') their predictions were testable. and in fact falsified. Yet instead of accepting the refutations the followers of Marx re-interpreted both the theory and the evidence in order to make them agree. In this way they rescued the theory from refutation; but they did so at the price of adopting a device which made it irrefutable. They thus gave a 'conventionalist twist' to the theory; and by this stratagem they destroyed its much advertised claim to scientific status.

HISTORICAL DETERMINISM

Marx's theory of history is considered a variant of historical determinism linked to his reliance on dialectical materialism as an endogenous mechanism for social change.

"At a certain stage of development. the material productive forces of society come into conflict with the existing relations of production or - this merely expresses the same thing in legal terms - with the property relations within the framework of which they have operated hitherto. From forms of development of the productive forces these relations turn into their fetters. Then begins an era of social revolution. The changes in the economic foundation lead sooner or later to the transformation of the whole immense superstructure."

The concept dialectic emerged from the dialogues of the ancient Greek philosophers but was brought out by Hegel in the early 19th century as a conceptual framework for the often opposing forces of historical evolution. Historical determinism has also been associated with scholars like Arnold Toynbee and Oswald Spengler but in recent times this conceptual approach has fallen into disuse.

In an effort to reassert this approach to an understanding of the forces of history. P.R. Sarkar criticised the narrow conceptual basis of Marx's ideas on historical evolution. In the 1978 book The Downfall of Capitalism and Communism. Ravi Batra pointed out crucial differences in the historical determinist approaches of Sarkar and Marx. "Sarkar's main concern with the human element is what imparts universality to his thesis. Thus while social evolution according to Marx is governed chiefly by economic conditions. to Sarkar this dynamic is propelled by forces varying with time and space: sometimes physical prowess and high-spiritedness. sometimes intellect applied to dogmas and sometimes intellect applied to the accumulation of capital (pg. 38)... The main line of defence of the Sarkarian hypothesis is that unlike the dogmas now in disrepute. it does not emphasise one particular point to the exclusion of all others: it is based on the sum total of human experience - the totality of human nature. Whenever a single factor. however important and fundamental. is called upon to illuminate the entire past and by implication the future. it simply invites disbelief. and after closer inspection. rejection. Marx committed that folly. and to some extent so did Toynbee. They both offered an easy prey to the critics. and the result is that today historical determinism is regarded by most scholars as an idea so bankrupt that it can never be solvent again. "

SUPPRESSION OF INDIVIDUAL RIGHTS

In the *Communist Manifesto*. Marx also set out a ten point programme of reform that he thought would be applicable to all modern industrial nations. with suggestions that included the redistribution of land and production as the basis of a transitional society before communism. Some liberal theorists argue that any redistribution of property is a form of coercion.

Various pro-capitalist economists have argued that a socialist state would by its very nature erode the rights of its citizens. The American economist Milton Friedman argued that under socialism. the absence of a free market economy would inevitably lead to an authoritarian political regime. Friedman's view was also shared by Friedrich Hayek and John Maynard Keynes. who both believed that capitalism is a precondition for freedom to flourish in a nation state.

IMPLEMENTATION OF COMMUNISM

Anarchists have often argued that Marxist communism will inevitably lead to coercion and state domination. Mikhail Bakunin believed Marxist regimes would lead to the "despotic control of the populace by a new and not at all numerous aristocracy." Even if this new aristocracy were to have originated from among the ranks of the proletariat. Bakunin argued that their new-found power would fundamentally change their view of society and thus lead them to "look down at the plain working masses."

ETHICAL

Marxism has been criticised for engendering the belief that ends justify the means. However. Marx himself may not have believed this. Marx wrote: An end which requires unjustified means is no justifiable end. Leon Trotsky emphasized the importance of revolution and believed that the end justifies the means:Dialectic materialism does not know dualism between means and end. The end flows naturally from the historical movement. Organically the means are subordinated to the end.

Stalin and Mao. both prominent Marxists are widely regarded as taking this view.Opposition to the ends justifying means was voiced by Max Weber in his 1919 lecture *Politics as a Vocation*:

We must be clear about the fact that all ethically oriented conduct may be guided by one of two fundamentally differing and irreconcilably opposed maxims: conduct can be oriented to an 'ethic of ultimate ends' or to an 'ethic of responsibility.'...

...Whosoever contracts with violent means for whatever ends—and every politician does—is exposed to its specific consequences. This holds especially for the crusader. religious and revolutionary alike.

Although he does not specifically name Marxism. Gandhi notes the importance of means in his work Satyagraha. which outlines his philosophy of non-violence. The theory of Satyagraha sees means and ends as inseparable. The means used to obtain an end are wrapped up and attached to that end. Therefore. it is contradictory to try to use unjust means to obtain justice or to try to use violence to obtain peace. As Gandhi wrote:

They say. 'means are. after all. means'. I would say. 'means are. after all. everything'. As the means so the end...

ECONOMIC

Marxian economics have been criticized for a number of reasons. Some critics point to the Marxian analysis of capitalism while others argue that the economic system proposed by communism is unworkable.

The Austrian School of economics charges Marx's economic system with being based on the classical labour theory of value. It argues this fundamental theory of classical economics is false. and prefers the subsequent and modern theory of value the subjective theory of value put forward by Carl Menger in his book Principles of Economics. The Austrian School of Economics was not alone in criticizing the Marxian and Classical belief in the Labour Theory of Value. British economist Alfred Marshall attacked Marx saying. "It is not true that the spinning of yarn in a factory... is the product of the labour of the operatives. It is the product of their labour. together with that of the employer and subordinate managers. and of the capital employed." Marshall points to the capitalist as sacrificing the money he could be using now for investment in business. which ultimately produces work. By this logic the capitalist contributes to the work and productivity of the factory because he delays his gratification through investment. Marshall. through the Law of Supply and Demand. attacked Marxian theory of value. According to Marshall. price. or value. is determined not just by supply but by the demand of the consumer. Labour does contribute to cost. but so does the wants and needs of consumers. The shift from labour being the source of all value to subjective individual evaluations 'creating' all value undermines Marx's economic conclusions and some of his social theories.

John Maynard Keynes referred to *Das Kapital* as "an obsolete textbook which I know to be not only scientifically erroneous but without interest or application for the modern world".

Distorted or absent price signals

The economic calculation problem is a criticism of socialist economics. or more precisely central economic planning. It was first proposed by Ludwig von Mises in 1920 and later expounded by Friedrich Hayek. The problem referred to is that of how to distribute resources rationally in an economy. The free market solution is the price mechanism. wherein people individually have the ability to decide how a good should be distributed based on their willingness to give money for it. The price conveys embedded information about the abundance of resources as well as their desirability which in turn allows. on the basis of individual consensual decisions. corrections that prevent shortagesand surpluses; Mises and Hayek argued that this is the only possible solution. and without the information provided by market prices socialism lacks a method to rationally allocate resources. Those who agree with this criticism argue it is a refutation of socialism and that it shows that a socialist planned economy could never work. The debate raged in the 1920s and 1930s. and that specific period of the debate has come to be known by economic historians as *the Socialist Calculation Debate.*

Reduced incentives

Some critics of utopian or egalitarian socialism argue that income sharing reduces individual incentives to work. and therefore incomes should be individualized as much as possible. Critics of socialism have argued that in any society where everyone holds equal wealth there can be no material incentive to work. because one does not receive rewards for a work well done. They further argue that incentives increase productivity for all people and that the loss of those effects would lead to stagnation. John Stuart Mill in*Principles of Political Economy* (1848) said:

It is the common error of Socialists to overlook the natural indolence of mankind; their tendency to be passive. to be the slaves of habit. to persist indefinitely in a course once chosen. Let them once attain any state of existence which they consider tolerable. and the danger to be apprehended is that they will thenceforth stagnate; will not exert themselves to improve. and by letting their faculties rust. will lose even the energy required to preserve them from deterioration. Competition may not be the best conceivable stimulus. but it is at present a necessary one. and no one can foresee the time when it will not be indispensable to progress. However. he later altered his views and became more sympathetic to socialism. particularly Fourierism. adding chapters to his Principles of Political Economy in defence of a socialist outlook. and defending some socialist causes. Within this revised work he also made the radical proposal that the whole wage system be abolished in favour of a co-operative wage system. Nonetheless. some of his views on the idea of flat taxation remained. albeit in a slightly toned down form.

The economist John Kenneth Galbraith has criticized communal forms of socialism that promote egalitarianism in terms of wages/compensation as unrealistic in its assumptions about human motivation:

This hope [that egalitarian reward would lead to a higher level of motivation]. one that spread far beyond Marx. has been shown by both history and human experience to be irrelevant. For better or worse. human beings do not rise to such heights. Generations of socialists and socially oriented leaders have learned this to their disappointment and more often to their sorrow. The basic fact is clear: the good society must accept men and women as they are.

EMPIRICAL AND EPISTEMOLOGICAL

Arguments against Marxism are often based on empirical or epistemological reasoning. Others are based on the assertion that the Marxian conception of society is fundamentally flawed.

The Marxist stages of history. class analysis. and theory of social evolution have been criticized. Robert Conquest argues that detailed analyses of many historical periods fail to find support for "class" or social evolution as used by Marxists. Sartre concluded that "class" was not an homogenous entity and could never mount a revolution but continued to advocate Marxist beliefs. Marx himself admitted that his theory could not explain the internal development of the "Asiatic" social system. where much of the world's population lived for thousands of years.

Many notable academics such as Karl Popper. David Prychitko. and Francis Fukuyama argue that many of Marx's predictions have failed. Marx predicted that wages would tend to depreciate and that capitalist economies would suffer worsening economic crises leading to the ultimate overthrow of the capitalist system. The socialist revolution would occur first in the most advanced capitalist nations and once collective ownership had been established then all sources of class conflict would disappear.

Popper has further argued that historical materialism is a pseudoscience because it is not falsifiable. Popper believed that Marxism had been initially scientific. in that Marx had postulated a theory which was genuinely predictive. When Marx's predictions were not in fact borne out. Popper argues that the theory was saved from falsification by the addition of ad hoc hypotheses which attempted to make it compatible with the facts. By this means a theory which was initially genuinely scientific degenerated into pseudo-scientific dogma.

Marxists respond that the social sciences are inherently unfalsifiable because they rely upon interpretation and analysis of complex events. which are never fully conclusive. unlike the experimentation of hard science. As an example of this. orthodox economists themselves have difficulty predicting economic developments using their own analyses. Popper agreed on the non-falsifiability of the social sciences. but instead used it as an argument against central planning and all-encompassing historiographical ideologies. Thomas Kuhn rejected Popper's theory of falsifiability and instead proposed that a gradual emergence of contrary data eventually leads to a paradigm shift in which scientists re-evaluate their underlying theoretical beliefs and even metaphysics. thus inadvertently describing Marxism as pseudoscientific himself. Popper devoted much attention to dissecting the practice of using the dialectic in defence of Marxist thought. which was the very strategy employed by V. A. Lektorsky in his defence of Marxism against Popper's criticisms. Among Popper's conclusions was that Marxists used dialectic as a method of side-stepping and evading criticisms. rather than actually answering or addressing them:

Hegel thought that philosophy develops; yet his own system was to remain the last and highest stage of this development and could not be superseded. The Marxists adopted the same attitude towards the Marxian system. Hence. Marx's anti-dogmatic attitude exists only in the theory and not in the practice of orthodox Marxism. and dialectic is used by Marxists. following the example of Engels' Anti-Dühring. mainly for the purposes of apologetics - to defend the Marxist system against criticism. As a rule critics are denounced for their failure to understand the dialectic. or proletarian science. or for being traitors. Thanks to dialectic the anti-dogmatic attitude has disappeared. and Marxism has established itself as a dogmatism which is elastic enough. by using its dialectic method. to evade any further attack. It has thus become what I have called reinforced dogmatism.

7

Libertarian Socialism

Libertarian socialism (sometimes called social anarchism. left-libertarianism and socialist libertarianism) is a group of political philosophies within the socialist movement that reject the view of socialism as state ownership or command of the means of production within a more general criticism of the state form itself as well as of wage labour relationships within the workplace. Instead it emphasizes workers' self management of the workplace and decentralized structures of political government asserting that a society based on freedom and equality can be achieved through abolishing authoritarian institutions that control certain means of production and subordinate the majority to an owning class or political and economic elite.Libertarian socialists generally place their hopes in decentralized means of direct democracy and federal or confederalassociations such as libertarian municipalism. citizens' assemblies. trade unions. and workers' councils. All of this is generally done within a general call for libertarian and voluntary human relationships through the identification. criticism. and practical dismantling of illegitimate authority in all aspects of life.

Past and present political philosophies and movements commonly described as libertarian socialist include anarchism (especiallyanarchist communism. anarchist collectivism. anarcho-syndicalism. and mutualism) as well as autonomism. communalism.participism. revolutionary syndicalism. and libertarian Marxist philosophies such as council communism and Luxemburgism; as well as some versions of "utopian socialism" and individualist anarchism.

OVERVIEW

Libertarian socialism is a western philosophy with diverse interpretations. though some general commonalities can be found in its many incarnations. Its proponents generally advocate a worker-oriented system of production and organization in the workplace that in some aspects radically departs from Neo-classical economics in favour of democratic cooperatives or common ownership of the means of production (socialism). They propose that this economic system be executed in a manner that attempts to maximize the liberty of individuals and minimize concentration of power or authority (libertarianism). Libertarian socialists are strongly critical of coercive institutions. which often leads them to reject the legitimacy of the state in favour of anarchism. Adherents propose achieving this through decentralization of political and economic power. usually involving the socialization of most large-scale private property and enterprise (while retaining respect for personal property). Libertarian socialism tends to deny the legitimacy of most forms of economically significant private property. viewing capitalist property relations as forms of domination that are antagonistic to individual freedom.

The first anarchist journal to use the term "libertarian" was *Le Libertaire. Journal du Mouvement Social* and it was published in New York City between 1858 and 1861 by French anarcho-communist Joseph Déjacque. "The next recorded use of the term was in Europe. when "libertarian communism" was used at a French regional anarchist Congress at Le Havre (16–22 November 1880). January the following year saw a French manifesto issued on "Libertarian or Anarchist Communism." Finally. 1895 saw leading anarchists Sébastien Faure and Louise Michel publish *La Libertaire* in France." The word stems from the French word *libertaire*. and was used to evade the French ban on anarchist publications. In this tradition. the term "libertarianism" in "libertarian socialism" is generally used as a synonym for anarchism. which some say is the original meaning of the term; hence "libertarian socialism" is equivalent to "socialist anarchism" to these scholars. In the context of the European socialist movement. *libertarian*has conventionally been used to describe those who opposed state socialism. such as Mikhail Bakunin.

The association of socialism with libertarianism predates that of capitalism. and many anti-authoritarians still decry what they see as a mistaken association of capitalism with libertarianism in the United States. As Noam Chomsky put it. a consistent libertarian "must oppose private ownership of the means of production and wage slavery. which is a component of this system. as incompatible with the principle that labour must be freely undertaken and under the control of the producer."

In a chapter recounting the history of libertarian socialism. economist Robin Hahnel relates that thus far the period where libertarian socialism has had its greatest impact was at the end of the 19th century through the first four decades of the twentieth century.

Early in the twentieth century. libertarian socialism was as powerful a force as social democracy and communism. TheLibertarian International– founded at the Congress of Saint Imier a few days after the split between Marxist and libertarians at the congress of the Socialist International held in The Hague in 1872– competed successfully against social democrats and communists alike for the loyalty of anticapitalist activists. revolutionaries. workers. unions and political parties for over fifty years. Libertarian socialists played a major role in the Russian revolutions of 1905 and 1917. Libertarian socialists played a dominant role in the Mexican Revolution of 1911. Twenty years after World War I was over. libertarian socialists were still strong enough to spearhead the social revolution that swept across Republican Spain in 1936 and 1937.

On the other hand a libertarian trend also developed within marxism which gained visibility around the late 1910s mainly in reaction against Bolshevism and Leninism rising to power and establishing the Soviet Union. Contemporary libertarian Marxist Harry Cleaverdescribes the situation as follows:

Outside and against this process of turning of Marxism into an ideology of domination. however. were various revolutionary tendencies which still drew on Marx's work to inform their struggles and which rejected both social-democratic and Marxist-Leninist versions of his theory. The most interesting of these. those that are relevant to my current purpose. have been those which insisted on the primacy of the self-activity and creativity of people in struggle against capitalism.

Within the space of these tendencies there has developed a coherent critique of "orthodox Marxism" that includes not only a rejection of the concept of "the transition" but a reconceptualization of the process of transcending capitalism that has remarkable similarities to Kropotkin's thinking on this subject.... Thus one of the earliest political tendencies within which this approach appeared after the Russian revolution of 1917 was that of "Council Communism" which saw the "workers councils" in Germany. or the soviets in Russia. as new organizational forms constructed by the people.

As with the anarchists. they too saw the Bolshevik take-over of the soviets (like that of the trade unions) as subverting the revolution and beginning the restoration of domination and exploitation.... Over the years this emphasis on working class autonomy has resulted in a reinterpretation of Marxist theory that has brought out the two-sided character of the class struggle and shifted the focus from capital (the preoccupation of orthodox Marxism) to the workers.... As a result. not only has there been a recognition that capitalism seeks to subordinate everyone's life (from the traditional factory proletariat to peasants. housewives and students) but that all those peoples' struggles involve both the resistance to this subordination and the effort to construct alternative ways of being.

ANTI-CAPITALISM

Libertarian socialists are anti-capitalist. and can thus be distinguished from right-wing libertarians. Whereas capitalist (and right-libertarian) principles concentrate economic power in the hands of those who own the most capital. libertarian socialism aims to distribute power. and thus freedom. more equally amongst members of society. A key difference between libertarian socialism andcapitalist libertarianism is that advocates of the former generally believe that one's degree of freedom is affected by one's economic and social status. whereas advocates of the latter focus on freedom of choice within a capitalist framework. This is sometimes characterised as a desire to maximize "free creativity" in a society in preference to "free enterprise."

Within anarchism there emerged a critique of wage slavery which refers to a situation perceived as quasi-voluntary slavery.where a person's livelihood depends on wages. especially when the dependence is total and immediate. It is a negatively connoted term used to draw an analogy between slavery and wage labour by focusing on similarities between owning and renting a person. The term *wage slavery* has been used to criticize economic exploitation and social stratification. with the former seen primarily as unequal bargaining power between labour and capital (particularly when workers are paid comparatively low wages. *e.g.* in sweatshops). and the latter as a lack of workers' self-management. fulfilling job choices and leisure in an economy.

Libertarian socialists believe if freedom is valued. then society must work towards a system in which individuals have the power to decide economic issues along with political issues. Libertarian socialists seek to replace unjustified authority with direct democracy. voluntary federation. and popular autonomy in all aspects of life. including physical communities and economic enterprises. With the advent of the industrial revolution. thinkers such as Proudhon and Marx elaborated the comparison between wage labour and slavery in the context of a critique of societal property not intended for active personal use. Luddites emphasized thedehumanization brought about by machines while later Emma Goldman famously denounced wage slavery by saying: "The only difference is that you are hired slaves instead of block slaves.".

Many libertarian socialists argue that large-scale voluntary associations should manage industrial manufacture. while workers retain rights to the individual products of their labour. As such. they see a distinction between the concepts of "private property" and "personal possession". Whereas "private property" grants an individual exclusive control over a thing whether it is in use or not. and regardless of its productive capacity. "possession" grants no rights to things that are not in use.

ANTI-AUTHORITARIANISM AND OPPOSITION TO THE STATE

Libertarian socialists generally regard concentrations of power as sources of oppression that must be continually challenged and justified. Most libertarian socialists believe that when power is exercised. as exemplified by the economic. social. or physical dominance of one individual over another. the burden of proof is always on the authoritarian to justify their action as legitimate when taken against its effect of narrowing the scope of human freedom. Libertarian socialists typically oppose rigid and stratified structures of authority. be they political.

economic. or social. In lieu of corporations and states. libertarian socialists seek to organise society into voluntary associations (usually collectives.communes. municipalities. cooperatives. commons. or syndicates) that use direct democracy or consensus for their decision-making process. Some libertarian socialists advocate combining these institutions using rotating. recallable delegates to higher-level federations. Spanish anarchism is a major example of such federations in practice.

Contemporary examples of libertarian socialist organizational and decision-making models in practice include a number of anti-capitalist and global justice movements including Zapatista Councils of Good Government and the Global Indymedia network (which covers 45 countries on six continents). There are also many examples of indigenous societies around the world whose political and economic systems can be accurately described as anarchist or libertarian socialist. each of which is unique and uniquely suited to the culture that birthed it. For libertarians. that diversity of practice within a framework of common principles is proof of the vitality of those principles and of their flexibility and strength.

Contrary to popular opinion. libertarian socialism has not traditionally been a utopian movement. tending to avoid dense theoretical analysis or prediction of what a future society would or should look like. The tradition instead has been that such decisions cannot be made now. and must be made through struggle and experimentation. so that the best solution can be arrived at democratically and organically. and to base the direction for struggle on established historical example. They point out that the success of thescientific method comes from its adherence to open rational exploration. not its conclusions. in sharp contrast to dogma and predetermined predictions. To libertarian socialists. dogmatic approaches to social organization are doomed to failure; and thus they reject Marxist notions of linear and inevitable historical progression. Noted anarchist Rudolf Rocker once stated. "I am an anarchist not because I believe anarchism is the final goal. but because there is no such thing as a final goal".

Because libertarian socialism encourages exploration and embraces a diversity of ideas rather than forming a compact movement. there have arisen inevitable controversies over individuals who describe themselves as libertarian socialists but disagree with some of the core principles of libertarian socialism. For example. Peter Hain interprets libertarian socialism as minarchist rather than anarchist. favoring radical decentralization of power without going as far as the complete abolition of the state and libertarian socialist Noam Chomsky supports dismantling all forms of unjustified social or economic power. while also emphasizing that state intervention should be supported as a temporary protection while oppressive structures remain in existence. Proponents are known for opposing the existence of states or government and refusing to participate in coercive state institutions. Indeed. in the past many refused to swear oaths in court or to participate in trials. even when they faced imprisonment or deportation.

CIVIL LIBERTIES AND INDIVIDUAL FREEDOM

Libertarian socialists have been strong advocates and activists of civil liberties that provide an individual specific rights such as the freedom in issues of love and sex (free love) and of thought and conscience (freethought). In this activism they have clashed with state and religious institutions which have limited such rights. Anarchism has been an important advocate of free love since its birth. Later a strong tendency of free love appeared alongside anarcha-feminism and advocacy of LGBT rights. In recent times anarchism has also voiced opinions and taken action around certain sex related subjects such as pornography. BDSM and thesex industry.

Anarcha-feminism developed as a synthesis of radical feminism and anarchism that views patriarchy (male domination over women) as a fundamental manifestation of compulsory government. It was inspired by the late 19th-century writings of early feminist anarchists such as Lucy Parsons. Emma Goldman. Voltairine de Cleyre and Virginia Bolten. Anarcha-feminists. like other radical feminists. criticise and advocate the abolition of traditional conceptions of family. education and gender roles. Also the council communist Sylvia Pankhurst was a feminist activist as well as a libertarian marxist. Anarchists also took a pioneering interest in issues related to LGBTI persons. An important current within anarchism is free love. Free love advocates sometimes traced their roots back to the early anarchist Josiah Warrenand to experimental communities. viewed sexual freedom as a clear. direct expression of an individual's self-ownership. Free love particularly stressed women's rights since most sexual laws discriminated against women: for example. marriage laws and anti-birth control measures.

Libertarian socialists have traditionally been skeptical of and opposed to organised religion. Freethought is a philosophical viewpoint that holds opinions should be formed on the basis of science. logic. and reason. and should not be influenced by authority. tradition. or other dogmas.The cognitive application of freethought is known as "freethinking." and practitioners of freethought are known as "freethinkers." In the United States. "freethought was a basically anti-Christian. anti-clerical movement. whose purpose was to make the individual politically and spiritually free to decide for himself on religious matters. A number of contributors to *Liberty* (anarchist publication) were prominent figures in both freethought and anarchism. The individualist anarchist George MacDonald was a co-editor of *Freethought* and. for a time. *The Truth Seeker*. E.C. Walker was co-editor of the...free-thought/ free love journal *Lucifer. the Light-Bearer*". *Free Society* (1895–1897 as *The Firebrand*; 1897–1904 as *Free*

Society) was a major anarchist newspaper in the United States at the end of the nineteenth and beginning of the twentieth centuries. The publication staunchly advocated free love and women's rights. and critiqued "Comstockery" – censorship of sexual information. In 1901. Catalan anarchist andfree-thinker Francesc Ferrer i Guàrdia established "modern" or progressive schools in Barcelona in defiance of an educational system controlled by the Catholic Church. The schools' stated goal was to "educate the working class in a rational. secular and non-coercive setting". Fiercely anti-clerical. Ferrer believed in "freedom in education". education free from the authority of church and state. Later in the 20th century Austrian freudo-marxist Wilhelm Reich became a consistent propagandist for sexual freedom going as far as opening free sex-counselling clinics in Vienna for working-class patients as well as coining the phrase "sexual revolution" in one of his books from the 1940s. During the early 1970s the anarchist and pacifist Alex Comfort achieved international celebrity for writing the sex manuals *The Joy of Sex* and *More Joy of Sex*.

VIOLENT AND NON-VIOLENT MEANS

Some libertarian socialists see violent revolution as necessary in the abolition of capitalist society. Along with many others. Errico Malatesta argued that the use of violence was necessary; as he put it in *Umanità Nova* (no. 125. September 6. 1921):It is our aspiration and our aim that everyone should become socially conscious and effective; but to achieve this end. it is necessary to provide all with the means of life and for development. and it is therefore necessary to destroy with violence. since one cannot do otherwise. the violence that denies these means to the workers.Pierre-Joseph Proudhon argued in favour of a non-violent revolution through a process of dual power in which libertarian socialist institutions would be established and form associations enabling the formation of an expanding network within the existing state-capitalist framework with the intention of eventually rendering both the state and the capitalist economy obsolete. The progression towards violence in anarchism stemmed. in part. from the massacres of some of the communes inspired by the ideas of Proudhon and others. Many anarcho-communists began to see a need for revolutionary violence to counteract the violence inherent in both capitalism and government.

Anarcho-pacifism is a tendency within the anarchist movement which rejects the use of violence in the struggle for social change. The main early influences were the thought of Henry David Thoreau and Leo Tolstoy. It developed "mostly in Holland *(sic)*. Britain. and the United States. before and during the Second World War".Opposition to the use of violence has not prohibited anarcho-pacifists from accepting the principle of resistance or even revolutionary action provided it does not result in violence; it was in fact their approval of such forms of opposition to power that lead many anarcho-pacifists to endorse the anarcho-syndicalistconcept of the general strike as the great revolutionary weapon. Later anarcho-pacifists have also come to endorse to non-violent strategy of dual power.Other anarchists have believed that violence (especially self-defence) is justified as a way to provoke social upheaval which could lead to a social revolution.

ENVIRONMENTAL ISSUES

Green anarchism. or ecoanarchism. is a school of thought within anarchism which puts a particular emphasis on environmental issues. An important early influence was the thought of the American anarchist Henry David Thoreau and his book *Walden*. as well as Leo Tolstoy and Elisee Reclus. In the late 19th century there emerged anarcho-naturism as the fusion of anarchism and naturist philosophies within individualist anarchist circles in France. Spain. Cuba and Portugal. Important contemporary currents are anarcho-primitivism and social ecology. An important meeting place for international libertarian socialism in the early 1990s was the journal *Democracy and Nature* in which prominent activists and theorists such as Takis Fotopoulos. Noam Chomsky. Murray Bookchin and Cornelius Castoriadis wrote.

The journal promoted a green libertarian socialism when it manifested as its aims that:

- ...the public realm has to be extended beyond the traditional political domain to the economic and broader social domains so that the reintegration of society with the economy. polity and Nature can be achieved. In this sense. democracy should be seen as irreconcilable with any form of inequity in the distribution of power. that is. with any concentration of power. political. social or economic. Consequently. democracy is incompatible with commodity and property relations. which inevitably lead to concentration of power. Similarly. it is incompatible with hierarchical structures implying domination. either institutionalised (*e.g.*. domination of women by men). or "objective" (*e.g.*. domination of the South by the North in the framework of the capitalist division of labour). and the implied notion of dominating the natural world. Finally. democracy is fundamentally incompatible with any closed system of beliefs. dogmas. or ideas. So. democracy. for us. has nothing to do with the present dominant liberal conception of democracy... "Our aims" by Democracy and Nature"

POLITICAL ROOTS

WITHIN EARLY MODERN SOCIALIST THOUGHT

Peasant revolts in the post-reformation era

For Roderick T. Long libertarian socialists claim the seventeenth century English Levellers among their ideological forbears. Various libertarian socialist authors have identified the written work of English Protestant social reformer Gerrard Winstanley and the social activism of his group. the Diggers. as anticipating this line of thought. For anarchist historianGeorge Woodcock although (Pierre Joseph) Proudhon was the first writer to call himself an anarchist. at least two predecessors outlined systems that contain all the basic elements of anarchism. The first was Gerrard Winstanley (1609-c. 1660). a linen draper who led the small movement of the Diggers during the Commonwealth. Winstanley and his followers protested in the name of a radical Christianity against the economic distress that followed the Civil War and against the inequality that the grandees of the New Model Army seemed intent on preserving.

In 1649–1650 the Diggers squatted on stretches of common land in southern England and attempted to set up communities based on work on the land and the sharing of goods. The communities failed. but a series of pamphlets by Winstanley survived. of which *The New Law of Righteousness* (1649) was the most important. Advocating a rational Christianity. Winstanley equated Christ with "the universal liberty" and declared the universally corrupting nature of authority. He saw "an equal privilege to share in the blessing of liberty" and detected an intimate link between the institution of property and the lack of freedom." For Murray Bookchin "In the modern world. anarchism first appeared as a movement of the peasantry and yeomanry against declining feudal institutions. In Germany its foremost spokesman during the Peasant Wars wasThomas Muenzer; in England. Gerrard Winstanley. a leading participant in the Digger movement. The concepts held by Muenzer and Winstanley were superbly attuned to the needs of their time — a historical period when the majority of the population lived in the countryside and when the most militant revolutionary forces came from an agrarian world. It would be painfully academic to argue whether Muenzer and Winstanley could have achieved their ideals. What is of real importance is that they spoke to their time; their anarchist concepts followed naturally from the rural society that furnished the bands of the peasant armies in Germany and the New Model in England."

The Enlightenment

For Roderick T. Long libertarian socialists also often share a view of ancentry in the eighteenth century French encyclopedists alongsideThomas Jefferson and Thomas Paine". A more often mentioned name is that of English enlightenment thinker William Godwin.For Woodcock a more elaborate sketch of anarchism. although still without the name. was provided by William Godwin in his *Enquiry Concerning Political Justice* (1793). Godwin was a gradualist anarchist rather than a revolutionary anarchist; he differed from most later anarchists in preferring above revolutionary action the gradual and. as it seemed to him. more natural process of discussion among men of good will. by which he hoped truth would eventually triumph through its own power. Godwin. who was influenced by the English tradition of Dissent and the French philosophy of the Enlightenment. put forward in a developed form the basic anarchist criticisms of the state. of accumulated property. and of the delegation of authority through democratic procedure."

During the French Revolution. Sylvain Maréchal. in his *Manifesto of the Equals* (1796). demanded "the communal enjoyment of the fruits of the earth" and looked forward to the disappearance of "the revolting distinction of rich and poor. of great and small. of masters and valets. of governors and governed." The term "anarchist" first entered the English language in 1642. during the English Civil War. as a term of abuse. used by Royalists against their Roundhead opponents.

By the time of the French Revolution some. such as the *Enragés*. began to use the term positively. in opposition to Jacobin centralisation of power. seeing "revolutionary government" as oxymoronic. By the turn of the 19th century. the English word "anarchism" had lost its initial negative connotation.

The Romantic era and "Utopian Socialism"

Kent Bromley. in his preface to Peter Kropotkin's book *The Conquest of Bread*. considered early French socialist Charles Fourier to be the founder of the libertarian branch of socialist thought. as opposed to the authoritarian socialist ideas of Babeuf and Buonarroti. AnarchistHakim Bey describes Fourier's ideas as follows: "In Fourier's system of Harmony all creative activity including industry. craft. agriculture. etc. will arise from liberated passion — this is the famous theory of "attractive labour." Fourier sexualizes work itself — the life of the Phalanstery is a continual orgy of intense feeling. intellection. and activity. a society of lovers and wild enthusiasts." Fourierism manifested itself "in the middle of the 19th century (where) literally hundreds of communes (phalansteries) were founded on fourierist principles in France. N. America. Mexico. S. America. Algeria.

Yugoslavia. etc. Pierre-Joseph Proudhon. Friedrich Engels. and Peter Kropotkin all read him with fascination. as did André Breton and Roland Barthes. Herbert Marcuse in his influential work *Eros and Civilization* praised Fourier saying that "Fourier comes closer than any other utopian socialist to elucidating the dependence of freedom on non-repressive sublimation."

Anarchist Peter Sabatini reports that in the United States "of early to mid-19th century. there appeared an array of communal and "utopian" counterculture groups (including the so-called free love movement).

William Godwin's anarchism exerted an ideological influence on some of this. but more so the socialism of Robert Owen and Charles Fourier. After success of his British venture. Owen himself established a cooperative community within the United States at New Harmony. Indiana during 1825.

One member of this commune was Josiah Warren(1798–1874). considered to be the first individualist anarchist".

Anarchism

As Albert Meltzer and Stuart Christie stated in their book *The Floodgates of Anarchy*. anarchism has:

...its particular inheritance. part of which it shares with socialism. giving it a family resemblance to certain of its enemies. Another part of its inheritance it shares withliberalism. making it. at birth. kissing-cousins with American-type radical individualism. a large part of which has married out of the family into the Right Wing and is no longer on speaking terms. (*The Floodgates of Anarchy*. 1970. p. 39.)

Pierre-Joseph Proudhon. who is often considered the father of modern anarchism. coined the phrase "Property is theft" to describe part of his view on the complex nature of ownership in relation to freedom. When he said property is theft. he was referring to the capitalist who he believed stole profit from laborers. For Proudhon. the capitalist's employee was "subordinated. exploited: his permanent condition is one of obedience."

Seventeen years (1857) after Proudhon first called himself an anarchist (1840). anarchist communist Joseph Déjacque was the first person to describe himself as a libertarian. Outside the United States. "libertarian" generally refers to anti-authoritarian anti-capitalist ideologies.

Libertarian socialism has its roots in both classical liberalism and socialism. though it is often in conflict with liberalism (especially Neo-liberalismand right-libertarianism) and authoritarian State socialism simultaneously. While libertarian socialism has roots in both socialism and liberalism. different forms have different levels of influence from the two traditions. For instance mutualist anarchism is more influenced by liberalism whilecommunist and syndicalist anarchism are more influenced by socialism. It is interesting to note. however. that mutualist anarchism has its origins in 18th- and 19th-century European socialism (such as Fourierian socialism) while communist and syndicalist anarchism has its earliest origins in early 18th-century liberalism (such as the French Revolution).

Anarchism posed an early challenge to the vanguardism and statism it detected in important sectors of the socialist movement. As such "The consequences of the growth of parliamentary action. ministerialism. and party life. charged the anarchists. would be de-radicalism and embourgeoisiement. Further. state politics would subvert both true individuality and true community. In response. many anarchists refused Marxist-type organisation. seeking to dissolve or undermine power and hierarchy by way of loose political-cultural groupings. or by championing organisation by a single. simultaneously economic and political administrative unit (Ruhle. Syndicalism). The power of the intellectual and of science were also rejected by many anarchists: "In conquering the state. in exalting the role of parties. they [intellectuals] reinforce the hierarchical principle embodied in political and administrative institutions". Revolutions could only come through force of circumstances and/or the inherently rebellious instincts of the masses (the "instinct for freedom" (Bakunin. Chomsky)). Thus. in Bakunin's words: "All that individuals can do is to clarify. propagate. and work out ideas corresponding to the popular instinct".".

Marxism

Marxism started to develop a libertarian strand of thought after specific circumstances. "One does find early expressions of such perspectives in(William) Morris and the Socialist Party of Great Britain (the SPGB). then again around the events of 1905. with the growing concern at the bureaucratisation and de-radicalisation of international socialism". Morris established the Socialist League in December 1884. which was encouraged by Friedrich Engels and Eleanor Marx. As the leading figure in the organization Morris embarked on a relentless series of speeches and talks on street corners. in working men's clubs and lecture theatres across England and Scotland. From 1887. anarchists began to outnumber socialists in the Socialist League. The 3rd Annual Conference of the League. held in London on 29 May 1887 marked the change. with a majority of the 24 branch delegates voting in favour of an anarchist-sponsored resolution declaring that "This conference endorses the policy of abstention from parliamentary action. hitherto pursued by the League. and sees no sufficient reason for altering it." Morris played peacemaker but sided with the anti-Parliamentarians. who won control of the League. which consequently lost the support of Engels and saw the departure of Eleanor Marx and her partner Edward Aveling to form the separate Bloomsbury Socialist Society.

However. "the most important ruptures are to be traced to the insurgency during and after the First World War. Disillusioned with the capitulation of the social democrats. excited by the emergence of workers' councils. and slowly distanced from Leninism. many communists came to reject the claims of socialist parties and to put their faith instead in the masses." For these socialists. "The intuition of the masses in action can have more genius in it than the work of the greatest individual genius". Luxemburg's workerism and spontaneism are exemplary of positions later taken up by the far-left of the period – Pannekoek. Roland Holst. and Gorter in Holland. Sylvia Pankhurst in Britain. Gramsci in Italy. Lukacs in Hungary. In these formulations. the dictatorship of the proletariat was to be the dictatorship of a class. "not of a party or of a clique"." However within this line of thought "The tension between anti-vanguardism and vanguardism has frequently resolved itself in two diametrically opposed ways: the first involved a drift towards the party; the second saw a move towards the idea of complete proletarian spontaneity...The first course is exemplified most clearly in Gramsci and Lukacs...The second course is illustrated in the tendency. developing from the Dutch and German far-lefts. which inclined towards the complete eradication of the party form."

In the emerging Soviet state there appeared Left-wing uprisings against the Bolsheviks which were a series of rebellions and uprisings against the Bolsheviks led or supported by left wing groups including Socialist Revolutionaries. Left Socialist Revolutionaries. Mensheviks. and anarchists. Some were in support of the White Movement while some tried to be an independent force. The uprisings started in 1918 and continued through the Russian Civil War and after until 1922. In response the Bolsheviks increasingly abandoned attempts to get these groups to join the government and suppressed them with force. *"Left-Wing" Communism: An Infantile Disorder* is a work by Vladimir Leninhimself attacking assorted critics of the Bolsheviks who claimed positions to their left.

For "many Marxian libertarian socialists. the political bankruptcy of socialist orthodoxy necessitated a theoretical break. This break took a number of forms. The Bordigists and the SPGB championed a super-Marxian intransigence in theoretical matters. Other socialists made a return "behind Marx" to the anti-positivist programme of German idealism. Libertarian socialism has frequently linked its anti-authoritarian political aspirations with this theoretical differentiation from orthodoxy... Karl Korsch... remained a libertarian socialist for a large part of his life and because of the persistent urge towards theoretical openness in his work. Korsch rejected the eternal and static. and he was obsessed by the essential role of practice in a theory's truth. For Korsch. no theory could escape history. not even Marxism. In this vein. Korsch even credited the stimulus for Marx's Capital to the movement of the oppressed classes. "

In rejecting both capitalism and the state. some libertarian marxists align themselves with anarchists in opposition to both capitalist representative democracy and to authoritarian forms of Marxism. Although anarchists and Marxists share an ultimate goal of a stateless society. anarchists criticise most Marxists for advocating a transitional phase under which the state is used to achieve this aim. Non-etheless. libertarian Marxist tendencies such as autonomist Marxism and council communism have historically been intertwined with the anarchist movement. Anarchist movements have come into conflict with both capitalist and Marxist forces. sometimes at the same time. as in the Spanish Civil War. though as in that war Marxists themselves are often divided in support or opposition to anarchism. Other political persecutions under bureaucratic parties have resulted in a strong historical antagonism between anarchists and libertarian Marxists on the one hand and Leninist Marxists and their derivatives such as Maoists on the other. In recent history. however.

libertarian socialists have repeatedly formed temporary alliances with Marxist-Leninist groups for the purposes of protest against institutions they both reject. Part of this antagonism can be traced to the International Workingmen's Association. the *First International*. a congress of radical workers. where Mikhail Bakunin. who was fairly representative of anarchist views. and Karl Marx. whom anarchists accused of being an "authoritarian". came into conflict on various issues. Bakunin's viewpoint on the illegitimacy of the state as an institution and the role of electoral politics was starkly counterposed to Marx's views in the First International. Marx and Bakunin's disputes eventually led to Marx taking control of the First International and expelling Bakunin and his followers from the organization. This was the beginning of a long-running feud and schism between libertarian socialists and what they call "authoritarian communists". or alternatively just "authoritarians". Some Marxists have formulated views that closely resemble syndicalism. and thus express more affinity with anarchist ideas. Several libertarian socialists. notably Noam Chomsky. believe that anarchism shares much in common with certain variants of Marxism such as the council communism of Marxist Anton Pannekoek. In Chomsky's *Notes on Anarchism*. he suggests the possibility "that some form of council communism is the natural form of revolutionary socialism in an industrial society. It reflects the belief that democracy is severely limited when the industrial system is controlled by any form of autocratic elite. whether of owners. managers. and technocrats. a 'vanguard' party. or a State bureaucracy."

In the mid-20th century some libertarian socialist groups emerged out of disagreements with Trotskyism which presented itself as leninist anti-stalinism. As such the french group*Socialisme ou Barbarie* emerged out of the Trotskyist Fourth International. where Castoriadis and Claude Lefort constituted a Chaulieu–Montal Tendency in the French Parti Communiste Internationaliste in 1946. In 1948. they experienced their "final disenchantment with Trotskyism". leading them to break away to form Socialisme ou Barbarie. whose journal began appearing in March 1949. Castoriadis later said of this period that "the main audience of the group and of the journal was formed by groups of the old. radical left: Bordigists. council communists. some anarchists and some offspring of the German "left" of the 1920s". Also in the United Kingdom the group Solidarity was founded in 1960 by a small group of expelled members of the Trotskyist Socialist Labour League. Almost from the start it was strongly influenced by the French *Socialisme ou Barbarie* group. in particular by its intellectual leader Cornelius Castoriadis. whose essays were among the many pamphlets Solidarity produced. The intellectual leader of the group was Chris Pallis (who wrote under the name Maurice Brinton).

In the People's Republic of China (PRC) since 1967. the terms Ultra-Left and left communist refers to political theory and practice self-defined as further "left" than that of the central Maoist leaders at the height of the GPCR ("Great

Proletarian Cultural Revolution"). The terms are also used retroactively to describe some early 20th-century Chinese anarchist orientations. As a slur. the Communist Party of China (CPC) has used the term "ultra-left" more broadly to denounce any orientation it considers further "left" than theparty line. According to the latter usage. in 1978 the CPC Central Committee denounced as "ultra-left" the line of Mao Zedong from 1956 until his death in 1976. "Ultra-Left" refers to those GPCR rebel positions that diverged from the central Maoist line by identifying an antagonistic contradiction between the CPC-PRC party-state itself and themasses of workers and "peasants" conceived as a single proletarian class divorced from any meaningful control over production or distribution. Whereas the central Maoist line maintained that the masses controlled the means of production through the Party's mediation. the Ultra-Left argued that the objective interests of bureaucrats were structurally determined by the centralist state-form in direct opposition to the objective interests of the masses. regardless of however "red" a given bureaucrat's "thought" might be. Whereas the central Maoist leaders encouraged the masses to criticize reactionary "ideas" and "habits" among the alleged 5per cent of bad cadres. giving them a chance to "turn over a new leaf" after they had undergone "thought reform". the Ultra-Left argued that "cultural revolution" had to give way to "political revolution" – "in which one class overthrows another class".

In 1969 french platformist anarcho-communist Daniel Guerin published an essay called "Libertarian Marxism?" in which he dealt with the debate between Karl Marx and Mikhail Bakunin at the First International and afterwards he suggested that "Libertarian marxism rejects determinism and fatalism. giving the greater place to individual will. intuition. imagination. reflex speeds. and to the deep instincts of the masses. which are more far-seeing in hours of crisis than the reasonings of the 'elites'; libertarian marxism thinks of the effects of surprise. provocation and boldness. refuses to be cluttered and paralysed by a heavy 'scientific' apparatus. doesn't equivocate or bluff. and guards itself from adventurism as much as from fear of the unknown." In the US from 1970 to 1981 there existed the publication *Root and Branch* which had as a subtitle "A Libertarian Marxist Journal".

Autonomist Marxism. Neo-Marxism and Situationist theory are also regarded as being anti-authoritarian variants of Marxism that are firmly within the libertarian socialist tradition. For libcom.org "In the 1980s and 90s. a series of other groups developed. influenced also by much of the above work. The most notable are Kolinko. Kurasje and Wildcat in Germany. *Aufheben* in England. Theorie Communiste in France. TPTG in Greece and Kamunist Kranti in India. They are also connected to other groups in other countries. merging autonomia. operaismo. Hegelian Marxism. the work of the JFT. Open Marxism. the ICO. the Situationist International. anarchism and post-68 German Marxism."Related to this were intellectuals who were influenced by Italian left communist Amadeo Bordiga but who disagreed with his leninist positions and so these included the french publication *Invariance* edited by Jacques Camatte. published since 1968 and Gilles Dauve who published *Troploin* with Karl Nesic.

NOTABLE LIBERTARIAN SOCIALIST TENDENCIES

CLASSICAL ANARCHIST TENDENCIES

In a chronological and theoretical sense. there are classical — those created throughout the 19th century — and post-classical anarchist schools — those created since the mid-20th century and after.

Mutualism

Mutualism is a political and economic theory largely associated with Pierre-Joseph Proudhon. Proudhon argued that "all capital. whether material or mental. being the result of collective labour. is. in consequence. collective property." This meant that artisans would manage the tools required for their own work while. in large-scale enterprises. this meant replacing wage labour by workers' co-operatives. He argued "it is necessary to form an ASSOCIATION among workers... because without that. they would remain related as subordinates and superiors. and there would ensue two... castes of masters and wage-workers. which is repugnant to a free and democratic society." As he put it in 1848:

"Under the law of association. transmission of wealth does not apply to the instruments of labour. so cannot become a cause of inequality.... We are socialists... under universal association. ownership of the land and of the instruments of labour is *social* ownership... We want the mines. canals. railways handed over to democratically organised workers' associations... We want these associations to be models for agriculture. industry and trade. the pioneering core of that vast federation of companies and societies. joined together in the common bond of the democratic and social Republic."

Mutualists believe that a free labour market would allow for conditions of equal income in proportion to exerted labour. As Jonathan Beecher puts it. Proudhon's aim was to. "emancipate labour from the constraints imposed by capital". Proudhon supported individual possession of land and argued that the "land is indispensable to our existence. consequently a common thing. consequently insusceptible of appropriation." He believed that an individual only had a right to land while he was using or occupying it. If the individual ceases doing so. it reverts to unowned land. Mutualists hold a labour theory of value. arguing that in exchange labour should always be worth "the amount of labour necessary to produce an article of exactly similar and equal utility." and considering anything less to be exploitation. theft of labour. or usury. Mutualists oppose the institutions by which individuals gain income through loans. investments. and rent. as they believe the income received through these activities is not in direct accord with labour spent. In place of these capitalist institutions they advocate labour-owned cooperative firms and associations. Mutualists advocate mutual banks. owned by the workers. that do not charge interest on secured loans.

Most mutualists believe that anarchy should be achieved gradually rather than through revolution. Some individualist anarchists. such as Benjamin Tucker. were influenced by Proudhon's Mutualism. but unlike Proudhon. they did not call for "association" in large enterprises.

Mutualist ideas found a fertile ground in the XIX century in Spain. In Spain Ramón de la Sagra established anarchist journal *El Porvenir* in La Coruña in 1845 which was inspired by Proudhon´s ideas. The catalan politician Francesc Pi i Margall became the principal translator of Proudhon's works into Spanish and later briefly became president of Spain in 1873 while being the leader of the Democratic Republican Federal Party.

According to George Woodcock "These translations were to have a profound and lasting effect on the development of Spanish anarchism after 1870. but before that time Proudhonian ideas. as interpreted by Pi. already provided much of the inspiration for the federalist movement which sprang up in the early 1860's." According to the *Encyclopaedia Britannica* "During the Spanish revolution of 1873. Pi y Margall attempted to establish a decentralized. or "cantonalist". political system on Proudhonian lines." Kevin Carson is a contemporary mutualist theorist who is the author of *Studies in Mutualist Political Economy*.

Collectivist anarchism

Collectivist anarchism (also known as anarcho-collectivism) is a revolutionary doctrine that advocates the abolition of the state and private ownership of the means of production. Instead. it envisions the means of production being owned collectively and controlled and managed by the producers themselves. For the collectivization of the means of production. it was originally envisaged that workers will revolt and forcibly collectivize the means of production Once collectivization takes place. workers' salaries would be determined in democratic organizations based on the amount of time they contributed to production.

These salaries would be used to purchase goods in a communal market. This contrasts with anarcho-communism where wages would be abolished. and where individuals would take freely from a storehouse of goods "to each according to his need." Thus. Bakunin's "Collectivist Anarchism". notwithstanding the title. is seen as a blend of individualism andcollectivism. Collectivist anarchism is most commonly associated with Mikhail Bakunin. the anti-authoritarian sections of the First International. and the early Spanish anarchist movement.

Anarchist communism

Anarchist communism (also known as anarcho-communism and occasionally as free communism) is a theory ofanarchism which advocates the abolition of the state. markets. money. capitalism and private property (while retaining respect for personal property). in favour of common ownership of the means of production. direct democracy and a horizontal network of voluntary associations and workers' councils with production and consumption based on the guiding principle: "from each according to his ability. to each according to his need".

Anarcho-communism developed out of radical socialist currents after the French revolution but was first formulated as such in the Italian section of the First International. The theoretical work of Peter Kropotkin took importance later as it expanded and developed pro-organizationalist and insurrectionary anti-organizationalist sections. Some forms of anarchist communism. such as insurrectionary anarchism. are strongly influenced by egoism and radical individualism. believing anarcho-communism is the best social system for the realization of individual freedom. Most anarcho-communists view anarcho-communism as a way of reconciling the opposition between the individual and society. To date. the best known examples of an anarchist communist society (*i.e.*. established around the ideas as they exist today and achieving worldwide attention and knowledge in the historical canon). are the anarchist territories during the Spanish Revolution and the Free Territoryduring the Russian Revolution. Through the efforts and influence of the Spanish Anarchists during the Spanish Revolution within the Spanish Civil War. starting in 1936 anarchist communism existed in most of Aragon. parts of the Levante and Andalusia. and in the stronghold of Anarchist Catalonia before being crushed by the combined forces of Francoism. Adolf Hitler. Benito Mussolini. Spanish Communist Party repression (backed by the USSR) as well as economic and armaments blockades from the capitalist countries and the Spanish Republic itself.During the Russian Revolution. anarchists such as Nestor Makhno worked to create and defend—through the Revolutionary Insurrectionary Army of Ukraine—anarchist communism in the Free Territory of the Ukraine from 1919 before being conquered by the Bolsheviks in 1921. Anarcho-communist currents include platformism and insurrectionary anarchism.

Within individualist anarchism

Individualist anarchism refers to several traditions of thought within the anarchist movement that emphasize the individual and his or her willover external determinants such as groups. society. traditions. and ideological systems. Josiah Warren is widely regarded as the first American anarchist. and the four-page weekly paper he edited during 1833. *The Peaceful Revolutionist*. was the first anarchist periodical published. For American anarchist historian Eunice Minette Schuster "It is apparent...thatProudhonian Anarchism was to be found in the United States at least as early as 1848 and that it was not conscious of its affinity to the Individualist Anarchism of Josiah Warren and Stephen Pearl Andrews...William B. Greene presented this Proudhonian Mutualism in its purest and most systematic form.".

Later the american individualist anarchist Benjamin Tucker "was against both the state and capitalism. against both oppression and exploitation. While not against the market and property he was firmly against capitalism as it was. in his eyes. a state-supported monopoly of social capital (tools. machinery. etc.) which allows owners to exploit their employees. *i.e.*. to avoid paying workers the full value of their labour. He thought that the "labouring classes are deprived of their earnings by usury in its three forms. interest. rent and profit."... Therefore "*Liberty* will abolish interest; it will abolish profit; it will abolish monopolistic rent; it will abolish taxation; it will abolish the exploitation of labour; it will abolish all means whereby any labourer can be deprived of any of his product."...This stance puts him squarely in the libertarian socialist tradition and. unsurprisingly. Tucker referred to himself many times as a socialist and considered his philosophy to be "Anarchistic socialism."

French individualist anarchist Emile Armand shows clearly opposition to capitalism and centralized economies when he said that the individualist anarchist "inwardly he remains refractory – fatally refractory – morally. intellectually. economically (The capitalist economy and the directed economy. the speculators and the fabricators of single are equally repugnant to him.)" The spanish individualist anarchist Miguel Gimenez Igualada thought that ""capitalism is an effect of government; the disappearance of government means capitalism falls from its pedestal vertiginously...That which we call capitalism is not something else but a product of the State. within which the only thing that is being pushed forward is profit. good or badly acquired. And so to fight against capitalism is a pointless task. since be it State capitalism or Enterprise capitalism. as long as Government exists. exploiting capital will exist.

The fight. but of consciousness. is against the State." His view on class division and technocracy are as follows "Since when no one works for another. the profiteer from wealth disappears. just as government will disappear when no one pays attention to those who learned four things at universities and from that fact they pretend to govern men. Big industrial enterprises will be transformed by men in big associations in which everyone will work and enjoy the product of their work. And from those easy as well as beautiful problems anarchism deals with and he who puts them in practice and lives them are anarchists.... The priority which without rest an anarchist must make is that in which no one has to exploit anyone. no man to no man. since that non-exploitation will lead to the limitation of property to individual needs".

The anarchist writer and bohemian Oscar Wilde wrote in his famous essay *The Soul of Man under Socialism* that "Art is individualism. and individualism is a disturbing and disintegrating force. There lies its immense value. For what it seeks is to disturb monotony of type. slavery of custom. tyranny of habit. and the reduction of man to the level of a machine." For anarchist historian George Woodcock "Wilde's aim in *The Soul of Man under Socialism* is to seek the society most favorable to the artist... for Wilde art is the supreme end. containing within itself enlightenment and regeneration. to which all else in society must be subordinated.... Wilde represents the anarchist as aesthete." In a socialist society. people will have the possibility to realise their talents; "each member of the society will share in the general prosperity and happiness of the society." Wilde added that "upon the other hand. Socialism itself will be of value simply because it will lead to individualism" since individuals will no longer need to fear poverty or starvation. This individualism would. in turn. protect against governments "armed with economic power as they are now with political power" over their citizens. However. Wilde advocated non-capitalist individualism: "of course. it might be said that the Individualism generated under conditions of private property is not always. or even as a rule. of a fine or wonderful type" a critique which is "quite true." In this way socialism. in Wilde's imagination. would free men from manual labour and allow them to devote their time to creative pursuits. thus developing their soul. He ended by declaring "The new individualism is the new hellenism".

Anarcho-syndicalism

Anarcho-syndicalism is a branch of anarchism that focuses on the labour movement. Anarcho-syndicalists view labour unions as a potential force for revolutionary social change. replacing capitalism and the state with a new society democratically self-managed by workers.

The basic principles of anarcho-syndicalism are Workers' solidarity. Direct action and Workers' self-management. Workers' solidarity means that anarcho-syndicalists believe all workers—no matter their race. gender. or ethnic group—are in a similar situation in regard to their boss (class consciousness). Furthermore. it means that. within capitalism. any gains or losses made by some workers from or to bosses will eventually affect all workers. Therefore. to liberate themselves. all workers must support one another in their class conflict. Anarcho-syndicalists believe that only direct action—that is. action concentrated on directly attaining a goal. as opposed to indirect action. such as electing a representative to a government position—will allow workers to liberate themselves. Moreover. anarcho-syndicalists believe that workers' organizations (the organizations that struggle against the wage system. which.

in anarcho-syndicalist theory. will eventually form the basis of a new society) should be self-managing. They should not have bosses or "business agents"; rather. the workers should be able to make all the decisions that affect them themselves.

Rudolf Rocker was one of the most popular voices in the anarcho-syndicalist movement. He outlined a view of the origins of the movement. what it sought. and why it was important to the future of labour in his 1938 pamphlet *Anarcho-Syndicalism*. The International Workers Association is an international anarcho-syndicalist federation of various labour unions from different countries. The Spanish Confederación Nacional del Trabajo played and still plays a major role in the Spanishlabor movement. It was also an important force in the Spanish Civil War.

LIBERTARIAN MARXIST TENDENCIES

Libertarian Marxism refers to a broad scope of economic and political philosophies that emphasize the anti-authoritarian aspects of Marxism. Early currents of libertarian Marxism. known as left communism. emerged in opposition to Marxism–Leninism and its derivatives. such as Stalinism. Maoism. and Trotskyism. Libertarian Marxism is also critical of reformist positions. such as those held by social democrats. Libertarian Marxist currents often draw from Marx and Engels' later works. specifically the *Grundrisse* and *The Civil War in France*; emphasizing the Marxist belief in the ability of the working class to forge its own destiny without the need for a revolutionary party or state to mediate or aid its liberation. Along with anarchism. Libertarian Marxism is one of the main currents of libertarian socialism.

Libertarian Marxism includes such currents as Luxemburgism. council communism. left communism. *Socialisme ou Barbarie*. the Johnson–Forest tendency. world socialism.Lettrism/Situationism and operaismo/autonomism. and New Left. Libertarian Marxism has often had a strong influence on both post-left and social anarchists. Notable theorists of libertarian Marxism have included Anton Pannekoek. Raya Dunayevskaya. CLR James. Antonio Negri. Cornelius Castoriadis. Maurice Brinton. Guy Debord. Daniel Guérin. Ernesto Screpanti and Raoul Vaneigem.

De Leonism

De Leonism. occasionally known as Marxism-Deleonism. is a form of syndicalist Marxism developed by Daniel De Leon. De Leon was an early leader of the first United States socialist political party. the Socialist Labour Party of America. De Leon combined the rising theories of syndicalism in his time with orthodox Marxism. According to De Leonist theory. militant industrial unions (specialized trade unions) are the vehicle of class struggle. Industrial Unions serving the interests of the proletariat will bring about the change needed to establish a socialist system. The only way this differs from some currents in anarcho-syndicalism is that. according to De Leonist thinking. a revolutionary political party is also necessary to fight for the proletariat on the political field. De Leonism lies outside the Leninist tradition of communism. It predates Leninism as De Leonism's principles developed in the early 1890s with De Leon's assuming leadership of the Socialist Labour Party; Leninism and its vanguard party idea took shape after the 1902 publication of Lenin's "What Is to Be Done?". The highly decentralized and democratic nature of the proposed De Leonist government is in contrast to the democratic centralismof Marxism–Leninism and what they see as the dictatorial nature of the Soviet Union and the People's Republic of China and other "communist" states. The success of the De Leonist plan depends on achieving majority support among the people both in the workplaces and at the polls. in contrast to the Leninist notion that a small vanguard party should lead the working class to carry out the revolution.

Council communism

Council communism was a radical Left movement originating in Germany and the Netherlands in the 1920s. Its primary organization was theCommunist Workers Party of Germany (KAPD). Council communism continues today as a theoretical and activist position within Marxism. and also within libertarian socialism. The central argument of council communism. in contrast to those of Social democracy and Leninist communism. is thatworkers' councils arising in the factories and municipalities are the natural and legitimate form of working class organisation and government power. This view is opposed to the reformist and Bolshevik stress on vanguard parties. parliaments. or the state. The core principle of council communism is that the state and the economy should be managed by workers' councils. composed of delegates elected at workplaces and recallable at any moment. As such. council communists oppose state-run "bureaucratic socialism". They also oppose the idea of a "revolutionary party". since council communists believe that a revolution led by a party will necessarily produce a party dictatorship. Council communists support a workers' democracy. which they want to produce through a federation of workers' councils.

The Russian word for council is "soviet". and during the early years of the revolution worker's councils were politically significant in Russia. It was to take advantage of the aura of workplace power that the word became used by Vladimir Lenin for various political organs. Indeed. the name "Supreme Soviet". by which the parliament was called; and that of the Soviet Union itself make use of this terminology. but they do not imply anydecentralization. Furthermore. council communists held a critique of the Soviet Union as a capitalist state. believing that the Bolshevik revolution in Russia became a "bourgeois revolution" when a party bureaucracy replaced the old feudal aristocracy.

Although most felt the Russian Revolutionwas working class in character. they believed that. since capitalist relations still existed (because the workers had no say in running the economy). the Soviet Union ended up as a state capitalist country. with the state replacing the individual capitalist. Thus. council communists support workers' revolutions. but oppose one-party dictatorships. Council communists also believed in diminishing the role of the party to one of agitation and propaganda. rejected all participation in elections or parliament. and argued that workers should leave the reactionary trade unions and form one big revolutionary union.

Left communism

"Left communism" is the range of communist viewpoints held by the communist left. which criticizes the political ideas of the Bolsheviks at certain periods. from a position that is asserted to be more authentically Marxist and proletarian than the views of Leninism held by theCommunist International after its first and during its second congress. Left Communists see themselves to the left of Leninists (whom they tend to see as 'left of capital'. not socialists). Anarchists (some of whom they consider internationalist socialists) as well as some other revolutionary socialist tendencies (for example De Leonists. who they tend to see as being internationalist socialists only in limited instances). Although she lived before left communism became a distinct tendency. Rosa Luxemburg has heavily influenced most left communists. both politically and theoretically. Proponents of left communism have included Amadeo Bordiga. Herman Gorter. Anton Pannekoek. Otto Rühle. Karl Korsch. Sylvia Pankhurst and Paul Mattick.

Prominent left communist groups existing today include the International Communist Current and the International Bureau for the Revolutionary Party. Also. different factions from the old Bordigist International Communist Party are considered left communist organizations.

Johnson–Forest tendency

The Johnson–Forest tendency. sometimes called the Johnsonites. refers to a radical left tendency in the United States associated with Marxist theorists C.L.R. James and Raya Dunayevskaya. who used the pseudonyms J.R. Johnson and Freddie Forest respectively. They were joined by Grace Lee Boggs. a Chinese-American woman who was considered the third founder. After leaving the trotskist Socialist Workers Party. Johnson–Forest founded their own organization for the first time. called Correspondence. This group changed its named to the Correspondence Publishing Committee the next year. However. tensions that had surfaced earlier presaged a split. which took place in 1955. Through his theoretical and political work of the late 1940s. James had concluded that a vanguard party was no longer necessary. because its teachings had been absorbed in the masses. In 1956. James would see the Hungarian Revolution of 1956 as confirmation of this. Those who endorsed the politics of James took the name Facing Reality. after the 1958 book by James co-written with Grace Lee Boggs and Pierre Chaulieu. a pseudonym for Cornelius Castoriadis. on the Hungarian working class revolt of 1956.

Socialisme ou Barbarie

Socialisme ou Barbarie (Socialism or Barbarism) was a French-based radical libertarian socialist group of the post-World War II period (the name comes from a phrase Friedrich Engels used. and was cited by Rosa Luxemburg in a 1916 essay. 'The Junius Pamphlet'). It existed from 1948 until 1965. The animating personality was Cornelius Castoriadis. also known as Pierre Chaulieu or Paul Cardan. Because he explicitly both rejected Leninist vanguardism and criticised spontaneism...(for) Cornelius Castoriadis the emancipation of the mass of people was the task of those people; however. the socialist thinker could not simply fold his or her arms. Castoriadis argued that the special place accorded to the intellectual should belong to each autonomous citizen.

However. he rejected *attentisme*. maintaining that. in the struggle for a new society. intellectuals needed to "place themselves at a distance from the everyday and from the real"." Political philosopher Claude Lefort was impressed by Cornelius Castoriadis when he first met him. They published *On the Regime and Against the Defence of the USSR*. a critique of both the Soviet Union and its Trotskyist supporters. They suggested that the USSR was dominated by a social layer of bureaucrats. and that it consisted of a new kind of society as aggressive as Western European societies. Later he also published in *Socialisme ou Barbarie*.

Situationist International

The Situationist International was a restricted group of international revolutionaries founded in 1957. and which had its peak in its influence on the unprecedented general wildcat strikes of May 1968 in France.

With their ideas rooted in Marxism and the 20th-century European artistic avant-gardes. they advocated experiences of life being alternative to those admitted by the capitalist order. for the fulfillment of human primitive desires and the pursuing of a superior passional quality. For this purpose they suggested and experimented with the *construction of situations*. namely the setting up of environments favorable for the fulfillment of such desires. Using methods drawn from the arts. they developed a series of experimental fields of study for the construction of such situations. like unitary urbanism and psychogeography. In this vein a major theorectical work which emerged from this group was Raoul Vaneigem´s *The Revolution of Everyday Life*. They fought against the main obstacle on the fulfillment of such superior passional living. identified by them in advanced capitalism. Their critical theoretical work peaked on the highly influential book *The Society of the Spectacle* by Guy Debord. Debord argued in 1967 that spectacular features like mass media and advertising have a central role in an advanced capitalist society. which is to show a fake reality in order to mask the real capitalist degradation of human life. To overthrow such a system. the Situationist International supported the May '68 revolts. and asked the workers to occupy the factories and to run them with direct democracy. through workers' councils composed by instantly revocable delegates.

After publishing in the last issue of the magazine an analysis of the May 1968 revolts. and the strategies that will need to be adopted in future revolutions. the SI was dissolved in 1972.

Autonomism

Autonomism refers to a set of left-wing political and social movements and theories close to the socialist movement. As an identifiable theoretical system it first emerged in Italy in the 1960s from workerist (*operaismo*) communism. Through translations made available by Danilo Montaldi and others. the Italian autonomists drew upon previous activist research in the United States by the Johnson–Forest Tendency and in France by the group Socialisme ou Barbarie. Later. post-Marxist and anarchist tendencies became significant after influence from the Situationists. the failure of Italian far-left movements in the 1970s. and the emergence of a number of important theorists including Antonio Negri. who had contributed to the 1969 founding of *Potere Operaio* as well as Mario Tronti. Paolo Virno. Franco Berardi"Bifo" etc.

Unlike other forms of Marxism. autonomist Marxism emphasises the ability of the working class to force changes to the organization of the capitalist system independent of the state. trade unions or political parties. Autonomists are less concerned with party political organization than other Marxists. focusing instead on self-organized action outside of traditional organizational structures. Autonomist Marxism is thus a "bottom up" theory: it draws attention to activities that autonomists see as everyday working class resistance to capitalism. for example absenteeism. slow working. and socialization in the workplace.

All this influenced the German and Dutch Autonomen. the worldwide Social Centre movement. and today is influential in Italy. France. and to a lesser extent the English-speaking countries. Those who describe themselves as autonomists now vary from Marxists to post-structuralists and anarchists.

The Autonomist Marxist and *Autonomen* movements provided inspiration to some on the revolutionary left in English speaking countries. particularly among anarchists. many of whom have adopted autonomist tactics. Some English-speaking anarchists even describe themselves as *Autonomists*. The Italian *operaismo* movement also influenced Marxist academics such as Harry

Cleaver. John Holloway. Steve Wright. and Nick Dyer-Witheford. Today it is associated also with the publication *Multitudes*.

OTHER TENDENCIES

The post-classical anarchist tendencies as well as tendencies which cannot be easily classified within the anarchist/marxist division presented before.

Within the labour movement and parliamentary politics

Pierre-Joseph Proudhon ran for the french constituent assembly in April 1848. but was not elected. although his name appeared on the ballots in Paris. Lyon. Besançon. and Lille. France. He was successful. in the complementary elections of June 4. The catalan politicianFrancesc Pi i Margall became the principal translator of Proudhon's works into Spanish and later briefly became president of Spain in 1873 while being the leader of the Democratic Republican Federal Party. For prominent anarcho-syndicalist Rudolf Rocker: "The first movement of the Spanish workers was strongly influenced by the ideas of Pi y Margall. leader of the Spanish Federalists and disciple of Proudhon. Pi y Margall was one of the outstanding theorists of his time and had a powerful influence on the development of libertarian ideas in Spain. His political ideas had much in common with those of Richard Price. Joseph Priestly. Thomas Paine. Jefferson. and other representatives of the Anglo-American liberalism of the first period. He wanted to limit the power of the state to a minimum and gradually replace it by a Socialist economic order." Pi i Margall was a dedicated theorist in his own right. especially through book-length works such as *La reacción y la revolución* (en:"Reaction and revolution" from 1855). *Las nacionalidades* (en:"Nationalities" from 1877). and *La Federación* from 1880.

There was a strong left-libertarian current in the British labour movement and the term *libertarian socialist* has been applied to a number ofdemocratic socialists. including some prominent members of the British Labour Party. The Socialist League was formed in 1885 by William Morris and others critical of the authoritarian socialism of the Social Democratic Federation. It was involved in the New Unionism. the rank and file union militancy of the 1880s–90s. which anticipated syndicalism in some key ways (Tom Mann. a New Unionist leader. was one of the first British syndicalists). The Socialist League was dominated by anarchists by the 1890s.

The Independent Labour Party. formed at that time. drew more on the Non-Conformist religious traditions in the British working class than on Marxist theory. and had a libertarian socialist strain. Others in the tradition of the ILP. and described as libertarian socialists Michael Foot and most importantly. G. D. H. Cole.Labour Party minister Peter Hain has written in support of libertarian socialism. identifying an axis involving a "bottom-up vision of socialism. with anarchists at the revolutionaryend and democratic socialists [such as himself] at its reformist end". as opposed to the axis of state socialism with Marxist-Leninists at the revolutionary end and social democrats at the reformist end. Another recent mainstream Labour politician who has been described as a libertarian socialist is Robin Cook. In 1974 the journal*Libertarian Communism* was started in the United Kingdom by a group inside the Socialist Party of Great Britain.

Defined in this way. libertarian socialism in the contemporary political mainstream is distinguished from modern social democracy and democratic socialism principally by its political decentralism rather than by its economics. The multi-tendency Socialist Party USA also has a strong libertarian socialist current.

Katja Kipping and Julia Bonk in Germany. Femke Halsema in the Netherlands and Ufuk Uras and the Freedom and Solidarity Party in Turkey. are examples of a contemporary libertarian socialist politicians and parties operating within a mainstream government. In Chile the autonomist organization *Izquierda Autonoma* (Autonomous Left) in the Chilean general election. 2013 gained a seat in the Chilean Parliament through Gabriel Boric. ex leader of the 2011–13 Chilean student protests.

Georgism

Georgism (also called Geoism or Geonomics) is an economic philosophy and ideology which holds that people own what they create. but that things found in nature. most importantly land. belong equally to all. The Georgist philosophy is based on the writings of the economist Henry George (1839–1897). and is usually associated with the idea of a single tax on the value of land. His most famous work. *Progress and Poverty* (1879). is a treatise on inequality. the cyclic nature of industrialized economies. and the use of the land value tax as a remedy. Georgists argue that a tax on land value is economically efficient. fair. and equitable; and that it can generate sufficient revenue so that other taxes (*e.g.* taxes on profits. sales or income). which are less fair and efficient. can be reduced or eliminated. A tax on land value has been described by many as a progressive tax. since it would be paid primarily by the wealthy. and would reduce economic inequality.

Georgist ideas heavily influenced the politics of the early 20th century. Political parties that were formed based on Georgist ideas include the Commonwealth Land Party. theJustice Party of Denmark. the Henry George Justice Party. and the Single Tax League. Several communities were also initiated with Georgist principles during the height of the philosophy's popularity. Two such communities that still exist are Arden. Delaware. which was founded in 1900 by Frank Stephens and Will Price. and Fairhope. Alabama. which was founded in 1894 by the auspices of the Fairhope Single Tax Corporation. Christian anarchist Leo Tolstoy was enthused by the economic thinking of Henry George. incorporating it approvingly into later works such as Resurrection. the book that played a major factor in his excommunication.

Guild socialism

Guild socialism is a political movement advocating workers' control of industry through the medium of trade-related guilds "in an implied contractual relationship with the public". It originated in the United Kingdom and was at its most influential in the first quarter of the 20th century. It was strongly associated with G. D. H. Cole and influenced by the ideas of William Morris.

Guild socialism was partly inspired by the guilds of craftsmen and other skilled workers which had existed in England during the Middle Ages. In 1906. Arthur Penty published *Restoration of the Gild System* in which he opposed factory production and advocated a return to an earlier period of artisanal production organised through guilds. The following year. the journal *The New Age* became an advocate of guild socialism. although in the context of modern industry rather than the medieval setting favoured by Penty. The Guild Socialists "stood for state ownership of industry. combined with "workers' control" through delegation of authority to national guilds organised internally on democratic lines.

About the state itself they differed. some believing it would remain more or less in its existing form and others that it would be transformed into a federal body representing the workers' guilds. consumers' organizations. local government bodies. and other social structures." In 1914. S. G. Hobson. a leading contributor to *The New Age*. published *National Guilds: An Inquiry into the Wage System and the Way Out*. In this work. guilds were presented as an alternative to state-control of industry or conventional trade union activity. Guilds. unlike the existing trade unions. would not confine their demands to matters of wages and conditions but would seek to obtain control of industry for the workers whom they represented. Ultimately. industrial guilds would serve as the organs through which industry would be organised in a future socialist society. The theory of guild socialism was developed and popularised by G. D. H. Cole who formed the National Guilds League in 1915 and published several books on guild socialism. including *Self-Government in Industry* (1917) and *Guild Socialism Restated* (1920).

Revolutionary syndicalism

Revolutionary syndicalism is a type of economic system proposed as a replacement for capitalism and an alternative to state socialism. which uses federations of collectivised trade unions or industrial unions. It is a form of socialisteconomic corporatism that advocates interest aggregation of multiple non-competitive categorised units to negotiate and manage an economy. For adherents. labour unions are the potential means of both overcoming economic aristocracy and runningsociety fairly in the interest of the majority. through union democracy. Industry in a syndicalist system would be run through co-operative confederations and mutual aid. Local syndicates would communicate with other syndicates through the Bourse du Travail(labour exchange) which would manage and transfer commodities.

Syndicalism is also used to refer to the tactic of bringing about this social arrangement. typically expounded by anarcho-syndicalism and De Leonism. in which a general strike begins and workers seize their means of production and organise in a federation of trade unionism. such as the CNT. Throughout its history. the reformist section of syndicalism has been overshadowed by its revolutionary section. typified by the Confédération Générale du Travail (CGT) in France. IWW. the Federación Anarquista Ibérica section of the CNT.. the Unione Sindacale Italiana and theCentral Organisation of the Workers of Sweden (SAC).

Christian anarchism

Christian anarchism is a movement in political theology that combines anarchism andChristianity. It is the belief that there is only one source of authority to which Christians are ultimately answerable. the authority of God as embodied in the teachings of Jesus. More than any other Bible source. the Sermon on the Mount and Jesus' call to not resist evil but turn the other cheek. are used as the basis for Christian anarchism.

Christian anarchists are pacifists and oppose the use of violence. such as war. The foundation of Christian anarchism is a rejection of violence. with Leo Tolstoy's *The Kingdom of God Is Within You* regarded as a key text. Christian anarchists denounce the state as they claim it is violent. deceitful and. when glorified. a form ofidolatry.

The Tolstoyans were a small Christian anarchist group formed by Tolstoy's companion. Vladimir Chertkov (1854–1936). to spread Tolstoy's religious teachings. Prince Peter Kropotkin wrote of Tolstoy in the article on anarchism in the 1911 Encyclopædia Britannica while in hundreds of essays over the last twenty years of his life. Tolstoy reiterated the anarchist critique of the state and recommended books by Kropotkin andProudhon to his readers. whilst rejecting anarchism's espousal of violent revolutionary means. Dorothy Day was an American journalist. social activist. devout Catholic convert; she advocated the Catholic economic theory of distributism.

Day "believed all states were inherently totalitarian." and was a self-labeled anarchist. In the 1930s. Day worked closely with fellow activist Peter Maurin to establish the Catholic Worker movement. a Non-violent. pacifist movement that continues to combine direct aid for the poor and homeless with Non-violent direct action on their behalf. The importance of Day within catholicism goes to the extent that the cause for Day's canonization is open in the Catholic Church.

and she is thus formally referred to as a Servant of God. Ammon Hennacy was an Irish American pacifist. Christian. anarchist. social activist. member of the Catholic Worker Movement and a Wobbly. He established the "Joe Hill House of Hospitality" in Salt Lake City. Utah.

Gandhism

Gandhism is the collection of inspirations. principles. beliefs and philosophy of Mahatma Gandhi (Mohandas Karamchand Gandhi). who was a major political and spiritual leader of India and the Indian Independence Movement. It is a body of ideas and principles that describes the inspiration. vision and the life work of Gandhi. It is particularly associated with his contributions to the idea and practice of Non-violent resistance. sometimes also called civil resistance. Gandhian economics are the socio-economic principles expounded by Mohandas Gandhi. It is largely characterised by its affinity to the principles and objectives of Non-violent humanistic socialism. but with a rejection of violent class war and promotion of socio-economic harmony.

Gandhi's economic ideas also aim to promote spiritual development and harmony with a rejection of materialism. The term "Gandhian economics" was coined by J. C. Kumarappa. a close supporter of Gandhi. Gandhian economics places importance to means of achieving the aim of development and this means must be non-violent. ethical and truthful in all economic spheres. In order to achieve this means he advocated trusteeship. decentralization of economic activities. labour intensive technology and priority to weaker sections. Gandhi also had letter communication with Christian anarchist Leo Tolstoy and saw himself as his disciple.

Gandhi challenged future Indian Prime Minister Jawaharlal Nehru and the modernizers in the late 1930s who called for rapid industrialization on the Soviet model; Gandhi denounced that as dehumanizing and contrary to the needs of the villages where the great majority of the people lived. After Gandhi's death Nehru led India to large-scale planning that emphasized modernization and heavy industry. while modernizing agriculture through irrigation. Historian Kuruvilla Pandikattu says "it was Nehru's vision. not Gandhi's. that was eventually preferred by the Indian State." Gandhi was a self-described philosophical anarchist. and his vision of India meant an India without an underlying government.He once said that "the ideally Non-violent state would be an ordered anarchy."

While political systems are largely hierarchical. with each layer of authority from the individual to the central government have increasing levels of authority over the layer below. Gandhi believed that society should be the exact opposite. where nothing is done without the consent of anyone. down to the individual. His idea was that true self-rule in a country means that every person rules his or herself and that there is no state which enforces laws upon the people.

Gandhian activists such as Vinoba Bhave and Jayaprakash Narayan were involved in the *Sarvodaya* movement. which sought to promote self-sufficiency amidst India's rural population by encouraging land redistribution. socio-economic reforms and promoting cottage industries. The movement sought to combat the problems of class conflict. unemployment and poverty while attempting to preserve the lifestyle and values of rural Indians. which were eroding with industrialisation and modernisation.

Sarvodaya also included *Bhoodan*. or the gifting of land and agricultural resources by the landlords (called *zamindars*) to their tenant farmers in a bid to end the medieval system of *zamindari*. *The Conquest of Violence: an Essay on War and Revolution* is a book written by dutch anarcho-pacifist Bart de Ligt which deals with non-violent resistance in part inspired by the ideas of Gandhi. Anarchist historian George Woodcock reports that *The Conquest of Violence* "was read widely by British and American pacifists during the 1930s and led many of them to adopt an anarchistic point of view".

Platformism

Platformism is a tendency within the wider anarchist movement based on the organisational theories in the tradition of Dielo Truda's*Organizational Platform of the General Union of Anarchists (Draft)*. The document was based on the experiences of Russian anarchistsin the 1917 October Revolution. which led eventually to the victory of the Bolsheviks over the anarchists and other groups. The *Platform*attempted to address and explain the anarchist movement's failures during the Russian Revolution.

Today there are platformist groups in many countries including the Workers Solidarity Movement in Ireland. North Eastern Federation of Anarchist Communists (NEFAC. or*Fédération des Communistes Libertaires du Nord-Est*) in the northeastern US. the *Union Communiste Libertaire* in Quebec. Common Cause in Ontario. the *Organización Comunista Libertaria* (OCL) in Chile. the Federation of Anarchists of Greece (OAE) in Greece. *Anarchist Communist Initiative* (AKI) in Turkey. *Organizacion Socialista Libertaria* (OSL) in Argentina. the *Federazione dei Comunisti Anarchici* (FdCA) in Italy. the *Coletivo pró Organização Anarquista em Goiás* in Brazil. *Grupo Qhispikay Llaqta* in Peru. the Libertarian Communist Organization (France) in France. the *Alianza de los Comunistas Libertarios* (ACL) in Mexico. Melbourne Anarchist Communist Group (MACG) and Sydney Anarchist Communist Trajectory (SACT) in Australia. the Zabalaza Anarchist Communist Front (ZACF) in South Africa. and Revolutionary Confederation of Anarcho-syndicalists (RKAS) by the name of N.I.

Makhno an international anarcho-syndicalist. platformist confederation (sections and individual members of RKAS exist in Ukraine. Russia. Georgia. Germany. Latvia. Bulgaria and Israel). Platfomist organizations also founded the now defunct International Libertarian Solidarity. The Web site Anarkismo.net is run collaboratively by Platformist organisations from all over the world.

Within the New Left

The emergence of the New Left in the 1950s and 1960s led to a revival of interest in libertarian socialism. The New Left's critique of the Old Left's authoritarianism was associated with a strong interest in personal liberty. autonomy and led to a rediscovery of older socialist traditions. such as left communism. council communism. and the Industrial Workers of the World. In the United States this was caused by a renewal of anarchism from the 1950s forward through writers such asPaul Goodman and anarcho-pacifism which became influential in the Anti-nuclear movement and anti war movements of the time and which incorporated both the influences of gandhism and toltoyan Christian anarchism. In Australia the Sydney Push was a predominantly left-wing intellectual subculture in Sydney from the late 1940s to the early 1970s which became associated with the label "Sydney libertarianism". The New Left also led to a revival of anarchism in the 1960s in the United States. Journals like *Radical America* and *Black Mask* in America. *Solidarity*. *Big Flame* and *Democracy and Nature*. succeeded by *The International Journal of Inclusive Democracy*. in the UK. introduced a range of left-libertarian ideas to a new generation. Social ecology. autonomism and. more recently. participatory economics (parecon). and Inclusive Democracy emerged from this. The New Left in the United States also included anarchist. countercultural and hippie-related radical groups such as the Yippies who were led by Abbie Hoffman.

The Diggers. Up Against the Wall Motherfuckers and the White Panther Party. By late 1966. the Diggers opened free storeswhich simply gave away their stock. provided free food. distributed free drugs. gave away money. organised free music concerts. and performed works of political art. The Diggers took their name from the original English Diggers led by Gerrard Winstanley and sought to create a mini-society free of money and capitalism. On the other hand the Yippies employed theatrical gestures. such as advancing a pig ("Pigasus the Immortal") as a candidate for President in 1968. to mock the social status quo. They have been described as a highly theatrical. anti-authoritarian and anarchist youth movement of "symbolic politics". Since they were well known for street theater and politically themed pranks. many of the "old school" political left either ignored or denounced them. According to ABC News. "The group was known for street theater pranks and was once referred to as the 'Groucho Marxists'."

Social ecology and Communalism

Social ecology is closely related to the work and ideas of Murray Bookchin and influenced by anarchist Peter Kropotkin. Social ecologists assert that the present ecological crisis has its roots in human social problems. and that the domination of human-over-nature stems from the domination of human-over-human.

Bookchin later developed a political philosophy to complement social ecology which he called Communalism (spelled with a capital *C* to differentiate it from other forms of communalism). While originally conceived as a form of social anarchism. he later developed Communalism into a separate ideology which incorporates what he saw as the most beneficial elements of anarchism. Marxism. syndicalism. and radical ecology.

Politically. Communalists advocate a network of directly democratic citizens' assemblies in individual communities or cities organised in a confederated fashion. The method used to achieve this is called libertarian municipalism and involves the establishment of face-to-face democratic institutions which grow and expand confederally with the goal of eventually replacing the nation-state. Unlike anarchists. Communalists are not opposed to taking part in parliamentary politics—especially municipal elections—as long as candidates are libertarian socialist and anti-statist in outlook.

Participism

Participism is a twenty-first century form of libertarian socialism. It comprises two related economic and political systems called Participatory economics or "Parecon" and Participatory politics or "Parpolity".

Parecon is an economic system proposed primarily by activist and political theorist Michael Albert and radical economist Robin Hahnel. among others. It uses participatory decision making as an economic mechanism to guide the production. consumption and allocation of resources in a given society. Proposed as an alternative to contemporary capitalist market economies and also an alternative to centrally planned socialism or coordinatorism. it is described as "an anarchistic economic vision". and it could be considered a form of socialism as under Parecon. the means of production are owned by the workers. It proposes to attain these ends mainly through the following principles and institutions: Workers' and consumers' councils utilizing self-managerial methods for decision making. balanced job complexes. remuneration according to effort and sacrifice. and Participatory Planning. Under Parecon. the current monetary system would be replaced with a system of non-transferable "credit" which would cease to exist upon purchase of a commodity.

Parpolity is a theoretical political system proposed by Stephen R. Shalom. It was developed as a political vision to accompany Parecon. Participism as a whole is critical of aspects of modern representative democracies and capitalism arguing that the level of political control by the people isn't sufficient. To address this problem Parpolity suggests a system of "Nested Councils". which would include every adult member of a given society. Under Participism. the state as such would dissolve into a mere coordinating body made up of delegates which would be recallable at any time by the nested council below them.

Inclusive Democracy

Inclusive Democracy is a political theory and political project that aim for direct democracy. economic democracy in a stateless. moneyless and marketless economy. self-management (democracy in the social realm) and ecological democracy. The theoretical project of Inclusive Democracy (ID)). as distinguished from the political project which is part of the democratic and autonomy traditions. emerged from the work of political philosopher. former academic and activist Takis Fotopoulos in *Towards An Inclusive Democracy* and was further developed by him and other writers in the journal *Democracy and Nature* and its successor *The International Journal of Inclusive Democracy*. anelectronic journal freely available and published by the International Network for Inclusive Democracy.

According to Arran Gare. *Towards an Inclusive Democracy* "offers a powerful new interpretation of the history and destructive dynamics of the market and provides an inspiring new vision of the future in place of both neo-liberalism and existing forms of socialism". Also. as David Freeman points out. although Fotopoulos' approach "is not openly anarchism. yet anarchism seems the formal category within which he works. given his commitment to direct democracy. municipalism and abolition of state. money and market economy".

An artificial market is proposed by this tendency as a solution to the problem of maintaining freedom of choice for the consumer within a marketless and moneyless economy. an artificial market operates in much the same way as traditional markets. but uses labour vouchers or personal credit in place of traditional money. According to Takis Fotopoulos. an artificial market "secures real freedom of choice. without incurring the adverse effects associated with real markets".

Insurrectionary anarchism

Insurrectionary anarchism is a revolutionary theory. practice and tendency within the anarchist movement which emphasizes the theme of insurrection within anarchist practice. It is critical of formal organizations such as labour unions and federations that are based on a political programme and periodic congresses. Instead. insurrectionary anarchists advocate informal organization and small affinity group–based organization. Insurrectionary anarchists put value in attack. permanent class conflict. and a refusal to negotiate or compromise with class enemies.

Contemporary insurrectionary anarchism inherits the views and tactics of anti-organizational anarcho-communism and illegalism. So. "between 1880 and

1890". with the "perspective of an immanent revolution". who was "opposed to the official workers' movement. which was then in the process of formation (general Social Democratisation). They were opposed not only to political (statist) struggles but also to strikes which put forward wage or other claims. or which were organised by trade unions." But "While they were not opposed to strikes as such. they were opposed to trade unions and the struggle for the eight-hour day. This anti-reformist tendency was accompanied by an anti-organisational tendency. and its partisans declared themselves in favour of agitation amongst the unemployed for the expropriation of foodstuffs and other articles. for the expropriatory strike and. in some cases. for 'individual recuperation' or acts of terrorism." A resurgence of such ideas happened "in the peculiar conditions of post war Italyand Greece."

Zapatismo and Magonism

The Zapatista Army of National Liberation (*Ejército Zapatista de Liberación Nacional*. EZLN) often referred to as the *Zapatistas* is a revolutionary leftist group based in Chiapas. the southernmost state of Mexico. Since 1994. the group has been in a declared war "against the Mexican state." though this war has been primarily Non-violent and defensive against military. paramilitary. and corporate incursions into Chiapas. Their social base is mostly rural indigenous people but they have some supporters in urban areas and internationally.

Their main spokesperson isSubcomandante Marcos (currently a.k.a. Delegate Zero in relation to "the Other Campaign"). Unlike other Zapatista spokespeople. Marcos is not an indigenous Maya. Since December 1994. the Zapatistas had been gradually forming several autonomous municipalities. called Rebel Zapatista Autonomous Municipalities (MAREZ). In these municipalities. an assembly of local representatives forms the *Juntas de Buen Gobierno*or Councils of Good Government (JBGs). These are not recognised by the federal or state governments; they oversee local community programmes on food. health and education. as well as taxation. The EZLN political formations have happened in two phases generally called*Aquascalientes* and *Caracoles*.

The group takes its name from Emiliano Zapata. the agrarian reformer and commander of the Liberation Army of the South during theMexican Revolution. and sees itself as his ideological heir. *Zapatista* originally referred to a member of the revolutionary guerrilla movement founded about 1910 by Zapata. His Liberation Army of the South (Ejército Libertador del Sur) fought during the Mexican Revolution for theredistribution of agricultural land. Zapata and his army and allies. including Pancho Villa. fought for agrarian reform in Mexico. Specifically. they wanted to establish communalland rights for Mexico's indigenous population. which had mostly lost its land to the wealthy elite of European descent. Zapata was partly influenced by an anarchist from Oaxacanamed Ricardo Flores Magón. The influence of Flores Magón on Zapata can be seen in the Zapatistas' Plan de Ayala. but even more noticeably in their slogan (this slogan was never used by Zapata) "*Tierra y libertad*" or "land and liberty". the title and maxim of Flores Magón's most famous work. Zapata's introduction to anarchism came via a local schoolteacher. Otilio Montaño Sánchez – later a general in Zapata's army. executed on May 17. 1917 – who exposed Zapata to the works of Peter Kropotkin and Flores Magón at the same time as Zapata was observing and beginning to participate in the struggles of the peasants for the land.

In reference to inspirational figures. in nearly all EZLN villages exist murals accompanying images of Zapata. Che Guevara. and Subcomandante Marcos. The ideology of the Zapatista movement. Zapatismo. synthesizes traditional Mayan practices with elements of libertarian socialism. anarchism. and Marxism. The historical influence of Mexican Anarchists and various Latin-American Socialists is apparent on Zapatismo; with the positions of Subcomandante Marcos also adding a distinct Marxist (according to the New York Times) element to the movement. A Zapatista slogan is in harmony with the concept of mutual aid: "For everyone. everything. For us. nothing" (*Para todos. todo. Para nosotros. nada*).

Left wing market anarchism

Left wing market anarchism. a form of left-libertarianism. individualist anarchism and libertarian socialism is associated with scholars such as Kevin Carson.Roderick T. Long. Charles Johnson. Brad Spangler. Samuel Edward Konkin III. Sheldon Richman. Chris Matthew Sciabarra. and Gary Chartier. who stress the value of radically free markets. termed *freed markets* to distinguish them from the common conception which these libertarians believe to be riddled with statist and capitalist privileges. Referred to as left-wing market anarchists or market-oriented left-libertarians. proponents of this approach strongly affirm the classical liberal ideas of self-ownership and free markets. while maintaining that. taken to their logical conclusions. these ideas support anti-capitalist. anti-corporatist. anti-hierarchical. pro-labour positions in economics; anti-imperialism in foreign policy; and thoroughly liberal or radical views regarding such cultural issues as gender. sexuality. and race.

The genealogy of contemporary market-oriented left-libertarianism—sometimes labeled "left-wing market anarchism"—overlaps to a significant degree with that of Steiner–Vallentyne left-libertarianism as the roots of that tradition are sketched in the book *The Origins of Left-Libertarianism*. Carson–Long-style left-libertarianism is rooted in 19th-century mutualism and in the work of figures such as Thomas Hodgskin and the individualist anarchists Benjamin Tucker and Lysander Spooner. While. with notable exceptions. market-oriented libertarians after Tucker tended to ally with the political right. relationships between such libertarians and the New Left thrived in the 1960s.

laying the groundwork for modern left-wing market anarchism. Left wing market anarchism identifies with Left-libertarianism (or left-wing libertarianism) which names several related but distinct approaches to politics. society. culture. and political and social theory. which stress both individual freedom and social justice. Unlike right-libertarians. they believe that neither claiming nor mixing one's labour with natural resources is enough to generate full private property rights. and maintain that natural resources (land. oil. gold. trees) ought to be held in some egalitarian manner. either unowned or owned collectively. Those left-libertarians who support private property do so under the condition that recompense is offered to the local community.

Communization

Communization mainly refers to a contemporary communist theory in which we find is a "mixing-up of insurrectionist anarchism. the communist ultra-left. post-autonomists. anti-political currents. groups like the Invisible Committee. as well as more explicitly 'communizing' currents. such as *Théorie Communiste* and *Endnotes*. Obviously at the heart of the word is communism and. as the shift to communization suggests. communism as a particular activity and process...."

The association of the term communization with a self-identified "ultra-left" was cemented in France in the 1970s. where it came to describe not a transition to a higher phase of communism but a vision of communist revolution itself. Thus the 1975 Pamphlet *A World Without Money* states: "insurrection and communisation are intimately linked. There would not be first a period of insurrection and then later. thanks to this insurrection. the transformation of social reality. The insurrectional process derives its force from communisation itself." The term is still used in this sense in France today and has spread into English usage as a result of the translation of texts by Gilles Dauvé and*Théorie Comuniste*. two key figures in this tendency. In collaboration with other left communists such as François Martin and Karl Nesic. Dauvé has attempted to fuse. critique. and develop different left communist currents. most notably the Italian movement associated with Amadeo Bordiga (and its heretical journal *Invariance*). German-Dutch council communism. and the French perspectives associated with *Socialisme ou Barbarie* and the Situationist International.

In the late 1990s a close but not identical sense of "communization" was developed by the French post-situationist group Tiqqun. In keeping with their ultra-left predecessors. Tiqqun's predilection for the term seems to be its emphasis on communism as an immediate process rather than a far-off goal. but for Tiqqun it is no longer synonymous with "the revolution" considered as an historical event. but rather becomes identifiable with all sorts of activities – from squatting and setting up communes to simply "sharing" – that would typically be understood as "pre-revolutionary". From an ultra-left perspective such a politics of "dropping-out" or. as Tiqqun put it. "desertion" — setting up spaces and practices that are held to partially autonomous from capitalism — is typically dismissed as either naive or reactionary. Due to the popularity of the Tiqqun-related works *Call*and *The Coming Insurrection* in US anarchist circles it tended to be this latter sense of "communization" that was employed in US anarchist and "insurrectionist" communiques. notably within the Californian student movement of 2009–2010.

CONTEMPORARY LIBERTARIAN SOCIALISM

A surge of popular interest in libertarian socialism occurred in western nations during the 1960s and 1970s. Anarchism was influential in the Counterculture of the 1960s and anarchists actively participated in the late sixties students and workers revolts. In 1968 in Carrara. Italy the International of Anarchist Federations was founded during an international anarchist conference held there in 1968 by the three existing European federations of France. the Italian and the Iberian Anarchist Federation as well as the Bulgarianfederation in French exile. The uprisings of May 1968 also led to a small resurgence of interest in left communist ideas. Various small left communist groups emerged around the world. predominantly in the leading capitalist countries. A series of conferences of the communist left began in 1976. with the aim of promoting international and cross-tendency discussion. but these petered out in the 1980s without having increased the profile of the movement or its unity of ideas. Prominent left communist groups existing today include theInternational Communist Party. International Communist Current and the Internationalist Communist Tendency.

The housing and employment crisis in most of Western Europe led to the formation of communes and squatter movements like that ofBarcelona. Spain. In Denmark. squatters occupied a disused military base and declared the Freetown Christiania. an autonomous haven in central Copenhagen.

Around the turn of the 21st century. libertarian socialism grew in popularity and influence as part of the anti-war. anti-capitalist. and anti-globalisation movements. Anarchists became known for their involvement in protests against the meetings of the World Trade Organization (WTO). Group of Eight. and theWorld Economic Forum. Some anarchist factions at these protests engaged in rioting. property destruction. and violent confrontations with police. These actions were precipitated by ad hoc. leaderless. anonymous cadres known as *black blocs*; other organisational tactics pioneered in this time include security culture. affinity groups and the use of decentralised technologies such as the internet. A significant event of this period was the confrontations at WTO conference in Seattle in 1999. For english anarchist scholar Simon Critchley "contemporary anarchism can be seen as a powerful critique of the pseudo-libertarianism of contemporary neo-liberalism...One might say that contemporary anarchism is about responsibility. whether sexual. ecological or socio-economic; it flows from an experience of conscience about the manifold ways in which the West ravages the rest; it is an ethical outrage at the yawning inequality. impoverishment and disenfranchisment that is so palpable locally and globally."

International anarchist federations in existence include the International of Anarchist Federations. the International Workers' Association. and International Libertarian Solidarity. The largest organised anarchist movement today is in Spain. in the form of the Confederación General del Trabajo (CGT) and the Confederación Nacional del Trabajo (CNT). CGT membership was estimated to be around 100.000 for 2003. Other active syndicalist movements include in Sweden the Central Organisation of the Workers of Swedenand the Swedish Anarcho-syndicalist Youth Federation; the CNT-AIT in France; the Union Sindicale Italiana in Italy; in the US Workers Solidarity Alliance and the UKSolidarity Federation. The revolutionary industrial unionist Industrial Workers of the World. claiming 2.000 paying members. and the International Workers Association. an anarcho-syndicalist successor to the First International. also remain active.

Libertarian socialists in the early 21st century have been involved in the alter-globalization movement. squatter movement; social centers; infoshops; anti-poverty groups such asOntario Coalition Against Poverty and Food Not Bombs; tenants' unions; housing cooperatives; intentional communities generally and egalitarian communities; anti-sexistorganizing; grassroots media initiatives; digital media and computer activism; experiments in participatory economics; anti-racist and anti-fascist groups like Anti-Racist Actionand Anti-Fascist Action; activist groups protecting the rights of immigrants and promoting the free movement of people. such as the No Border network; worker co-operatives.countercultural and artist groups; and the peace movement etc.

Libertarian socialism has also more recently played a large part in the global Occupy movement. in particular its focus on direct participatory democracy.

Bibliography

Alan Woods: *Reformism or Revolution : Marxism and Socialism of the Twenty-First Century: Reply to Heinz Dieterich*, Aakar Books, Delhi, 2009.

August Bebel: *Woman and Socialism*, All India Democratic Women's Association (AIDWA), Delhi, 2001.

Che Guevara: *Global Justice : Liberation and Socialism*, Leftword Books, Delhi, 2004.

Horace B. Davis: *Nationalism and Socialism : Marxist and Labor Theories of Nationalism to 1917*, Aakar Books, Delhi, 2011.

Irfan Habib: *On Socialism : Selections from Writings of Karl Marx, Frederick Engels, V.I. Lenin, J.V. Stalin, Mao Zedong*, Tulika Books, Delhi, 2009.

Istvan Meszaros: *Socialism or Barbarism : From the "American Century" to the Crossroads*, Aakar Books, Delhi, 2007.

Istvan Meszaros: *The Alternative to Capital's Social Order : From the "American Century" to the Crossroads: Socialism or Barbarism*, K.P. Bagchi and Company, Kolkata, 2001.

Istvan Meszaros: *The Challenge and Burden of Historical Time : Socialism in the Twenty-First Century*, Aakar Books, Delhi, 2009.

Jag Pal Singh; Virendra Kumar Vijay; Vivek Kumar and Satbeer Singh: *Philosophy of Democratic-Socialism : Equal Opportunity to Grow (EOTG)*, Himanshu Publication, Delhi, 2004.

K Sinha; Uma Sinha and Priyam Krishna: *Whither Socialism : Quest for a Third Path*, Serials Publication, Delhi, 2008.

Kaushik Chakraborty: *Relocating the Origins of the First World War (1914) : Imperialism, Finance Capital, Socialism, Nationalism, Power Rivalry, War Aims and War Guilt or Kriegeschuldfrage (1870-1914)*, Readers Service, New York, 2008.

Leo Huberman and Paul M. Sweezy: *Introduction to Socialism : Including "The ABC Of Socialism*, Aakar Books, Delhi, 2010.

Leo Panitch: *Renewing Socialism : Transforming Democracy, Strategy and Imagination*, Aakar Books, Delhi, 2010.

M.M. Sankhdher and Stuart Nagel: *Capitalism Socialism and Democracy : Combining for Welfare Justice and Equity : New Perspectives in Political Theory*, Deep and Deep Publication, Delhi, 2002.

Martin Hart-Landsberg and Paul Burkett: *China and Socialism : Market Reforms and Class Struggle*, Aakar Books, Delhi, 2006.

Michael A. Lebowitz: *Build It Now: Socialism for the 21st Century*, Daanish Books, Delhi, 2006.

Paul M. Sweezy and Charles Bettelheim: *On the Transition to Socialism*, Aakar Books, Delhi, 2010.

Prabhat Patnaik: *Re-envisioning Socialism*, Tulika Books, Delhi, 2011.

R. C. Gettel and W. A. Dunning: *Socialism : A political Reader*, Cosmo Publication, Delhi, 2004.

Randhir Singh: *Contemporary Ecological Crisis : A Marxist View (Crisis of Socialism : Notes in Defence of a Commitment—Vol. 5)*, Aakar Books, Delhi, 2009.

Randhir Singh: *Indian Politics Today : An Argument for Socialism-Oriented Path of Development (T. Nagi Reddy Memorial Lecture)*, Aakar Books, Delhi, 2009.

Randhir Singh: *Marxism, Socialism, Indian Politics : A View From the Left*, Aakar Books, Delhi, 2008.

Randhir Singh: *Struggle For Socialism : Some Issues*, Aakar Books, Delhi, 2010.

Ravindra Sharma: *Paradoxes of Chinese Socialism*, Manak Publication, Delhi, 2007.

Rosaline Jamir: *Romance of Socialism and Feminism : In Poetics of Temsula Ao, Monalisa Changkija and Robin S. Ngangom*, Swastik Publications, Delhi, 2011.

Santanu Bagchi: *Ideas on Socialism and Social Justice : A Study of Jawaharlal Nehru, Rammanohar Lohia and Asoke Mehta*, Kanishka Publication, Delhi, 2002.

Saral Sarkar: *Eco-Socialism or Eco-Capitalism? : A Critical Analysis of Humanity's Fundamental Choices*, Orient Blackswan, Hyderabad, 2000.

U. Srivastava: *Capitalism Socialism and Indian Politics*, Kunal Books, Delhi, 2011.

Vandita Varma: *From Marxism to Democratic Socialism : The Deeper Roots of Affinity*, Books India International, Delhi, 2005.

W H Mallock: *Critical Examination of the Socialism : From Beginning to Modern Times*, Dominant Publication, Delhi, 2009.

William Ash: *Workers' Politics : The Ethics of Socialism*, Aakar Books, Delhi, 2010.

Index